PENGUIN BOOKS

ALL THAT IS SOLID

'As Danny Dorling's powerfully argued new book makes
clear . . . the need for serious action has never been greater'
Ed Cumming, *Daily Telegraph*

'Dorling has bravely gone to the root of the issue'
Owen Hatherley, *Guardian*

'*All that is Solid* is a powerful, important book for these times . . .
It has an angry urgency . . . the stock answer is that we should simply
build more, but this is one of the many myths Dorling demolishes'
Tim Hall, *The Times Higher Education*

'Dorling grasps the importance of the issue. His urgency is warranted'
John McDermott, *Financial Times*

'A carefully researched, well argued and generally convincing analysis'
Douglas Osler, *Scotsman*

'Clearly argued and comes with a wash of facts'
Douglas Murphy, *Icon Magazine*

'Offers a radical solution to the housing crisis in Britain . . .
He cuts to the heart of things' Anthony Cummins, *Metro*

DANNY DORLING

All that is Solid

*How the Great Housing Disaster
Defines Our Times, and What
We Can Do About It*

PENGUIN BOOKS

PENGUIN BOOKS

UK | USA | Canada | Ireland | Australia
India | New Zealand | South Africa

Penguin Books is part of the Penguin Random House group of companies
whose addresses can be found at global.penguinrandomhouse.com.

First published by Allen Lane 2014
Published in Penguin Books with a new Afterword 2015
001

Set in 9.35/12.5pt Sabon LT Std
Typeset by Jouve (UK), Milton Keynes
Printed in Great Britain by Clays Ltd, St Ives plc

A CIP catalogue record for this book is available from the British Library

ISBN: 978–0–141–97819–2

All photographs by Gemma Thorpe.
Gemma Thorpe is a freelance photographer specializing in social
documentary, with a particular interest in youth issues, migration and identity.
She has published and exhibited her work in the UK, China and Europe.
For more info see: www.gemmathorpe.com

www.greenpenguin.co.uk

To Stacy – for four decades of friendship

Contents

List of figures and tables

FIGURES

self-interest on building society risk-taking and market structure, *c.* 1880–1939', Discussion Papers in Economic and Social History No. 86, University of Oxford, January 2011, Figure 14.)

Figure 6 (p. 93). UK average land prices and house prices, 1983–2009. (Source: M. Griffith, *We must fix it: delivering reform of the building sector to meet the UK's housing and economic challenges*, London: Institute for Public Policy Research, 2011, p. 7.)

Figure 7 (p. 123). The modern London Kensington mansion, an artist's impression, 2012. (Source: redrawn from Ben Hasler's original image of a Kensington mansion, O. Wainwright, 'Billionaires' basements: the luxury bunkers making holes in London streets', *Guardian*, 9 November 2012. http://www.guardian.co.uk/artanddesign/2012/nov/09/billionaires-basements-london-houses-architecture)

Figure 8 (p. 144). Proportion of residents receiving cash allowances for rental costs, by OECD country, 2009. (Source: OECD, given in A. Hull and G. Cooke, 'Together at home: a new strategy for housing', Institute for Public Policy Research, report, 21 June 2012, p. 53. http://www.ippr.org/publication/55/9279/together-at-home-a-new-strategy-for-housing)

Figure 9 (p. 164). Income changes in the UK. (Source: Oxfam, *The perfect storm: economic stagnation, the rising cost of living, public spending cuts and the impact on UK poverty*, Oxford: Oxfam, 2012.)

Figure 10 (p. 169). Maximum weekly local housing allowance permitted after April 2013, England and Wales. (Source: R. Ramesh, 'Camden Council plans to move 761 poor families from London', *Guardian*, 13 February 2013. http://www.guardian.co.uk/uk/2013/feb/13/london-council-relocation-benefits-cap)

Figure 11 (p. 173). Three-month on three-month housing price change, 1983–2012, UK, and trend lines. (Source: Halifax House Price Index, all buyers, seasonally adjusted data, analysis by author, trends added.)

TABLES

Acknowledgements

Tom Penn at Penguin both came up with the idea for this book at the very start and radically rearranged the final manuscript at the very end, beyond normal editorial duties – thank you. My agent, Antony Harwood, argued in 2012 that the idea was worth pursuing and, as ever, I am very grateful to him. However, my gratitude goes much further back in time, as I have been looking at housing, on and off, for a quarter of a century now. I must thank the Housing and Society Research Group at the University of Newcastle upon Tyne, and in particular Tony Champion, for giving me my first academic job that involved researching housing, in 1991. Much more recently I should thank the Royal Irish Academy for inviting me to Dublin to lecture on the crisis in early 2013 and for giving much useful advice, not least from Michael Higgins, who told me a thing or two that I did not know about economics and the Irish housing crisis after my presentation at the Academy (which I wished he had told me beforehand!).

This is now a much better book than my original draft because so many people have helped to edit it and have commented on earlier drafts and lectures. Tom Penn cut out a great deal of the original hype, and made me be far clearer than I otherwise would have been. However, his comments came only after many other people had helped to organize my thoughts better than I could alone. Editing started with David, Bronwen and Alison Dorling, who read the first drafts. I am also very grateful to Charlotte Shepherd, Housing Aid Officer at Sheffield City Council, and to Andrew Parfitt, Head of Housing Policy Division at the Department of Work and Pensions, who both commented in a personal capacity. I am indebted to Joe, Theo and others at the Squatters' Action for Secure Homes, who kindly allowed me to present my early findings to an open house meeting of squatters and would-be squatters in south London. I am grateful for advice to Sarah Blandy and Benjamin Hennig, both then at the University of Sheffield; Fern Elsdon-Baker of the Institute of Community Cohesion; Carl Lee at Sheffield College; Tony Champion of what was the University of Newcastle upon Tyne (now 'Newcastle University'); Rob Kitchen at the National University of Ireland, Maynooth; Alex Fenton and Christine Whitehead at the LSE; Sebastian Kraemer of the Tavistock Clinic; Kat Smith of the University of Edinburgh; Becky Tunstall at the University of York; Gemma Thorpe, photographer, who took all the shots used here; and, lastly, Paul Coles, then of the University of Sheffield, who kindly redrew all the graphics. And thanks to David Dorling and Stacy Hewitt, who read it all again at the end to check it still made some sense, and then read it a second time after I completely rewrote the first half yet again, partly due to events in the housing market!

Finally I must thank Donna Poppy for copyediting the manuscript and turning my enthusiastic claims into much more readable prose, Richard Duguid for steering the final production so smoothly and Krishna Prasad and colleagues at the typesetters for working through the Christmas and New Year holidays. All errors remain my responsibility, but I could not have written this book without everyone's help.

1
Crisis

If people hoarded food on the basis that its value was sure to go up when others began to starve and would pay anything, we would stop their hoarding. But hoarding is now happening with shelter in the most unequal and affluent parts of the world. Increasingly it is the financing of housing that is our biggest problem: the mortgage or rent, the bills and the inequitable taxes.

When we talk about our housing and wealth, ultimately what we are talking about is our freedom. When a great disaster looms in housing so, potentially, does a disastrous loss of freedom. We become less free of fear of the future. We become less free in our ability to choose where we live, and less free than those in countries not suffering a housing crisis.

Lack of access to housing, a growing sense of insecurity over how we are to be housed, is lack of access to the freedom to feel secure; it constitutes a growing restriction on the right of the majority to be free to live a good and safe life.

In the past in the UK we had greater freedom over where we could live. Fewer areas were too expensive to live in, and there were fewer areas that you would desperately try to avoid living in. Far less of our income was spent on housing, and we did not need to rely on our homes to provide us with financial security in our old age.

In the last five years our dependence on housing for our economic survival has become starkly apparent. Our national economic well-being appears so tightly entwined with the housing market that the Chancellor of the Exchequer devoted the majority of new financial commitments in his March 2013 budget to measures intended to boost the housing market, trying as hard as he could to sustain high and rising prices in the south of England.

Almost everywhere in Britain rents are rising, but in many places outside of the south of England housing values are continuing to fall. Housing has become a problem for everyone. While it is an acute problem in England as a whole, it is especially so in the south-east and south-west for those who do not own, who want to rent or who are trying to buy but then have to pay back huge mortgages.

Housing is a national obsession in the UK because housing equity represents as much as 61% of England's net worth, or around £4 trillion.[1] That may even be an underestimate. According to alternative estimates, if Wales and Scotland are included and non-mortgage debt secured on housing is excluded, this figure rises to £5.5 trillion.[2] The exact value of our housing stock depends upon when you value it; whether you subtract the value of additional loans secured on property (i.e. loans other than primary mortgages); and whether account is made of depreciation. But, whichever way you measure it, 61% or more is an astonishing proportion of the UK's national wealth.

How did housing come to represent such a huge percentage of the UK's net worth? Is the fact that the majority of our savings are tied up in our homes precisely why governments feel unable to tackle the inequities of the housing market? How did the British come to have so little in their pension pots, so little in their savings accounts, such miserly state pensions and hence, for many, so much financial interest tied up in their homes? And what future is there for all those who haven't bought or who aren't planning to buy housing, for the renters – a large and growing majority of young adults – and for the equally large and growing group of those who are precarious purchasers? This last category includes people who have tried to buy with a mortgage but at some point have been forced to give up and move back into renting or living with family or friends; among them are increasing numbers of hoodwinked 'consumers' who, over the course of their lives, take out several mortgages but never complete payments on any.

Over-reliance on housing for financial security in the UK accounts for the obsession of our newspapers with housing. There are many exaggerated media responses to even the smallest rise or the slightest dip in house prices. In 2010 this obsession resulted in small dips in housing prices generating headlines such as 'UK "value" falls by £94 billion'. During 2009 the apparent fall in the value of Britain's homes accounted for most of a large decline in national wealth, a decline equivalent to the annual costs of running the NHS.[3]

The decline in national wealth was apparent, because most potential sellers simply did not try to sell at lower prices. Transactions on the open market halved in the years following 2008. It was also only apparent because there is little other than market confidence, political intransigence and planning tradition holding prices up at all. Had the journalist involved consulted another source, he could have reported UK 'value' falling by over £1 trillion a year earlier!

The fall in national wealth of over £1 trillion was in the year to 2008, and most of that huge decline was due to the falling value of residential housing.[4] Over £1 trillion is a ten times larger collapse than £94 billion, but for much of the press a big number is simply a big number. The big numbers can also spoil all those stories about small fluctuations, concentration on which adds credence to the myth that prices are relatively stable and that what has happened recently to the British housing and rental markets is unusual, local and will not be repeated or protracted.

When the housing market stalled in 2008, private builders largely stopped building. Government then stepped in with schemes to try to boost the supply of new housing. However, by 2012 figures for government-assisted home-building revealed that the number of what were called 'affordable housing starts' for 2011–12 had resulted in just 15,698 properties being built nationally in an entire financial year. This represented a 68% fall on the figures released for the previous year.[5]

By early 2013 the housing starts figures had worsened still further. But the drop in subsidized building became evident only after Andrew Dilnot, the Chair of the UK Statistics Authority, castigated the coalition government for its earlier misrepresentation of housing statistics and demanded that clearer statistics should be presented.[6]

By the end of summer 2013 the satirical magazine *Private Eye* was noting how Grant Shapps, the Conservative Party Chairman and recent Minister of State for Housing, appeared to be strangely quiet about the possible benefits from house prices once again rising in the south of the country. The magazine's writer noted that in 2011 Shapps had suggested that price stability should be the aim of government policy, by which Shapps meant prices rising by 2% less than earnings.

In 2012 and 2013, as average earnings fell, national average housing prices rose. Shapps's 2011 suggestion that people should 'see their homes as places to live rather than as investments'[7] began to ring hollow. Landlords and the very rich were investing again, especially in the south of England. Shapps had hardly expanded the social rented sector at all; hardly any affordable homes had been built. But this wasn't some mistake or a cock-up: when the last few years were examined afresh, it became clear just who had taken advantage of others, what they had wanted to achieve, and who had aided them in their efforts.

'GENERATION RENT'

The stark drop in younger people owning a home presents a long-term challenge for all political parties but especially the Conservatives. Research shows that private renters and people living in social housing are less likely to vote Tory.

– Nick Faith, Policy Exchange researcher, 2013[8]

By 2013 it had become evident that what the UK government had planned was not an expansion of social housing construction. What it had wanted, and got, was a massive expansion of the private rented sector. This was achieved not through new building, but through private landlords buying homes that had recently been vacated. In many parts of the south-east of England private landlords now own the majority of houses on streets that until recently were home to families with mortgages. In autumn 2013 the Prime Minister countered criticism of this very recent trend, saying that he would ensure it became easier for ordinary families who were renting to take out massive 95% mortgages, but he did not explain how they would ever be able to pay back the borrowed money.[9]

The coalition government appeared unaware of the long-term political implications of its policies, not least of how this would influence the way people might in future vote. Government appeared more interested in upholding its core supporters' short-term financial interests than in thinking about the long term. The policy shift that encouraged 'Generation Rent' to grow became apparent in dribs and drabs during 2012 and was then made formal in the budget of spring 2013.

Take, for example, the response to a report Grant Shapps commissioned from Sir Adrian Montague, Chairman of the multinational private equity and venture capital company 3i, that was published in August 2012.[10] Although the coalition had not officially accepted the recommendations of Sir Adrian's report, it quietly agreed – to fall in with his report's recommendations – to waive a mandatory quota of affordable homes in new housing developments. That waiving, Sir Adrian suggested, 'would allow developers to create more properties for letting to boost the private rented market'. Thus, although the minister talked about more affordable social housing being made available, what he actually did was to boost the private rented market. He also promised to try to reduce what he saw as the 'excessive regulation' on this sector – a statement that should have resulted in more criticism than it did because Britain has one of the least regulated private rented sectors in Europe.

When one of the UK's main TV news channels, ITN, first ran the Adrian Montague story on its website, it was titled 'Report offers "blueprint" to expand private rented sector' – a title that was quickly changed to 'Demand for homes doubles the rate houses are built'. The web address of the story preserves the original headline. Maybe a sub-editor at ITN sympathetic to the government changed the headline; or maybe ITN were leant on? We will probably never know. The letters 'ITN' stand for Independent Television News, but that does not tell you what their news is supposed to be independent of.[11]

Eleven months after the ITN story ran, even the government's critics, including those on the political fringe, appeared to forget that the coalition once had a plan to boost the social housing supply. By summer 2013 the details of a new 'help-to-buy' scheme – using a massive £12 billion of taxpayers' money to guarantee up to £130 billion[12] of new mortgage lending – was announced.[13] Initially it was set to run from January 2014, and mortgage lenders would have to collect a declaration from any buyer using the scheme stating that they did not already own property. However, each member of a couple could easily finance a property through the scheme and then rent one out, transfer that to one partner and the other partner buy a third and so on and on. The coalition government says it is up to lenders to ensure that such transgressions do not take place, but it gave them little time to prepare. Then, at the end of September 2013, the Prime Minister brought forward the start date of 'help-to-buy' to the first week of October. He wanted to be able to tell Conservative Party members at his annual conference speech that the government was doing all it could to boost the housing market higher and higher.[14] The October 2013 'help-to-buy' scheme grew out of an earlier 'funding-for-lending' scheme, but was much larger and far riskier.

The government's 'funding-for-lending' scheme had been aimed at business enterprise in general, but ended up fuelling a buying spree by landlords. It helped grow 'Generation Rent'. When it was introduced, few realized who the money was mostly going to, but sceptics were warned by its introduction to look more carefully at future schemes.

The proposed £12 billion 'help-to-buy' scheme hit stony ground when announced, and many thought it would not make its 2014 implementation. It had vocal critics ranging from the International Monetary Fund to the Office for Budget Responsibility and even the Bank of England. The criticism was that this scheme would not really help renters become buyers. Instead it would simply lead to prices going higher and higher, as a few more people bought using massive loans, many of whom would soon rent out these properties and charge the mortgage plus a profit to new renters. Criticism from such heavyweights could not be ignored by the mainstream media, but it was at first only grudgingly reported, even when the head of strategy at the bank Société Générale described the policy as being 'moronic'.[15] But even that did not stop the first phase starting in April 2013, or the bringing forward to October 2013 of the supposed main 2014 'help-to-buy' initiatives.

When 'help-to-buy' began in April 2013 it had been targeted solely at new-build property buyers. It allowed up to a fifth of the mortgages of buyers of new-build properties to be provided by government, thus ensuring that government, and hence we collectively, would take the first hit were the price of new-build housing to fall. Banks were then willing to lend mortgages when just a 5% deposit was put down, safe in the knowledge that they would not lose out even if prices fell by 25%: the government (i.e. all of us) would pay up instead. That these government loans are interest-free for the first five years adds to the collective hit taken by taxpayers. When buyers are let off paying interest, everyone else is paying to help private home-builders sell houses at higher prices than the market says they are worth; the subsidies, in effect, are causing people to buy their homes at inflated prices.

If housing prices then do fall, government spending will have to rise to cover some of the very large mortgage defaults. The one saving grace of the original policy is that, in theory, it should have encouraged new house-building, which can be useful where more homes are needed, but does not help in other areas of the country. Furthermore, given current trends, many of the homes being built are likely to end up in landlords' hands once they are sold, as previously mentioned, so what purports to be a 'help-to-buy' scheme may well end up being no such thing. Many people may find that the April 2013 scheme will help them to buy a new-build property and to live in it for a short time. But, if any of the following happens to the buyer or their partner, they may be forced to sell: losing their job; being demoted; salaries falling behind inflation; becoming ill; splitting up; or suffering a rise in interest rates. More often than not they will be selling at a loss to a landlord.

What, though, of the second stage of George Osborne's policy: the extension of the guarantee to large parts of all mortgages taken out on property valued up to £600,000? This was planned to be the greatest state intervention in the private property market ever undertaken. The former Governor of the Bank of England, Lord King, has said the scheme is 'too close for comfort to a general scheme to guarantee all mortgages'.[16] The second stage now applies to all existing dwellings valued up to £600,000, not just new-build. Its aim is obvious: simply to hold up and possibly further increase prices; it is not designed to boost supply.[17] Holding up housing prices also allows rents to remain high. The policy may even dampen demand for newly built properties, as now the government will subsidize you when you buy any older property. Why risk buying an often more expensive newly built property whose value has not yet been determined by the market?

If there is to be a surge in new home-building in Britain in the years to come, it will mostly be building on behalf of the private buying and private rental market, while much more public sector money will flow to both the landlords and the banks, and huge sums will be made available for underwriting many of their risks in the event of any fall in prices. The profits will be privatized and the risks will be nationalized, a trend that began under New Labour and is accelerating under coalition rule.

Housing in the UK has become so unstable that government now feels it has to prop up the private market with these massive subsidies to give the impression of stability. However, there is a growing realization that this is a policy only for the short term, one that could work up until the next general election, but that might not work once people recognize how much the housing market is being manipulated. If new potential buyers begin to get cold feet, if people try to live at parents' or friends' homes even longer than they currently do before they rent, if confidence begins to quiver – what then? Plan A is for government to boost the private market so that house values rise and rise as average incomes fall, with the result that debt grows too. The coalition has no Plan B. When houses cost too much for most people to buy, more and more have to rent.

Already under many existing coalition government schemes more taxpayers' money than ever before is being used to underwrite landlords' risks when they buy new property to rent. From 2012, £10 billion in loan guarantees has been on offer to these landlords by government. In October 2012 the then new Housing Minister, Mark Prisk, announced, 'We're offering £10 billion in loan guarantees to provide up to 15,000 new homes for rent, putting £19.5 billion in public and private funding into an affordable homes programme.'[18] Mark was shuffled out of the housing job a year later, in October 2013. No MP ever seems to stay for long as Housing Minister; and, perhaps for this reason, even more money than that, and much more than ever before, also flows in landlords' direction from another pot: the housing benefit bill, which has risen massively since 2009.

The housing benefit bill rises because ever increasing numbers of households cannot afford their rising rent costs. Of the rise in claims since 2009, 85% has been from households where at least one member is in work.[19] The original expansion of housing benefit payments going to private landlords, which, by 1989, had risen to £5 billion a year, has recently been described as 'Brilliantly evil in retrospect'.[20] That same government subsidy for landlords, but for the period 2012–14, has now risen to £35 billion. This huge bill rose by more than a third since the coalition took power.[21] And, as more and more people are forced to rent, it will continue to rise, even as the government insists the bill will be reduced. These are all monies that go directly to landlords.

The £35 billion housing benefit bill that keeps rents high by actually paying those high rents; the £10 billion underwrite of the future risks of large private landlords who are currently building new housing to rent out at great profit; the October 2013 extra 'help-to-buy' underwrite of the lending 'risk' of banks and other mortgage lenders to the tune of £12 billion – factor in all of these, and you begin to see a staggering amount of government money going into the hands of some of the richest 'players' in the private housing market. All this keeps rents and prices high. All this puts more and more people into ever greater debt.

Government may say that their massive current underwriting of risk will probably never have to be realized, but that will happen only if housing remains prohibitively expensive – so expensive, in fact, that most people will find it increasingly difficult to work out just how to get housed, without having to expose themselves to levels of debt their parents would never have believed possible, let alone countenanced, or without having to rely on the state to pay at least part of their rent.

The coalition government in Britain presents state support for the private renting and buying sectors as an alternative to building more social housing. The suggestion is that the private sector is better at building and managing homes than the state, and also better than charities such as housing associations; it is just that the private sector needs a little encouragement. But what if the underlying problem of housing in Britain is not too few homes, but too many homes too poorly shared out? And far too many homes priced far too highly? Expanding the private sector tends not to reduce inequalities in provision. It could result in more second homes being built in and around London, not more first homes for people currently living in crowded conditions, those living with other families, unable to get some space.

The rental sector in Britain is not as large as in many other European countries, and a good case can be made for expanding it. But the unregulated rapid expansion we have seen in recent years will result in ever greater profits for landlords and ever greater precariousness for tenants. In the year to 2013 median rents in London rose by 9%, while median London earnings rose by only 2%; and the typical young renter has been forced to move out (on average) every twelve months by his or her landlord to enable that landlord to find a new tenant to pay the higher rent.[22]

The new-builds for rent are chiefly designed for poorer people, for those who cannot afford the highest or even average rents. But we have learned from experience that services designed for poor people tend to be poor services. One in three privately rented homes in England today is still not currently up to the government's 'decent' standard. Complaints against landlords rose by 27% in the three years to July 2012, many of which concerned landlords allowing hazards that posed an imminent risk to the health of tenants.[23]

Services initially designed for a wide range of people that later become services for poor people almost always become poorer services. This is what happened to British council housing, as it was residualized, and it could be what is happening to the private rental sector now. Services remain good services or improve when those using them have clout, and especially when they have a choice over whether to use them or not. When rents are as high as they are in Britain today, most people who rent simply have to choose the least bad home they are offered. Many landlords are now reaping great profits because they devote only a tiny proportion of the rent money to making these properties good homes in which to live. Tenants simply don't have the power to shop around and reject what's not good enough. And British landlords know this.

In mainland Europe much of the private rental sector works so much better than in the UK. This is not only because it is a larger sector that spans most of the Continental mainland, but also because it is maintained to support a far wider range of tenants in terms of social background and age. As a result, governments control rents and preserve rights. Rented homes are far better insulated and sound-proofed, and also tend, on average, to be larger. When the private sector in Europe works well it is usually because of good government control. After all, the 'market' was originally a place where local government controlled where and how goods could be traded. Without that control, profit maximization in housing leads to growing inefficiency. Satisfying short-term goals by hiking prices up leads to long-term trouble.

When it comes to private sector house-building, David Richie, the Chief Executive of Bovis, one of the largest building firms in Britain, explains that, following what he calls the 'severe slowdown in the northern half of the country', it became 'financially safer' for developers 'to build below a line drawn from Cheltenham in the west to Cambridge in the east'.[24] The private market will always gravitate to wherever the most money is to be made and will act, build, buy and sell when and wherever profit can be maximized, nothing more, and nothing less. It does not maximize happiness or utility when left to its own devices. It does not try to best arrange our transport to work, nor to ensure that we pollute as little as possible as we commute. It works only to satisfy each player's immediate desires, or, at most, the desires of a pair of players, a buyer and a seller.

Inequalities are exacerbated by the fact that a few people have far better knowledge of markets than the majority. Individuals can never become experienced consumers of housing unless they have a terribly unsettled life, moving so often that they become familiar with a wide range of tenures, mortgage offers and landlords, and so get to know when and where the 'best deals' come up. Any life lived with such an obsession over housing is unlikely to be especially fulfilled. Government can, and should, act on behalf of all of us, so that each of us need not become a housing expert. But sometimes government acts more in the interests of landlords and banks than in the interests of most households and most people.

It is not necessary for a government to be Machiavellian for its actions to result in almost all voters' personal economic positions

There were no structural problems with these houses, which are currently boarded up. They were once solid dwellings, but are now in the wrong city and, even more importantly, in the wrong part of that city. The buildings shown here are all that remains, in 2013, of over 130 houses that were the subjects of compulsory purchase orders in 2008. The rest were demolished, and all but this half-dozen are now nothing but air. They were demolished because they came to be seen as being in the wrong place at the wrong time, located in the poor enclave of Fir Vale, in Sheffield. They were built when different industries dominated. Had these same houses been built elsewhere, it is likely that they would have been lovingly renovated. In other places where there is once again ageing housing that isn't being looked after, many of those homes could suffer a similar fate to these, should the market crash again, regardless of how many people badly need housing.

being harmed. It simply requires enough members of parliament to believe that what is best for a few landlords (and for even fewer bankers) is best for us all. Even if that condition is not met, and many politicians have their doubts over bankers, if enough believe that it is essential that housing prices (and hence also rents) stay high, the results will be much the same. They may not be in cahoots with the financiers but they may as well be.

Government, and many in the policy world, in the media and in academia, may believe that action to support and even to increase high housing prices is essential, at least for the coalition to be voted into office in future. This may account for the resistance encountered by those who make suggestions for real change, as well as the recent series of desperate policies of subsidy and underwriting in an effort to delay the inevitable readjustment.

Housing is of greater political consequence than most other areas of government policy. It's as near as most people personally get to what is called the greater economy. Employment comes a close second to housing, but most pensioners, children and many others are not employed, whereas everyone is directly affected by housing, all of the time. Conversely, many people, especially those without young children, may not care much about what is happening to education, and those who are well can easily pay less attention to changes to our health services.

Most people are not affected by the level at which benefit payments are set, or by how the minimum wage is determined. Cut benefits, and crime may rise, but few make such links and often those that do simply demand more prisons. (Prisons have been the only form of state housing that has expanded in recent decades in the UK, but it is also a form in which rates of overcrowding are rising fast too, as many cells designed for one person to sleep in, and use a toilet, now house two or three.)

Those who are most adversely affected by housing policy believe they have little power to alter politics. And usually they are right. They are the least powerful in the areas where they live, so politicians can reduce social security spending on the poorest without losing much popular support. Politicians can increase overcrowding in prisons, in social housing and in much private renting housing; and, in the short term, they can get away with it. However, as their housing policies begin to impact on a greater and greater share of the population, and on the large majority of young adults, it becomes harder to sustain such policies. But it also becomes harder to end them. A particular constituency has become reliant on prices remaining high and rising.

Policy on housing is different from policy on employment, crime, defence, health or education. Policy on housing touches everyone. For example, make renting less problematic and you reduce the incentive to buy, so policies that help tenants might be seen to harm the interests of those who own outright and are trying to sell at a high price.

We all need a home to go to, whether we are of school age or of pensionable age, in good health or poor, not paid, badly paid or well paid. When our housing feels insecure, we feel insecure. That insecurity can range from feeling a little bit less wealthy, as at some point in the near future the value of your Notting Hill townhouse (once subdivided into flats) falls, to despairing about being forcibly relocated away from where you grew up because there is apparently no longer any space for you in Newham. Clearly, losing a little wealth is far less of an issue than having to leave your home town or borough, but the wealthy mansion owner might be happier to see you go rather than lose a fraction of his equity. If equality were to grow, he might eventually have to subdivide his property again, so that there would be some space for people like you to stay in part of that building. He knows it happened before. If the forces of Conservatism don't triumph, it could happen again.

Many of us worry that there may not be enough homes to go round. We worry that we could easily be evicted were we to be late with the rent or mortgage payment. If we are homeowners, we worry that the home we own outright has a monetary value that is as solid as quicksand and that the future we thought was secure will turn out to have been a pipedream. Few people find reassurance through the ways in which we have come to organize how we are housed.

Of those that have won out in the housing lottery – unless they have no children, no relatives and care for no friends who are in situations somewhat different from their own – they too should still have worries. If we carry on as we are, how will society be able to function in a way that allows people to respect each other? How will all our children be housed? How big will their debts be?

Housing has become the defining economic issue of our times because housing finance is at the heart of the current economic crisis. So many of us put so much money and faith into these little individualized pockets of risk, at least at one point in our lives, that we can easily become more concerned about our home and neighbourhood than the wider picture.

When we concentrate our worry on our housing, we worry less about the wider economy becoming dysfunctional. Worry about housing distracts us from the disaster of millions of young adults having no work, of income inequalities rising relentlessly. We worry about our individual property value or rent level; about paying the mortgage each month; about whether the profit on our sale will pay the nursing home fees; or about why we failed to try much harder to buy when we were younger.

If housing prices are rising and you have bought a home, none of the other trends appear to matter that much, because you, and your family, are doing all right, even if society as a whole appears to be in more of a mess than it was when people did not overwhelmingly profit from the rising value of their bricks and mortar rather than from their labour.

DISASTER CAPITALISM

There is the risk of a property-driven boom in the UK ...

– Antony Jenkins, Chief Executive Officer,
Barclays Bank, 2013[25]

Our personal housing experiences both encapsulate and engender the particular kind of capitalism that we are currently living through: Disaster Capitalism. That is what occurs when people are allowed to profit out of a crisis. The term was first widely used to describe how great profits were made in the aftermath of hurricane Katrina hitting the Louisiana coastline of the United States in 2005 and decimating New Orleans.[26]

In the United Kingdom the banks and larger landlords are now making huge profits from the housing crisis. Many of their risks are being covered by the taxpayer through the new underwriting schemes. Furthermore, in both the UK and the US, government currently lends to banks (in effect, to their shareholders) at near-zero interest rates, while banks still lend to us at much higher rates and very much higher rates for those deemed to be more of a risk.

For every hidden subsidy to the rich that you discover, there appears to lurk behind it an even greater sum of money that is being lent, risked or raised to try to maintain the crooked state of our housing system. After all, it was the housing subprime financial crisis that triggered the trillions of pounds and dollars now spent on 'quantitative easing'. And what is it exactly that this huge quantity of money is supposed to ease? Everything appears to be being done to restore things to how they were, to maintain the gross inequalities, to prevent a substantial readjustment.

You might think this situation will not change, but it has not always been like this. Today the poorly and insecurely housed are not a group that can be sidelined. This is partly because the housing precariat have become such a large group.[27] This book focuses on the UK housing market, but the UK is not the only set of nations where so much has been invested, both financially and emotionally, in housing. Across much of the rich world, levels of confidence in our individual economies are, to a greater or lesser extent, now more reliant on the housing market than they have ever been. This is not safe. Trying to return to business as usual following the 2008 crash, to relying so greatly on housing as a financial store of wealth, is a policy that will expose us to yet more insecurity in the future.

When the housing market appears buoyant, people spend more and the economy does better in general. Demand rises, not just for goods related to housing, not just for sales of carpets and curtains, but for holidays and cinema trips. It would be better if we mostly replaced carpets and curtains only when they were worn out, if the cinemas were cheaper, and if a good holiday was not necessarily an expensive one. However, given the current way in which economic growth is measured, the more that is spent, and the more frequently it is spent, and the quicker we throw possessions away and replace them, the better off we are all said to be.

Looking at the financial crisis through the prism of housing leads us to the nub of what's gone wrong. And to what will be required to make us both be, and feel, more secure again. Neither show-homes nor insecure homes make us happy. We need to know that we are living on solid ground, that our homes are safe. We should not have to live with the perceived need to present our home to others kitted out like a newly refurbished hotel. We need to organize how we are housed, so that we neither have to fear for our basic shelter, nor behave as if the fabric of our homes reflected our status and achievements. Currently too many people are too poorly housed and a rich subset are too expensively housed, overprovided for at the expense of the majority.

Fundamentally it is the linking of housing to social status that allows prices and rents to be increased beyond what the cost of providing the dwelling might be, or beyond what the value of the land might be if it were turned to other purposes. It was Karl Marx and Friedrich Engels who first wrote of how a house could be made to appear to be a hovel, should a mansion be built next to it. It was the economist Robert H. Frank who came to notice this occurring again over 150 years later, but in the contemporary US rather than in nineteenth-century Europe (where Karl and Friedrich first made the observation). To illustrate the issue of status, Frank included the floor-plan reproduced below, way back in 2001, to show what was happening in the US at that time. To understand the point being made, you need to look at this floor-plan and this picture of a house, and think how nice it would be to live there. But please look carefully, and also think about whether you really would need a three-car garage that has both windows and curtains.

This book is mainly concerned with the UK housing market, but events overseas both drive what occurs in Britain and also offer a portent for what may soon occur here. In particular, what has happened

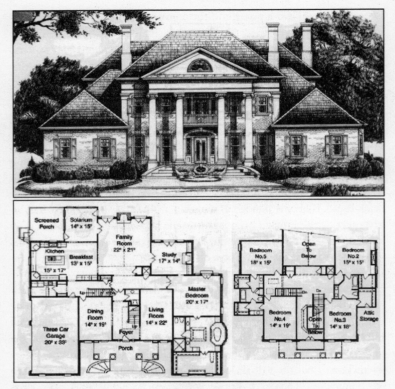

Figure 1. Dream home: 6,000-square-foot house, front elevations and floor plans, United States, 2001.

recently in the UK began to happen earlier in the US. People at the top in the US began to want more, much more, than they had, and they found ways to take it.

Better-off individuals in the US recently became much better off. The top 1% now takes home a fifth of all national income, leaving just 80% for the other 99%. To envisage what this means, imagine going to a school that serves 100 children in three classes (or 33, 33 and 34 children in each). In one of those classes is a single child who receives $20 a day in pocket money. The other 99 children in the school each, on average, receive the equivalent of 80¢ a day in pocket money, but not evenly.

Other children in the rich boy's class, which happens to be the class of 34 children, receive, on average, $2 a day. In the next class average pocket money is just 50¢ a day. But in the third class it is almost nothing. That is how unequal the US has become in terms of income inequality, and that growing inequality in ability to buy has had consequences about what people subsequently want.

Everybody, understandably, wants more when they each have so little in comparison with their peers. Those who have almost nothing want more; those who have just 50¢ would much prefer $2 and cannot see what is unreasonable about that; and those who receive $2 know this is only a tenth of what the richest boy in the class has, so they too can feel poor. But it is the rich boy who is most isolated, who cannot see the other children as his peers; they are not, in effect, his peers, so even he does not have all he might want.

As the rich in the US began to take a greater and greater slice of the American pie, they needed new ways to show how successful they were. One option was to purchase American 'dream homes'. The picture and floor plan opposite shows a small version of one of these, perhaps built for someone who had only just made it into the top 1% of US society in the early 2000s. It may look to you like a large home, but then (if it does) you are probably like those children who have 'only' $2 a day pocket money each: a child in the top class out of three, but not in the richest half of that class. What do you know? It is easy to be on above-average earnings (or pocket money) and feel poor when inequality is so high and people are so segregated in their education, in their employment or in their residential neighbourhoods.

In the UK the top 1% do not yet take home as much as a fifth of all national income, but their share is currently rising. The picture and floor plan above may appear even more ostentatious to a UK readership, as there is less land to build on in the UK, but if inequalities within the UK continue to grow this could become an example of an expensive home that more of the affluent in the UK will soon desire to one day own, one that so few do own now. What matters about the floor plan is where it first appeared in print. This is because its publication illustrates that all the problems of housing that have been discussed so far in this book are well known to the elite and have been understood in their circles for some time. It also suggests that just because they are well known does not mean they are manageable.

The image of a dream home and floor plan is taken from a book published in 2007, which was itself based on an academic lecture given in 2001.[28] In the lecture the US economist Robert H. Frank explained how a few people wanting more and more ended up making everyone else less happy. Slowly, and at first most clearly from the example set by the United States of America, we are learning that disaster unfolds if you fail to curtail the excesses of the rich, if you fail to regulate housing, and if you fail to see shelter as a right, not something to be sold freely and bought by the highest bidder to the detriment of the majority. At a certain age every child needs a little pocket money, but no child needs $20 a day, especially if, like space for housing, that money is coming out of a fixed pot.

Robert Frank is co-author with Ben Bernanke of a series of mainstream economic textbooks published in the US. Bernanke was until very recently the Chairman of the US Federal Reserve, a post he had held since 2006, before the crash. Those in the elite at the top of US society knew they had a bubble long before it burst; they just didn't know how to deal with it. They also knew they had a severe problem with rising economic inequalities. But they did not know how to reduce them, or at least how to do so in a way that they could present as acceptable in the US political climate of the time.

Those at the top of UK society knew of the problems rising inequality brings almost as well. They'd heard it from the horse's mouth. In September 2006 Frank explained all this at a seminar held within No. 11 Downing Street, then the office of Gordon Brown, Chancellor of the Exchequer. The slides he showed can still be viewed on the web.[29] The young men and women of the Treasury who were listening found it to be a very impressive lecture. They knew growing inequality in housing was bad, but they just didn't know what to do about it.

RECENT INEQUALITY

If you want the American Dream, go to Finland.

– Ed Miliband, 2012[30]

The United States is one of the few countries in the rich world where inequalities in income between households are even greater than those found within the UK. The best-off tenth of households in the US receive each year, on average, 15.9 times as much to live on as the worst-off tenth. In the UK that ratio is 13.8 to 1; in the Netherlands it is 9.2 to 1; in Denmark 8.1 to 1; in Germany 6.9 to 1; and in Finland 5.6 to 1.[31] As the incomes of those at the top in both the UK and US rose in recent decades, housing prices and rents at the top rose too, but those increases dragged the prices and rents of slightly cheaper properties up – especially cheaper property near the most expensive housing. The rises in housing prices rippled out, and, although there was less of a hike lower down the hierarchy, the rise was always higher, proportionately, than the salary and wage increases received by the people further down. For a time this continued regardless of the fact that less well-off people soon simply didn't have the money to pay for their housing. Everyone just had to be otherwise poorer, often getting into greater debt, to keep up. In the UK, for the poor, the state stumped up more and more of the growing bill. In the US, trailer parks grew larger and multiplied.

Eventually the gap between housing costs and earnings became too great for many people in the middle of the income distribution in the US. It was not surprising that the housing crisis began there. It was, and remains, the most economically unequal of rich countries. People had been tempted into buying on the pretext that if prices carried on being pulled up, they would be forced to rent for the rest of their lives if they did not buy now. If you can sympathize with such fears, that may have as much to do with your own housing history and what you have experienced, as with your general levels of empathy.

Poorer families in the early noughties in the US were offered mortgages at interest rates that started cheap but later rose – though what real choice did they have? In contrast, in those countries that are more equitable, renting is considered to be an acceptable option for people higher up the scale and their rents, as well as everyone else's, are lower. There are also, by definition, fewer poorer households in more equitable countries, and the rich are less rich.

Across most of the more equitable rich countries of the world, housing prices are not inflating away at the top, because incomes are not soaring at the top. More sensible decisions over where to live are possible in places other than the most expensive parts of the world's inequitable rich countries. In contrast, within the rich world, in societies such as those found in the US and the UK, growing inequalities are having an increasing influence on both residential location decisions and housing prices. For example, it becomes more and more important to live in a good area if you want to get your children into a good school. This is because when economically mixed neighbourhoods become rarer, it is harder to find schools with a mixed social intake.

Growing income inequalities allow people to segregate more through their housing choices, but, when this happens, choosing where to live becomes less of a choice and more of a burden. Where you want to live always seems just out of reach. Everyone can end up feeling poorer when a few get richer, including many of those who materially appear to have much more than others around them.

There are many effects of rising income inequalities on housing decisions. Unequal incomes necessarily fuel the growth of bubbles in the housing market, because individually it makes sense to spend as much as you can on a home when inequalities are growing. People worry about not getting on the ladder and borrow whatever they can to leap on to it. As a result poorer areas become relatively even poorer again. Then folk ask, 'Who would want to live there?' – which becomes a self-fulfilling prophecy. But such imparities must eventually end. There is usually nothing fundamentally wrong with the land in poorer areas, and nothing particularly special about the land in richer areas, other than that richer people live there. Left unchecked, prices will rise and rise where they start off highest – until almost no one can afford to live there – and then who would be fool enough to buy or rent there? This is how a new cycle of volatility begins.

It is not just housing prices that rise as inequalities grow; so too do rents, and for much the same reason: because it becomes increasingly important to avoid poorer areas and poorer regions as inequalities rise and those places that started off a little disadvantaged become more evidently poor. A precariously housed population, one that is always temporarily renting, then grows. More and more people have no way of knowing when their landlord might decide they have to leave their home. The higher the rent you pay, the less likely it is that you will be made to leave, but it is still no guarantee.

Precarious living is not just about precarious employment; it is also about being precariously housed. The effects of constantly having to move home, not when you choose but when you are forced to, are known to be worst for children and the elderly. They are the most vulnerable members of poorer households. They, and impoverished childless adults, have the least choice in housing. It is the most money, not the most needs, that gains you the most space.

In the UK one result of paying as high a rent as you could afford to, and charging as much as you could get away with, was that in the UK the housing benefit bill was allowed to balloon. This was the money government was paying directly to landlords for people who could not afford to pay the rent themselves. Government in the UK is now trying to reduce that taxpayer subsidy to landlords, but it is doing so by harming tenants, casualties of the coalition's continuing fundamental belief that the unfettered market is the best route to allocating housing. Tenants are now being harmed in many ways: most well known is when they are told they must leave their home because it has one room too many in relation to the size of their family, but there are no smaller properties for them; least well known is the growing illicit private market in renting out single rooms to entire families, or even unheated garden sheds (such is the growing desperation for housing).

To see what can happen to the majority of the population when you allow the housing market to run to extremes, it is necessary to look overseas. And you don't have to look that far. Ireland should be close enough to cause some fear; or even Spain and Portugal, of which more later; but to end this introductory chapter on the current crisis let's take the US and examine what happened there when prices and rents rose astronomically and median wages began to fall in absolute terms, year after year, without apparent end – ever since the late 1970s, in fact.[32]

Many people who had recently bought property in the US in the years up until 2008 did so on what turned out to be unsustainable mortgages. Often, once they defaulted on the mortgage, they would walk out of the property, leaving the keys behind and trying to leave the debt with the home. Others were evicted. As more and more property became vacant, vandals moved in. Because the bottom had fallen out of the market in many parts of the US, when the banks tried to auction the empty dwellings, in many cases they could find no buyers. As a result banks stopped auctioning most properties in many states.

The graph below shows how quickly banks' attitudes changed to the huge numbers of people unable to meet their mortgage payments following the crash of 2008. US banks simply gave up trying to evict defaulting mortgagees in many places, letting people remain in their property long after they had stopped paying. In some states this applied to the majority of defaulters.[33]

So badly had the housing market slumped, and so widespread was the problem, that the banks often felt that the game just wasn't worth the candle. This was just a couple of years ago, remember, not the 1930s of the Great Depression. There were also campaigns against eviction, but these were less effective than the knock-on effects of the evictions themselves: the banks soon came to realize that leaving properties empty reduced what little value was left in them and so was ultimately not in the banks' best financial interests.

By late 2012, across all of New York State, the average defaulting borrower was being allowed to remain in his or her home for almost three years, rent and mortgage free. In the US as a whole, the average time for defaulting mortgagees living-for-free had risen to over a year (and had more than tripled since 2007, when it was normal to evict people within about four months). However, none of this apparently increased leniency was enjoyable either for the overexposed lenders or for the bankrupt borrowers, who faced a precarious future in their now bank-owned properties. All these residents could, at any time, be evicted and made homeless.

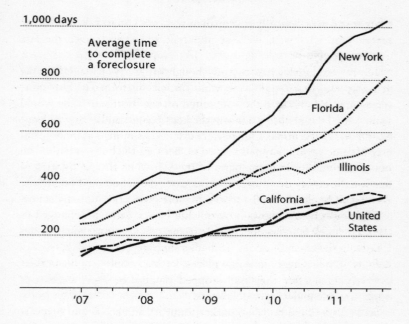

Figure 2. Average number of days to complete a foreclosure in the US by state, 2007–12. The time to complete a foreclosure has nearly tripled in the US nationwide, from about four months in 2007 to nearly a year in 2011.

In the years following 2008 something fundamental changed in the US. Both banks and buyers learned a lesson that had been forgotten for decades: that free market madness leads to misery. The bottom can fall out of markets when those markets are left to their own devices and when the vast majority of participants in the market are ill-informed in comparison with a few insiders. And even most of those insiders were burnt in the process! In hindsight just a few of the few, the insiders' insiders, came out with a profit. The vultures of this particular Disaster Capitalism were those banks and investors that had bet on the crash occurring. Maybe they had read the right books and looked at that picture of a dream home in the same way that Robert Frank had. Maybe they realized that at some point it would all have to end and they positioned themselves well to take advantage of that ending.

Many people outside of the US are unaware that not only is a near-complete housing market collapse possible, but also that it has just happened to a market as large and rich as the US's. The European press appeared averse to reporting these trends from across the Atlantic, despite being happy to talk endlessly of US celebrities. You have to look to the US press to find the reports. Perhaps writing on housing misery does not sell newspapers. Perhaps the collective interests of the European banks, the press moguls, the politicians and all the rest of those with money tied up in the system were so great that it was thought to be a bad idea for people to start thinking that housing was not very safe, that it was no longer a solid investment. In Ireland, Iceland, Portugal, Spain, Italy and Greece people are more wary. In the UK they are not.

Reporting just how bad a financial crisis has become may appear as both unpatriotic and as scaremongering; but, if it is not done, the way is opened for something worse to occur in the near future. This book tells the story that has been repeatedly ignored in the UK and suggests what might be done to effect change for the better. It begins with this chapter on **crisis**, because we are in crisis, but it should be remembered there are many routes out of a crisis. Not all is doom and gloom, but to see where we might get to requires a clearer picture of where we have been.

Chapter 2 concerns the **planning** and thinking behind housing: how housing has once again come to reflect so closely our class structure and social polarization. Issues of freedom and greed, efficiency and inequality, are first dealt with in detail here. Lessons from the (Roaring) 1920s and (Depression) 1930s are considered with a view to seeing whether our behaviour following the 2008 crash could have been predicted on the basis of what happened after 1929.

Chapter 3 considers the **foundations** of housing in Britain: what underlies our homes. How housing finance began as a form of saving small sums for those who were careful, but then came to be intricately bound up with generating wealth and with growing economic inequality. The claim being made here is that it was a shift in values and priorities that led to our current market volatility, but also that what happened in the past is not necessarily a sure guide to the future: the failure of history to precisely repeat itself increases uncertainty.

Chapter 4 concerns the **building** and upkeep of housing. Through the 1920s to the 1970s, when we were becoming more economically equal, housing for the poor was being built to better and better standards, while housing for the rich was subdivided or, at the other extreme, turned into open homes for the public to view. We are now rapidly moving away from that time and back towards the inequalities of the Roaring Twenties.

Chapter 5 looks at how we are **buying** housing: how we rent it; borrow to buy it; try but often fail to ensure our homes are affordable. It is not just that Britain began to become more unequal after the 1970s, but that London began to grow in population terms again; the capital city had been becoming less crowded and its citizens better housed decade after decade from 1911 up until then. Now the new, rapidly regrowing London is Europe's only mega-city, a place in which even the extremely well paid can struggle to find a one-bedroom flat. What are the implications for housing in Britain of current attempts to try to clear the poor from London, of allowing it to grow so rapidly and so differently from before?

Chapter 6 turns to the current **slump** in housing and asks why it is said that there is not enough housing for all. This is worth questioning, given that, in aggregate and per capita, we have never had so much housing available to be lived in. If we need to build great numbers of new homes, why is so much of the existing stock empty? Why are so many homes left empty for part of the week just because they are someone's second or third home? And why are so many more people now, as opposed to ten or twenty years ago, occupying such large homes so inefficiently if we have an overall shortage on such a large scale?

Chapter 7 considers how **speculation** in housing has got us into this mess: the rent arrears, repossessions and homelessness that result from rampant speculation. Changes in how we are housed can cause great changes in society. They can foster selfishness and be used by those who want to label large sections of the population as feckless. Growing housing insecurity has been shown to contribute to rising ill-health and to the deep-rooted anxiety and insecurity that feelings of helplessness engender, especially when people are forced to declare themselves homeless or bankrupt, or to succumb to massive borrowing in order to cope.[34]

Chapter 8 ends by offering up **solutions**, suggesting that extending already existing but little used legislation to allow people to stay in their homes when they are the victims of speculation could lead to a future where there is both less profit to be drawn from housing for a few, and more security to be enjoyed by the many. But to get to that future we must again work towards separating housing from wealth.

Throughout this book graphs and charts illustrating the current crisis are interspersed with photographs of housing in the city of Sheffield, where the first draft of this book was written. The images should serve as a reminder that housing is primarily about shelter, about our most basic needs, not about the extremes of poverty and affluence. And, although London is mentioned very often in these pages, this is mostly a story of people's struggle outside the capital.

The final draft was finished in Oxford, in September 2013, by then the 'most unaffordable city anywhere outside London'.[35] Writing a book on housing while moving between two such different cities will have coloured the pages that follow. In neither city can most people quite believe how people are housed in the other place when it is described to them. Both cities have acute housing problems: Sheffield has the longest social housing waiting list in the UK, Oxford the highest prices outside of London. Housing, like so much else in life, is ultimately about geography – about how we all get to fit in.

This image may look as if it is nothing unusual. All it shows is a bed in a corner of a room. It is an old bed; the mattress is covered with a single fitted sheet and a duvet is thrown across it. The pillow still shows the imprint of the head of the person who slept in the bed last night, and, if you look closely, you'll see that the walls of this bedroom have been papered over crudely but effectively. Your view of this bed may change once you know that it is a bed in a hostel for homeless young people in Sheffield. Above all else, housing is about bedrooms, about a place in which to sleep and feel secure. This bed has recently been home to dozens of youngsters, all of whom lack secure housing. Beds in hostels, in prisons, in hospitals and in communal halls and lodging houses are not included in the official statistics on how many beds there are in Britain. Behind the housing statistics there are missing numbers, and behind the missing numbers, and the bricks, mortar, plaster, wallpaper, beds and bedding, there are stories about how people fit into society – or not. Our homes are the slots we fit into in space. Our families are the slots we fit into in time. Making housing harder to come by makes being part of society, even being part of a family, all the harder to achieve.

2

Planning

The UK has one of the most persistently volatile housing markets, with four boom and bust cycles since the 1970s. These cycles distort housing choices, drive up arrears and repossession rates, inhibit house-building and heighten wealth inequalities.

– Mark Stephens, Professor of Economics
at the University of Glasgow[1]

Superficially, the current housing crisis can appear to be a crisis of land and building. The leading housing charity Shelter claims that 'The ultimate solution to England's housing crisis is to build more homes.'[2] The government's Business Secretary, Vince Cable, first called for an 'aggressive programme' of house-building in his speech at the 2012 Liberal Democrats' annual party conference,[3] a sentiment that was echoed by the Prime Minister later that year.[4]

At certain times not enough land appears to be available on which to build homes and not enough builders appear willing to build, even when the big building firms have control of so much of the land that is actually available. Speculators can force up the price of land far faster than that of housing. Professor Mark Stephens is right in saying that some house-building has been inhibited by the volatility of the UK market. At times in the past, and just after a price fall, it does not appear worthwhile to build new homes, because they will sell for too little; at other times it appears worth holding on to the land and building later, because prices are rising and rising. But fundamentally

Shelter is wrong: the 'ultimate' problem in recent decades has not been too little building, but growing inefficiency in our use of the housing stock that we have.

Growing income and wealth inequalities mean that housing is both chosen and allocated less and less by need and more and more by taste. And inadequate housing is increasingly put up with simply in desperation. A council maisonette that was built in northern England to house a family of three or four might today be bought by a single professional in need of somewhere cheap, someone who feels the need of a study, a spare bedroom and lots of living space (albeit possibly in a not very desirable area). The family who could have lived there is housed badly elsewhere, but there isn't enough money to provide for their greater need. More better-off people are single for longer; we live longer; and we break up more frequently and take longer to start another serious relationship than we used to – so we can easily come to occupy housing less efficiently. When we married young and stayed married, we fitted better into the housing stock; but it is not our changing demographics that are causing the shortage of housing, but rather the growing inequities in our economics.

Families tend to be much smaller than in the recent past, and people start them far later. In theory, two small households could share one large home, but you hardly ever hear of two lone-parent single-child households, a group of four people, sharing a home. Even if they wanted to, they probably could not afford it. That is what is key.

Go back not too long ago in history and you hear of how common it was for people to be packed far more tightly into housing. I'm not suggesting we need to do that, but I am suggesting that we should start worrying much more than we currently do about how many of our buildings are empty for so much of the time and of how many rooms are unused, even in buildings that are not vacant. It is worth going back to when there was almost no unused housing, in 1929, and to look at how the market crash was dealt with then, back when what was normal in Britain was to rent; and when there really were not enough habitable homes to go round.

The last time there was a depression as deep and as long as the one that Europe and most of the rest of the rich world are currently experiencing there was a very different response from the housing sector.

Between 1920 and 1938, Britain experienced a boom in both mortgage lending and house-building. This was despite wages being stagnant and unemployment rising. As Figure 3 below shows, the boom started in the three years up to the General Strike of 1926, slowed, and then took off again with a vengeance in 1933 and 1934. The figure also shows that it was fuelled by the provision of additional mortgage advances – by greater lending and growing debt. Some commentators might well suggest that if it worked then, why could such a house-building programme not work now?

The boom was not necessarily sustainable. If it had not been for the start of the war in 1939, there may have been a further economic crash. But this example nevertheless illustrates a population becoming progressively better and more fairly housed, even in the midst of a great economic crisis and fear. It has happened before; it happened then. However, from the 1920s to 1939 Britain was also becoming a much more equitable society. Half of the fall in income inequality that occurred between 1918 and 1978 occurred in just those twenty years.[5] Slums were beginning to be demolished. The first homes for (modest) heroes were built at the end of the First World War; the last new state-funded homes were built for their grandchildren at the end of the 1970s. It is for their great-grandchildren that the crisis is worse.

It could be argued that the 1920s and 1930s are too far back in

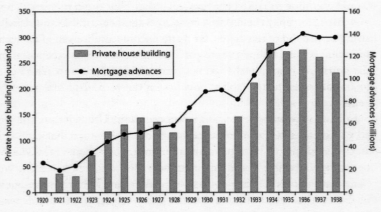

Figure 3. Private house-building and mortgage lending in the UK, 1920–38.

time for us to learn from, or that the lessons of those years are not applicable because we never got to see them fully played out. It is easy to come to believe that the Second World War alone prevented a further market crash. (An alternative theory is that the US New Deal and UK Keynesian equivalents did get us out of the hole, but they were possible only because they were coupled with growing austerity for the rich.) However, when we look back to how, despite the overall growth in income equality then, the salaries of financiers were allowed to get out of control in those years, or to how large the gap between rich and poor remained, despite the narrowing of that gap, the relevance to our own time becomes clearer. Thus the years between the world wars are worth considering in a little more detail, before we move forward in time.

Today, advocates of building our way out of the current crisis say that five years after the 1929 crash almost 300,000 homes were built in the UK, and, according to the graph opposite, over £100 million of mortgages were being issued a year, a huge sum for those times.[6] The majority of housing media pundits today appear to call for a similarly aggressive increase in lending and home-building now. But what they almost all ignore is that in the 1920s and 1930s that building was coupled with growing income *equality*. Simply building new housing in isolation did not alleviate the housing crisis of the 1920s and 1930s; *more and more people had to come to be able to afford to buy that housing*. More had to see their wages rise, and to know that they would continue to rise in the future, so that they could take up debts and afford to repay them. Most people's wages were stable and slowly rising by the end of the 1930s, while the income and wealth of the rich was, on average, falling every year[7] (though there were exceptions in the worst years and in the worst areas of unemployment). You have to go back even further to see how taxing the very rich more actually began.

In 1894 inheritance tax was introduced in the UK, but only for the very largest estates, and only at a rate of 7.5%. By 1930 that rate had risen to nearly 40%.[8] Furthermore, income taxes had been raised earlier, during the First World War, and not reduced much thereafter. We built more homes for the poor partly by depriving the richest of much of their recent extravagance. Thus, by the 1930s, great wealth was being seriously taxed for the first time through those higher death duties. Incomes at the top of the distribution were being curtailed, partly through taxation but even more so through restraint.

By the 1940s high rates of taxation deterred people at the top from trying to secure excessive pay rises. What was the point? They would receive only a small fraction of the extra money when top tax rates were taken into account. To imagine what it was like, think of what the re-introduction of higher taxation today might mean. A chief executive could receive as little as 10% today on earnings of over £500,000 a year, if they could be taxed at 90%. There would therefore be little point asking for pay rises once you were on £500,000 a year. Double your pay after that, to a nominal £1 million a year, and you would receive only an extra £50,000 for all your supposedly additional efforts. When those at the top take home less, they have less money to spend trying to buy up more housing, and the less well paid could receive more.

Recent research has determined that housing was becoming more equally shared out at the same time as more was being built. New council housing was allocated on the basis of need, and so was filled up with families that could use all the rooms. New-build private sector housing was bought because a family needed more space or was forming a new household as a couple, perhaps after living with one pair of their parents. Now they could start a family and no longer have to fit their new family within the original family home. This recent research, by Professor Rebecca Tunstall of the University of York, has shown that the allocation of space in housing became much more equitable between the censuses of 1921 and 1931, and 1931 and 1951[9] – a conclusion that she reached by comparing the amount of space occupied by the best-off tenth with that of the worst-off tenth in England and Wales using the census records. Before that, from 1911 to 1921, inequalities in allocation had been growing.

Today, the situation is very different. What little housing is being built is being even more unfairly shared out than it was a decade, or two or three decades, ago. New housing is not going to those most in need. Contrast this with the period throughout the 1950s and 1960s, and between 1971 and 1981, when housing was becoming ever more fairly allocated. Fairness over the course of the last century comes into relief when the decadal population and housing censuses are used to measure how many rooms people had, how crowded they were. Census data tells us that in the period 1921–81 the housing problem was, in aggregate, constantly being successfully addressed. It is true that part of the end of that run did include system-built high-rise flats. Mistakes were made in the past. But after 1981 different mistakes began to be made, mistakes we had not seen since just before the 1920s. Those who had the most were once again allowed to take more.

Professor Tunstall's research shows that between 1981 and 1991 those who started off with more space ended up, on average, gaining more of any additional space as compared with any other group in society. They were mostly likely to extend their property or to move home to an even larger property, despite having started with so much. Shortly before 1981, at the point at which we had become most equal, the best-off 10% of households still had 3 times as many rooms in their homes per person as the worst-housed tenth; by 2001 that ratio had risen to 3.7 times, the highest inequality recorded post-war. Rising inequality in housing provision mirrors rising inequality in income and wealth overall.[10]

In the 1930s, there was – as there is today – a perceived chronic shortage of housing. Yet the situation was very different. Then there was an absolute shortage of housing, not just a very poor distribution of a large amount of housing, as is the case today; neither was there such a vast amount of often unoccupied housing. Social divisions were very high, similar in extent to today. The top 1% took a similar share of income in 1936 as they did in 2008, but back in 1936 they had been taking less and less each year for the past twenty years; and they would continue to take less and less for the next forty. By contrast, the very best-off today have been taking more and more for at least the last thirty years and, as yet, show few signs of slowing down their land, housing and wealth grab.[11]

In England in the 1930s, the promise of a 'semi in the suburbs' appeared to be a way out of poverty, a route away from the slums. The slums were cleared by public spending, while the very rich increasingly found that death duties meant they had to donate their largest homes to the National Trust, and to downsize. Grand townhouses in London were converted into flats. But what worked then may not work now. Housing cannot be viewed in isolation from other social trends, and it could be quickly improved in the past and become more affordable because society as a whole was then becoming more equitable.

Council maisonettes in Batemoor, Sheffield, viewed from a child's eye-line. Each apartment was originally built to house a small family. Some have now been sold under the right-to-buy scheme that was brought in by Margaret Thatcher's government during the 1980s. You can perhaps tell where different styles of window have been used to replace old frames, or where the styles of the door panels differ. Those are the signs of home ownership or, more likely nowadays, of private rentals. While it is mainly still families off the waiting list who are housed in the council-owned property, slightly more affluent single people often buy those apartments that are on the open market. What were once family housing units are now sometimes single adult homes. Later on they may rent them out to another person like themselves, or to a couple, but rarely to a middle-class couple with children. As economic inequality grows, fewer and fewer people use up more and more housing space and land.

The 1930s was the time when large numbers of people were first able to put down deposits to borrow money to buy their homes. Some of these deposits were as low as 5% of the property value. And house-builders often helped even with those modest deposits, lending or even gifting that supposedly 'saved' money to prospective purchasers. This was to stimulate growth in the housing market, and in a way is very similar to what the UK government has been doing with its schemes to help people buy new-build homes today. But lending too much was frowned upon, both then and now, as it could inflate the market and, as both then and now, people were living in the aftermath of an economic crash.

There are other similarities between the 1930s and today. Mortgage repayment periods lengthened from 20 years to 25 or 27 years, despite the much lower life-expectancy at the time. In 1930 the median age of death for men was 67 and for women it was 71. By 2010 these figures were 82 and 85 respectively.[12] But by the noughties people had started to take out mortgages much later in life and also for longer, so they could again be paying back the bank until their old age. There are other possible similarities between the 1930s and now. Back then the lack of available housing was partly blamed for very few children being born, for a dip in fertility. In some quarters the same is suggested as being a strong possibility today, even during the current mini-baby-boom.

HOUSING DEMAND

We are in a housing crisis that extends from the homeless on the street well into the middle class. We have couples deciding not to have children because they do not have the space to house them. We have people paying extortionate rents, and the lowest rate of new home construction in almost a century. Yet ministers just sit there like gouty old men in the 19th hole . . .

– Nick Cohen, *Spectator*[13]

Britain is not undergoing a mini-baby-boom where the cost of housing is highest. In 2011 the fertility of the UK was 1.91 children born per woman, but the lowest number was in London, at 1.84 children.[14] Furthermore, there is extensive out-migration from London of families with children. No doubt the near-impossibility, for many, of being able to provide their children with much space within Britain's most crowded city is a large part of the reason for the annual exodus of so many children from the capital. Central London in particular is not child-friendly, with by far the largest annual net migration of children routinely recorded as being from there.[15] However, that annual out-migration has been curtailed since the crash of 2008. When young families with very small children can't move out of inner London, there is suddenly a huge shortage of primary school places, soon set to reach 118,000 places.[16]

A century ago, to try to alleviate the severe housing problems and to prevent landlords from profiteering during and after the First World War, the government imposed rent control, from 1914 onwards. At that time, paying rent of less than a third of your income was generally a 'danger-signal' that something was very wrong with the rooms.[17] There was great agitation in society; revolution had just taken place in Russia. Neville Chamberlain, as Health Minister in 1923, introduced a Housing Act that subsidized private sector housebuilding. The first ever Labour government to gain power was elected in 1924, having won almost enough votes in 1923. It promised many things, among them the addressing of the housing problem of those times. It introduced the Housing (Financial Provisions) Act, now known as the Wheatley Act, which encouraged house-building by local authorities. Then, exactly ten years later, in 1934, the Special Areas (Development and Improvement) Act was introduced by the coalition government to boost spending in the more depressed industrial regions. Next, in terms of milestones, the 1944 coalition government pledged 'a separate house for every family that wishes to have one'.[18] The Labour government of 1945 began the building needed. Change takes time. The achievement of each decade was hard won, and would often have appeared nearly impossible to imagine just a generation earlier.

In retrospect, we can see that the period from 1918 through to 1945 was one of ever greater intervention in the provision of housing by the state. The period that followed, from 1945 to 1970, is now famous for alternating Labour and Conservative administrations vying to demonstrate which could build the most state housing. There was a boom in private sector building too. The population became increasingly well housed. Although the 1971 census still recorded whether a home had hot running water or not, it did so to help local authorities determine where most improvements in housing stock were needed.

Great plans were made by the late 1960s Labour governments to improve housing even further, culminating in the census of 1971, which was the most detailed survey of the nation's housing ever made. However, by the early 1970s, Britain was lurching through a series of financial crises, and the aspiration that every family that wished to have a separate home should be able to have one suffered a setback. Inflation was soaring, and there was a squeeze on the provision of mortgages as interest rates rose and rose, being well over 10% a year for many years to come. Part of the reason there was a policy turn-around by 1981 was because of public disquiet over these crises – a disquiet that allowed a group of politicians to come to power in 1979 and instigate policies that benefited the best-off in society. In doing so they sowed the seeds of our current crisis.

Again, a comparison with the 1920s and 1930s shows that, follow-ing the economic crashes of 1929 and 2008, interest rates were kept low. (The financial crises of the 1970s were minor, and very different in comparison with either of these crashes: interest rates rose rather than fell as inflation rose, but they were seized on by the rich as an opportunity to allow economic inequalities to grow again, and, in so doing, to stoke up greater inequity in housing.)

The economic crash of 2008 and the ensuing slump was uncannily similar to that of 1929. In response to the latter, the UK government tried to create a housing boom by lowering interest rates in a way very similar to what the Bank of England did post-2008, and has con-tinued to do until at least 2014. When interest rates are set very low, the incentive to borrow, including possibly borrowing to build, is very high. But this can be a risk if institutions and people find it difficult later to pay back the cost of that borrowing when interest rates rise.

Take a look at the graph below, which shows how, in 1929, the three-month Treasury Bill rate plummeted along with the Bank of

England base rate. Treasury Bills, known as sovereign bonds, are short-term investments that can be bought from the government, which pays what is, in effect, interest at a 'rate' advertised when they are sold, but received only when the bonds mature. The base rate is normally lower than this, being the rate at which the Bank of England will lend to other banks.

In 1932 the base rate fell to 2%, bringing down interest rates for borrowers too, not quite to the historically low rates of today, but still to some of the lowest base rates ever recorded. Note also how flat the trend shown in the graph below was five years after the crash (from 1934 onwards, through to 1939). That is very similar to what the new Governor of the Bank of England, Mark Carney, suggests will happen from 2013 to 2018, although many do not believe him.[19] He says he will keep the rates low until unemployment falls below 7%. He may, but the official rate of unemployment was not much higher than 7% when he said this, and the official rate can easily come down if more people are forced to take a few hours of very low-paid part-time work (docked benefits would be the result if they fail to accept the work on

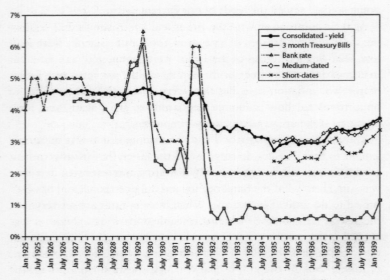

Figure 4. Interest rates in the UK by type of loan and Treasury Bills, 1925–39.

offer, no matter how unsuitable). Back in the 1930s there was far less part-time work. A job was a job, and there simply were not enough jobs to go round.

The graph shown above was drawn not in the 1930s but in 2008, the year the current crisis began, by George Speight, then Senior Manager at the Bank of England, responsible for the Systemic Risk Reduction Division.[20] One result of the policies of the 1930s, Speight remarked in 2010, was that the 'housing market looked increasingly unstable – [with] risk of a vicious circle of falling prices, rising repossessions, financial pressure on building societies, reduction in the supply of mortgage lending'.[21] Speight thought it worth comparing what was being planned for the UK after 2010 with what had happened during the 1930s.

A single lifetime later, and again there are concerns that the housing market is becoming increasingly unstable and that government policies – by causing prices to rise and building up a new bubble – may even be fuelling the growing instability. During summer 2013 financial experts began to call for a turnaround in policies when it appeared that a housing price bubble was once more forming.[22] Earlier, in his lecture at the Ashmolean in Oxford, George Speight had said that we had no way of now knowing whether the low-interest-rate-fuelled lending frenzies of the 1930s would have spiralled out of control and that all that had saved the lending societies was the onset of the war. He explained that the cost of rearmament increased prices overall, which helped to raise house prices and hence to reduce the size of housing-related debt. Then, during wartime, the government itself guaranteed mortgage payments and there was further inflation.

In other words, the last time the housing finance system in Britain was in as much of a mess as it is today, the saviour proved to be a cataclysmic event – a world war. The much more stable economy we enjoyed after the war was partly the product of the war's economic conditions; and the continued growth in economic equality was partly the product of the war's pragmatism and solidarity. Back then it was accepted that everyone needed to be decently housed, and that until that had been achieved no one should have too much. After the era of rationing, people understood that you all did better when you shared out better what you had.

Part of what is different this time is that there is, hopefully, no world war looming. But subsequently there seems to be nothing to stop the current housing crisis turning into a housing disaster. During wartime, housing reverts to what it should be: shelter. And bankers to what they should be: accountants employed to protect us from gamblers and gambling. Today there is no collective memory of 'all being in it together', of sharing by rationing. Rather, there is a widespread ethos instilled by Thatcherism that you need to put yourself first, to get into the top half of society and then you'll be OK; or, if you are already in the top half, to get into the top tenth; and, if you are in the top tenth, to become one of the best-off 1%. There is remarkably little understanding that the 1% can only ever be 1% of the population.

But what is also different now – and why we should not draw too many parallels with the 1930s building spree – is that then we had far too few homes for the number of people living in Britain. In 1931 there were, on average, 4.2 people for every dwelling that existed. Today that figure is 2.3, but for the first time since the war it is actually rising slightly.[23] Orthodox economic theory suggests that, because of this, housing prices could start to recover overall and building resume, because there is now an increasing absolute demand to be met, not a demand largely created by an increased inequality in supply. But that demand has very little money behind it, and the ratio of people to homes has still risen by only a fraction. What is more, overcrowding as traditionally measured is rising most where there is the least space to build, in London.

Overcrowding caused when young adults are unable to set up on their own is also rising. Altogether, a fifth of parents in Britain with children aged twenty-one to forty now have at least one living with them who cannot afford to move out; and a tenth have one who, they say, could just about afford it but who chooses not to.[24] This is worse than it has been recently in Britain, but it does not compare with the time of those children's great-grandparents, in the 1930s, when there simply was not enough housing to go round, even after so many of the big houses were subdivided. More had to be built.

In the present day, as in the 1930s, interest rates are very low and taxes need, in effect, to be raised to pay for the deficit. Or, put another way by Professor Nicholas Crafts: 'The aspect of the 1930s that is especially relevant for today is that it represents the only experience that the UK has had of attempting fiscal consolidation when nominal interest rates are close to the lower bound and reductions in interest rates cannot be used to offset the impact of tighter fiscal policy on aggregate demand.'[25] Although somewhat of a mouthful, academic thinking such as this has led for repeated calls in the broadsheet press for us to learn from the 1930s,[26] and in some ways we can.

Some aspects of the past are very familiar. During the late 1920s and into the 1930s, rather like the 1990s and 2000s, the pay of top mortgage financiers rose rapidly. Back then these were the directors of the large building societies, such as the Abbey Road Building Society (ARBS, which became Abbey National) and the Co-operative Permanent Building Society (CPBS, which became the Nationwide). Today the equivalents to those highly paid building society men of the past are the CEOs of the biggest banks. The graph below shows just how quickly top financiers' pay rose in the years up to 1940.[27] However, you would have to multiply these averages by at least one thousand to get to the rate of remuneration of even the most lowly of current financial directors today. Only a small part of that increase is due to inflation.

A large part of the reason why the pay of 'top' bankers is so much higher now is due to differences between the times that preceded the crashes of 1929 and of 2008. Bankers back then were largely not aristocrats; certainly the building society directors whose pay is being plotted here were not. The landed gentry were far richer then, as were many merchants and industrialists, in comparison with the 'City men' of that time. But today it is the bankers who rule the financial roost. Industrialists and merchants are paid less, and many of the gentry have sold their mansions to a banker to make ends meet. Contemporary top financiers have been far greedier than their equivalents were eighty years ago, but note how in all but one case top pay stopped rising after 1929. The one exception was the pay of the man in charge of the Woolwich Equitable Building Society. Ironically it is now owned by Barclays, but the man at the top of that bank in 2008, Bob Diamond, was out of his job a few years after the crash and was not replaced by someone who was even more expensive than him.

Today the equivalents of top building society directors of the 1930s,

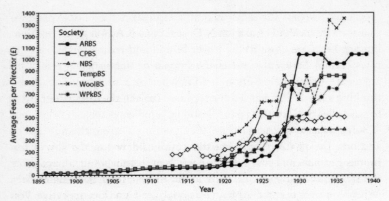

Figure 5. Building society Director fees in the UK, 1895–1940.

still almost exclusively men, are the highest-paid employees at Barclays, RBS, HSBC and Lloyds. These are the men who head the four major UK banks. Each of these banks has a balance sheet over £1 billion. These are the four banks that are all too big to fail. Their size, it has been claimed, guarantees them a £34 billion advantage through what is in effect state insurance.[28]

Being seen as too large to fail helps the largest banks to pay their executives such enormous sums. Banks are now so enormous and so complex, they argue, that only a few people in the world are qualified to run them. These institutions have come to be of crucial importance to all of us because all of us have to bail them out if they crash. In theory, by law, collectively we are insuring all deposits up to £85,000 in all these banks. All the time!

We have been here before, but the reason to worry more now is that the last time we were in such a mess with our housing war curtailed the excesses at the top. In the 1930s the country was becoming more equal, but the financiers were taking more and more. Now we are becoming less equal, partly *because* the financiers are taking more and more. As the graph above shows, the last time top financiers' pay rose as fast, excessive pay was slightly held in check by the events of 1929, but it wasn't fully controlled until 1939. And in comparison with the greed of today, the boardroom excesses of the 1930s look like peanuts.

AVARICE AND IGNORANCE

*Please don't make me sound like a prat for not knowing how
many houses I've got.*

– David Cameron, 2009[29]

In 2009 David Cameron almost certainly knew exactly how many
homes his wife and he owned, or had 'got' – four – but he probably
did not want all those who were about to vote for him to know this.
When you own several homes, you no longer own them to live in: you
own them to generate and maintain wealth, a lot of wealth.

The number of households renting privately rose by 1.1 million in
the UK between 2007 and 2011, to 4.7 million. A further 4.9 million
were renting from a social landlord.[30] The last time as many people
rented was in the 1960s, and by then the proportion had been falling
for at least half a century. Even though we are now so much better
housed, you have to go back to just before the First World War to find
a time when the trends were worsening as they are now. Back then, as
many people in Britain were as insecurely housed as they are today,
and faced a future of even greater insecurity, in large part because a
few people relied on their property portfolios to maintain their wealth
and privilege. Every working-class family and much of the middle
class rented. But top incomes coming from earnings were lower then;
it was incomes from rent that were higher. The great housing disaster
of our times is the return to such great financial inequality, now supposedly based on a few being worth so very much not for what assets
they have inherited but for what they do.

Growing income inequality in the UK, led by bankers' pay rises at
the very top, makes housing increasingly insecure for the majority,
and it is in the interests of the bankers that this should be the case.
The more times people start new mortgages or fail to complete old
ones; borrow money to buy because they cannot afford the rent; or
borrow money to buy houses to rent out – the more times all that
happens, the more money banks make. Stability and security are bad
for profiteering.

When we had more stability, we had building societies that worked as charities, made no profit for any shareholders and, after 1939, controlled the pay of their staff well. But almost all of the building societies were sold off in the 1980s and 1990s, when the law was changed to make that possible. Thus it has been the planned advancement and general tolerance of rising avarice that has brought us to where we are. But the key word here is 'planned': this did not happen by accident. Changes in legislation over recent decades have actively encouraged the extreme greed of a few who have gained wealth through the ignorance of a large majority of us.

Rent controls had been maintained in the UK all the way from the First World War to 1977, when they were consolidated in the Fair Rent Act: this ensured that landlords could increase the rent only every two years, and only if rents of similar properties were being increased. The effect of this legislation was to make it hard for landlords to profit excessively and easier for people to come to own their own home, as builders built homes to sell to individuals rather than to landlords. This state of affairs obtained until the Fair Rent Act was, in effect, repealed, in the late 1980s. The provisions of that previous Act still apply, but only to those who are still alive, have not moved home and took out tenancies before 1988. And, as only a landlord's solicitor could put it, 'Property investors need to be aware of this, as often investment properties are available at low prices because redevelopment is not possible, as the tenants are protected and cannot be evicted.'[31] You can make more money as an investor when you can evict.

The phrase 'property investor' has now entered the language. Estate agents will ask potential buyers of property whether their interest is in 'residential' or 'investment' – the latter means to become a landlord. Shelter estimates that no more than around 2% of people in Britain are landlords. The number of landlords does not rise greatly when more and more people have to rent privately: what happens is that a few people and institutions end up acquiring a huge amount of property. The assured short-hold tenancy brought in by the 1988 Housing Act allowed this process to slowly begin, coming shortly after the big bang of 1986 when the City was deregulated and the old building societies, with their models of responsible lending, were subsumed.

The great housing insecurity of our times has been brought about by a minority becoming the hoarders of property, and this hoarding has been facilitated by successive governments. It has not always been like this and it need not continue, but the hoarding will get worse if we do not acknowledge it and once again make it undesirable for a few to stockpile housing. We will also need to address the acute inequalities in income that have arisen since 1980 and have made buying an extra property with ready cash an option for a tiny but very influential minority.

As pointed out at the very start of this book, if people hoarded food on the basis that its value was sure to go up when others began to starve and would pay anything, we would stop their hoarding. But hoarding is now happening again with shelter in the most unequal parts of the affluent world. Because of this, because of the selfish actions of a few, many younger householders in the UK are now spending 50% of their income on housing, often just to rent or to cover the monthly payments on an interest-only mortgage. The average housing costs of all households in the UK fell from 21% to 20% of total expenditure between 2008 and 2010, when interest rates fell.[32] This average includes all those households that own outright and hence have very low housing costs. Exclude the outright owners and it rises to nearly a third of total expenditure for most, and more than half for some. This is similar to what was recorded for most families in 1913.[33]

There is a point of view that says that none of this matters. Some people suggest that in a free market people are not forced to pay the prices homes are being sold for or rented at; that they could always buy something cheaper. But it becomes very hard to find somewhere cheaper that your family can fit into when housing greed cascades down from above to damage us all. Although cheap property can be found, it is often in areas of acute social deprivation or in parts of the country where there's no work, in those places where the crisis has impacted particularly badly. Renting in areas where there are more jobs is often more expensive than buying. High rents then force up home sale prices, because they make those prices look low in comparison with renting when interest rates are low, and they also make the entire market more volatile.

When people are buying property at prices they do not think are reasonable, it does not take much for some, at some point, just to hold back a little. All that is underpinning the housing market in the south of England right now is a general feeling of confidence based on a perceived lack of alternatives.

In those parts of Britain where unemployment has not risen, there is now almost nothing left on the open market for the people who, in the past, would have bought the cheapest property, so many more have to rent than did previously. With more people renting, more property lies vacant between lets. Finding somewhere to live as a tenant becomes more difficult, with the result that more people resort to hostels, more sleep rough, more have to squat, more stay with parents until their forties, more are overcrowded. It is not that this might happen: it has happened. That is a crisis. Later chapters in this book give the statistics on rising homelessness. Those statistics need to be understood in the context of why less housing is available for most people, despite our having more housing in Britain, per person, than ever before.

A few people are becoming very rich by speculating on housing, owning homes they do not need, often renting them out to give themselves a great profit, but sometimes leaving them empty for prolonged periods. Why do people, especially those with great assets, appear to behave so selfishly? And why is their attitude so different from that of their parents, who did not behave as badly? It appears to be the case that the entire culture around property has changed in the last thirty years or so – that we have recently been taught to adopt attitudes towards it that are not the same as those of our parents. Part of the teaching is subconscious. Changing attitudes to housing mirror general changes that result from growing inequalities in society. As we become more unequal, we begin to think differently. Recent research has shown that as inequality rises, richer people become more selfish,[34] poorer people become more confused,[35] and the overall attitudes, in general, of all of us shift to the right, to being less collective, to thinking our futures depend largely on our individual actions.[36] In fact our futures depend far more on what happens to the people all around us than on those individual actions.

How people think is greatly influenced by their times as well as by their personal circumstances. In May 2013 the right-wing economic historian Niall Ferguson claimed that the man most credited with ending the last housing and economic crisis as significant as today's, John Maynard Keynes, thought as he did because he was gay and childless.[37] This was meant as an insult to Keynes, who was a Liberal, but who would be seen as left-wing today. Ferguson later apologized for implying that being gay or not having children was some kind of limitation.[38] The implication was that Keynes could not see the value of holding on to wealth within rich families. But perhaps his personal circumstances did help Keynes to view the world with a little less self-interest than people like Niall Ferguson.

To better understand the mess we are currently in over how we are housed, we need to understand how some of the very rich might think. To caricature: the rich know they will die, but some hope that their ideals, their stewardship of the world, will cause the future to be shaped in a particular way, so their way of life can live on. But that is just one possible explanation for hoarding. Or perhaps they are just frightened for their children, if they have children, and are very much less concerned about the children of others.

Could it be that some of the rich amass housing because they believe that passing on great wealth to their children will protect them? As inequalities grow and the future looks more precarious, and more and more families in society are precariously housed, the incentive to hoard may grow. Could it be as simple as that? But within the more selfish world that they are creating, their children may also have less secure futures even if they start off richer, because there will be more opportunities for failure. Rising economic insecurity could lead wealthy people to become even greedier. They might need all that money. They never know!

A particularly astute social commentator, Oscar Wilde, who did not live long enough to see the downfall of Victorian society, suggested in 1891 that: 'Selfishness is not living as one wishes to live, it is asking others to live as one wishes [them] to live. And unselfishness is letting other people's lives alone.'[39] Today, as we regain Victorian inequalities, selfishness becomes asking others to live in ways that support your lifestyle but that you yourself would not tolerate: in cramped conditions, in debt and anxious. Others need to live like this if you are to live as you wish and have as much as you want, with spare homes and much spare space in your homes, just in case you might need it.

I think it is charitable to suggest that, because of increased volatility, because all is suddenly not so solid, a small group is again doing its best to leave a huge inheritance; and a larger group mistakenly believes that they have the moral right to do so. But before we arrived at our current levels of extreme inequality, we had achieved more stable times. However, there were a few back then who grew up to hate that stability and predictability. Inequalities did not rise again by accident; they had to be driven upwards. Perhaps we need more people who can think as broadly and as unconventionally as Wilde and Keynes once did. Bubbles of avarice always need pricking, but each bubble is different from the last. Wilde gave two reasons as to why we keep on repeating our past mistakes: 'The evolution of man is slow. The injustice of men is great.'[40] They remain apposite.

We all know that many of the next generation will do things that their parents disapprove of. We need to remember that most rich families in the past saw their wealth frittered away by one or other of their children, or, if not by them, then by their grandchildren. Almost all charitable foundations end up being wound up within a few decades of the founder's death. Their names do not live on. Almost all buildings named after the great and the good get renamed. Good ideas and good deeds live on far longer in the collective memory than does any dedication of money.

This section began by quoting the Prime Minister on how many homes he owned, but he was last asked that question when he was in opposition. David and Samantha Cameron will one day inherit a great deal of money, more from her side than his. Their wealth, even that amassed before their full inheritance is received, will allow them to own many more properties in future, leaving aside all the future earnings he might make on the lecture circuit, or she might receive for designing expensive notebooks for people with expensive tastes.

Many thought that in 2009, back when David said 'Please don't make me sound like a prat', their kind were a dying breed. Many thought that property ownership was still spreading to more and more households, that wealth could still be diluted, especially in the aftermath of the economic crash. Now we need to realize that owning just four homes may be a low point for people as rich as the Prime Minister and his wife; in future the wealthy are set to have more, but not all of the wealthy.

Considering today's extremely affluent people we tend to see only their successes. We see only those families who have successfully sheltered their wealth, those families who married within the world of the affluent and didn't water down the legacy. These are the families and the trusts and foundations that are still around. We do not see that, just as money can't buy you love, it is also no sure guarantor of the long-term security of your descendants. If we saw wealth differently, we would have fewer problems providing good housing for all, because all of our descendants could one day depend on what we collectively provide and how we collectively act.

This book began with the argument that is central to the case it makes. It concerns our current dilemma's foundation. Debates about the arrangement of housing and wealth are ultimately debates about freedom. The point being made here is that when there is a great disaster looming in housing, there is also the potential for a disastrous loss of wider freedoms. When all that is solid about our housing system becomes uncertain, our freedom to live without fear of the future diminishes. Similarly our freedom to choose where we live is curtailed. We are less free to move home, to live in other places just across the other side of our town, let alone across our country. We become fearful of how much further our right to be sheltered well will be impacted upon by those who always want more. More and more people become victims of a peculiar type of market failure, one that deprives us of the right to live where many of our parents did.

HOPE AND FREEDOM

This is such an egregious example of market failure, and threatens to transform a once socially diverse capital into an exclusive playground for the jet-set and a cash cow for absentee landlords. It's time we start thinking about who has the right to the city.

– Giles Fraser, Priest-in-Charge at St Mary, Newington, by the Elephant and Castle (former Canon Chancellor of St Paul's Cathedral, who resigned in 2011 over the threat to use force to remove the Occupy protesters)[41]

Lack of access to decent housing and a growing sense of insecurity about how we are to be housed equates to a lack of access to freedom and a growing restriction on the right of the majority to live a good and safe life. To ensure our freedom to be well housed, we should look to where those freedoms are most curtailed and be concerned first with those who are the least free to choose. And when it comes to housing, it is the homeless who are the least free. As Jeremy Waldron, Professor of Law and Philosophy at NYU,[42] explained in the aftermath of the huge rise in homelessness that took place in the United States during the Reagan years (1980–88):

> If homelessness raises questions even in regard to the most basic principles of liberty, it is an issue that ought to preoccupy liberal theorists every bit as much as more familiar worries about torture, the suppression of dissent, and other violations of human rights. That the partisans of liberty in our legal and philosophical culture have not always been willing to see this (or say it) should be taken as an indication of the consistency and good faith with which they espouse and proclaim their principles.[43]

What Professor Waldron was saying, in 1991, is that people who talk of freedom but who are not concerned about housing – and about the extreme of homelessness – are not really concerned about freedom at all. They might be concerned about their personal freedom to do what they like and live as they like, but they are apparently less concerned that others should have the most basic freedom of having somewhere safe to live. Often people who advocate what they think of as the great freedom of the 'free market' find it hard to consider the basic freedoms of others.

You are likely to be reading this book because you believe that housing is a crucial issue of our times. You are very unlikely to be homeless or even to have been homeless. However, we all need to be concerned, not only about homelessness and those who are very insecurely housed, but also about the very rich, and the affluent, and the average, and the modest, and the poor and other minorities, if we are to ensure that the current deleterious housing situation improves. The way to guarantee greater freedom is to think more widely than just about ourselves and our families. If there is to be enough good housing for all, and if our friends and family are to be well housed in the future, we cannot just look after our own short-term interests.

It is when everyone concentrates too much on their own interests that those very interests are harmed: we find that most of us are squeezed into too little space to be well housed, and that the growing wealth of a few affluent landlords and multiple property owners translates into growing insecurity and financial volatility for the majority. Ultimately, when the super-rich are encouraged to speculate on housing, they fuel a property bubble that grows exponentially with their wealth before it bursts. Those who find they have invested in whatever is next most profitable, often out of luck, become the new rich. But they know their position could easily be usurped. Each person acting purely from self-interest creates a future that is in almost nobody's interest. It is in how well or how badly we are housed that this becomes most evident, day in, day out.

There are wider arguments than greater efficiency for demanding that we better manage our housing. The way we currently organize housing literally makes many of us sick with worry; it is a grossly unfair allocation of scarce resources. Ultimately we have to recognize that housing is not just central to our well-being but also to our environment, and to environmental sustainability. A more socially divided country sees its citizens experience longer and more polluting commutes to work, a less efficient use of land and space overall, more wasted building, more empty buildings. More become homeless and fewer are well housed when a fraction of the population is encouraged to speculate in ways that do more harm than good – when they are encouraged to treat property as a financial investment.

3

Foundations

We need to avoid turning a housing crisis into a homelessness disaster.

– Kathleen Kelly, Joseph Rowntree Foundation, 2012[1]

Housing sells news. It sells magazines on how to do up your home and keep it looking good. It keeps local newspapers afloat financially by providing inside pages full of property adverts. It generates TV shows and newspaper articles of 'property porn', images of wonderful dream homes being renovated or designed by determined couples – almost always couples – couples locating, couples relocating, couples buying a second or holiday home, couples with grand plans. Housing becomes entwined with the promise of successful personal relationships, with success in careers, in business and in almost all other aspects of life. Often the stories about beautiful homes (and beautiful people) sit side by side with tales of housing woe: the couple that cannot get on the ladder, the family being evicted who can no longer pay the rent, and the unsuccessful, the less 'beautiful people'.

Every year books like this one are published complaining about how we house so many people so poorly, even in countries as affluent as the UK. For each book that is published, thousands of disenchanted newspaper articles are written. Almost all of these articles consist of one lament after another, concerning lack of supply, high prices, extortionate rents, the poor quality of some of our homes, or the need for the extra homes we wish we could live in, the homes we wish could be built. Housing creates controversy and concern. And when our nests appear to be under threat, when our offspring struggle to secure their own home, there seems to be one obvious answer: build more.

This book is different: it is a book about housing, but it does not advocate building many more homes. This book does not add support to many of the usual solutions offered. It does not suggest that so-called affordable housing schemes are good, or that we necessarily need thousands of new 'council homes' to be built. It does suggest that the housing problem requires a more serious solution than merely building more homes. This conclusion has resulted partly from concerns about the near-future, not about the present. Solutions such as home-building, which look as if they might solve some of our present woes, may not be the panacea many imagine if we continue to allow a few to get richer and richer through exploitation of what the housing system has become. Building more may result in the wealthy owning even more houses, more families renting some of those homes, but more being empty at any one time and in greater future inequality, unless we address rising inequalities in how housing is shared out.

We are currently sowing the seeds of a housing disaster, a disaster that is yet to come. It will happen if those in affluent countries carry on housing themselves through the vehicle of accrued wealth, when property ownership becomes just another investment, a money spinner. We need to look at where we are heading, given what we are currently doing. I suggest that Britain presents an extreme case, in which the disaster has already loomed into view, and that the commonly suggested solutions have so far been inadequate for the long term.

Many suggestions have been made about how the housing disaster could be averted, apart from more mass home-building: from reintroducing rent controls to bringing in completely new land taxes, from rationing bedrooms in social housing to self-building new green homes. But what needs to be stressed is that none of these solutions will work if we continue to tolerate the rising polarization in wealth. This message may sound repetitive, but the underlying cause of our problems is repetitive, and our failure to understand it means that solutions have been proposed that would make the problem of inequality worse. Why ration rooms in social housing even more when that is already the most cramped sector and those concerned are not sitting on a home simply to see their wealth grow? The majority of our national wealth is held in the form of housing, and that wealth is becoming more unevenly shared out as our incomes become more unequal year after year. Polarization in house price trends exacerbates the divides begun by growing income inequalities. Is it any wonder we have a housing crisis?

Currently far too many of the very affluent believe that, if they neglect to pass on a little wealth to their friends or family, they will impoverish them, that they will have failed. Some feel they need to buy their sons and daughters houses when they are university students so that they have an 'investment'. The grandchildren of the very richest in society also need some property purchased in their names, just to be secure in future. Such behaviour will not necessarily protect the relatives of the rich, but it will certainly ensure that another family does not get to secure a mortgage on the home that is part of a toddler's property portfolio.

For the very affluent, transfers of money, often avoiding taxation, to help with 'grandchildren's school fees, higher education costs[2] and the deposit on a first home'[3] are trifling sums, amounts to help with everyday costs, written about as if Granddad were lending a tenner. However, it is not normal to pay school fees: only 7% of children attend private school. It is not normal to have your university fees paid for by rich relatives: it is normal to get into debt. And it is not normal for grandparents to be rich enough to give their grandchildren large amounts of money, even on their death. When for a small group all these things become normal, they become unconcerned with issues such as the quality of state schools, rising student debt or the housing crisis. Some may even see it as being in their grandchildren's competitive interests for the lives of those whom they are by-passing to be made worse. The children of the rich might find it easier to win in a race when the schools of the majority are underfunded.

Above the affluent group being considered here are people so rich that none of these issues matter for them. For them, even very expensive housing is just a minor expense. Because of the existence of this very rich group above them, the affluent often do not think of themselves as rich or fortunate. They think of themselves as normal, having to worry about where the school fees might come from. When they put property in trust, for instance, on behalf of a toddler, they see their behaviour as careful, good and moral. They may even see themselves as 'average people', or as average among those whom they consider to be hard working and able, 'people like us', as they might say.

In Britain, by 2008–10, a tenth of households had net assets worth at least £970,000. Most in that tenth had far more than that; and, during 2013, the criterion for entry into the richest tenth of households exceeded £1 million as property prices in London rose. Contrast that tenth with the bottom tenth, where, in 2008–10, those households had only £13,000 in assets, most having far less and many with practically no assets at all.[4] And, again, the gap will have been widening since those recent years. The best-off of the poorest will now have less. The richest tenth of children by household in Britain are growing up in families with well over *one hundred times* as much wealth as the poorest tenth.[5] As a result rich and poor children in Britain currently lead parallel lives, their paths rarely cross, and their perceptions of what is normal are easily distorted. The poor believe that the rich must be happy; the rich believe that the poor must be dangerous.

In British society today, far too many believe that they have to become more affluent for the purpose of just looking after their family's future well-being, especially their housing. If they were just a little better off, all would be fine, people say. However, once they get into that better-off group, they quickly acclimatize to the norms of that group. It is very hard not to acclimatize. Who are you to disagree with the majority of the new group you have joined? 'Don't be skinflints', you may hear. You 'have to look after yourself, as nobody else will'. In a way, so long as growing numbers think like that, they may be right.

Too many of the affluent believe that you must buy the biggest home you can to ensure you are safe in future, or hold more than one home in a portfolio of 'investments'. That kind of thinking makes us all badly off and all, in one way or another, badly housed. And it also makes housing as a whole extremely volatile. It is also not necessarily a good idea (socially, psychologically or politically) for the very affluent to be corralled in a few areas of expensive housing, near the fee-paying schools where they send their children. And for many of the very rich there is always the fear that their tax dodging will be found out, or that their legal tax avoidance will be redefined as tax evasion. Taxes may rise, share markets may fail. The wealth they think is so necessary to their well-being is a target for many others, and that can be frightening.

No matter who you are – multimillionaire landlord or in-debt tenant – you can have little firm idea of what the future may hold when it comes to housing. But millions of people are starting to rely on housing as a source of finance, and not just hoping for an uncertain windfall. Already, two million existing pensioners plan to sell their home to boost their pension.[6] However, even if you are mildly well off you cannot necessarily rely on your home to pay for your retirement. In 1995 the median fifty-year-old in Britain had net wealth of £66,000. By 2005 that had risen to £187,000 because of the housing boom, but then prices fell.[7] Prices cannot rise as greatly again without an influx of hundreds of thousands of incredibly wealthy immigrants spreading out from central London. If you are hoping that the rising value of your home will be your pension, that immigration is what you are hoping for. Furthermore that average gain of £121,000 did not come out of the ether: it was a transfer from young to old.[8] The younger generation is now paying the price of the older generation's house price inflation windfall. This is widely recognized, even on the political right.[9]

Suppose you are richer than the median but not quite in the top 10%. You might think you would then be OK relying on your housing 'investment', but, even if you own property outright in a 'good' area, it might plunge in value just at the point when you need its value. Most people take their home off the market at that point, but you might not have that choice. You can't choose when you become ill or redundant, or necessarily have much control over when your relationship breaks down. Housing is becoming a casino investment. Even the modern-day landlord may find himself with a great liability on his hands in future. What if fewer people go to university in the future and more of those who do choose to stay at home? So the market in student lets falls. Whatever happens, there will be winners and losers, and they need not be the same generations, groups or places as before; times change.

The message of this era of greed is: try to make as much money as you can out of housing as soon as you can, and give up renting if you possibly can. If you can't – then you're a loser. If you buy or sell at the wrong time, you're a loser. If you don't exploit others, you're a loser. If you spend money maintaining your property, it may not increase its value, but cosmetic changes just before you come to sell can boost its price – just quickly paint over the rotting woodwork.

Prices are rising; and prospective buyers will be told by estate agents how unlikely they are to fall. As one fund analyst put it in August 2013: 'We are back in a time where, as Mr Gekko said, "greed is good". And, once again, in one form or another, it would appear "it's legal".'[10] It is in many people's legal interests to cajole others into staying in the casino. It is in the interests of mortgage brokers and of estate agents; even the Treasury does well, as it collects stamp duty on sales. But eventually almost everyone in a casino ends up a loser.

It is not just in the UK that there are these problems. In the West in general, housing is in crisis – and all parts of society are at risk. People who think of themselves as being of modest means in the West are, when viewed from a worldwide perspective, among the richest on earth. When sorted by income, most of the world's 1% richest people live in what are often described as 'modest homes' worth $200,000 to $400,000. It is because these can fall in value just at the wrong time for their retirement, or for a job change, or for the end of a relationship, that even people this well off do not think of themselves as well off.[11]

Often the children of the best-off tenth of each affluent society in the world (the top 1% of the world income parade) find it very hard to get on the housing ladder, and they are the lucky ones. By 2013 the average deposit required by a first-time buyer in London was £64,000![12] No wonder people panic about amassing wealth to try to help their kids. Their children will hardly have to live in slums, but they will be borrowing vast sums just to buy what is usually a very poky flat, and putting down £64,000 for the 'privilege'. And, what is more, hardly any of them will ever complete that mortgage. Most don't expect to. These are 'starter homes'. They will sell it on to another young person, who will, in turn, have to borrow greatly and pay huge amounts of money in interest, even if the rates are historically 'low', just for the privilege of having somewhere to sleep. If they move back to renting, they may have to pay a penalty fee for redeeming the mortgage early. If prices fall at all, it is their £64,000 that will be lost first.

It is because the very well-off suffer as well as the very poor that housing is everyone's problem. The well-off suffer less, but they still have their lives made worse, more insecure, by the way we allocate housing in Britain, in comparison with the well-off in more equitable countries. In more equitable affluent countries the well-off have a smaller share of national wealth, but they tend to do better than their richer counterparts in more inequitable countries in terms of their mental health; they also receive other, less immediate benefits from living in a much more social environment. Crime rates are lower in more equitable countries, so the rich need fear robbery and burglary less; schooling is cheaper, with far fewer private schools and much lower university fees; and a wider range of jobs is well paid in more equitable countries, allowing the rich to expand beyond a narrow group of occupations.[13]

The UK is a good example for study, better than many others, if you want to see just what a problem housing can become when economic inequalities rise. Sitting economically between the US and mainland Europe, the UK combines the excesses of Anglo-Saxon capitalism with royalist attitudes towards the sanctity of accumulated wealth.

In the UK successive governments, both influenced by and influencing changes in culture, have turned the housing market, and the financial sector that relies on it, into one of the few remaining props of the UK economy. That economy has now become so reliant on the housing market 'doing well' that much else is subordinated to it. Interest rates are kept low in part because raising them would immediately throw huge numbers of homeowners into negative equity. The value of their properties would fall because potential buyers' ability to pay would be reduced. By keeping interest rates as low as they are now, the government (via the Bank of England) is in effect lending banks money at almost no cost. (When banks give people mortgages, almost all the interest is paid to the banks; only a tiny fraction need be paid back to the Bank of England.)

George Osborne's very lopsided 2013 budget announcements, his very weak autumn statement of that year, Mark Carney's tentative winter interventions, and all the arguments that followed (about whether he was blowing up a bubble or preventing a crash), are the result of many longer-term changes that made housing pivotal to UK economics. The disaster, in this respect, is the incredibly unbalanced economy: it is what happens when the south-east bubble pops and house prices fall into line with the rest of the country; or, perhaps equally disastrously, what happens when they don't and an economic apartheid opens up between north and south.

When trying to determine what should be done, the UK is well placed to learn from its neighbours. However, when it comes to housing, commentators often suggest that the island of Britain is somehow insulated from events overseas, both near and far away. But Britain has never been insulated. Just because housing has become a national obsession in Britain does not mean that housing works completely differently here from how it does in similar countries. There are differences, but they do not mean that lessons cannot be learned from nearby. In fact, within the UK, housing works very differently in Northern Ireland compared to Scotland and Wales, and the greatest differences are found within England.

Housing in Middlesbrough, Mexborough, Maidenhead and Merton might as well be housing in four different countries. Prices and rental levels vary greatly when you compare these four places, and the gaps in housing costs and expectations are widening all the time. The price of a palace in the poorest district will barely buy you a garage in the richest. The definition of decent quality is also wildly divergent in places as disparate as these. Fittings and fixtures in the poorest districts remind visitors from the richest areas of how homes used to be kitted out a quarter of a century ago. In the richest quarters of England homes are now so expensive, and rents so high, that buyers think nothing of furnishing their dwellings like four-star hotels; tenants paying a fortune in rent expect to be stunned by the 'quality' of the bathroom. Even the most basic of bathrooms was not too long ago considered a luxury; having somewhere inside the home to go to the toilet was rare in my grandparents' youth, before the Second World War. Now bathrooms in expensive areas are routinely being remodelled as a fashion item. In the most expensive of homes it may be a sign that something is amiss if one of the many bathrooms has not been redecorated within the last three or four years.

Perhaps people restyling their fixtures and fittings, toilets and towel rails, should be taken as a sign that something has gone very wrong. Renovation acceleration occurs when local housing markets begin to overheat. Often these local buying frenzies were fuelled by much the same cheap money as that which fuelled subprime US mortgage growth. During this period, when housing prices rose quickly, rents could rise quickly too: high rents look less ridiculous set against a supposedly high housing price for what were once 'normal' homes.

The UK has not had the worst housing crisis in the rich world, but it has been badly hit by the crisis because so much of the UK economy is reliant on housing. In Europe the housing crash has been most abrupt in Spain and Ireland. The blame for the crash in Ireland is partly assigned to the government, which made the decision to bail out the banks, but it is also laid at the doors of the banks themselves.

The Irish housing bubble was initially inflated through the greed of bankers, builders and developers; left unchecked by government, it gradually infected the entire country, and the Celtic Tiger went from being a term of praise to a pejorative term in a matter of just a few years. Although the bubble may have been internally generated, it required overseas monies to blow it up to the size it eventually reached. Much of this money came from overseas banks. In March 2013 the veteran US academic Noam Chomsky put it bluntly: 'the housing bubble which was fuelled by Spanish and indeed German banks – you know they were the lenders – went way out and caused a great crisis for which the public is now paying.'[14]

International observers use Ireland to illustrate just how fast and how far a housing market can fall. Commentators in Ireland appear to be moving on from pointing the finger of blame, however, because fixing the problem is far harder than identifying where it began. They all accept it began with the far too cosy relationships between banks, builders, developers and government. By contrast, in the UK, blame for the long economic recession is attributed by the coalition (and by many on the right of the commentariat including most of the press) to New Labour government spending, not to the bankers. This is despite UK gross debt being very low under that New Labour government just before the crisis began. In 2007 accumulated government debt was just 47% of GDP, in comparison with the then OECD average of 73%, and the annual deficit was just 2.7% of GDP.[15] By May 2013, after the banks had been bailed out and as the costs of the recession were mounting, accumulated debt was 75% of GDP, or £1.2 trillion.[16] And the annual deficit had become three times as big as in 2007.[17] Britain lost its triple-A credit rating in February 2013, the first such loss since 1978.[18]

The wish of those on the right to attribute Britain's current housing problems to the last government may be responsible for a reluctance by the British press to cover similar problems when they are seen in other countries. Perhaps this reluctance is also linked to a fear that what has happened to housing prices in Spain, Ireland and elsewhere could still, at least partly, happen in the UK. We try not to talk about the problems occurring elsewhere because we want to think that the British housing market is somehow immune to even greater volatility. So many people in Britain don't want to think of the consequences of the price bubble bursting that they don't even look to their nearest neighbour, Ireland, to learn from that country's debates about who is now going to shoulder all the debt incurred by the property bubble of the Celtic Tiger years.[19]

HOME TRUTHS

> It does indeed at first sight seem possible for the earth to become the exclusive possession of individuals by some process of equitable distribution. 'Why,' it may be asked, 'should not men agree to a fair subdivision? If all are co-heirs, why may not the estate be equally apportioned, and each be afterwards perfect master of his own share?'
>
> – Herbert Spencer, eugenicist and *Economist* magazine subeditor, 1851[20]

One hundred and fifty years, or two lifetimes, ago, leading thinkers speculated over the possibility of land division (Spencer in the UK), land tax (Henry George in the US), nationalization, communism, and the concept of property being theft. Housing was slowly improved. Around seventy-five years, or one lifetime, ago, across almost all the rich world, we spent much less of our annual incomes on housing. For example, even in New York City, then far more crowded than it is today, households spent 32% of their income on housing in 1933–4, including lighting and heating their homes. By 1950 housing costs had fallen to 28% of household income; but by 2002–3 that cost had risen again, to 38%,[21] exceeding the costs of the 1930s, just as income inequality in the US now exceeds the very high levels last recorded at that time too.[22] I would suggest that it is partly because income inequality is now so high that housing again consumes so much of most people's incomes.

The UK is the European country that has followed the US pattern of inequalities – rising abruptly since 1980 and reaching historically high levels in the present day – most closely. As a result people on near-average incomes can today find they have very little to get by on, despite being in the middle. The BBC took the example of a couple with a child living on £22,000 a year, around the median level, and found that in a third of England they would have had to pay out at least 35% of their annual income on housing costs if they rented, even for the very cheapest rental property in the area. Alternatively, if they took out a mortgage, after having saved or been given £20,000, in almost 30% of districts in England they would not be able to afford even the cheapest property on the market.[23]

Today, in a bad year, for younger adults housing costs can easily consume over half their take-home pay. Pay tends to be much lower for the young, and the majority of the best job opportunities for many young adults are concentrated in the most expensive parts of the country in which to live. Sadly, the young have become used to being exploited, taking on huge debt and trying not to think too far into the future.

Without the memory of different times, the extremes of today can appear normal. Further down, towards the bottom of the housing 'market', a few landlords become very rich as the state indirectly pays them well to provide what is often a shoddy service. In the UK, where housing benefit payments end up with the landlords and where rent controls remain almost non-existent, a few people are profiting greatly due to the misery of the majority. It is because of these profits, and the intense interest in continuing to secure them among the most power-ful, that the clamour for change that already exists, but that has no focus, is consistently rejected, dampened down or ignored.

What is happening is not a simple case of demand outstripping housing supply. You just have to count how many homes there are in relation to the number of households. Throughout the developed world there has never been more housing than there is today: we have – in theory – more bedrooms, more square metres per person, more space to live in.[24] You have to keep on asking: if there is all this space available, why do we have a problem?

I hope it is already clear that this book is, in effect, concerned not with an absolute lack of housing, but with the problem of how that housing is distributed, and of how together we might begin to solve the problem of apparently ever increasing inequality. Ultimately it is about the need to control greed. Housing has been transformed into a very badly regulated market, and this lack of regulation inevitably allows some to take advantage. Markets, when they have worked, have always relied on regulation in order to prevent the greedy from taking undue advantage.

In the UK recent governments have promoted a kind of winner-takes-all capitalism, propped up by a one-choice-then-you're-out housing allocation policy for the poor. Most social housing tenants are made just one offer of housing on a take-it-or-leave-it basis, and that applies only to those families whom the authorities are forced to house by law, mostly those with children. In England alone millions of people are on the waiting list for social housing. In the 1990s less than a million households were waiting for the council to house them, but by 2008 that figure had reached 1.8 million; the count is now above two million.[25] One household has been on that list for fifty-seven years.[26] In the UK as a whole, there are an estimated 600,000 people officially registered as homeless,[27] while at least 240,000 people have now relied on squatting in one form or another so that they can avoid becoming street homeless.[28]

Homelessness is becoming one of the defining issues of the protracted financial crisis. Street homelessness in the UK rose by 17% between

Buildings labelled as 'an exclusive development of 2, 3 and 4 bedroom homes', currently under construction in Sheffield. Home-building is continuing in 2012–14, but at a much slower pace than before. Homes are still mainly being built for sale at a profit and are still very often being marketed with the suggestion that buying new property will help you to elevate your social status. The implication is that by moving to somewhere 'exclusive', you will also become more exclusive, more posh. These apartments are styled with old-fashioned chimneys, more for effect than for use. Many are marketed as investment opportunities for buy-to-let landlords, to rent out to whoever is willing to pay the highest rent. Again, the supposed social cachet of having the right address is presented as a justification for charging the higher rent. Such schemes can appear good for the individual, but not good for society as a whole: they devalue all the areas that are not 'exclusive', which (the advertising implies) you should try to avoid living in if you possibly can.

2008, at the start of the crisis, and the end of 2011.[29] Total homelessness then rose by 26% in the two years after that.[30] By 2013 it was estimated that 20,000 to 50,000 people were currently squatting in the United Kingdom, occupying between 2% and 4% of empty commercial properties and far fewer of the 737,500 empty residential properties. It is estimated that these empty properties alone could house two million people if fully occupied.[31] Many of these properties are empty because they're simply being traded for investment purposes, and not for purposes of actual use. It is true that there are worse stories from a few places elsewhere in Europe, where squatting has become the only way to live for families in some areas,[32] but even more shocking tales emanate from North America, where so many families have been evicted from their homes in recent years.

A key reason why the homeless and squatters receive so little attention is because so many politicians own so many homes. Often they claim they need to because of the precarious nature of their jobs, but routinely minor members of parliament in Britain, and the congress in America, are embarrassed when their home-ownership levels are revealed. Because this behaviour often spans political divides, it curtails debate.

Too many politicians have a vested interest in not wanting to talk too much about their vested interests. In Britain this problem was widely discussed in 2001 when the phrase 'Twelve Homes Meacher', concerning the property-buying habits of a minister in the Labour government, first appeared. His property portfolio may not number exactly twelve, of course, because 'Mr Meacher does not want to come clean on exactly how many homes he owns. His entry in the register of members' interests says tersely "Flats let in London".'[33] When both political parties are cursed by this problem, it becomes clear that it is widespread. However, it is in American examples that we can most clearly see how both profiteering and the embarrassment over profiteering go right to the political top.

Just as the housing market crash was beginning to gain speed in the US, in 2008, Senator John McCain was the Republican nominee for President. Senator McCain made an error that David Cameron would repeat in the UK two years later. Unlike Mr Meacher, however, neither Cameron nor McCain was honest enough simply to say that he did not wish to say. Instead, when asked, both replied that they could not recall how many homes they had. McCain came over as the more plausible of the two, as he had a greater number of homes to remember than Cameron.

The Democratic Party candidate for President, the then obscure Barack Obama, reported it like this:

> Then there was another interview, where somebody asked John McCain, 'How many houses do you have?' He said, 'I'm not sure, I'll have to check with my staff.' True quote! So they asked his staff and they said, 'At least four.' By the way, the answer is, John McCain has seven homes.[34]

Unfortunately for McCain, seven homes was too high a number for a presidential candidate in 2008, a year in which many voters faced possible eviction in the aftermath of the crash. He did not appear to have any connection with the ordinary voter. What's more, his staff had been economical with the truth. Obama – who, until he moved into the White House, had had only one home – had, understandably, underestimated McCain's property holdings. The *New York Times* listed ten properties held in McCain's name.[35]

When McCain was making his gaffe about his gaffs, and claiming to be unsure about the number of homes he had, millions of other very different Americans were being made homeless, often within only a few months of defaulting on their mortgages. The term for being behind on your mortgage payments is 'mortgage delinquency' in the US; in the UK it is 'mortgage arrears'. The US crisis in housing resulted in a legal conveyor belt of repossession orders, what came to be called 'an eviction mill'. The numbers of those who were put through that mill, as well as those who feared they might be, rose rapidly in the years up to 2013.

Later in this book some of the connections between housing and health are discussed, but it is worth stating here that the stress of basic issues concerning housing has greatly damaged people's health across the US. Indeed, overall US life expectancy fell in 2008. That fall is now thought to be as much related to the 'eviction mill' as it is to any other aspects of the crash.[36] There is growing evidence that the crisis is very bad for health in many ways, possibly leading to the first fall in life expectancy in the UK to be recorded since the 1930s. This doesn't normally happen in affluent countries outside of wartime,[37] further evidence that these are not normal times.

What the housing crisis does, more than any other type of social crisis, is affect entire neighbourhoods and cities. Huge numbers of people are harmed. This harm occurs both when housing becomes too expensive to afford and when it plummets in value. When one home is abandoned, people living all around it worry about what might happen to their street. When a street is abandoned, people worry about the neighbourhood. When a neighbourhood appears largely abandoned, when no one can sell, people worry about the town. And when a town as large as Detroit goes bankrupt, people worry about other towns. In July 2013 that city stopped issuing death certificates because it could not afford to buy the paper to print them on.[38] It really had gone bankrupt. At the time of writing, no one knows how long it will be before it is solvent again.

From the subprime lending crisis, to the foreclosure epidemic, to the bankruptcy of entire cities – as things have got worse, governments have insisted they would soon get better. The overall economic situation deteriorated in the US because a few sought to make excessive profits from lending and receiving interest. In those countries within the rich world where people are best housed, there are usually quite strict controls preventing the few from making huge profits at the expense of the many. The same is true of those affluent countries that have the best results in terms of overall health and educational outcomes.

In general, it is not how much is spent on health or education or housing that has most influence on whether a population is well cared for, or well educated, or well housed, but how that spending is spread around.[39] Affluent countries report better health and education outcomes when their resources are more evenly distributed, and the same is true for housing.

Often the evidence that housing issues are at the heart of many social problems is only circumstantial, but rates of imprisonment, the proportions of children given up for adoption and many other indicators of social strife are higher where it is harder to be housed. By 2008, 136,000 children a year were being adopted in the US, 15%

more than in 1990.[40] Over 2.2 million people were imprisoned in the US by 2008,[41] up from 1.1 million in 1990. These figures dwarf those of other nations. Per person, only Rwanda imprisons more people than the US and then only if prisoners of war are included.[42]

If we want to feel secure about our societies, cities, neighbourhoods and, more precisely, the home in which we live, we need some better choices and greater overall freedom. We need to be able to rent where we want to live, but also to be able to buy when and where that makes sense – but never with the intention of profiting through the owner-ship of bricks, mortar and land. Profits made out of securing essential living standards have a tendency to reduce overall living standards.

One person's housing profit is another's cost and misery. The profit will be quickly assimilated and largely forgotten – quietly accepted like accidentally acquired ill-gotten gains – but the misery may be felt for a long time. Thus, in aggregate, we are better off when housing is made more like health, instead of left as an arena for profiteering. Per-haps many of today's estate agents will one day be viewed much as the way we now view people who sold snake oil or who performed other forms of quackery in medicine in the past. No doubt the quacks said they were providing a vital service, and some may have believed that they were, but most people today agree that we are better off without them. We will always need people to help arrange how we are housed. But we need people with everyone's best interest at heart, not what might best line their or their firms' pockets.

Wherever we live we need to see new rules introduced or old ones restored in the interests of the vast majority who do not own much of the national wealth. Old rules that worked so well in the past and that still work well elsewhere today include rent controls. New rules might be to tax land on the basis of its value. If people choose to hoard it, they can, but they must pay for the privilege. Most important are rules about wealth and freedom. Rules about freedom involve the protection and introduction of rights. One right suggested later in this book is the 'right-to-sell' your home but stay in it as a tenant. This would be a counterbalance to the 'right-to-buy' and a way of reducing both evictions and the stigma attached to certain areas. If your neigh-bours could stay in their home, even after having completely defaulted

Gleadless Valley tower blocks, as seen from Meersbrook Allotments, in Sheffield. These tower blocks were built to replace slum housing – a fact that is often forgotten today by those who view them as an eyesore. However, compared to what they replaced, the tower blocks were an improvement in the landscape. High-density living allows spaces to be left open and green, and such buildings are often prized in many cities in the world. Tower blocks become an eyesore when, in a polarizing society, they are viewed as the homes of people with the least choice. Tower blocks similar to these, but overlooking a park in central London, are regarded as prime investments on the worldwide housing market. Housing becomes good housing when there are more opportunities to live a good life in the space around that housing. Homes must be damp-free, spacious enough, well soundproofed, insulated and let in enough light; but they also need to sit within a neighbourhood in which children feel safe and can play, in which adults are happy to live, and in which the elderly are not trapped in their homes through fear of the outside.

on a mortgage, as long as they paid their rent upon becoming tenants in the same property, would it still be worthwhile buying in a 'posh' area? Would posh areas stay as posh if people did not have to leave such neighbourhoods so quickly when they fell on hard times? And, if such areas became less posh, would prospective buyers be quite so willing to spend a fortune to live there?

The alternative to the introduction of such new rights, to the restoration of such old freedoms, is the housing disaster that comes closer and closer every day.

THE APPROACHING DISASTER

Housing is at the heart of the economic crisis, and getting housing right will be part of its answer. It is also one of the toughest of political quandaries, one whose obvious answer is so unpalatable that no government has had the courage to face it. The quandary is this: housing costs too much, but for millions of people, security depends on the value of their bricks and mortar.

– Guardian editorial, September 2012[43]

For many people – speculators, landlords or simply homeowners who have been forced to take the gamble of getting on to the 'property ladder' – a 'housing disaster' means a fall in property prices.

In November 2012 the Royal Institute of Chartered Surveyors' annual assessment of the Portuguese housing market ran with the headlines: 'Prices and rents continue to fall'; 'Confidence index remains quite negative'; 'Lettings activity indicators weaken'.[44] In Spain, just two months later, it was reported that there were still an estimated one million houses on the market, most of them new-builds, all unsold. Such a glut meant that prices were expected to drop a further 20%.[45] Around the same time the ratings agency Fitch announced that it expected house prices in Ireland to decline by a further 20% from current levels.[46] All these predictions cast a pall over those countries during 2013. Whatever slight increases in prices did occur in any area were seen as a chimera, a statistical by-product of the low volume of sales (just a few sales could be recorded as an indication of a price rise), the result of a few opulent properties being sold off at low prices. And as prices continued to fall, people were less and less surprised. By August 2013 Spanish prices had fallen a further 9.3%, down nearly 40% from their 2008 peak.[47]

None of this happened out of the blue. There were warnings, and governments did try to prevent housing crises from turning into social disasters. Ireland's housing market crash was said by one commentator to have begun at 10 p.m. on 2 October 2008, when Irish home-buyers watching the nightly news saw an incoherent display from the chief executive of the Financial Regulator: 'they saw him and said, Who the fuck was that??? Is that the fucking guy who is in charge of the money??? That's when everyone panicked.'[48] The man was trying to reassure them. The government that he worked for wanted the problem sorted, but it was too late. Other sources disagree about the precise timing: some say panicking began a few days earlier, on 30 September, when the bank guarantee was introduced – but it all took place within just a few days. A crisis can begin that quickly. The repercussions from those initial attempts to avert disaster took a good deal longer to fully emerge: four years, in fact.

In 2011 Michael Lewis, writing in *Vanity Fair*, reported events as an almost complete capitulation to international money markets in Ireland. He suggested that what had most obviously changed in the country's politics had been the role that began to be played by foreigners. Foremost among the foreigners was the Troika of the European Commission, the International Monetary Fund (IMF) and the European Central Bank (ECB), which laid down the austerity measures Ireland had to follow if it was to receive bailout funding once international investors were no longer willing to risk their money following the 2008 crash. The Irish government and Irish banks by 2011 were crawling with representatives of the Troika as well as American investment bankers and, in Michael's words, 'Australian management consultants and faceless euro-officials, referred to inside the Department of Finance simply as "the Germans". Walk the streets at night and, through restaurant windows, you see important-looking men in suits, dining alone, studying important-looking papers.'[49] It may not have been quite as bleak as that, but it certainly felt that bleak. By April 2013 the Troika had succeeded in getting Dublin to publish legislation making it easier for property to be seized and for residents in arrears with their mortgages to be evicted.[50] Ironically, just four months after that, Irish experts (alongside some of those now returned management consultants) were warning that an Australian market crash might be imminent, given current signs.[51] Nowhere is completely safe.

What occurred in Ireland in 2013 could have been very different. By late 2012 the Irish seemed to have tired of the foreign technocrats; some had looked across the ocean northwards, to Iceland, and learned that there was an alternative to doing what the bankers say you must do. Put in a similar situation by a very few bankers and colluding government officials, Iceland had decided to default on its sovereign debt. Today many of the headquarters of Iceland's former banks remain empty in the tiny Borgartún quarter of Reykjavik, and there has been a popular revolt against the bankers there. However, the old Icelandic banking families remain powerful. A member of one was reported in 2011 (by journalist and writer Peter Geoghegan) to be overheard claiming, at what he thought was a private dinner, that it was still possible to turn Reykjavik into Europe's Hong Kong.[52] By not doing what the bankers said, Iceland had avoided the worst aspects of possible austerity: by not paying its debts to richer creditors overseas, it was saying that bondholders had taken a risk, that risk had turned bad, and Iceland would now look at how to recoup internally. Iceland's example inspired much discussion and some progress in Ireland, and, in the long run, it could still provide inspiration to many countries throughout the world.

In October 2012 the Irish government announced that it planned to introduce a bill encouraging banks to cut substantially the amount that borrowers owed on their mortgages: a programme of massive mortgage write-downs, in fact. The Irish government suggested that this was a step that no other major country had so far been willing to take on such a broad scale to deal with the current crisis. The initiative was designed to lower each borrower's monthly payments, thereby preventing a tide of foreclosures, and removing the uncertainty that would otherwise hang over the Irish housing market for many years to come. The *New York Times* suggested that 'If it works, the plan could provide a road map for other troubled countries.'[53] From the outside, it began to look as if the Irish were beginning to take control of their own fate. What was possible had, itself, changed. But then the banks countered that any blanket debt forgiveness would result in 'strategic default among customers who could afford to pay their mortgages',[54] and the Troika had the measures reversed. This development was less than a year ago, however, and we do not know how this story will end. We do know that an entire generation in Ireland, and their children, will never trust bankers and developers again.

It is when what is possible changes that real change begins. Real change is not change within an existing set of parameters. It is not the raising and lowering of interest rates or the building of a few state subsidized homes. Real change came when it first became the state's business to build homes. It came when people first started to gamble on property prices rising more and more, and so, for a time, they did. It is the housing landscape itself that will change, not just the seasonal features within it. If the Irish government does introduce a land tax, this will make a similar future tax in the UK more realizable. A land tax means there is less economic sense in one family owning as many homes and as much land as possible, as it becomes more expensive to own more than you need. After the tax has been applied, housing will be valued more for its 'use' than for its 'exchange' value. It is an example of what one eminent academic geographer calls 'a post-capitalist imagination'.[55] It is what many would call common sense.

Sadly, for every optimistic turn reported in Iceland or Ireland or elsewhere, there always appears to be some banker sitting in the corner trying to prevent its taking place. In Ireland the government decides to forgive much debt and prevent evictions; the Troika steps in to demand the law is changed back again. In the case of Iceland it was the old rich families and the man Peter Geoghegan overheard talking at that dinner about turning Reykjavik into a finance casino who are trying to subvert the will of the majority.

In Ireland the bankers, the firms and the old rich families to which they are most closely connected are also responsible, not just the

Troika and the credit reference agencies. Professor Rob Kitchin and his colleagues from the University of Maynooth found that these groups were subverting attempts to realign the Irish economy. On closer inspection by those Irish academics, some of the Irish government's recent apparent boldness appears to prove illusory. What the government has actually done, the researchers from the National Institute for Regional and Spatial Analysis suggest, is to have kept many developers and speculators in business. These were the people who had been responsible for inflating the property bubble. Along with the banks they had 'blocked the growth of more resilient players or new start-ups in the wake of the crash, whilst doing little to protect homeowners and tenants struggling to pay mortgages and rent'.[56] Thus there is much scepticism about some of the latest moves being proposed and about the actual intent of many in government. Moves to allow borrowers to pay back a little less were partly seen as more of the same, not yet a sea-change. But a sea-change is possible, and here, possibly and despite recent set-backs, Iceland still leads the way. There will always be small cohorts of vested interests trying as hard as they can to return to business as usual. Sometimes they will succeed. But now there are increasing numbers of journalists, writers, activists and academics looking more and more sceptically, in ways they have not looked before, at an area – housing – for so long considered humdrum and boring. All this attention is making it far harder for the corruption of the past to continue unchecked.

In Iceland, unlike in Ireland, the government allowed the country's largest banks to fail after 2008. At the same time, debt relief was awarded to households in difficulties with their mortgages and local businesses facing bankruptcy. A sceptic might say that this is just keeping a firm that should fail to stay in business, but time will tell which policies are best. On 8 June 2012 two former banking executives of the Byr Savings Bank, Jon Thorsteinn Jonsson and Ragnar Zophonias Gudjonsson, were sentenced to four and a half years in prison by Iceland's Supreme Court, having been found guilty of committing fraud. This was a major step forward in Europe. However, the former Prime Minister, Geir Haarde, was given no punishment, even when found guilty of having not convened enough cabinet meetings to properly monitor the situation.[57]

There were downsides as well to Iceland's partial defiance of our current banking hegemony. Inflation recently reached almost 20% in one year and it remains high, but inflation usually reduces the inequality between those who have nothing and those who have the most wealth. However, inflation can also increase the cost of housing for many, bring it up and out of proportion with earnings. The best inflation is inflation in the prices of things you do not need, in the prices of luxury goods such as overseas holidays, expensive jewellery and fast cars.

There were also costs for Britain when Iceland chose to be deviant, which could be a portent of what might occur if any of George Osborne's new multibillion pound internal UK loans, mortgage and bank deposit guarantees ever have to be called upon. The British government bailed out UK speculators in the Icelandic banks, which included a number of English local authorities that had 'invested' their deposits to try to maximize incomes. The British also lent heavily to Ireland, to enable the government to guarantee all deposits held in failed banks there (this was in addition to the Troika bailout). In 2010 the British government lent Ireland £3.2 billion; in 2011 it cut the interest rate on that loan; and in December 2012 that cut was made retrospective, so that a further £7.7 million less interest had to be paid back to the UK that month. No explanation was given as to why this was done, other than that 'The links between our financial systems, particularly in Northern Ireland, mean that there is a strong economic case to provide financial assistance to Ireland.'[58] Could Ireland really not afford a sum just short of €10 million? Was it that close to being bankrupt? In many ways Britain has been trying very hard to maintain business as usual, not just within the UK but also nearby. Perhaps this was partly due to fears over the pound. Or, more likely, due to fear of what a greater banking collapse in Ireland might mean for the UK housing market. The market in the south of England was like a fragile house of cards that could be upset at any moment by a nearby house's fall.

If Ireland had copied the Icelandic response to the crisis early on – had not guaranteed all savers' deposits, no matter how large, had not accepted the Troika's intervention and had then (when even that was not enough) not accepted additional loans from the British that had to be repaid by 2020, albeit at lower and lower interest rates – the great economic chaos in that country might very easily have spread over the border and across the Irish Sea. Ireland's being within the euro may have made British support easier. At the end of the day all the support that was extended to Ireland – from within the eurozone, from the Troika and, eventually, from the British – did not 'save' Ireland but rather resulted in average house prices in Ireland falling to 60% of their 2006 value by 2013; in most cases this was under half what they had been selling for at their 2008 peak. By November 2013 claims were increasingly being made that the Irish housing market had finally bottomed out, but evidence of stability had yet to be amassed.[59] Even when Icelandic housing prices are measured in euros, the falls since the peak have been less in Iceland than in either Ireland or Spain.[60]

It is remarkable that Spain, Ireland and Iceland are so little discussed in Britain, when they are nearby models of the chaos that can so easily come to housing markets. Go directly south in 2013 and prices are still falling in Spain; go directly west and we cannot even be sure they are yet flat-lining in Ireland; go north and the first country you hit is Iceland, whose recent tales the UK also defiantly ignores. All these examples should cause the British to be more cautious; if only we were not so insular.

At several points during the last few years the Icelandic króna fell in value to roughly half its previous peak. The pound has fallen by half that amount, but a comparison is never made, and we hear few discussions today of possible runs on the pound. We need to look to Iceland to know what that would mean. In Iceland the cost of imports consequently doubled and currency controls had to be established in 2008, after the collapse of the króna, to stop the wealthy moving their monies abroad. The British even tried to use anti-terror legislation to get some of its own speculators' monies out! When the full story of the crisis is finally revealed, Britain may well not come out of it well, but may instead be seen as the country that stood most squarely behind the interests of the banks and those who had most to lose: the wealthy.

Meanwhile the people of Britain carried on borrowing largely in ignorance of what had so recently been happening around them. They could see no alternative. Britain is such a socially divided society and, for most, the only way into the top half is through trying to buy a home in the right place at the right time. Home ownership status and social class are almost one and the same thing in the UK today. Usually the middle class buy and eventually own; the working class rent or buy but then risk defaulting.

Not all is well in Iceland, but at least it is one island where they are all in it together. As Professor of Economics at the University in Reykjavik, Thorolfur Matthiasson, explains, the Icelanders have been looking after their own: 'Taking down a company with positive cash flow but negative equity would in the given circumstances have a domino effect, causing otherwise sound companies to collapse ... Forgiving debt under those circumstances can be profitable for the financial institutions and help the economy and reduce unemployment as well.'[61] In contrast, in Britain, firms began to go to the wall and many housing projects stalled when the crash came in 2008, and there was little subsequent debt forgiveness.

It is not just Iceland, Ireland, and Spain from where we can learn lessons. Portugal is the most similar country in Europe to the UK in terms of income inequalities, and there the market has also collapsed, so the impact on a similarly socially divided society can be seen from that example. Housing markets in Italy and Greece have also been thrown into chaos along with the rest of the peripheral regions of Europe. But, in contrast, and at exactly the same time, although now at Europe's core, it is reported that in far more socially equitable Germany housing prices have increased sharply over the last two years because investors are looking for solid returns and safe havens in the midst of the euro crisis, and think they will find them there; but, in doing so, they may just be helping to bring about exactly the situation they were trying to avoid.[62]

Rising housing prices within parts of Germany have caused 'some people to worry about the formation of a bubble that could collapse if the German economy falters'.[63] The old models of speculation and accumulation appear to be faltering, even in what is seen as the solid core of Europe. This is beginning to spread disquiet where recently all had appeared most solid. In Germany wages may on average be higher, but a quarter now live on low wages, and, though unemployment has fallen, temporary employment has increased.[64] Divisions there are rising. But they have a long way to rise. Inequalities are nothing like they are in Britain, where people are paid far less in large numbers and unemployment is much higher. In Britain in 2013 you could buy a terraced house in a rundown part of Stoke on Trent for £1, while the grandest terrace in the land was being put on the market at £250,000,000.[65] Almost no one in Britain is shocked by such divisions any more. But they should be, because they do not bode well.

The context we are in today is one in which there is little certainty and a sense of rising insecurity, even at the heart of Europe. At the periphery – from Cyprus to Malta, through Greece, Italy, Spain, Portugal, and up through Ireland to Iceland – there is more uncertainty than ever before. Some fifteen political parties contested the elections in Iceland in April 2013, twice as many as at the previous election. The centre-right parties regained control by promising not to seek shelter in the euro, and the Pirate Party won its first seats in any national election anywhere in the world. Iceland is still in some obvious disarray and appears to be oscillating politically from left to right again. However, it is now looking at relatively stable housing prices and rents. They are neither rising nor falling but have settled – not as low as the falls elsewhere in Europe, but much lower than any price falls recorded so far in the UK. The cost of living in Iceland remains exorbitant due to high import costs, but maybe a lesson has been learned about speculation that will not be forgotten quickly, at least not for a generation.

Perhaps partly as a result of what has happened in Iceland, it is mainly in the most affluent parts of Germany where housing prices have risen most quickly recently, especially where 'crisis-ridden Greeks, Italians and Spaniards buy like crazy, the "concrete gold" that some German real-estate is assumed to represent'.[66] Again, it is worth restating that a lesson on the errors of speculation is soon to be learned where it is least expected, in the very heart of Europe. And, if you think that is too much Jeremiah-style doom-saying, then what about London and the south-east of England?

In many ways more akin to Germany than Ireland, parts of south-east England were experiencing what appeared to be a renewed property boom as I was writing this book in 2013. To experience a boom you have to believe that a crash is near-impossible, or at least enough people need to believe that. But simultaneously, alongside prices rising in the south-east, the British periphery, like the European periphery, continued to see most housing prices fall. Some falls were very large: 14.6% in the year to July 2013 in Powys and 2.2% for the whole of Wales. Northern England suffered similar falls in particularly depressed areas.[67]

Perhaps people in the south think they no longer live in the same country as those in Newcastle, Liverpool or Stoke? Or perhaps they feel they have no choice but to buy at ever inflating prices and pray that they have not just bought at the wrong time? But do people really have no choice but to spend most of what would otherwise be their disposable income on rent or mortgage repayments, just to have a good job, or to live near their family and friends?

What do UK politicians have to say about the situation? Take one with a seat in the north but leading a party whose support is mostly located in the south of England. During the leadership debates in the run-up to the 2010 UK general election, Liberal Democrat leader Nick Clegg said that the issues most people talked about to door-stepping politicians concerned 'the cost and availability of housing'.[68] Yet Clegg soon followed in the time-honoured tradition of MPs, who, after gaining office, fail to suggest solutions to the problems they acknowledge while in opposition.

Housing in Britain is unlikely to be greatly improved by incremental adjustments to existing policies. Acting against any minor beneficial measures are the forces of speculation and accumulation, of a few trying to get rich quickly through property. If you think the remaining powers of wealthy vested interests in Iceland or Ireland are a problem, just imagine what a brake on progress the City of London remains. When it comes to international financial policy, it is surely the City of London that eggs on the UK government to offer extra loans to Ireland, outside of the Troika arrangements, to help it guarantee all deposits, which suggests it is fine to sit by as other countries struggle and also to invoke terrorist legislation against Iceland when it does default.

The UK trends are not good. Prices in the housing market polarized further during 2012 and into 2013, and even more people are worried

Newly refurbished flats in Sheffield can be seen to the left. To the right over the walkways are the old Park Hill flats, dwellings that are currently undergoing redevelopment. The graffiti on the walkway connecting these blocks reads 'I love you, will you marry me?' It is now being used as an advertising slogan to try to sell the refurbished apartments, but as of spring 2013 they were selling slowly and the vast majority of the blocks of flats in the complex as a whole were empty, awaiting redevelopment monies that appear to be slow in coming. These iconic buildings sit above Sheffield train station, just two hours and fifteen minutes' journey-time from the heart of London. If the private housing market recovers in the north of England, they will be transformed. If it moves only slowly, for years most of these potential homes may remain empty. Sheffield has a very long waiting list for housing. The tale of the man who sprayed the graffiti and the woman he painted it for did not end happily. It featured in a BBC Radio 4 play, broadcast a few years ago to entertain the (mostly) middle-class listeners of that radio station, the very people who are now the target market for those refurbished flats, flats that were once the crowning achievement of a past era of slum clearance. The walkways were so wide that they were called streets in the sky, and a milk-float drove along them each morning making deliveries to the original working-class tenants, who could not believe how lucky they were to live there. Now most homes in Park Hill remain derelict.

about housing now, as compared with when the crisis first hit – how to get it, how to keep it, how to sell it, when to buy it, when to sell it. Where most 'top' bankers live, property prices are rising. Outside of London, where most bank customers live, they are not. The falls have been greatest since 2008 in places where the property prices were lowest to begin with, in cities such as Hull, Belfast, Glasgow and Swansea.

In February 2013 the Royal Institute of Chartered Surveyors announced a commission to investigate what even it called 'the UK housing crisis'.[69] The surveyors explained that the further you travel from London, the less prices were expected to rise in future. Even being optimistic, 'In Wales, prices won't return to their average peak of £154,696 until 2021 with the current market value more than £20,000 down to less than £132,000.'[70] In real terms, taking account of inflation, this is a predicted permanent fall. Many, including the surveyors, consider a housing 'disaster' to consist of a falling market, although some also want to prevent housing price bubbles forming, so that people do not suffer in the consequent fall. The surveyors would also like to see the establishment of some affordable areas to buy within London, where, by the end of 2013, increases of up to 30% were being reported in the space of just a few months. But if prices were to rise greatly in the poorest parts of London and in places that are further away from London, people there would have even less to spend than they already do, following the recent falls in average household incomes.[71] Cheaper housing could be better housing, but not better for speculators.

Reaction was surprisingly muted when, in his budget of 21 March 2013, Chancellor George Osborne's main announcements involved only those new policies to try to shore up the housing market described in the first chapter of this book. Osborne was fearful of contagion – the prospect of falling prices in the north of England, Wales, Ireland and Scotland spreading southwards, threatening the still buoyant housing market in the south-east.

In response to Osborne's March 2013 budget, Angela Brady, the President of the Royal Institute of British Architects, greeted the Chancellor's announcement by saying: 'The construction industry shrank by 8% last year and we are continuing to see disappointingly low levels of house-building.' And she continued: 'Although the announcements today for further spending on housing and infrastructure are to be welcomed, it [sic] will barely make a dent in the delivery of the sustainable new homes and communities we desperately need.'[72] No one challenged Angela. No one asked why homes could not be delivered at lower prices, why rising prices were so desirable to her and the vested interests she represented. No one appeared to point out how much it actually costs to build a home: how much goes in profit to architects, to builders, to surveyors' firms and their bosses and shareholders – and, by contrast, how much less is paid to the labourers, the people on the ground. And, as far as I can tell, no one in the mainstream media responded to the announcements by asking whether we might not have a great many homes already, homes that are being underused, and whether in a time of austerity it might be better to try to make better use of them rather than risk government money on trying to boost prices in the private housing market.

As 2013 progressed, cynicism on government housing policy grew. *Private Eye* noted that one scheme set up to encourage 100,000 new home sales had only achieved 1.5% of that target number.[73] This was 'FirstBuy', the coalition's immediate successor to Labour's 'HomeBuy Direct' scheme. In both schemes (and later in 'NewBuy' for all buyers) government lent first-time buyers who were not on top incomes most of the deposit on a home, so that they could really overextend themselves in debt. Almost a year before *Private Eye* put the boot in, one analyst remarked, 'We should also question the assertion that, by encouraging first-time buyers, this will somehow have a laxative effect on the congested market. Once again, these are new-builds, chain-free properties.'[74] It was perhaps criticism like this, suggesting that the Chancellor's schemes were having little influence, that led Osborne to boost the schemes and to offer to underwrite so many more billions from January 2014 onwards.

The Chancellor knew he had to do something. As the effects of the economic crisis rippled out, housing across all sectors was being impacted on in numerous damaging ways. Just as he was writing the 2013 budget, it became known that the number of students going to universities was falling, and a conglomerate of major university student landlords was going bust. Often these bankruptcies were reported as separate local stories, so only someone with a housing obsession could link them. For instance, in Nottingham, the local press announced that 'After sinking £48 million into the complex two miles north of University Campus, Opal has gone into administration.'[75] But at least twenty very similar major landlords suffered the same fate in the preceding three weeks; thirteen companies in Manchester alone went under early in 2013.[76]

Companies that had recently built housing, in this case university housing, were not doing well. Enticements to build when most families are getting poorer, by helping to shore up the long-term debt of those families, is unlikely to add much real confidence to the market, although it can easily inject a short-term boost by helping those who are desperate to buy – people who cannot afford the repayments and who would normally be rejected by the banks for that reason. Since 2010 through to 2013 the average hourly wage in Britain has fallen by 5.5%. This is one of the largest wage falls to be found across all of Europe.[77] Only in Greece, Portugal and the Netherlands have the falls been greater, but in all of those countries the average cost of housing is lower. At the same time, in London, more than 2,000 bankers are paid well over a million euros each a year. In all of France only 162 are on such salaries, and in Germany just 170, but the good news is that there have been slight falls in the number of such highly paid London bankers since 2010, and their average salaries have fallen to '€1.44 million in 2011, down from €2.3 million in 2010'.[78] Change is possible, and it has in some ways begun, but those who want to return to the old ways have regrouped and are working very hard to hold back the tide. That is hardly surprising, given that, in effect, it is what they are paid to do. Banks will not make such great profits in their good years in future if we do change how we behave towards how we are housed.

It is in the interests of the vast majority that we change how we behave – that we change the foundations of how housing has been provided, managed, exchanged, cared for and built. Some of that change is already beginning. From self-build schemes to squatting, a small number of people are housing themselves differently, but governments are also slowly changing. The headlines are dominated by those trying to keep the old order in place just a little longer, but away from the headlines policies are beginning to be considered that would tax mansions and other excessive forms of housing opulence. Legislation is already in place in Britain that allows mortgagees to stay in their homes and become tenants to avoid eviction; it just isn't used much and it needs adapting, but it is there. There are also plans afoot within some political parties to increase tenants' rights,[79] but these must be set against plans by others to reduce their rights, increase evictions, reintroduce mass private renting and let the already rich get even richer. It's a battle that the minority at the top currently appears to be winning. To see how they are doing that, we need to work up from the foundations to ask how housing is built, financed and held.

4
Building

Houses in London are so expensive these days that the mind somewhat boggles at the thought that there are actually enough rich people around to buy them all. And of course there aren't. It's all debt. That special sort of debt that is perfectly serviceable and safe just so long as nothing whatsoever changes at all.

My experience, though, is everybody's future. House prices are soaring everywhere, aided by the low interest rates we can't afford to change and the government's bizarre, cynical help-to-buy scheme. Home ownership, once seen as a ladder out of poverty, has become a millstone of the middle. It's where all our money goes, meaning that it can't go anywhere else, meaning that we grow ever richer on paper, but with nothing left to spend. Monetary sadhus we are, balanced precariously on piles of borrowed cash.

– Hugo Rifkind, *Spectator*, 2013[1]

When Hugo Rifkind describes the middle classes of Britain as *sadhus* – ascetic monks who have left behind all material attachments – because it costs them so much just to pay for somewhere to sleep, he is perhaps exaggerating a little, but he is clearly agitated. Rifkind, a highly successful young journalist from a family not devoid of money and power, is finding it hard to get by.

Housing has become everyone's problem. This is yet another reason why the current crisis is leading to a disaster – one in which current acute discomfort with how we are housed turns into despair, as so many of us come to see the housing element in our cost of living rise even higher, our security departing, our living conditions deteriorating and even our health suffering if, as Hugo puts it, we are balancing 'precariously on piles of borrowed cash'. This disaster is different from previous near-housing crashes, even from the 1930s Depression. At its heart lie new extremes of avarice and ignorance.

To see how we got here, go back to basics. Consider who holds the land on which most homes are built, why they don't build on all of it, and who the building is for. Issues of migration need to be considered. If immigration levels stay buoyant and emigration levels do not increase, the need for new housing to be built in future will continue to grow. However, the type of housing being built and whether it is for rent or eventual ownership will be strongly influenced by whether economic inequalities in Britain rise or fall in future. Greater economic equality also tends to coincide with higher-quality rental property being made available at lower prices and with less profit being drawn out of housing sales. Similarly, the extent to which we bring empty property back into use and renovate old property, rather than build new, will depend on choices yet to be made, and on the overall political direction we will come to take.

In Britain, more than in almost any other affluent country, the precise location of property is seen to matter greatly, because, increasingly, geography reveals the most detail about your class. Tenure is only a very crude class divider: owning/buying or renting/defaulting. Within the housing classes, precisely where you buy or where you rent gives away most of the rest of your status. Because of that we are now careful not to directly ask people in Britain where they live when we first meet them, just as we were once careful not to ask directly about any religious beliefs.

It used to be whether you lived upstairs or downstairs, in the servants' quarters or the master's rooms, that revealed the most about you. Then, as we became more equal, and both the servants and the servant-keeping classes disappeared, suburbs became more similar. Now, as social classes segregate anew, whether we build and what we build changes again. So the recent fate of different groups, from the poorest in London to the super rich, also has to be considered.

To what extent do we put our wealth into housing because our houses define our status and signal who we are? A growing part of housing is the material reality and projection of the 'profession'. Place increasingly reflects the person, and even the way people dress now reflects where they most likely live. Put another way, most people can tell that you probably rent a cheaper property just by looking at your overalls. Conversely, if that suit is tailor-made, and those are the right kind of leather shoes, more likely your mortgage is on a detached home rather than a semi, if outside of London. Inside central London, someone owning a detached house might well dress down. They know they are rich.

Housing is intertwined with all other social, economic and political issues. Consider how attitudes to race affect housing and even influence how many homes are built in Britain. Fear of newcomers and a little old-fashioned racism can encourage governments to restrict legal immigration even further. Wives and husbands of British citizens are now locked out of Britain unless their income is substantial. Governments have been known to encourage the fear of others, as this distracts from the state's own failures to provide enough school places, jobs and homes.

It is easy to suggest that too few resources are the fault of immigrants. A policy to further reduce immigration, if effective, would also be a policy to reduce the need for new home-building for an ageing and shrinking society. But further immigration controls, restricting demand, could make the housing market even more volatile than it already is. The top end of the London housing market is now almost completely reliant on a steady stream of new rich immigrant 'investors'. Curtail their immigration, tamper with their non-dom status and prices at the top could crash. The bottom of the private rental market in cities like Sheffield is similarly partly held up by continued immigration, but in this case of some of the poorest people to arrive. Volatility in housing prices and rents is not new to the UK, but it has been growing in magnitude in recent decades. All kinds of solutions have been suggested.

Many commentators today advocate fewer planning restrictions as one solution to the problem of too few homes. They want more building on land designated as green belt as well as the lifting of other restrictions. They point to the US and to how its housing sector survived the last depression. But in the US, the greatest economic beneficiary of the Second World War, the story was different to that in the UK. There, the 1930s house-building boom was helped by the motorcar opening up whole new swathes of green land – to which virtually no geographical planning restrictions were applied. The UK never had much open space between its cities, so the two countries, in this respect, are not comparable.

Financial restrictions on housing finance were put into place in post-Depression America, and their impact was a long-lasting one. In 1933 the Glass–Steagall Act was passed by Congress to stop banks using savers' money to gamble madly. The Act prevented banks from selling off their mortgage loans for others to gamble with; and banks had to use savers' monies to support the lending they did. The Act helped to prevent a repeat of the widespread fraud that occurred in the years leading up to the crash of 1929. But it was repealed in 1999 following extensive lobbying by large banks.

The story of what followed is by now well known. The eight years following 1999 appear in hindsight to be very much a repeat of the eight years leading up to 1929, the Roaring Twenties: 'Once again, banks originated fraudulent loans and once again they sold them to their customers in the form of securities. The bubble peaked in 2007 and collapsed in 2008.'[2] Between 1933 and 1999 there were no similar great bank crashes and no similar housing market crashes in the United States. But that did not mean that less geographically restricted house-building meant homes for everyone. It meant more homes, and more space in those homes for most people, until the early 1980s; but not homes for all.

Even before widespread economic inequalities rose again there were specific groups who were clearly very badly housed in both North America and Europe. Post-war, US suburbanization continued apace with only occasional minor downturns, but it was suburbanization for the majority. By the 1970s white Americans had never been better housed. The same was true in the far more spatially restricted

UK: by the 1970s most white people had also never been better housed. But if you were black it was a different story. For example, in the US the government backed loans to homeowners to the tune of $120 billion between 1934 and 1962, but 98% of these went to white people, despite African-Americans then constituting a tenth of the population.[3] In the UK it was routine in the 1970s to see signs in lodging-room and B&B windows saying 'no blacks'. All was far from utopia, but the road to utopia was being walked.

In the UK, planning restrictions were brought in after the Second World War through the Town and Country Planning Act of 1947; as a result, building became concentrated in existing urban areas, and, initially, most housing construction was state-planned and state-funded. There were a few exceptions, such as the new towns, of which the largest was Milton Keynes, but land supply was consequently strictly controlled in the UK, unlike the US. Some think that this may have prevented a fall in house prices in the UK private sector after 2008 at a time when prices in the US were plummeting, but it also means like-for-like housing prices are often higher in the UK than in the US. Ireland and Spain followed the US model more closely, allowing building to take place largely unfettered by planning, and, possibly as a consequence, those two countries have so far experienced some of the greatest drops in home prices during the housing crisis.

It is possible that a great fall in prices for the UK is yet to come, and that the readjustment has been postponed only by extreme government and Bank of England action: the bailing out of banks; keeping the bank rate at near zero; and the creation of ever more expensive schemes to encourage ever greater private borrowing. Many books are currently being published saying that what the US and UK governments are doing is folly. What is most striking, however, is how the authors of these books range from revolutionaries to estate agents. In one such book, Andrew Smithers, an investment manager, suggests that these attempts to boost demand will not work, because there are longer-term structural problems that stretch across the rich world.[4] To try to work out which point of view is more plausible – that of the government, or that of its many and disparate critics – we need to look at some of the basics of supply and demand.

LAND AND MIGRANTS

London property prices are racing ahead with figures today
confirming that the city is skewing averages for the whole
country higher – but not all areas of the capital are booming.

– *Daily Mail*, 'This is Money' website, 17 September 2013[5]

Housing prices in the UK rose sixfold from 1983 to 2007, but land prices increased sixteenfold.[6] Similar patterns are always found whenever and wherever people are allowed to hoard land, untaxed, and housing is allowed to be accrued as an asset rather than being used primarily for shelter. When housing is hoarded as an asset, what is called its 'exchange value', its price, starts to rise until this far exceeds its 'use value', the price worth paying just to live in it. If a home were simply worth what it cost to maintain it, the price-to-rent ratio would be stable. Prices rise much higher when people speculate on the likelihood that they will rise even higher in the near future.

In May 2013 the Organisation for Economic Co-operation and Development (OECD) released a report suggesting that average housing prices were currently overvalued by 31% in the UK in comparison with rents, and by 21% in comparison with income. Put simply, our housing prices are higher than can be justified, even by orthodox economics. The UK was found not to be alone in the list of countries where property was now, in general, greatly overvalued; but, according to the OECD, in all the countries where there were problems, including the UK, 'these countries are heavily reliant on their property market and have seen households build up big mortgage debts.'[7] In other words there is continued wishful thinking going on. What is particularly interesting about this OECD report is that in the UK it was greeted without scepticism, including by newspapers that usually seek to boost house prices. The quote from the report cited above was reported on the *Daily Mail*'s financial website. Now even the commentariat on the right say prices are too high.

A generation of homeowners is delighted with the profits they have

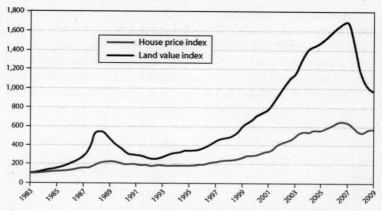

Figure 6. UK average land prices and house prices, 1983–2009.

apparently made simply by having sat tight and watched the housing market overheat. But now they are beginning to worry. Some are beginning to wonder where the money has come from. And some are concluding that it has been stolen from the next generation, who are now paying for it through their high rents and house prices. If the newspapers that the middle class read also reaffirm this, including papers on the political right, the uncertainty over whether homes are really worth their current price tag grows. And house price fear spreads into the general psyche.

Some people 'generously' help their children with their deposits. However, rarely are the amounts enough for the next generation to acquire a first house that is of the same quality as the older generation had enjoyed; nor is the help usually enough to allow the younger generation to buy without also first having to save money of their own. The average age of first-time buyers is now widely reported to be people in their mid-thirties. A twenty-five-year mortgage might not be paid off until the buyers reach their sixties, or later. In such circumstances housing 'consumers' begin to see that, when land prices rise, as they have risen in the UK, someone is making a mint out of doing nothing but starting off rich. Only those who start off rich can own great quantities of land and then buy more. Government ministers pretend they disapprove of this, but they do little or nothing to prevent it.

Consider, for instance, Nick Boles, the UK coalition Planning Minister, who, in 2012, said: 'I think everyone has the right to live somewhere that is not just affordable but that is beautiful and has some green space nearby ... a basic moral right, like healthcare and education. There's a right to a home with a little bit of ground around it to bring your family up in.'[8] Currently, however, this vision appears a long way off for most. Maybe for most it is meant to remain as a vision, an aspiration, not a reality, as something to spur on those who might otherwise not work hard enough. This may sound a bit harsh, but Boles must know that for everyone to have some green space nearby, the rich cannot be allowed to continue to take more and more of it.

In Britain the large private home-builders are known to be hoarding land for which planning permission to build has already been obtained. They are waiting until it rises in value. Then the homes they will build on that land will be worth far more. What the builders look at is evidence such as the graph above, showing that UK land, by 2007, was worth sixteen times more than its value in 1983. Even after the adjustments following the crash, it was still worth at least ten times as much in 2009 as it was in the early 1980s. Private builders imagine that such a rise might happen again, that if they simply hold on to their land and build on only a little of it, they might make a hundredfold profit on an early 1980s investment, rather than a tenfold profit now. They believe another tenfold rise in future land values would bring this about, but their calculations do not take account of whether anyone in the future will be able to afford these prices.

By summer 2013 private builders had secured planning permission on enough land to build 400,000 homes in England, but not one of those homes had been built. That June the Labour opposition leader was reported as saying: 'All options should be on the table, including giving local authorities real power to say to the worst offenders that they should either use the land, or lose the land.'[9] In response the head of one of Britain's largest builders suggested that 'land is generally in short supply.'[10] The implication is that some other landholders are hoarding as well as the builders, and this encourages the builders to hoard what they hold too. Some of the largest landowners in the country are complicit, including pension funds, utility companies, the royal family, the Church, various charities, Oxbridge colleges, members of the aristocracy and other rich landowners.[11] If land is in short supply, it is only because we allow it to be; a land value tax would encourage all these owners to diversify a little out of land, freeing more to be built upon.

One reason why land rose in value far faster than the housing built on it was because, as incomes in Britain polarized, the rich got so much richer from the very early 1980s onwards. The rich saw land as a safe investment for their surplus money. They joke about how it is a fixed resource; about how no one will ever make more land. The price of land rose quickly at times when stock and shares were not giving the rich similar 'returns'. It was partly because the rich got richer and spent more of their monies on land that the builders began to wait a little longer before building to reap the rewards of inflation. There is now often a three- or four-year period between new land purchases by builders and property construction upon that land. Building faster might easily lose the building firm and its shareholders money if prices are rising.

By waiting for land prices and hence the apparent value of homes to rise further, the builders themselves are helping to shore up demand and to create further inflation in both land and housing prices. This is their job. They are private builders. Their job is to make as great a profit as they can. It is not primarily to build homes. If it were, they would build more.

What happens when builders don't use the land they possess to increase the available housing supply? One possibility (but an unlikely one) is this: 'Emigration from the UK rose, up to 353,000 from 336,000, with the number of people leaving the UK for a definite job up to 127,000 from 108,000 the previous year.'[12] The UK could become a more and more expensive place in which to live. People who can no longer afford to live in southern England may have to leave to live in cheaper countries, while those rich enough to come in will be encouraged with further inducements to settle. It is unlikely that fewer may migrate in than emigrate out, but this is what those who would like to see Britain go the way of Singapore are actually wishing for. Singapore is one of the few countries in the rich world with higher income inequalities than those to be found either in the UK or in the

US. Singapore maintains this by enticing wealthy incomers in with tax breaks and ensuring that servants hired from overseas have no right to remain in the country after they are no longer needed by the wealthy.

Emigration from Britain rose during 2012 when rates of immigration to the UK fell. More people were still coming in than going out, but the gap between those two figures was falling. People may leave places if there is not enough housing that they can afford. They may look at cheaper housing prices in many parts of booming Australia[13] and in most of New Zealand if they want more space for their money, more rooms as well as more sunlight. Fewer then come to live here. There is a case for building more homes, if just to reduce emigration and aid immigration, an inward movement of the young and not too expensive labour that an ageing Britain needs.

Many elderly people are so frail that they need a carer to visit them regularly. In January 2013 Gail Foster, an elderly woman, died when her carers were arrested by the UK Border Agency and so failed to turn up to feed her for nine days. The immigrants who had been feeding her were to be deported to hit government targets. It was because of those targets that Mrs Foster, at age eighty-one, 'was left to starve'.[14] Meanwhile, young British people are told that they need to aspire to the highest-paid jobs, and most know they would find it hard to survive long on a carer's wage. Pundits often suggest that greater immigration deprives us of housing, but they rarely explain how greater immigration can help us live longer and happier lives. We are almost always better housed at home than in a hospital bed.

The UK government would like people in Britain to blame poorer immigrants for the cost of housing being high, not bankers, private builders, landowners or speculators. The Labour Party toys with blaming immigration for various woes, most obviously when it talks of 'British jobs for British workers': even the Green Party has some elements within it that see immigration as adding to greenhouse-gas emissions. And some Liberal Democrats in Tower Hamlets have distributed leaflets that link the area's housing shortages with black and Asian people.[15] Put housing and immigration together and you get a toxic mix in almost any policy forum.

The coalition government has never understood the case for building homes for the growing numbers of completely new households that Britain should expect to be home to in the near future. It also does not understand that an ageing population would benefit from an influx of younger adults. Instead, Theresa May, the UK Home Secretary, suggested around Christmas time 2012 that 'House prices could be 10% lower over twenty years if the government cut net migration to zero.' She said this within two weeks of those emigration figures being released.[16] The statistics were those showing an increase in the numbers of people leaving the UK. They showed that although net immigration was still positive, it was falling. Her implication was that housing prices are high not because of issues such as the hoarding of land and the lowering of most people's incomes during austerity but because of immigration. She also assumes that the electorate she wants to appeal to are innumerate as well as prejudiced. A reduction of 10% over twenty years, or much less than 0.5% a year, is negligible.

London Mayor Boris Johnson rebuffed May's comment, saying that 'I don't think it is sensible to say that to keep down property values we should keep people out, or investors out, in order to allow property values to decline. That would lead to a fall in the equity of everyone and, for the life of me, I cannot see the logic.'[17] When people like Boris Johnson – or Planning Minister Nick Boles for that matter – talk of 'everyone', they don't mean tenants; or those about to buy at inflated prices in order to 'get on to the housing ladder'; or those who have no equity; or those in communal establishments such as retirement homes, prisons, military barracks or student halls. They mean outright owners and property landlords.

The two great economic crashes that followed the Roaring Twenties and never-had-it-so-good noughties have been compared in some detail earlier in this book. However, one great difference between 1929 and the years after 2008 in the UK is that, whereas in the 1930s there was a great growth in home-building, in the noughties, since the peak year of 2006/7 when over 192,000 homes were built in the UK, there has been a collapse in construction. We still have more homes and more rooms in homes than we have ever had, but we are now building more slowly than we have ever done. These two facts could, of course, be related, but we are not building slowly because everyone is now well housed but because builders are waiting for the time when greater profits are to be made. They have shareholders to satisfy or, for the smaller firms, mouths to feed.

By 2011/12 fewer than 110,000 permanent dwellings were being completed a year in Britain, and only 31% of those by housing associations for social renting (social renting means dwellings to be released for rent below supposedly free market prices). Local authorities, which used to build more houses than any other sector in some years, built just 2.7% of all homes in the 2011/12 financial year, fewer than 3,000 in total across all of the UK, and a third of those were in Scotland! However, as few as 130 council homes were built nationally in 2004/5, so, out of context, this minuscule rise in building could be represented as a great increase by a cynical politician.[18]

Sometimes there can be too many too dramatic claims being made about how dire the current situation is. This book has probably been guilty of a little of that, and so it is worth stepping back a bit. When you research issues of how many homes are being built you can quickly tire of the repeated claims that recent statistics are the worst since reliable records began. What almost no one says is that, even while our new-build rates slowed, the number of bedrooms potentially available to the people of Britain continued to rise and rise. We may not be building that many more new dwellings, but we have rapidly added rooms to what we already have.

Extensions were mostly built to turn three-bed into four-bed homes, at the same time as family sizes continued to fall. Often those extensions were built on to homes that had been purchased through 'right-to-buy', and not on to homes that remained council property. Precise annual figures are hard to come by, but a comparison of annual census returns for small areas shows just how many rooms have been added over the course of the last ten years.[19] Although it is true that in particular parts of the country and within particular tenures (say, smaller council-owned property), overcrowding rates have increased, despite all the roof conversions and all the building of bedrooms over the garage, there are, nonetheless, more bedrooms overall in the British housing stock now than there were ten years ago – more per family, even more per person.

Those who argue for renewed home-building tend to avoid looking at why so much of the existing stock of housing in Britain is so under-used, and how many properties could still be easily extended, should a little more space be needed. Those who would like to see more building now are a very wide group of individuals, ranging from the Chancellor of the Exchequer, George Osborne, through to the British Chambers of Commerce, the Labour Party and the charity Shelter.[20] But most of these advocates of house-building programmes tend to say little about the way existing housing stock is underused – and very little about stock that isn't used at all. As one newspaper financial editor explains:

> We fetishize the idea that grannies and granddads must stay in their family homes all their life. Why? So they can close off rooms, as they are too expensive to heat? It's understandable that people have an emotional attachment to their homes, and no one can or should be forced out. The idea of spending one's final years in a poky one-bed flat with nightmare neighbours horrifies me as much as anybody else. But a decent-sized, well-managed two-bed mansion-block flat, a lift, shops and GP services within close walking distance? No car to worry about, space for family to visit, a park close by? What's not to like?[21]

There's quite a bit not to like about leasehold mansion blocks: all manner of hidden costs in the way of service charges and huge lump sums demanded without notice for potentially fictitious building repairs. Purchasing a leasehold in such a block can entail great insecurity. This is part of the reason why most of the spare housing capacity in Britain is not held in land-banks, nor is it in boarded-up homes. Our spare housing capacity is, in fact, mostly in homes that are only very partially occupied. Later I'll provide figures to show that most bedrooms are not slept in most nights in the UK! This is not because people are secretly sneaking out of their bedroom and into someone else's bed; it is because we have so many spare bedrooms. We have enough, in fact, to allow every family with children and every childless couple to have a spare bedroom, with many more left spare after that.

It is not that single elderly people should be forced out of larger homes. Almost all that occupy such homes own them outright. But almost any encouragement to downsize would help the situation greatly. If a person for some reason wishes to live in a mansion full of many empty bedrooms that should be their right, but it would be fair if their level of council or other property tax reflected the impact that exercising this right has on everyone else. At present they usually receive a 25% discount on their council tax for being a single-person household. That discount distorts how council tax could better work as an incentive for everyone to fit better into the stock we have, but there are many other policies that are needed as well. If measures were taken to move economic activity, government administration, university student places and much more towards areas with surplus housing, and if underoccupation was discouraged by revised property taxation, everyone in Britain could be adequately housed within the existing stock. The principle would be akin to 'the polluter pays', but replace the word 'polluter' with 'hoarder'.

I am not saying that more homes being built would not help; I am saying that more homes alone are not the answer. There is one scenario, already touched upon above, where it would make sense to begin a great home-building programme, and it is a scenario that should not be ignored, given two current global trends: the rising dominance both of the English language and of London as a point of attraction. If many more migrants were to come to Britain, much more home-building would be needed.

Should the government be serious about curbing immigration, or should the rest of Europe start to use English far more as the language of business in particular cities, home-building in the UK won't simply cease. Building homes is a little like building motorways in an area where population growth has been falling. If you build more roads in such an area, more and more people will drive alone, and more will drive further and for longer to work. Here in Britain, in contrast with more equitable affluent countries, better-off couples often own two homes, with one almost always empty. Thus, even without more people coming, we can find uses for more dwellings, but, as our income and wealth inequalities grow, these are usually not very efficient or often fair uses.

The analogy with rising single-occupant car use is worth thinking about a little longer. Clearly it is far better to have four people in a car than one. A little more fuel is used due to the additional weight, but not much, and much less in comparison with each of those four people driving their own car. However, the more scattered people's journeys become, and the more reliant people become on cars for other parts of their lives – to ferry children to childcare and later to and from school, for shopping and for recreation – the more likely you are to find more cars, often almost all cars, with just one person in them. This is even the case when at some points there are passengers in the car at the start of the journey. Once the schoolchildren are dropped off, the driver drives back alone.

Similarly, a dwelling that is just home to one person is almost as expensive to heat and light as one being used by several people. A row of single-occupant homes results in a row of dustbins all needing to be emptied, while many separate telephone and internet connections all need to be maintained. Separate water bills, a separate set of roofs and guttering to be looked after: the cost per person of low-density occupation is very high. None of these points mean that it is not possible for many people to live alone, should they wish to. In fact, it is in more equitable affluent countries that the highest proportions of solo-dwellers are found. Sweden has the highest proportion of anywhere in the world: single adults occupy 47% of all Swedish dwellings. In Norway, 40% of households have just one resident, and in similarly economically equitable Japan it is 30%.[22] But in all those countries this is achieved by not wasting so much of the rest of the housing stock through underoccupancy, and by having an increasing proportion of dwellings being built for (or converted for) solo-use.[23]

Building many more homes without many more people coming into the UK will not necessarily result in reduced overcrowding. A large part of the reason for this is that, as economic inequalities rise, poorer households are forced to crowd into whatever property they can get, allowing more affluent households to spread themselves out amongst the stock that is left. The affluent are then more likely to try to live away from the overcrowded poor, and so move further and further out of town, often in new-built homes. But they still need to drive or to take the train to work. In such circumstances, to see what happens if we were to build more homes in southern England, say, it may help to look at a surprising situation in an ex-colony. This time it is not the tiny island of Singapore, but the giant continental island of Australia.

Australia shows what occurs when there are few restrictions on home-building. Despite having a relatively low population, Australia has some of the longest commute times in the world, because the lack of planning restrictions has resulted in very low-density housing sprawl. What's more, Sydney has some of the highest housing prices in the world, because the private market was allowed to 'find its level', without much planning or intervention to consider the aggregate negative effects of every individual selfish action. One person choosing to build a home with a large garden does not just affect that one person. Everyone who then has to live further out of town has to drive past that garden. Multiply this by many thousands of dream one-acre plots and you each spend thousands of hours of your lifetime in extra unnecessary driving past all these enormous gardens, just to allow each of you to get to spend a few hours weeding your very large shrubberies.

The conventional wisdom in housing research proposes that there is enough pent-up 'demographic' demand to fill more homes, even if net immigration were to reduce to zero – especially in the overheated housing market of south-east England. Rising demographic demand – including all the divorces to come, staying single forever and ageing, which we hope we will get to enjoy – will cause housing to be used up by those who can afford it. As we live longer, there are more of us around to be housed. Advocates of the simplistic free-market approach say that rebalancing housing supply, as builders build, to meet this latent demand should reduce house prices, thereby making housing more affordable and turning latent demand into actual demand; but that works well only when all consumers are economically more equal.

The theory that prices will fall requires an assumption that 'hoarders' of vacant housing, and of the space occupied by very large gardens (on which new housing could be built), would put their stock and land on the market if they felt prices would not rise much further in future – that is, if now was exactly the right time to sell and delay would mean losing out. This point of falling prices is rarely achieved in Britain and usually then only fleetingly. However, the threat of being taxed in the near future for hoarding space would be an even greater incentive to sell than worry over falling future land values; and, of course, the threat of land taxation should lead to land values falling in future. Land upon which you pay an annual tax becomes uneconomic to hold empty.

But a market for smaller homes for smaller households requires those households to be able to buy and rent at lower levels than now – but not too low. All this, however, ignores how unevenly income and wealth – and hence effective demand – is now distributed in the UK. The gulf between rich and poor has become so great that either incomes at the bottom have to rise, or rents and prices have to fall greatly, before there can be much reconciliation. The usual suggestion to this quandary is simply to advocate more home-building – much more building.

Civic campaigns to build are again growing. At different times in the UK's recent and more distant past there has been rising and then falling public pressure to build. Today one group, Audacity, argues that there is a need to build five million homes within the next ten years, while also demolishing many substandard homes rather than patching them up. Audacity does have a point: housing doesn't last forever; it wears out. Audacity sees inertia as the result of a great contraction in the UK housing industry. It advocates a return to the energetic home-building that we last had in the 1930s, 1950s and 1960s.

Audacity suggests that most people in Britain expect to own their homes once their mortgages are paid off; or hope to get on the housing ladder; or are already outright owners. This trinity of tenure groups makes up a majority, they claim, that favours sustained house price inflation so that they can subsequently raise cash by releasing equity in their property. The problem, they suggest, is that a majority think they will benefit from the ladder itself being raised up. But the majority may well find out that they are wrong.

Even the very phrase 'housing ladder' entrenches the idea of property as a speculation. It implies that housing is a successful Ponzi scheme, one in which earlier investors' profits come directly from the input of later investors. Climb on board and you too will eventually win at the expense of some sucker below you. But all Ponzi schemes eventually fail. Everyone cannot get rich quick at the expense of future property buyers, especially as we have been having fewer than two children per couple in Britain for many decades now. Ponzi schemes work only for as long as there is a ready and ever larger supply of new customers to be duped.

The younger half of the population will not benefit from rising rents and housing prices. They need affordable and comfortable homes for themselves now, and value this need way above making a future profit. But many younger people cannot get even that, when a majority of the older age group, and especially a few much richer individuals, are allowed to profit greatly. Even among the elderly, sustained house price inflation divides the rich pensioner, who can leave their grandchildren a fortune, from the poor pensioners who rent and will leave very little.

The usual pattern of housing transitions is that people end up struggling for housing when they are young and then rattle around in oversized property when they are old. However, fewer and fewer people are now average in the income they receive; this pattern relied on far more predictable and fairly rewarded employment than we have today, evening out housing fortunes over a lifetime. It will be much harder to sustain into the future.

Even if Audacity were to manage to create an environment in which many homes could be built quickly, our employment profile has changed so much, so recently, that they could not simply all be bought by couples and individuals being lent money and paying it back in large monthly instalments (often some 300 such payments – twenty-five years times twelve months) without fault! You cannot just build and expect people to buy, reliably, when you no longer employ them reliably. Furthermore, very little housing in Britain is so badly deteriorated that it is at the end of its feasible 'life'. We don't yet have to build that much to replace what has to be replaced because it cannot be maintained. Only some really badly 'system built' property from the 1960s and 1970s is too expensive to renovate.[24]

RENOVATION AND REALITY

Full-scale refurbishment of the entire UK housing stock could support 4.7 million jobs and add £280 billion to the economy.

– Oxfam, 2012[25]

It is odd that today it has become the job of an anti-poverty charity to recognize how refurbishing property to create better housing, rather than building so much anew, could result in a better society. The UK government appears unable to see the links, let alone act, promoting a few loft-insulation schemes, but nothing that even approaches a tenth of what Oxfam suggests above. Oxfam's estimates are derived from research carried out by the Energy Saving Trust, and Oxfam itself says a more modest programme could also be implemented.

The full proposed programme of bringing existing UK housing up to scratch would have massive long-term benefits, such as saving £8.7 billion a year on domestic energy bills, and it is estimated that the resulting cuts in CO_2 emissions would be 48 million tonnes a year. Oxfam suggests that investing in retrofitting has the advantage of creating jobs quickly; the money remains in the UK, boosting the economy; more rooms could be added to property that is too small; and the environmental damage from huge amounts of new building is avoided. Reducing environmental damage is not necessarily an abstract concept. For instance, much land in the south that isn't built on is flood plain. It makes sense to leave it as that, if you wish to see fewer properties flooded each year.

Governments tend to believe that property-owners and property-buyers, landlords and mortgagors, have such a huge vested interest in their property that they will look after it well, building only where it is sensible to build, and maintaining housing to a good standard to maximize their rent or sale price. However, if renovating homes does not increase their sale value by more than the cost of the renovation, the incentive is not high, no matter how much such action might reduce energy consumption and waste in future. For landlords those are the tenants' problems and costs. For mortgagors and outright owners, future difficulties due to current neglect are mostly the problem of the people they will be selling on to. As the housing market in the south-east of England overheated in late summer 2013, sellers did not even bother to tidy up their property for viewers, let alone paint or plaster a few dodgy walls. They knew they could sell, regardless of how their home looked, as buyers were so afraid of missing the boat when prices rose.

Just as individuals cannot be expected to maintain the road surface outside their own home, or work out how to make a sewer system operate well, so too we cannot rely on individuals' self-interest to ensure that we adequately renew the housing stock. We need to ensure that what we have lasts for longer than it otherwise would, that it is as well insulated as it can be, and as comfortable to live in as possible. That has to be coordinated and properly planned. Occasionally there are schemes set up to help landlords and poorer homeowners to renovate their property, but as they stand these tend just to save landlords a little expense, and what we have done to date has not resulted in very high standards of residential building maintenance across the country. People who come to rent from abroad are often shocked by the state of what they are offered: by how cold many of our homes are, how badly soundproofed, how badly kept up.

A government with a different set of priorities could achieve a great deal. Imagine a more environmentally and socially aware government simply committed to achieving a tenth of the agenda suggested by Oxfam in the quotation above – generating 470,000 jobs in a refurbishment project that would save 'just' £870 million a year on energy bills. But to act so sensibly, collectively, requires both long-term planning and political courage, qualities that currently appear to be in short supply. It requires courage because financial experts opposed to such cooperative action will say it is economically impossible.

'Let the market find its own level' is the repetitive refrain of the right, treating housing as if it were a commodity, a consumer item that should find its correct price, its equilibrium level, through the apparent 'laws' of supply and demand. This supply-and-demand mechanism will, so the orthodox argument goes, balance out people and housing. Should there not be enough homes for people, the only thing stopping

This photograph shows the front of a Georgian-era home in Sharrow, Sheffield, formerly used as a squat. Note how even the small window above the door has been boarded up to make re-entry more difficult. When we pass such homes we need to ask why they are boarded up. There may be many superficial reasons, but underlying those is how we have chosen to arrange our economy. The more inequitably income and wealth are distributed in Britain, the more people there will be who cannot afford to rent or buy, and the more homes will stand empty, waiting for someone who can afford them. Squatting can be seen as an indicator of a housing system in crisis. The worse the normal housing system of allocating people to homes becomes, the more people will squat. Then the more draconian will become the defences set up to protect empty property from being used by squatters, until the whole exercise ceases to be economically sustainable. Millions of families in the United States are, in effect, squatting: they no longer pay the mortgage, but continue to live in the property.

more homes being built must be government regulation and, according to this way of thinking, less regulation is therefore needed. But those commentators who constantly call for less regulation ignore the way that so many homes were provided in the past: they were built by government, or built using monies lent or gifted by government. They also ignore the fact that people are usually better housed in those affluent countries that possess tight regulation and well-planned housing arrangements. They ignore the failure of the market in the past to supply enough housing of a high enough quality, as well as the pervasiveness of slum landlords and cowboy builders when and where regulation is absent.

All this brings us back to one of this book's central premises: that the fundamental problem in Britain – and in other Western countries – is not a shortage of homes. In July 2012 the property website rightmove.co.uk recorded a 1.7% drop in house prices that month, with two families trying to sell for every family trying to buy.[26] Prices fell by a further 2.4% the following month, and slightly again in September; they next rose by 3.4% in October, but fell by 2.6% in November, and then by a further 3.3% in December. You might think that this was because the summer is usually quieter, but by the next summer, that of 2013, prices were reported to be rising again in parts of the south-east and those drops were forgotten. Within five months of housing prices falling, the recording of a few rises in July and August 2013 resulted in talk of a bubble once again forming, talk reported earlier in the pages of this book. Then, September 2013, falls were reported in prices in Westminster (reported below in this book), all of which further illustrates just how volatile is the time that we are living through.

In January 2013 national average UK housing prices rose by just 0.2%, but then in February lending slumped 'by the biggest monthly amount in more than fifteen years'.[27] Both sales and prices were down. In the year to March 2013 there was a reported 16% fall in the number of properties being sold at prices of between £2 million and £3 million in London.[28] Three months later the summer newspapers talked of economic recovery and the prices of fairly average two-bed properties in central London soon routinely exceeding £1 million.[29] So, in March 2013, we had supply exceeding demand, but by August we had far more demand than supply for multimillion-pound London properties.

The extreme end of the market shows nicely how simple supply and demand balancing does not work for goods as bulky as housing. It is not possible to quickly and easily produce more homes when demand rises, especially when it comes to homes in the centre of London. But there, at least, demand is more about speculation and investment than need, although many people do need to be able to sleep close to the centre of the capital to do the jobs they do. Conversely, when prices fall it is not simply a matter of stabilizing the price, especially when people have to move home between cities for a new job, retirement or to house a growing family.

Real housing demand increases as families split up; as jobs are created in an area and people move in; as more children become adults and want to leave home to start their own family. When a single household is created by the merging of households, demand falls, but two households squeezing into one home is rare. It can occur when separated parents meet new partners and move in with them, bringing the children together to create a new merged family, but that requires more space in itself.

Supply is reduced when in-migration to an area and the splitting of households within it exceed the numbers of properties becoming vacant due to out-migration from an area, moves into retirement homes or simply the deaths of occupants. However, real housing demand is often not backed by the finance needed to make it 'effective' demand.

Part of the reason that we think we need more housing built now is that so many families divorce and do not quickly reconstitute into new families. A reconstituted family consists of a couple, where some of the children are his, and some are hers. Before there is any chance of such reconstitution of split-up households into new households, more and more children have a bedroom at Mum's, and also one at Dad's. Families splitting up and new families being formed mean that we need more space in our housing system as a whole to facilitate the musical-chairs game of sorting ourselves into new relationships. Higher rates of separation require more space in housing. And people are more likely to separate during a financial crisis, when greater unemployment and precarious employment add to everyone's stress.

An alternative joined-up housing and employment policy should recognize that the increase in income inequality since 1970 means we now use houses far more inefficiently: not only divorcing couples, but

New eco-homes built in the Arbourthorne neighbourhood in south-east Sheffield. Note the solar panels tilting to the sun on the roof of the property furthest away. In the north of England you need more of an angular advantage than in the south to catch enough sunlight. Homes built with the long-term interests of our environment in mind are often dismissed as costly extravagances, but if the extra effort required to avoid identikit modern boxes is qualified mainly as an increase in labour costs, then building eco-homes can create more jobs per home built than conventional construction. Changing how we build will take time. For homes like this to be built in greater numbers in places like Arbourthorne, upon land that has been used for building on in the recent past, there need to be more new jobs in Sheffield and fewer new jobs in the south of England, where almost all the expanses of spare land are now green belt.

second-, third- and fourth-home owners; couples (and even single adults) with no children but large dwellings; and those occupying private-sector family houses with many spare bedrooms. The growth of all these new household configurations, far more than an increase in population, contributes greatly to our overall housing shortage; this is then exacerbated by rich and super-rich multiple-home purchasing; more and more property that is often left vacant. All these problems are enhanced as more and more of the population tries to fit into the south-east of England, where there is the fewest number of homes for sale for those who need them the most.

Note that this point about under-use of the existing housing in Britain has almost nothing to do with the Bedroom Tax being applied to working-age social housing tenants, who on average use housing most efficiently of all. It is about the people who have little need for much of the space they have, not just one extra bedroom, but much more that they can afford to keep vacant. Almost all the empty property in the UK is owned by someone who knows it is empty, just as much of the housing in disrepair is owned by someone who could repair it, should they choose to. If a landlord claims that he does not have the money needed to refurbish a home, ask to what use he puts the rent he receives from his properties.

Maintaining a good stock of housing is not just about building replacement properties for those worn-out old homes. It is as much about repairing and maintaining existing property; homes can be repaired and refitted to remain fit for purpose well beyond their original design date. Often property is left empty because the owner has not bothered to get around to decorating it to rent out. But new policy is not encouraging this. On 15 November 2012 the British government changed the law on empty properties, so that they could be left empty by their owners for up to two years before any action might be taken by a local authority; previously Section 134(2)(a) of the Housing Act 2004, made law by the Labour government, had mandated six months.[30]

Governments have not been entirely toothless when it comes to the need to try to bring empty and abandoned property back into use. But when one government finally was a little bit innovative and introduced a law giving local authorities the power to intervene, the next government quickly watered down that law. Previously the authorities were allowed to intervene if nothing was done to what appeared to be an abandoned dwelling space, in an area where there was housing need. The change in this law will, of course, allow perfectly renovated property to stand empty for longer now; the owner can deliberately not market the property if they so desire. The point of the previous half-year limit was to encourage those with empty properties to rent them out, and, if they needed renovation or decoration, to do that quickly, before the local authority took over the property. Changing the time limit to two years encourages landlords to take their time. It encourages more hoarding of empty property. It keeps up the price of that property and makes housing in total more expensive. The 'use it or lose it after six months' policy, if better enacted rather than simply being rescinded, would help people to learn not to hoard and bring down prices, with rents then coming down as a consequence.

Clearly, ensuring that empty and dilapidated housing is quickly brought up to scratch is not a current policy priority; governments don't tend to get plaudits for ensuring that flimsy single glazing is replaced by double glazing, encouraging insulation of cavity walls and roofs, and so on. Social landlords can now get grants to insulate, funded from the green levies on fuel bills, but such grants were being cut towards the end of 2013, not long after they were introduced.[31] Voters do not appear to recognize that a government that helped to ensure that less housing was empty would help everyone fit in more easily. This – the everyday reality of the upkeep, filling and modernizing of our housing stock – sounds like bureaucratic red-tape and appears to be far less of a headline-grabbing initiative than 'building new homes'. Yet these are initiatives that governments might easily implement more widely and that all already exist in a limited form.

It is unlikely that the parties that form the current government think they will lose more votes from landlords than gain them from prospective tenants. There are many more tenants and prospective tenants, in comparison with the number of landlords. It has been suggested that as few as 2% of all people in Britain are landlords.[32] Why, then, does government allow so much property that could be rented out to be left standing empty for so long? Why does it fail to ensure that private property is brought up to a rentable standard if the building becomes empty for more than six months? It is hard not to conclude that when ministers increased the time limit before a local authority could act they did so because of lobbying from a few very rich and very well-connected people with vested interests – those who wanted to be free to keep a lot of their property empty until the market was right for them, those who own more property than they need. What other reason could there be?

When one generation or government neglects the maintenance of housing, the repair bill for the next grows disproportionately. Britain's New Labour government received little acknowledgement for all the homes it ensured were made decent while it held office, housing that had suffered decades of neglect. True, it did not boast about the figures, probably because it did not want to be seen to be especially favouring Labour's more traditional supporters, those who have the least. However, Labour could have made wider arguments to defend its large repair programme of so much social housing between the years 1997 and 2010. Keeping housing in good repair is remarkably more environmentally efficient in comparison with demolition and rebuilding. Concrete production is among the main sources of carbon pollution worldwide.

Large-scale refurbishment schemes do far more than improve the state of many individual houses. They can revitalize sink estates, ensure the upkeep of long-established roads and sewers built decades ago, and avoid the need for building on greenfield sites. Where the situation is one of extreme decay, the refurbishment solutions can be more radical. Narrow Victorian terraced housing can be adapted by knocking doors through the walls and converting two tiny properties into one desirable one. This has been done in several parts of the north of England, where otherwise the terraces may have faced demolition. But, of course, the question of repairing homes depends not on engineering but on economics. During the slum clearances of the 1960s large swathes of the London borough of Islington – largely nineteenth-century urban development – were earmarked for demolition. Protesters and local residents fought against the plans and won. Now, much of that old housing, once destined for demolition, is among some of the most expensive in the world. However, the economics of preserving and renovating nineteenth-century housing in the north of England, Wales, Northern Ireland and Scotland become harder and harder to sustain as the country tips economically on its axis, weighed down by the growing paper wealth of the south. The value of some northern terraces is now so low that knocking two into one, in places where there are fewer and fewer jobs, only produces good-sized houses in areas where people are no longer able to live. A good-sized house in the poorest parts of the north is not worth that much in monetary terms, but it is worth a lot as somewhere to call home.

Decaying stock can be maintained – even the rusted iron wall-ties that kept the brickwork of many very old homes straight in the past and ultimately stop a house collapsing can be replaced – if there is a will. But, if you leave all this to the market, rather than listen to protesters and others advocating a different policy, millions will be spent on privately retaining and greatly improving the decoration of just a tiny proportion of the national stock – money that could have been better spent spread over far more properties. It is not an either/or situation, but currently a disproportionate share of the nations' builders are working on makeovers of mansions that have not even had time to become slightly shabby since they were last redecorated, rather than spreading their work over the entire stock. A better public/private mix of building and renovation is needed.

Both protesters and planners can help to improve housing. Protesters have helped by protecting decent old stock from demolition, as in 1960s Islington; or by highlighting when old council estates are turned over to speculators who wish to build office blocks; or by spray painting the windows of estate agents moving into an area to try to gentrify it beyond the reach of locals' budgets. Planning regulations are often blamed for limiting housing supply, but they also ensure that homes are properly proportioned so that, for example, they can accommodate wheelchairs. As an ageing population, far more of us will be in those chairs in future. Far more of us will live long enough to spend our final years suffering from disabilities, including often becoming blind. In what kind of a home do you want to live and grow old?

When it comes to how we are housed, it's worth thinking not just of the property we might occupy, but of the sort of neighbourhoods where we might want to live. Do you want to enjoy one that has been planned and cared for; a place where people have worked to ensure that there are enough jobs, enough schools and enough shops nearby – or just a neighbourhood where people poorer than you cannot afford to live, and people richer than you would not want to live?

LOCATION, LOCATION

Most inner London boroughs are likely to become almost entirely unaffordable to low-income tenants on LHA [Local Housing Allowance] by 2016 ... The areas which remain affordable are characterized by high rates of multiple deprivation and unemployment among the existing population. We conclude that the reforms will intensify the spatial concentration of disadvantage in the city, and increase the segregation of poor and better-off households within London.

– Alex Fenton, Cambridge Centre for Housing
and Planning Research, 2011[33]

The way in which we choose to arrange and change our housing determines the way in which we live. In the UK we are currently choosing politicians who have a track record of picking policies that polarize society. It may be the prevailing political culture of our times, rather than the individual politicians themselves, but the effect of our recent choices has been to reward great selfishness, or what they might call aspiration, which then in turn makes us all want to aspire to having much more, of winning some lottery.

The quote above is from the conclusion of a farsighted 2011 report written by an academic then based at the University of Cambridge. The polarization that Alex Fenton talks about is not just currently occurring in London, or just in the south-east, or even just in the UK more broadly. But the UK situation is especially telling, because it illustrates what happens when societies grow increasingly unequal. London is ahead of the curve when it comes to housing policy that increases inequalities. It is the most economically unequal city in Britain, and – by wealth distribution – possibly the most unequal in the entire rich world.

Within less than a year of the coalition government gaining power in 2010, stories had begun to circulate that many of London's poor were soon to be rehoused outside the city. This most recent attack on the poor, which became an issue of segregation, happened first and most ferociously in London, because it is in London that more room is required for the middle and new upper classes of the country, and where they increasingly need to be.[34]

Over recent decades the proportion of upper-class individuals living outside of the capital, in its commuting hinterland, has fallen. It is not just that parts of the capital are gentrifying, but that the capital as a whole is becoming much posher.[35] For this to happen, fewer of those with less can be allowed to remain there. Perhaps those who can stay will soon be termed 'the deserving few'. The implication of recent nuances in official documents is that in some parts of London poorer people will have to work harder for the privilege of continuing to live in their homes, a privilege that could be reconsidered and renewed annually by council officers. Recently a document leaked from Hammersmith and Fulham Borough Council explained that from now on 'A social housing tenancy will need to be earned and its retention worked at. It will no longer necessarily be passed from one generation to the next.'[36] In other words, if you are a council home tenant in that borough, the grown-up child with learning difficulties who has lived with you for their entire life may be evicted from their home when you, the current tenant, die. Even before that point, however, you too might be evicted, to go to live in a more down-at-heel borough, if you do not continuously come up to scratch in some way. The same is not true for the private sector, where, at least outside most of London, modest homes – those whose value falls below the inheritance tax threshold (less than £325,000) – can be passed on to grown-up children who also reside only in that property without the fear that they will be evicted upon their parent's death.

The new edicts in places such as Hammersmith and Fulham Borough Council suggest that social housing in Britain may be becoming a gift to be bestowed on those who in future doff their caps well enough to retain their home. If their children do not show similar

A terraced street in the Sharrow neighbourhood of Sheffield showing, in the distance, one added skylight. For generations the way in which we have built and adapted housing has reflected our social structures. Most of the homes that were built early in our history were peasant hovels, of which little evidence remains. Then more solid homes were built for the working classes, often slightly larger properties on street corners for foremen's families. Today homes where the front door opens directly on to the street are seen as less desirable, whereas once they were coveted – better than living up an alley in a rookery. However, place the houses pictured above on a street in London's Notting Hill and suddenly, miraculously, they would again be seen as wonderful homes to live in, especially for the upper middle class and the upper class, and there would be many more expensive loft conversions and skylights put in. The extent to which all this is common sense to you, or a revelation, depends very much on where you live, in what kind of housing, and how old you are. The location of a property changes the nature of that property. When housing becomes segregated, it is not because of the housing but rather because of the changes in society, the economy and the politics in the places where that housing happens to be.

respect, do not (to paraphrase from above) 'earn the retention of their home by working at it', they will have to leave the parish (the borough). Working at it might mean never breaking the law, gaining a better job to pay the higher rent, getting credit from doing a bit of voluntary community service. This is a return to older, poorer sets of rights and laws. The leaked Hammersmith and Fulham document claimed that these measures were needed for 'Tackling Economic and Social Polarization'. In one way they will. A borough becomes less polarized if you evict the poor. As rents rise, but the local housing allowances, the housing benefit levels, do not keep pace, hundreds of families will be relocated from London to towns such as Stoke on Trent, Liverpool, Middlesbrough and further north and west. Even if this does not happen directly, it will occur indirectly.

Within Britain (and much of the rest of Europe) the debate over segregation, about who deserves and wishes to be housed where, is not only about rich and poor, but about black and white. In many localities this now increasingly translates into 'Muslim' and 'non-Muslim'. Responding to comments by Trevor Kavanagh, political editor of the *Sun*, one academic explained early in 2013 that there is widespread confusion over the current direction of segregation in housing in Britain today. He pointed out that Kavanagh's suggestion that Muslims in Britain were geographically segregated was not, in general, happening; that where it was happening it was not necessarily because of religion; and, even if it were due to that, that would not necessarily be a problem. He, Rob Ford, then finished his argument by pointing out that Kavanagh did not appear to be suggesting a solution to the straw problem that he had created. It is a complex argument but worth following up, because the current pernicious claim that Muslims are leading ever more parallel lives in the UK, including becoming ever more segregated by where they live, is so damaging. These suggestions of growing self-segregation and choosing parallel lives are repeatedly made and restated. Rob Ford went on to explain that:

> Even if segregation were a problem (which it generally is not), it is not clear what would satisfy Kavanagh as a solution. Maybe Muslims could integrate by moving away from areas where they are concentrated towards more homogeneously white areas, something University

of Manchester census analysts have shown all ethnic minority groups have been doing? This won't do for Kavanagh, who attacks it as Muslims 'colonizing the suburbs'. Leaving aside the absurd labelling of people often born and raised in Britain as 'colonizers', it is not obvious what Muslims caught in Kavanagh's Islamophobic catch-22 are supposed to do. If they stay in the inner city areas to which their families first migrated, they are attacked as setting up segregated 'Islamic Republics'. If they set out for the suburbs, they are attacked as 'colonizers' looking to impose their values on others.[37]

There is a group that has colonized housing in Britain. It is true. But they are (mostly) not immigrants, and hardly any of them are Muslim. Between 2006 and 2009 the chances of people aged over sixty-five, the affluent elderly, in Britain becoming a full (mortgage paid off) owner-occupier increased slightly, despite the overall proportion of households with a mortgage or being outright owners declining since at least 2002.[38] But there is a subgroup within the group of elderly and middle-aged families that does better than this: the very rich, especially the super-rich, who buy properties through their companies. Sometimes these companies are 'service' companies, set up (legally) for the purposes of tax avoidance. Houses are purchased by the service company as 'assets'; and the costs associated with doing them up are offset as 'liabilities'. The earnings of the rich are paid into the company too, and so often very little or no income tax is paid by these very rich individuals as a result of their property purchase, in which they might, or might not, choose to reside.

The super-rich do well whether they are young or old. They often pay no capital gains tax as long as they use an offshore-based company; they pay no inheritance tax if they claim 'non-dom' (not 'domiciled') status; and, if they set up their own company, no stamp duty, as they are not buying or selling a home but transferring shares in a company (as long as they can find a way of claiming that the property is not a residential home). Such a transfer would normally attract a 0.5% tax, but not for the super-rich; they know what they are doing. Many use an offshore trust, especially if buying property worth over £2 million, which, since March 2012, should attract 7% stamp duty.

The coalition government says it has been trying to tackle the avoidance of stamp duty – but its rate of progress has been extremely slow. For certain corporate bodies there are even ways around the introduction of a new 15% top-end stamp duty rate. That rate should, in theory, make prime location in central London a little less attract-ive, dampening down prices and helping to ensure places further afield in the south-east become a fraction more affordable (as some of those displaced from central London move back inwards). But, up until autumn 2013 at least, that has not happened. Perhaps this is because the continuation of many other loopholes will 'enable the residents of a total of £760 million worth of property [a year] to avoid British capital gains and inheritance tax'.[39] The rich get richer, those in the middle pay mortgage interest, and the poor can only dream of doing so. As a proportion of their income, the poor are now paying the most for the housing they get.

The poor pay the most to be housed because they rent. They never get to own the homes they live in. They also increasingly frequently suffer the indignity of being paid such low wages that their rent is paid for them by the state, implying that they cannot pay their way, while the fact is that they are denied decent work in a way their grand-parents were not. In the 1950s through to the end of the 1970s there was full employment, average wages rose in real terms year after year, and people could pay their own rent. Rents were also much lower than today, because so much of the rental sector was state owned.

The middle class pay more for their housing than their housing is worth, much more than their parents in absolute terms. Even when interest rates are low, more than half of what is paid back on a twenty-five-year mortgage doesn't pay off the loan; it pays a profit to the lender. The middle class often hope one day to own their property outright. Many of them do, but not all. However, because housing finance has become so skew-whiff, it is increasingly likely that their grown-up children will come to view part of the equity in those homes as the down-payment on an even larger mortgage in future. All the time the aggregate housing debt of the average middle-class family rises and rises.

Someone has to win from all of this, and it is those at the very top. They do not simply receive the bulk of mortgage interest payments, profits from building firms and rents from tenants; they also often live rent and mortgage free, if they put their properties in the hands of their private company or trust. You might say that they have in some way worked to earn the money for their homes, but there are only twenty-four hours in a day. How in that time can someone do enough useful work to earn the millions needed to buy the most expensive homes in the land?

In one way the extremely rich have worked hard: they have worked hard to achieve polarization in housing. They often influence politics and control newspapers, inducing the latter to peddle the line that individualism triumphs. They practise what they preach, buying and building their new homes in ways that allow them to avoid tax. For example Lord Rothermere, owner of the *Daily Mail*, was apparently not content to live just in his Eaton Square home in London's most expensive quarter, a place where grand townhouses had been built to accommodate many servants in the past. In 2004 another home, this time a neo-Palladian house, had to be built for him in a location described as 'deep in the Dorset countryside'. The property was called Ferne House and was said to be worth £40 million. It was constructed within the 220 acres of its own private grounds, but even that wasn't good enough for Lord Rothermere. In 2006 he had new east and west wings added to the house. Did he pay for these himself? No, apparently the 'money came in the form of bank loans for which Rothermere pledged eight million of his DMGT [*Daily Mail* and General Trust] shares, worth around £50 million. Except they weren't legally his shares. They belonged to the Bermudan company through which Rothermere family trusts control the *Mail* empire.'[40] In this way, the extremely rich build and buy mansions tax-free in Dorset or Kensington, while the newly impoverished are expelled to Stoke, Liverpool or Newcastle; or crowded into Newham, Barking or Dagenham in transit.

Recently it was claimed by the coalition government that Chancellor George Osborne had tried to close some of these complex property tax loopholes, but, again, the attempt to do so was at best half-hearted. A property developer was secretly filmed giving advice over how to avoid tax, having already helped other buyers engineer their way financially around the Chancellor's new provisions. Osborne's increase in stamp duty 'only affects *new* purchases of high-value homes by companies, those houses already owned in such a way [through an offshore company] – like those at Cornwall Terrace [bordering London's Regent's Park] – are not subject to the punitive stamp duty rate'.[41] The purchaser buys the service company created with the express purpose of owning that property, and as a result the registered owner of the property does not change: hey presto, no property sale has taken place, no stamp duty. The houses in Cornwall Terrace look, above ground, a little like the one shown in the picture below. Just as the finances are well hidden, so there is no way of knowing what so much property of this kind now looks like below ground.

The extremely rich have found a new way to hide their wealth and to remain inconspicuous in their consumption of it: through their creation of the vast, subterranean developments currently being built under many square miles of London's prime real estate. Own a property outright and you own the land underneath it. So, if money is no object, but going sideways or upwards is not possible, dig down.

All the effort that goes into making neo-Georgian property look as shiny as the day it was first built, all the carving out of subterranean playrooms, pools and servants' quarters,[42] could be effort spent renovating and repairing the homes that thousands of other, poorer, average people live in. There are only so many builders, plasterers, painters, carpenters and joiners. If more are working digging underground in Kensington or around Regent's Park, there will be fewer to undertake renovation above ground in Newham or Newcastle.

You may say that there are only so many mansions, but in 2011, 2012 and 2013 it was easy to spend far more than a day walking around London's most opulent streets watching builders at work, as the insides of grand townhouses were gutted and the innards sent through a series of chutes down into skips on the street – skips that are quickly whisked away to landfill to keep the neighbourhood looking its best. New interior walls are fitted, new staircases put in, a complete redecoration undertaken to allow all the latest fashions of home décor to be accommodated. And all that is before you dig down, and before the next purchaser moves in and wants it all changed around again. Perhaps every bedroom needs a walk-in wardrobe as well as an en suite. Lose a study here and a billiard room there and it can all be rejigged. The options are as endless as the depth of your wallet.

The housing crisis is a crisis of polarization: it illustrates in sharp

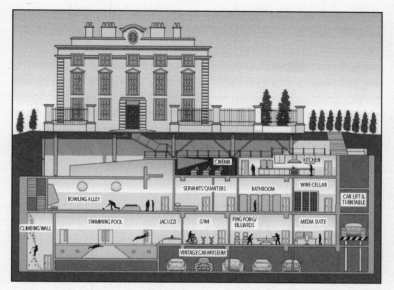

Figure 7. The modern London Kensington mansion, an artist's impression, 2012.

relief what occurs when the rich get richer and the poor poorer.[43] Almost everyone is unhappy with some aspect of their position along this spectrum: with how easy those above them have it, and how easily they themselves could slip down to live in what, for them, is the squalor of people housed in slightly worse circumstances than themselves: 'I couldn't live like that', they might say.

It is as the crisis deepens and the rise in the price of prime property accelerates in London, while over a quarter of the high street is closed in Blackburn,[44] that the issue of segregation begins to raise its ugly head again. This is not the supposed chosen segregation of one group wishing to live away from another; it is the enforced segregation that occurs when people who have been abandoned have to move to places that, increasingly, have also been abandoned. When this occurs it is not just rich and poor who become ever more separated. People can then become more divided by race and religion – especially if those labelled as being of a particular race or religion happen to be much better off, or poorer, than the norm.

The further away you move from a system in which a large proportion of housing is allocated by need (by government and housing associations), the more you reduce people's choices. You will get rising social segregation, area stratification along class lines if people can be housed only where they can pay high 'affordable rents' or at the whim of private landlords if they can just about pay their even higher rents. Fully privatize the housing system and polarization by wealth has the scope to grow and then mutate into segregation by race.

People mix more within and between areas in those countries where there is less differentiation in the cost of housing between areas. However, the relationship between prices and segregation is not simple. When prices in London first rose, the effect may have been to reduce racial segregation in that city. People increasingly had to live where they could afford to live. They could not be that choosy over whom their neighbours were. But once the stock of publicly owned housing began to dry up the situation changed. Private landlords in almost any part of London and the south-east were no longer interested in people who could not match market rents, resulting in less space for poorer non-white groups – less space not just in but also near expensive areas of the capital. By autumn 2013 the BBC revealed that letting agencies in London routinely told potential tenants that property was no longer available to rent if the tenants were African-Caribbean.[45] That is how segregation comes to increase.

HOUSING AND RACE

British society appears to be going backwards. Politics and the professions are dominated by an 'Old Boys' Network' ... and even though there is a more diverse population than ever before, Britain is still 'organized and shaped' by race.

– Doreen Lawrence, mother of Stephen Lawrence, 2013[46]

In 2010 the UK government introduced measures that it said were aimed to save £1 billion by spring 2015. The saving would come from reducing the cost of providing housing benefit payments, with poorer Londoners as a whole thought to be the most seriously affected. However, in 2011, analysis carried out on behalf of the Race Equality Foundation revealed that the 'reduction and capping of Local Housing Allowance will impact disproportionately on black and minority ethnic communities as many live in areas targeted by the cuts and will often need larger accommodation due to family size'.[47]

Just as our historic housing stock reflects our class structure and our past political decisions, so current changes in housing always reflect the particular prejudices of many in power through the impact they have on different ethnic and religious minorities. The impact is often obvious in retrospect. Take, for example, the rookeries adapted for the poorest of Irish and rural immigrants to London in the nineteenth century. Housing reform aided those groups in particular; lack of reform left them more destitute. Similarly, the lack of action today to improve the housing situation impacts on some groups more than on others.

As Raquel Rolnik, the UN Special Rapporteur on Housing, put it, recent cuts in housing benefit needed to be scrapped because they were a shocking breach of human rights, harming 'the most vulnerable, the most fragile, the people on the fringes of coping with everyday life'. The government chose to ignore her, with former Housing Minister Grants Shapps asking why we should listen to the views of someone from Brazil.[48] At least he didn't also point out that she was female as some other reason for ignoring her. But it is surprising that he thinks the UK is so well off, given how many people are struggling to survive.

In the UK, tenants who are so poor that they cannot afford to pay their rent have up to 100% of the rent paid to their landlord by the state through housing benefits. It is important to stress that the tenant never sees any of these rent subsidies, which – outside of the most expensive part of the country – are often at full market rates. The subsidies are paid directly to the landlord by the state. Soon in some areas they will not be. It will be paid to the tenants, who will then have to hand it over to landlords. The money is still a sum over which the household itself has no control. This is important because the media and the government often tacitly encourage the misapprehension that tenants are pocketing these rents, while it is the landlords who do the pocketing. It is also important to understand that since 2010, for the first time in decades, for many families even these benefits are now being cut, though not all families are equally affected.

When the coalition government introduced its complex cap on housing benefit in 2013,[49] despite ethnic minorities making up less than a fifth of housing benefit recipients, roughly a third of all households affected by the benefit cap contained at least one person from an ethnic minority background. The superficial reason for this was because of the concentration of people of minority backgrounds in London and because rents are higher in London. The deeper reason was the lack of any concentration of people in such circumstances among coalition members of parliament, or among the majority of their constituents. But, despite their ignorance, the increase in the number of evictions among people who are black and Asian was neither unforeseen nor unforewarned. Once introduced, it was criticized at the highest international level, as the UN Special Rapporteur's intervention made clear.

It was obvious when the housing benefit changes were first mooted that they would hurt some ethnic groups more than others. Even London Mayor Boris Johnson realized the implication of what the UK government was planning and promised that 'Kosovo-style social cleansing' in London ... would not happen 'on my watch.'[50] Two years later a landlord explained what was happening on Boris's watch as a result of evictions: 'The social cost is immeasurable. Lives are being wrecked ... I don't like ethnic cleansing, and that is what is happening.' He described the tenants he was in the process of evicting in London as 'exclusively non-white'.[51] Despite his pledge, and in the face of more and more evidence such as this, Boris Johnson did nothing.[52]

There were many instances of appalling treatment of the poor once the benefit changes had begun. A mother of four young children was told in spring 2013 that she and her children would be evicted from the London borough of Camden and moved to Liverpool because she was too poor to pay the rent and the state would no longer pay on behalf of her and her children. She explained: 'I want to stay where I am for my children's education. What it seems like is the government just wants London for the rich. They want to move people on benefits to poor areas.'[53] The London borough of Camden alone, just in the month of January 2013, was planning to evict a further 760 – mostly non-white – families with children. The 'ethnic cleansing' effect is perhaps unsurprising, given that the majority of families on low incomes in poorer parts of inner London are not white.

All this was foreseen by housing officials, who knew that many poorer people would no longer be able to pay the rent on a home that was big enough for all their children. Earlier, in 2012, an unnamed cabinet member for housing in one inner city borough was reported to have said: 'Let's face it, a lot of people with more than two or three children, and who are dependent on benefits in this borough, are not going to be here for very much longer.'[54] The officials were correct, although often the older children of relocated families are left in London to try to reduce the long-term impact on them of their family's eviction. They stay with friends' families so they can carry on at school in a neighbourhood they know, but they no longer see their parents very often.

The housing benefit cap is not a particularly new scheme when it comes to attempts to move poorer people away from richer areas. A generation ago the Conservative Party tried to achieve the same outcome, but more subtly. In 1986 the Conservative-controlled Westminster Council decided that the number of council house sales should be accelerated so that 'a natural and permanent Conservative majority could be manufactured in Westminster'.[55] Some 10,000 council homes were earmarked to be sold privately when the tenants in them either moved on or died. In other words, those tenants were not to be replaced with people from a similar demographic; Westminster was to be gentrified and the political balance shifted by selling homes that were located mainly in eight marginal wards. Eventually, the policy was found to be illegal, but not until January 1994, long after it had had its desired effects.[56]

A Westminster Council-style clearing of the poor, and especially poor black parents and children, is now under way again, but across most of London, not just in that one then famously corrupt Tory borough; and people are being moved not just to other parts of London, but to elsewhere in the country. The way in which people of different ethnicities are differently affected may be an unintended consequence, rather than something deliberately considered, but that does assume some degree of incompetence among those in power who failed to grasp the impact of their actions.

Another aspect of the housing benefit cap that will hurt some families more than others, especially the very poorest of larger families, is the overall maximum limit that will be applied regardless of need, even after deductions to benefits have been made. This will mean that if a family's costs push them over a prescribed limit – for instance because a child is disabled or they get a carer's allowance for an elderly family member – their rent may cease to be covered and they may have to leave their home. However, all these new regulations are very complex, and so will create confusion as well as distress. For instance, an elderly family member's attendance allowance might not be included because other adults aged over eighteen can be treated as a separate benefit unit even if living in the same household, although that might apply only if they keep their food in separate cupboards. It is almost impossible to work out until you are told what happens to you. None of this new red-tape was the product of a left-wing-created bureaucracy. The current housing benefit system was set up by the Conservatives in the 1980s: they wanted rents to be able to rise freely to encourage private landlords.

Many Londoners are now too young to know that in the 1980s it was Dame Shirley Porter, the daughter of the man who made Tesco Britain's most profitable supermarket, who was convicted of trying to clear away the poor from Westminster. She wanted to win a higher share of votes for her party in marginal seats in local elections. In 2009 she claimed to have written a book to refute all this but said she had decided not to publish it.[57] However, the key difference from today was that she was mostly only forcing families out to other parts of London, not to other parts of the country. Not to areas as far away as Newcastle, Plymouth, or Liverpool. Today if there is any gerrymandering going on, it is to ensure that much of London is so gentrified that the capital as a whole never returns a Labour mayor again. But who will staff the shops, fix the drains and teach the children? London becomes a worse place to live overall as a result.

It is not just to Liverpool, but also to other far-away cities, that evicted Londoners now have to go. Opposition politicians are finally

A British flag hangs from a balcony at Lansdowne flats in Sharrow, Sheffield. When you see a flag hanging like this today it makes you wonder why it is there. It may not be a racist or nationalist statement. It is, after all, not an England flag, but then it can't be about football, can it, and the Olympics were the year before this image was taken, so what is that flag doing there? Maybe it was put up as an ironic gesture or as a sign of solidarity by a family from a minority group, or by an enthusiastic child. Or maybe it was put up for the Olympics and never taken down. But, set between the satellite dishes, you begin to wonder whether you kind of know what it says, and then you worry about what that says about you. Then you might wonder how a family from a poorer part of London might feel, turning up for the first time outside these flats in a city they have never been to before, being housed next door to the flat with the flag. Even if that family from London is white, they might still be worried. If the north becomes a place to stow extradited people from the south, the image of the north will be harmed along with the lives of those who have been forcibly moved.

beginning to take note, very late in the day. Thus, at the end of 2012, it became clear to the main opposition party that 'The country is gripped by the worst housing crisis in a generation and the government's failed policies are making it worse not better ... hard-pressed London councils are faced with having to house those facing homelessness from Cornwall to Newcastle. To lose your home is a tragedy. To face then being uprooted from friends, family and work is absolutely wrong.'[58] However, it took the Labour Party almost another year for them to say that they would repeal the hated 'underoccupancy' penalty when in office, and that was only after the Scottish Nationalist Party councils banned Bedroom Tax evictions in March 2013.

What is taking place today through the coalition's housing policies is now widely recognized as prompting a new kind of social segregation in the UK, one occurring through government action. It is akin to actions most clearly seen in the US, where different parts of many cities are now home to people of very different ethnic origins.[59] There the private market plays a bigger role in moving people apart from each other, in maintaining segregation. That could now happen in Britain, as we begin to mimic ever more closely US laissez-faire social policy. So we need to look across the Atlantic to learn from there.

In 2012 in the US it was found that African-Americans living in the Detroit area were up to 70% more likely to end up being awarded a subprime loan than were white borrowers who had approached a mortgage broker in an almost identical financial situation. This was revealed through an analysis contained in the lawsuit being presented in a class action against the finance company New Century loans. The lawsuit was to recoup damages for the effect of loans that company had given out, high-cost loans that went far more often to African-Americans than to whites between 2004 and 2006.[60] So the key question for the lawyers was whether the company had targeted black families more than white families when both had similar financial characteristics.

So how did the case proceed? It was found that the 'similar financial characteristics' mentioned by the analysis were to be found in far fewer white borrowers in Detroit than black; and that the white group was far less likely to be targeted for subprime lending. Perhaps the mortgage broker thought that black borrowers were an inherently riskier option, although such a line of thinking breaks American anti-discrimination laws and subjects black borrowers to much higher than average interest rates because of this prejudice. In a similar way, it could be argued, white Londoners are far less likely to have been targeted for a cut in their housing benefits. More white Londoners on benefits are older; and pensioners escape the cuts outright.[61] In London fewer white families have children, so will have lower benefits bills to be cut. Many more of London's children are non-white in comparison with London's adults.[62]

When policies affect different ethnic groups differently, they can exacerbate the inequalities between different groups of children. When laws enshrine discrimination between parents, different groups' life chances are systematically altered. For example, in the US, subprime loans were supposed to be given out to people who would not normally qualify for a loan. Often they began with a low rate of interest, but eventually rose well above the average rate and became more and more unaffordable. There have been many repercussions, with families that took out subprime loans subsequently being far more likely to see themselves and their children made homeless.

A lawyer might say that subprime loans to buy (and in some cases build) housing were intentionally designed to become unaffordable if – as frequently happened – the mortgagor could not re-mortgage before the interest rate started to climb skywards. Mortgagors were not able to re-mortgage when the market crashed in 2008. Proportionately many more African-American than white mortgagors had to move into trailer parks or back to older ghettos as a result. This is why that class action lawsuit referred to above became possible: because so many people from one ethnic group were hurt by comparison with others. The same recourse to similar legislation is not impossible in the UK.

In the US, the memory of slavery, of having no right to hold any wealth, lies not far beneath the surface of the collective consciousness. In the UK, when all these housing stories are more fully revealed, when people in future tell of how their families were split up because of the cuts of 2012–15, attitudes to race, to class and servitude, and to lack of access to housing in the past, will be remembered.

Older memories of being housed badly often concern having to work in service, being a servant. A century ago in Britain almost all servants came from the countryside and were white. It was the most common occupation for women in 1911.[63] In London a century later, the new servants are now mostly non-white and come from further away. Often the woman pushing the pram in Knightsbridge can be identified as the nanny, and not as the mother of the child in the pram, by the colour of her skin (although more and more are now from Eastern Europe). Servants were defined by housing. They were employed to serve the household, did not usually have a home of their own and could not have children. Working as a servant still causes concern; people want to have their own home.

In the former capital of the British Empire race, like the history of working in service, is also an especially sensitive issue. This sensitivity was stoked up by Boris Johnson, who used the pejorative term 'piccaninnies' at one point when he was trying to ingratiate himself with those London voters most likely to swing towards him as their future choice. These might have been voters who saw Labour in London as favouring poorer Londoners, Londoners who are often black.[64] Richer people, people who tend to vote Conservative, can pay a lot of money for their homes. Most of the money that the rich invest in their housing is not for the bricks and mortar but for the location, and the value of the location increases the further away it is from the poor, or black people, or young people, and especially from poor young black people, from those Boris might have been thinking of as 'piccaninnies' when he used that word.

How you talk about people and housing, how you build homes, where you build homes, and whether you build homes – all of this depends on the type of society you want and how you believe that society should be arranged. What you think is fair when it comes to financing housing depends on what you more generally believe to be fair. For instance, if rent controls were reintroduced, greater income and wealth equality would result. Landlords could not become so rich, tenants would get to keep more of their incomes, the state would not lose so much housing benefit money to those landlords, and far fewer ethnic minority families in London would face eviction. You might say that rent controls would result in fewer homes being built, but, as it stands, at a time of considerable deregulation of the rental market, very few are being built today anyway.

An enhanced home-building programme will be needed if the demographics of the UK continue along the patterns of recent years – if more people come in from abroad to replace the children who have not been born since fertility slumped below two children per couple in the 1970s.[65] But such high rates of immigration continue for long periods only in countries that continue to be worth coming to, or at least more worth coming to than the nearby alternatives. Even if many more homes need to be built, for each that is built we should at least try to find one more through better use of what we already have. Convert one large old home into two flats for older people and you leave free the second large home those two older people may have occupied separately. There is a finite amount of space to build in, and finite financial and environmental resources to use to build, heat and also maintain our national housing stock.

Whether any future building programme should be left entirely to the private market, modified to make it more green or put largely in the hands of the state – these are political decisions that must be taken by the state. And because the state bought so much of our housing in the past, commissioning private builders to build it, many call for a new council house-building programme today. But back then we did not have the spare capacity within the housing stock that we have now. How many homes will be needed in future and hence how many will be built depends mostly on how well or badly we use what we already have.

A second consideration for our overall housing need is how many more people come into the country, or how many leave it, if the future is worse. There was net emigration after the recessions of the early 1970s, 1980s and 1990s.

A third consideration, and perhaps the most important of all, is how we might better pay for the housing we already have, its upkeep and maintenance, and pay for any new homes that we really do need. Should we really allow a few to profit so much from housing in the future?

5
Buying

We're condemning a whole generation to paying absurd prices for what is a basic human need – and it doesn't have to be this way.

– Faisal Islam, author of *The Default Line*, 2013[1]

For a home to be built and maintained someone has to pay for it. Most people buy housing by the month: by paying rent or a mortgage instalment. Those who have an interest-only mortgage are in effect renting (with a right to buy), but with some security of tenure. Similarly, people who rent council-owned property also have a right to buy outright on the property in which they live, and cannot be evicted on a whim. There used to be a clear dividing line between renting and owning. Now, in one way or another, we are almost all buying our monthly right to housing, but some of us end up richer as a result of how we pay for it, or how they make us pay for it. Most of us, though, end up poorer.

To see where we are heading, it is worth starting with those who are buying their right to be housed from social landlords – from councils or from housing associations. Examine the changing fortunes of this group, and you quickly begin to see how fewer and fewer people will have the option to buy in future and how more will be forced into the private rental sector. Landlords are skimming off more and more money for themselves and the waiting lists and rents grow as they do this.

At the heart of the current problems that the poorest have in buying housing are the implications of the Bedroom Tax. In September 2013 the UN Special Rapporteur on Housing said that this tax compromised tenants' human rights. One group that claims to be very much in favour of human rights – the coalition junior partners, the Liberal Democrats – came to declare that they had not understood what they were doing when they helped their Conservative allies to introduce that Bedroom Tax – or 'charge', 'penalty' or even excess 'subsidy', to use their terms.

Not all Liberal Democrats claimed that they did not understand what the Conservatives were doing. One MP, Sarah Teather, said she could not stand again as a Liberal Democrat MP because her party had become so callous. Hopefully she was beginning to see that a great problem arises in the housing market if a small group gets itself into a position in which it is able to make great profits from the majority of house-buyers. The greatest profits, suffice to say, are made by lending monies – at considerable interest – to others for house-buying. The more housing prices rise, and the longer the terms for paying back the mortgage, the greater is the profit to be made and the more expensive housing becomes. The prices rise not because the cost of building or of maintaining homes has suddenly become greater, but because a few have found better ways to more fully feather the nests of those with money to lend: the 'investors'.

Often landlords borrow monies from separate investors to buy property to rent. They then must not only pass on the interest costs but also make a profit on top of that; and, in a society that has been growing increasingly unequal and acquisitive, when landlords see people doing better than they are and making even more money, the incentive to charge more for rent increases too. A small group becoming very rich at the top of society results in many other not so small groups also trying to take more to just about manage to hang on to the coat-tails of those above them. Rents rise, prices rise, and soon any kind of property is beyond most people's grasp in many places.

In Britain, the government reacts to all of this by trying to create sheltered affordable housing – in effect admitting that most housing is unaffordable. But, even as it does this, looming over the entire housing landscape is the spectre of London: an overheated market in which housing prices appear to be spiralling out of control, one that has the makings of a perfect storm.

HOME OWNERSHIP

The Perfect Storm is a set of interlocking crises, and, while particular problems have particular solutions, there is a need for joined-up thinking, for example around how rethinking state support for housing can help to free up money to maintain social protection for all.

– Oxfam, 2012[2]

Within the next sixteen years a further 1.5 million people in the UK aged thirty and under will be forced to rent privately from landlords because of a lack of planned extra provision in social housing. A rise in those experiencing difficulty in accessing mortgages is also forecast. This is even if more homes are built for budding owner-occupiers, and even if more mortgages become available to help them do this. Such developments might be seen by both potential and existing private landlords as good news. The estimates of how many more would soon be forced to rent were calculated by the Joseph Rowntree Foundation in a report released during the summer of 2012.

The Rowntree report's authors proposed ways to avert what they described as a worsening crisis. What they wanted was a sustained programme of home-building. They also suggested that more 'stable private rented tenancies might be achieved through smarter incentives for landlords'.[3] However, in saying this, they signalled that there has been a sea-change in policy advocacy. We have now entered a new world, one where the aim has become to try to incentivize private landlords to behave well, rather than requiring them to do so. The Rowntree report proposed tax breaks for private landlords to encourage them to provide longer-term tenancies or to house vulnerable, disabled or poorer tenants. This might include those schemes where councils rent from private owners and in turn rent out the properties to families in need on the waiting list.

Significantly, a return to housing that is provided by housing associations and built by local councils, instead of the private sector, is no longer envisaged as even a remote possibility by many housing 'progressives'. People forget that councils were once allowed to use their monies to build housing, monies that were then repaid many times over in rent and reinvested in more housing. They forget that the private sector uses housing to make money for itself, not to make sure that everyone is securely housed in Britain. One generation may be safely housed, but their children will not be safely housed once the private sector has become dominant.

Just as the BBC exists 'to make good programmes popular, and popular programmes good', so the state and local government could make good housing more widely available, collectively, on our behalf. The state does not need to build housing for it to have better control, just as the BBC does not need to make many of its own programmes; but there does need to be an organization at the centre that does not have the profit motive at its heart, as there still is in education, in health and in television. That organization could be local government. If local government were to buy at the bottom end of the market, renovate and clear the new slums, they could also make cheaper housing better. If local government were allowed to tax housing more by introducing higher council tax bands with higher rates, they could also make popular housing more affordable.

The Rowntree report included no radical suggestions, such as giving local authorities the power to increase taxation, monitor housing supply or intervene as necessary. What it did usefully do was to project that the number of people in their twenties holding a mortgage would almost halve by 2020. In not challenging current trends, but simply rolling them forward, the report's authors were right in saying that it might be no bad thing if fewer young adults took on the financial risk and responsibility of maintaining the physical repair of a building; but they added that the young needed more of a choice than simple recourse to the private rented market.

The one and a half million people that the Rowntree report says will not be able to buy in future are a potentially powerful political force. These will be people who would have bought houses in the past, but who have now been deprived of the decision whether to rent or buy. They have also been deprived of choice when it comes to social housing, there isn't a very wide or attractive range on offer.

These people, as well as most of the families that they will form, will mostly have no choice but to rent privately using a short-hold tenancy – even if they are ready to settle down in one place, even if they have children for whom school and nursery places must be found. They can be moved out at any time during that tenure. The rules remain different in council housing, where once you are in, as long as you occupy all the rooms, you can stay, but there is so little now available. If rents keep rising as they are, soon these 1.5 million will have less real choice even within the private sector in future. They will be limited to what they can afford for as long as the landlord allows.

Social (not-for-profit) housing is both in decline and under threat of greater privatization. There are various ways in which social housing can be privatized. The biggest privatization in British history was the introduction of the 'right-to-buy' in the 1980s. Not necessarily a bad policy; later on I'll suggest how it simply lacked a 'right-to-sell' counter-weight for people with mortgages, or outright owners, who wanted to once again become tenants without having to move home. The 'right-to-buy' did give people the right to do up property, to decorate, to extend. But what Britain also needs is the right to give up that right: to revert to a tenancy if desired, with a landlord taking over such responsibilities.

Large-scale so-called 'voluntary' transfer of council stock to housing associations was another form of privatization that began in the 1980s. This becomes especially clear viewed alongside all the changes that have occurred to make housing associations less and less socially motivated and more and more profit-driven. Such changes include the increase in salaries now paid to their top officials. These have been similar to the increases enjoyed by building society executives in the 1920s and 1930s. If mutuality is not carefully guarded and preserved, what were once mutual organizations can gradually become much less mutual.

In the UK, by the recent Rowntree estimates, the number of adults aged under thirty who are able to access housing association tenancies and council housing is set to fall by almost a third by 2020, or to just 780,000 people. The number projected to end up sleeping on others' sofas or to become actually roofless as a result of the recent changes to the housing system is forecast by that same organization to rise to about 81,000 by the same year, a similar number to those being housed in prison. Far more adults will have to continue to live with their parents well into their thirties or forties – perhaps becoming parents themselves while never having left home. So, as we make less and less efficient use of our existing housing, some families will have to squeeze into fewer and fewer rooms in future.

The Rowntree report suggests that what underlies all these problems are 'the links between a long-running shortage of new housing supply and affordability. This shortage of housing supply affects both house prices and private sector rents.'[4] But – and this is of course one of the key questions posed by this book – is it as simple as that? We have not suddenly lost a large part of our housing stock. We have not recently had to demolish huge numbers of substandard buildings – at least not as many as when slums were cleared in the 1960s and before. It is not the balance between supply and demand that has changed most in recent times, but how housing is owned, managed and bought.

Millions of extensions – lofts, basements and so forth – have been added to existing property over the course of the last decade or so. Although house-building is at an historic low, as mentioned earlier the supply of dwellings and especially rooms per person has never been higher. This is because so many more rooms have been added to private sector property. But what has also changed most recently is who is able to own so much of this property: the large-scale private landlords.

Early in 2013 one private insurer, Prudential, announced that it was buying more than 500 homes to become a landlord in the south of England, as 'a calculated bet on years of good returns from "Generation Rent"'.[5] Two days later that same company announced that Prudential's boss had received £7.8 million in pay and benefits the previous year.[6] Had the announcements been made in the opposite order, the press might have been a little more critical of the Pru's new move into private renting. Imagine the headlines if the new (somewhat imprudent) pay level had been announced first, and then the move into profiting from moving into renting. How many hundreds of families would have to pay rent, all their rent, all year, just to pay that one man's huge salary?

What the Prudential's announcements, the coalition government's actions and the Rowntree report represent when all viewed together is the consensus of establishment thinking: a plan to manage growing wealth inequality as made manifest in the housing market, not a plan to reverse it. The Rowntree report tries to find a way of housing people better as incomes diverge, and as a large and growing section of society begins to realize that they will never be able to own their own homes. Furthermore, it is a plan that deals with the shrinking of the state: it aims to encourage private landlords to take over with a kind of renewed Victorian paternalistic control as social housing is privatized; to encourage more of the wealthy to 'invest' in housing by allowing them to write off any losses against their other tax liabilities;[7] to encourage old 'prudential' savings bodies to become landlords. The social rented sector is to be targeted at those 'most in need' – those whom no private landlord would otherwise care to house. Social housing, in other words, is to become a dumping ground for people seen as hopeless.

The political response in England to the Rowntree report was a public spat between the then coalition government Housing Minister, Grant Shapps, and his Labour 'shadow' counterpart, Jack Dromey. They argued about whether the government was actually building a few hundred 'affordable homes' or whether it wasn't even doing that. The row also concerned the demolition and clearing of older housing, some of which could perhaps have been preserved. The minister 'accused the previous Labour government of being second only to the Luftwaffe in destroying homes'.[8] In response Dromey, for Labour, made no pledge to reverse the trend towards more private landlords, but lamented the advent of 'Generation Rent'.

Some Conservatives countered the Labour spokesman by saying they would ensure the supply of housing for the needy by evicting people from social housing: that is people who could afford to rent privately. The Liberal Democrats, in the form of Lord Kirkwood and his like (on whom more below), simply gave a good impression of not

Solar panels can be seen now covering the roof of a home in the Gleadless Estate, Sheffield. Often a pair of homes will have been built originally by the council, but, by looking at how the fencing has been altered around the homes, at how the rendering or the windows have been changed, at the addition of an extension or a conservatory, you might be able to tell if one home is still in the social sector and another is not – although you cannot always tell simply by looking. In future social housing will become more obvious, as it will almost always be the most densely occupied form of housing. This is because the tenants in it are to be fined if they do not fill the home up completely. Meanwhile their neighbours are living in what was previously social housing, which now often looks less and less like social housing, and they can live in their private property at whatever density they wish with impunity.

knowing what was going on, so good in fact that it really is possible that some did not know. Like the child accompanying the school bully when he takes pocket money off a weaker child, and who later claims he did not know what was going on, the Liberal Democrats appeared to be very gullible coalition partners.

The wider point that needs to be made is that all the major parties have been fighting over comparatively minor issues rather than addressing the elephant in the room: the overall crisis. All have been suggesting policies that tinker at the margins. Some tinker to make things a little worse. For instance, in one London borough, the Conservatives announced plans to 'prevent couples who earn more than £40,000 living in a council home'.[9] A couple in London earning that amount from two wages is not well paid, but future council housing is to be reserved for the lowest paid and those out of work, or at least those who are lucky enough not to have been deported from the capital by their only 'offer' of housing being very far away.

While bickering among themselves, the coalition partners in Britain have also been trying to blur the boundary between private and social landlords. They do this partly to further privatize social housing. One way they have encouraged further 'self-privatization' is to announce that they will stop paying the rents of people living in social housing and relying on welfare benefits directly to the landlord from 2013. Polled before the move, some 80% of housing associations thought that direct payment of housing benefit to tenants would have a harmful effect on their association; 84% said rent arrears would rise as a result; 22% said that tenants no longer paying their rent would make it hard to pay back the loans the association itself owed; and 10% suggested that they might even go out of business as a result of this one policy change, or – in modern management speak – they might find it a 'great deal harder to meet their delivery commitments'.[10]

The reason given by the UK government for transferring rent payments to tenants is to try to make them better 'customers' and better able to shop around for their housing. The policy is about trying to encourage families to shop their way out of a council or housing association home into a supposedly cheaper private rented home. The plan is for them to move out of their own volition. But the private sector is not cheaper.

It is not hard to see why the coalition government is acting as it is. At present almost one in five people in Great Britain receives a cash allowance to help with rental costs. This is the highest proportion in all of the OECD countries for which there is data.[11] The proportion is this high because wages are so low and rents are so high. Rents escalated through a combination of removing rent controls and introducing greater housing benefits to compensate for the rises that occurred as a result. This was all done when Mrs Thatcher was Prime Minister. Today her successor government thinks it can reduce the housing benefit bill by getting those who receive these allowances to shop around for cheaper housing. It thinks it can encourage tenants to look harder by reducing the cash allowances of many. But it ignores people's needs to remain where they grew up, where their wider families and support networks are, and where their children's friends live. It also ignores how good landlords are at keeping rents high, if you allow that to be legal.

Research on markets has found that they operate well when there is more of a level playing field between consumers, not when some are very rich and others have very little.[12] What would really make people better 'customers' would be if they had incomes more similar to other people, as is the case in most of the other OECD countries, apart from the US. The US has trailer parks instead of a more equitable income and wealth distribution, and some of the highest homeless rates in the rich world. At any one time, even in winter, more than 600,000 people sleep rough in the US.[13] The threat of mass homelessness in the UK is used to justify transferring so much government money to landlords. The figure below shows just how great the subsidy to private landlords in the UK is, and which other countries are most similar.

When it comes to housing ownership, landlords have been taking a growing share of housing finance (through rents), not just in the private sector but in the state and charitable sectors too. Some supposedly not-for-profit providers have already become more like their private sector counterparts. There are now hundreds of very well-paid chief executives of housing associations, thousands of extremely well-remunerated finance officers and other 'top' officials on very high salaries.

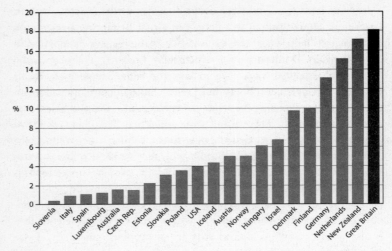

Figure 8. Proportion of residents receiving cash allowances for rental costs, by OECD country, 2009. (Note: data is for proportion of people, other than in Australia, Austria, Netherlands and New Zealand, where what is shown is the proportion of households.)

Once upon a time, each local authority employed a handful of people to be in overall charge of council housing, or, as it was referred to, 'the stock'. Some of these people even lived in that stock. People complained that they also did favours for their mates to get them a council home. Now hardly any housing managers live in the kind of home they manage.

For its annual summer conference in June 2013, held in Manchester, the Chartered Institute of Housing reported that it planned to host some '7,600 senior housing professionals, key providers, partners, suppliers and leaders'.[14] A two-day conference package cost £705, or 'just' £450 for a tenant representative. These were only the 'early-bird' rates. Some of the few tenants that turned up may have had to pay their own way, but the rest of those 'packages' will have been financed from rents, from tenants again. Even if no tenants had attended, if everyone had paid that £705 rate and all 7,600 'senior' folk had turned up, that amounts to a £5,358,000 conference bill. It's a lot of money to have a party in Manchester. My point here is that those who used to provide a service called housing now increasingly see themselves as being in the 'housing industry', needing to 'network', to understand 'strategic and operational' issues – but someone has to pay for them to do all this.[15]

By squeezing people into their properties more efficiently, housing associations aspire to becoming richer 'not-for-profit' businesses. People with an extra room in their property will be given the 'choice' of leaving their home or of somehow finding the spare money to hand over to the association, maybe by working 'on the side', or begging from relatives. Some will just find it all too much. In autumn 2012 Stuart Hodkinson, a housing researcher and lecturer based in the University of Leeds, explained that already

> quotas are being used to limit certain types of tenants from accessing new social housing . . . Since coming to power in May 2010, the coalition has gone to war on social housing and social tenants, especially in England and Wales . . . When I spoke recently to a tenant in Leeds already suffering from depression and unable to work and now faced with this appalling choice [of having to leave her home], she broke down in tears and said she was thinking about killing herself . . .[16]

What makes the current situation so infuriating is that it has been created by rising greed and selfishness, not by some national emergency or natural disaster. It is not that we have had more children and that they no longer fit into the homes we have, that the building and extending of housing has not kept pace with population growth. We have not just lost housing in a war or due to a huge earthquake. It is that a few people have chosen to make what was not necessarily a great housing system worse, and the effects are felt far and wide.

One reader commenting on Stuart Hodkinson's research findings concurred: 'People have to wait years on a housing list, and are made to feel like scum if they need to apply for housing benefit to pay a private landlord, if they can even have housing benefit in the first place. This government makes people suicidal just for not being able to afford to live.' That is what a crisis turning into a disaster feels like. Ultimately the reason for having social landlords is to prevent people from thinking of killing themselves.

This photograph, of the entrance to a tower block in the Sharrow area of Sheffield, could have been taken several decades ago and would have looked the same, but for the new keypad on the door. Those lucky enough to be allowed social housing nowadays, and so avoid the bottom end of the private sector, can now stay in it only as long as they have enough children to fill every room, or have well-enough-paid work or some extra source of income on the side. Social housing has come to be seen more as a transit camp for families with children most in need, and less as a permanent base. If a place is home, there is no need for a sign saying 'No ball games'. People either know not to play, or they get glass fitted that breaks less easily. Children need exercise and play, around a place that is home, but not around somewhere they are just passing through.

THE BEDROOM TAX

*A third of those hit by the 'spare room' tax are disabled, with
no exemption for divorced parents or foster parents with vis-
iting children. Families in Hartlepool and Liverpool who have
suffered the death of a child now face cuts for their empty
bedrooms. Nothing about housing policy makes sense. The
government is right that spending £23 billion a year on housing benefit is grossly wasteful, but why punish tenants when
most of it goes straight to landlords? They claimed these cuts
would make rents fall, but instead they rise.*

– Polly Toynbee, 2013[17]

The Bedroom Tax is a vile tax. Worse than the Poll Tax, it targets only
those with least, those who already need to rely on the state to help
pay their rent, but who happen to be deemed to have a spare room.
Maybe a room a child does their homework in, and then sleeps in,
when their brother or sister sleeps next door; or maybe a room for an
adult who coughs and wheezes all night; or maybe separate bedrooms
for the parents if they are just staying together for the sake of the
children. Remember that whenever possible all the children are
already expected to have doubled up. And also remember that in
many places there are far more three-bed than two-bed or one-bed
social housing units. If they ask to move, there is almost always no
locally available social housing appropriate to their circumstances.
The tax is wrong. But for the majority of people who hear of the Bedroom Tax, and who are not affected by it, the idea that people on
benefits should not be able to have a 'spare room' can at first sound
seductively sensible.

The way we run housing already contributes to social segregation
in Britain. In many ways the Bedroom Tax is set to exacerbate that
segregation by moving those who can't afford to pay it away from
areas where the homes have an extra room in them, towards two-bed
and one-bed flats. Alternatively it could be argued that in theory

national rates of ethnic segregation will be reduced by forcing poorer minority residents out of the capital. But in practice ethnic and religious segregation is already quickly falling in general in Britain, and has been since at least 1991.[18] Outside London the very large majority of people affected by the new Bedroom Tax will be white. The vast majority of households affected by the tax live a long way from London, where there are more spare rooms and often there is more spare housing.

You might have thought that the government in Britain, faced with an increasingly inefficient distribution of housing use, would try to introduce policies that would spread bedrooms out a little more evenly, and help people to stay in places where there are more rooms in order to reduce industrial decline. In the event, it did the opposite, while purporting to be taxing vacant bedrooms. With the introduction of the notorious Bedroom Tax in April 2013, the government has targeted the group of households that is already using housing most efficiently: people living in social rented housing who are not pensioners, those tenants who are already most crowded into smaller homes. The government is demanding that this group crowd even more tightly into their modest homes.

The Bedroom Tax (in effect, a reduction in housing benefit) applies to all social housing tenants in Great Britain who receive housing benefit and are deemed to be of working age. It can also be applied to new tenants who are pensioners.[19] The number of bedrooms a family is allowed is one for each adult couple and one for any other person over sixteen years; however, any two children below sixteen must share a bedroom, except when this would involve two children of the opposite sex over the age of ten having to share. So, if you are a father of a fifteen-year-old boy and a ten-year-old boy, you are allowed to have only a two-bedroom home or flat; for any extra bedroom you will have your benefit reduced. In the case of a separated or divorced couple, if one child also has a bedroom at their mother's home, and their mother is the main carer, any bedroom used at their father's home becomes subject to Bedroom Tax.

The Bedroom Tax restrictions were initially as tight as it is possible to imagine, other than that they excluded pensioners. At first, foster children were not acknowledged as part of the household for benefit

The Gleadless Valley is home to several housing estates in the south of Sheffield. This image shows a view of the main road up the valley. The Bedroom Tax will affect mainly people living in housing such as this, maisonettes where there may no longer be a child or a pair of children occupying every bedroom. As people's families age, as their children leave home – or if a child gets into university for example – they will become liable for the tax. Many families in these flats will now, in effect, be fined if any of these events occur and forced to try to find cheaper accommodation when they cannot pay the fine. If they could afford to pay the fine, they would not be eligible for benefits in the first place. There is almost no cheaper accommodation in Sheffield, and so they will have to eat less, or use the bus less frequently, or get into more debt more – just to get by.

purposes, so foster parents would be taxed for any rooms in which they might sleep. Later, the regulations were relaxed a little, but right up to the last minute before the tax (or 'charge') became law the rules kept on being changed. For instance, in March 2013, a month before the implementation of the tax, government ministers said that up to 5,000 foster carers would be exempt from the benefits deduction. Yet representatives of housing charities countered that the exemption would apply only to a single additional room, and would not apply to carers in receipt of housing benefit who looked after more than one foster child.[20]

The new Bedroom Tax also makes no allowance for disabled people, including people living in adapted or specially designed properties, unless local authorities choose to make such allowances available. If a disabled child needs his or her own bedroom,[21] well, bad luck: the child's family is still liable for the tax, though they can apply to a local discretionary fund in the hope of a handout to cover it. Most callously if a child dies and was the only occupant of a bedroom, the family is taxed until they vacate the home (or have another child to replace their dead one). Even if the dead child was sharing, if another sibling had a bedroom of their own, then, depending on that sibling's age, their brother or sister's death could mean that child now has to share, the third room of the home becomes vacant, and the family are liable for the tax. Dickens would have been able to describe this much better than I have – not just because he could write so well, but because he would have been familiar with the sentiment.

The Bedroom Tax is 14% of total rent (not just of the eligible housing benefit received) for one extra bedroom, or 25% if a family is deemed to have two spare rooms. Assuming a rent of £100 a week, the household, therefore, gets £14 a week less in benefits than it is deemed to need because of the definition of one room. They must make up the shortfall, probably out of benefits that they receive to feed themselves and their children. Housing association tenants are, on average, losing £16 a week for having a 'spare' room. Recent amendments mean that when Universal Credit comes in this will include any room used intermittently by a child who attends university for more than six months a year. As I write, Universal Credit is currently being piloted in a few areas and is set to be spread across all of the country by 2014, being fully implemented by 2017. It will affect millions of families and how they are housed.

The Bedroom Tax is a taste of what is to come from Universal Credit. The tax is already affecting an estimated 660,000 working-age social tenants, or 31% of existing working-age housing benefit claimants across the entire social housing sector. The majority of these people have only one extra bedroom, which, in many cases – as per the examples above – it is not really 'spare'.[22] If any comparison is made with living conditions for the rest of the population, it becomes even more obvious that these rooms would not normally be considered spare. People now often have more need of more room than they used to. Children are made to do more homework than when I was a child. People often now have to work part of the time from home.

With social housing being turned into dormitory housing, the line between the social rented sector and the private market is becoming starker, despite all the attempts to blur it. You might have the right to buy, but you no longer have the right to stay put. A not that highly paid university lecturer living in social housing in London wrote to me recently about this issue, saying that even he could not understand what was going on. He said 'even he' because he did research in this area, was supposed to be able to work out the details, but couldn't, despite the possibility of being adversely affected by it:

> I live in a flat block that is managed by Metropolitan Housing so get their newsletter. The recent one tried to explain whether, basically, you were about to lose your home due to the number of children, their ages, sexes, rooms, etc. In the end they just said, it's complicated, there's no way you could figure it out, so call us if you want. Looking at the criteria really did induce in me one of those 'out of place and time' feelings, like a wormhole somewhere in Whitehall had allowed the Chadwick Report to slip on to someone's BlackBerry.[23]

When he talks of a wormhole, this university lecturer is referring to Edwin Chadwick, a nineteenth-century lawyer whose report helped to usher in the notorious Poor Law Amendment Act of 1834. Under this Act, the aggregate of Poor Laws established over the centuries was abolished in an effort to cut costs; outside relief was ended; and the poor could receive help only through a centralized system of workhouse unions, made deliberately harsh in order to discourage them from seeking aid. One hundred and eighty years later in London, the parallels seem fairly obvious. A minority would like to turn the clock back to the immorality of early Victorian England, where the weakest were the most penalized.

In October 2012, six months before the Bedroom Tax's announcement, it was revealed that almost two thirds of all the tenants who would be affected by the tax had a disability; many of them were disabled children. In the past, it was precisely these households that had been deliberately allocated extra space. On hearing the announcement of this fact in the House of Lords, one Liberal Democrat member of the government that had introduced these draconian measures, Lord Archy Kirkwood, claimed: 'I was taken aback by the extent to which the client group [disabled people] will be affected by this policy change. I wish that I had known it during the passage of the bill.'[24]

Upon closer examination, Lord Kirkwood's comment appears to have been nothing more than an attempt to wash his hands of the responsibility. In 2011 Derek Long, head of the National Housing Federation's Northern Regions, had explained quite clearly that 'this policy will hit disabled people, foster carers and care sharers. The social sector is already four times more efficient than the market at matching people to homes.'[25] One respondent to Long's news, writing under a pseudonym,[26] explained that even earlier, in 2010, 'when analysts understood the consequences of welfare reforms and raised these issues with Grant Shapps [the Housing Minister], he confirmed that none of these reforms would affect existing tenants: this has proved to be a lie.'

It is very possible that a Conservative minister who might have been deceiving tenants was also perhaps not telling the whole truth to his coalition partners in government, but a politician with Lord Kirkwood's experience ought to have been able to separate fact from fiction. His and others' failure to do that will have considerable repercussions. Housing associations are concerned that, with the introduction of the Bedroom Tax, rent arrears will skyrocket as households fall behind, having no way to find the extra rent. The only other option, moving out, will prove financially prohibitive: moving home always comes at a cost. Today there are far fewer cheaper homes to move to than ever before.

There is another potential side-effect of the Bedroom Tax, one presumably unforeseen by policymakers, but spotted by affected tenants. Lorna Holden, who lived in Hartlepool, said of the tax: 'My personal opinion is that if you start adding Bedroom Taxes on and saying, "You're underoccupying", people are just going to occupy that space by having more kids. And then they get more benefit from the government because they've got more kids. So what they're really doing is punishing people who are trying to work, and bring up a family, and who need that extra bit of support to make ends meet. I just don't see how it's going to work.'[27]

Although housing charities said that from April 2013 around 670,000 so-called underoccupying tenants would have to pay between £11 and £20 a week extra for their apparent overuse of social housing, these figures were known far earlier than that. In June 2012 the BBC had tried to explain why the Bedroom Tax was doomed to failure, revealing National Housing Federation estimates that only 68,000 one-bedroom tenancies become available each year, while almost three times as many tenants would be officially overoccupying two-bedroom properties according to the April 2013 regulations. The BBC then reported the government Welfare Minister, Lord Freud, saying that the extra bedrooms were a 'luxury'.[28] This was despite the almost total non-existence of smaller properties for these tenants. The few that do exist have already been allocated to smaller newly homeless households. And there's a long waiting list to boot. It's time to take stock.

There are spare bedrooms in England, but they are almost all in privately owned homes that are not being rented. Perhaps if MPs were deprived of their taxpayer-subsidized London property whenever that property has a spare bedroom (perhaps the one that they use as a study), they might understand the issues better. Taking away 14% of the subsidy wouldn't work: MPs' salaries are such that they would hardly notice the difference. You would have to make the tax proportional to their disposable incomes, or include all the spare bedrooms in all their properties. Even then they would probably just feel angry, not very frightened, like the tenants affected by the Bedroom Tax. Similarly, if Lord Freud (whose personal wealth makes the average MP look like a pauper[29]) believes that having a single spare bedroom is a luxury, presumably he would be willing to live without any spare ones in any homes he might own? Or maybe just keep two or three spare ones and give up the rest? To someone who needs a bed? It would be worthwhile asking him: he has eight bedrooms in his London home. Lord Freud is remembered for recommending that more groups on benefits, such as some single mums, should be required to seek paid employment.

It is true that 'the days when having a baby got you a council property straight away are long gone'[30] (I quote this because it was never universally true). But, sadly, the days when you might have to have a baby if you want to stay in your home may well now be arriving in England. Urban legend has it that in Milton Keynes in the 1970s you could get a council house to move into on the day of your marriage, no child required. We so quickly forget those far more equitable times, as some of us return to older, outdated moralities.

The issue of people having babies to be able to secure welfare payments has a pedigree at least 180 years old. The 1832 Royal Commission that examined the reform of the Poor Laws, prior to the introduction of the Poor Law Amendment Act, was 'haunted [by] the image of women producing multiple bastards for profit'.[31] When parliament brought in the 1834 Act and reduced welfare, there was no reduction in what was then called bastardy, which had been an aim of the legislation, but there was a great rise in poverty. As a result the British eventually got social landlords – but it was a long, torturous and tortuous process from losing rights in 1834 to gaining them slowly over the course of the century that followed. Then, with devolution in Scotland and Wales in 1999, people in these countries gained even more control over their own housing. It seems that now it is mostly the English who are getting rid of much that remains of the original ethos of their social housing system and trying to turn it, at the extremes, into temporary, dormitory, skid-row housing. But it is only some of the English, and so far they have not been completely successful.

SKIMMING PROFITS

The number of families renting their home has doubled over the past ten years, as more and more people are priced out of home ownership.

— Shelter, 2013[32]

What tenants complain about most is not the bad treatment meted out by landlords, but the sense that they are slowly being bled dry of any potential small amount of wealth, and savings for their old age.[33] Most tenants cannot save as they pay so much rent. And because they cannot save, they cannot build up a deposit, which in turn means they cannot take out a mortgage. In the past, when prices were lower, mortgages were cheaper. Back then building societies dominated. These were organizations that existed to help tenants become buyers, and which did so without taking a profit; but most became banks in the 1980s and 1990s.

Barclays Bank, through its subsidiary the Woolwich – once a building society – tried to drum up mortgage business in summer 2012 by releasing figures suggesting that owning your home, rather than renting it, would save you £194,000 over fifty years. It added, 'this doesn't even include the value of the home you'll own at the end of it. While the total cost of mortgage repayments, maintenance and other costs of owning the average home would come to £429,000 over fifty years, renting a similar home over the same period would cost £623,000.'[34] If tenants in the private rented market feel bled dry, they have cause.

What the bank did not point out is who makes the most money out of lending the funds needed to raise a mortgage. The bank also omitted to highlight the flexibility of renting, and how much you lose if you fail to pay the mortgage of a home you are trying to buy. It will have been in the small print of their press release, for legal reasons, but it was not a prominent part of the story.

When your bank suddenly raises its interest rate, your best opt-out may be to try to sell your home. You could try to shop around for a better mortgage, but there are usually penalty fees to pay and nothing much better on offer. If your landlord raises the rent, you can quit the place far more easily and you don't need to find a buyer, but you may have trouble locating a new home. In the UK, tenants really don't have that many advantages – yes, there may be flexibility, but there's very little protection in an assured shorthold tenancy – not to mention the fact that rents are now going through the roof, while mortgage interest rates are, currently, flat-lining.

If being a private tenant were not so insecure, people might look a little more sceptically at the idea of becoming a mortgage-holder. Already many have lost what faith they once had in housing to secure them a little wealth, a little security, in later life. According to the world's most powerful central bank, the US Federal Reserve, the housing market crash had, by 2010, wiped out two whole decades of supposed wealth accumulation amassed by American families.

Adjusting for inflation, by 2007 the median family in the US had amassed a net wealth of $126,400, according to the US Federal Reserve. But by 2010 that had almost halved to $77,300 for the American family that was positioned centre-stage when every family was put in order according to wealth. In short, the median average American had become much less wealthy in the course of a very brief period of time. The *New York Times* reported that the housing market crash directly accounted for three quarters of that loss of apparently amassed wealth.[35]

It is not that every adult wants to be a homeowner. In fact privately renting tenants are often among the happier of tenure groups surveyed – but they also tend to be young and optimistic; after all there are almost two million university students in Britain and most of them rent privately. Renting also makes it easier to be mobile for employment opportunities, but it has its drawbacks when and where inequality is high.[36] The fact is that in very unequal countries such as the UK or US there are many reasons why people want to be in the top tenth of society as defined by income and wealth, and the top tenth tend to own property. In more equitable affluent countries the advantages of being rich are less obvious and the disadvantages of having less are greatly reduced.

It is far easier to rent and live well in a more equitable affluent nation. The same *New York Times* report found that, even despite the crash, 'Ranking American families by income, the top 10% of households still earned an average of $349,000 in 2010. The average net worth of the same families was $2.9 million.' Although it is only an average within the richest tenth, it is hardly surprising they would wish to try to protect their position, having got so far ahead of the rest. However, when average wages and wealth fall, the rest may come to realize that the rich can only become richer at the expense of the other 90% of US society. The average median American family now earn nearly an eighth of what the best-off tenth earn a year; median US family income fell to $45,800 in 2010 from $49,600 in 2007. In sterling $45,800 was then around £28,600 a year. That is Middle America. Half the population are poorer than that, many very much poorer.

Part of the reason the richest tenth became so extraordinarily wealthy in the US is because others there are so poor. By definition all 'successful' rich landlords are in the top 10%. They rely for their income on other people having to pay them rents, high rents, more money than those landlords need to live a good life. Others work in the finance industry giving out loans, as lawyers for banks, or as realtors (estate agents) who can do very well when the market is buoyant.

In Britain more and more estate agents were hired during 2012; they accounted for one in four of all new jobs created that year.[37] By 2013 one in every three new jobs in the UK was new (often temporary) employment as an estate agent.[38] Increasingly estate agents also work for landlords, managing properties on their behalf. Many landlords are rich enough not to need to interact with their tenants themselves. In both the UK and the US, if this trend carries on, we will reach a point where we see 'the whole upper tenth of a nation living with the insouciance of grand dukes and the casualness of chorus girls'. This was how F. Scott Fitzgerald, author of *The Great Gatsby*, succinctly described the inequities of 1920s America in *Tales of the Jazz Age*.[39] This is what the US is returning to, according to the statistics on inequalities in income and wealth just quoted above, and it is also what the UK is heading towards if it does not change course.

Almost a century ago Fitzgerald wrote of the casualness of the Roaring Twenties. Today average incomes are again falling in the US, just as they did back then. But national income then, Gross Domestic Product (GDP), was on average almost always rising. It is rising again now in both the UK and US. A few people are again getting very wealthy, so the reported mean take-home income of people in the States rises today as the median income falls. Mean average income of everyone can rise when just one rich person's income rises; but the median income rises only if most incomes rise. Something very similar is also happening in Britain: mean incomes are being recorded as rising even as the median national income falls and inequalities grow.[40]

This rise in income and wealth inequality is so important when it comes to housing that how it affects behaviour needs to be thought about carefully. Think again of that boy in the hypothetical school class mentioned right at the start of this book, but now let's make him British, so the boy is receiving £20 a day pocket money while all his classmates in the year, all ninety-nine of them in those three classes, receive, on average, 80 pence each a day. The mean average pocket money of that year group is then almost £1 a day. If all the rest of the year group see their pocket money drop, on average by 5 pence, but that one boy receives an extra £5 a day, mean average pocket money is said to have risen, even though almost everyone is worse off.

In the UK, as more and more people rented between 2001 and 2011, and as median incomes began to fall in real terms, the incomes of those at the top of society rose. A part of that rise was due to increasing rental incomes. Furthermore, the UK government also actively helped some of the best-off landlords in Britain to become wealthier. Think again about that boy in the class. Where did his extra pocket money come from? Well, suppose that his parents have bought some 'buy-to-let' flats and are renting them out to the parents of the other children in his school. Those parents will be a little worse off when the rent rises, and unable to give as much pocket money to their children, but his parents will have gained more. People don't rent out property because they are magnanimous. But government in the UK wants to encourage more individuals and corporations to become landlords, as well as the same old landlords to rent out more property.

On 1 February 2013 the UK coalition government set out a plan in which up to £10 billion would be handed out to private landlords. They gave an example, and, again, think of that hypothetical rich boy's parents as 'investors' to visualize how this will play out: 'An investor wants to build a block of 100 flats, which they will then offer for private rent [and] the value of the built flats will be £20 million. They can apply to the guarantee scheme for up to £16 million, or 80% of the end value.'[41] Now note, this is a guarantee, not a gift, but it is a guarantee to prevent the landlord from incurring any real risk to his investment. The government is, in effect, guaranteeing that, in the event that the flats can't be let, they can be sold, and sold at a loss that we will all be covering because it is government money. Government appears to believe that the money will always be repaid upon future sale – that is, that there will be no future price drops on the build investment. Nor does it believe that there will be future rent reductions. This is worryingly Gatsby-esque. If that hypothetical boy's parents were to build another 100 flats to rent out to other children's parents, they might get even richer; but if the scheme were to fail, all the other children's parents would have to make up their loss through their taxes; and their children might have to share some of the costs too in future tax payments, as national debt would rise, raising interest payments far into the future. All this could result from the government's encouragement of the best-off boy's parents' efforts to become even richer.

The government's underwriting of the investments of private landlords enables them to make significant profits in the UK's very lightly regulated rental market. From the point of view of tenants, the regulations in the UK market are weighted in favour of landlords. The government is guaranteeing the risks on the landlords' investments; the courts will help those landlords evict their tenants with just sixty days' notice. If everything goes pear-shaped and the landlord's scheme goes bust, taxpayers' money would cover 80% of any losses. The chances of government having pitched its policy 'just right' in order to give the private market exactly the right 'nudge' it needs are very low. By the end of 2013, Mark Carney, the new Governor of the Bank of England, was signalling that he thought there were problems with these schemes, but this was too late for all those that had already been approved in that year.

Private renting comes with many other problems. This is because individual landlords are, unsurprisingly, looking after their own interests. Clusters of privately rented property – for instances in university towns – can make an area unattractive to families who can afford to make genuine choices. Regulations have been introduced for housing in multiple occupation to try to control the clustering of masses of bedsits and very densely occupied homes with multiple tenants, but they are often ignored and local government enforcement officers are being sacked as cuts bite. The regulations also do not prevent the gardens of student houses becoming a bit of a tip. It soon becomes clear when and where the students and 'young professionals' are taking over. Meanwhile, despite incomes falling, rents are rising.

In late 2012 the National Housing Federation stated that 'The cost of privately renting a home has risen by 37% in the past five years, and is set to soar a further 35% over the next six years.'[42] In Britain, by 2010 rents were already the highest in Europe.[43] Very recently they have risen even faster. A large property services firm, LSL, regularly releases a 'buy-to-let' index of rental values. By October 2012 it showed that the average monthly rent across England and Wales had hit an all-time high of £744, which was the seventh month in a row of rent increases. It also revealed that average rents in London had risen in the year by 7% to now stand at £1,102 a month, rising by much more than twice the rate of inflation.[44] They rose again in the year to October 2013, by which time 'On a monthly basis, tenant finances feel impact, with total late rent up by £31 million.'[45] As rents carried on being raised, more and more tenants found it harder to keep up their payments.

At this point it might again be worth remembering that such price bubbles never last forever, but they can get very large before they burst. As I write (during late 2013) more and more outlying areas are being sucked into the orbit of the London bubble. If new jobs and 'wealth creation' are becoming more concentrated into this particular part of the country, there can appear to be some rationale for house prices and rents also rising correspondingly. Part of what may have been stoking up the bubble in London is austerity and lack of opportunity elsewhere in Europe, driving increasing numbers of young people to try their luck in Europe's only megacity.[46]

Before every fall in property values, before every fall in rents, comes a rapid rise. In the US, in the years following the end of war in 1918, it became evident that there was too little space for the returning troops and the children of the baby boom that followed their return. Average rents across the whole of the US went up by 10% in 1918–19, then by 20% in 1920 alone, then by a further 10% in 1921, increasing then each year by a further 8% in 1922, in 1923 and in 1924; so that in the period directly before the 1929 crash they had reached 168% of the pre-war, affordable, level.[47] The geographer David Harvey recently assigned to housing a very large part of the blame for the economic crashes both in 1929 and in 2008, and believes the current housing system is largely to blame for what underlies so much of our inequitable allocation of property.[48]

In England and Wales the share of households renting privately rose to 18% of all households by 2011, a sharp climb from 12% ten years before. Most of the rise was due to fewer people being able to get a mortgage and more small private apartments being built. Home ownership and buying (combined) fell from 69% to 64% of all households over that same decade. This left the reported national proportions of social rented households falling slightly from 19% to 18% of all households.[49]

By the financial year 2011/12 the average tenant of a social housing property in Britain had a median income of just £8,996 a year to live off. That money, £24.63 a day, might not be just for one person's needs: it could be an elderly couple, or a parent (or two) and children. In real terms that pittance is about 10% less than the same figure for 2005/6. Today fewer people have well-paid full-time work than they did then; it has been part-time work that has been increasing the most, as benefits are being cut, so even if unemployment falls, many people are not at all well off.[50] Unsurprisingly, given their very low incomes, some two thirds of all social housing tenants have no savings.[51]

Of those few social housing tenants who do have savings, half have less than £1,000. The cuts to local 'social' funds to help people buy cookers and the other essential items they need to live, and the cuts to the monies that councils once used to house homeless older teenagers, not to mention the introduction of the Bedroom Tax, are all biting hard. These changes are currently adding to the impoverishment of between a quarter and a third of all social housing tenants of working age in the UK – another slice of the knife of cuts on top of already falling standards of living.[52] However, when Raquel Rolnik, the UN Special Rapporteur on Housing, highlighted facts like this, she was accused of simply being unreliable, someone who, the *Daily Mail* claimed (by talking to her sister), had participated in witchcraft,

Velocity Tower, private apartments, located next to the inner ring road in Sheffield. Apartments such as these can be hard to let in the current climate: Sheffield has a glut of one- and two-bedroom private apartments built within its inner ring road, all targeted at affluent young professionals and the best-off students, who have, as yet, not arrived in the numbers needed to fill all the rooms. Rents remain too high for those older people who are being decanted out of social renting because they have too many rooms in their homes. And so more and more of the bedrooms within the city remain or become unoccupied, while the waiting list for housing continues to grow in Sheffield. The city already has the longest waiting list of any local authority in England.

someone who was, in effect, unhinged.[53] Campaigners against what is occurring are routinely either discredited or ignored, but rarely are they vilified to this extent. Fortunately there are many campaigners.

In June 2012 Oxfam declared that the UK was in crisis.[54] A significant part of the reason it gave for making such a declaration was the ongoing housing crisis. The charity cited evidence that the number of housing benefit claimants in work had more than doubled between November 2008 and February 2012. It pointed out that, even before the recession hit, there had been an acute housing shortage. Its researchers explained that by 2008 there were already 1.77 million households in England languishing on social housing waiting lists and that there were a further 489,400 households living in what were officially recognized as overcrowded homes. They then explained that government targets for the building of new homes had repeatedly been missed, and that housing construction had slowed to a crawl since the recession. They showed how the cost of housing had continued to rise; that this had occurred in spite of the recession; and that the rises in rents and prices could be seen in both the private and social rented sectors. They demonstrated that average rents were, by June 2012, at record highs (they have risen again quickly in the year and a half since) and that homes were already unaffordable in more than half of English local authorities by 2012 (again, before prices had risen even higher by winter 2013). They provided evidence that the numbers of newly homeless households had increased by 18% in England between 2010 and 2011.

What response did they receive from government? Nothing.

Oxfam drew the graphic below to illustrate the direction of recent change. Since that graphic was drawn, new evidence has emerged suggesting that, just below the level of directors and chief executives, people in the rest of the top fifth of income earners in Britain have received a cut in their disposable income as well as most people at the bottom of the heap, and that thus what is known as the UK's quintile income inequality ratio has finally begun to fall, as most people at the bottom started off with less to lose.[55] But the richest at the very top, the best-off tenth of the top tenth, the 1%, are still seeing their riches grow. A year after Oxfam's report was released, another major charity, the National Children's Bureau, produced yet another report showing that overcrowding and poverty among children was on the

Figure 9. Income changes in the UK, 2011–12, according to occupation of employees, in pounds sterling and percentages.

rise again, and that Britain faced a growing social apartheid between rich and poor when it came to where and how children were to be housed in future.[56] The National Children's Bureau was also ignored.

AFFORDABLE HOUSING

> Housing is central to health, well-being, prosperity and aspirations. There are significant economic, social and political returns to expanding and improving housing stock. Conversely, the housing market can play a destabilizing role in the wider economy and disrupt public policy intentions. Recognition of this, and a growing sense of crisis, has seen housing return as a key issue again . . .
>
> – Ben Marshall, Research Director of Ipsos MORI, 2012[57]

As the majority of people become poorer in real terms, ever growing numbers are finding housing less and less affordable, even in areas where rents are not rising and where prices are static or even falling. In this context, 'affordable housing' is a strange term. But it is a key plank of current government policy, one that originated in the days of New Labour.

In February 2013 a three-bed flat in Islington, north London, was put on the market at £705,000. It was stated that, if you had a household income of less than £77,200, and were a first-time buyer who lived outside the borough, you might be eligible to purchase a quarter of this property and pay a reduced rent on the rest of 'only' £2,425 a month. Why does this arrangement benefit only people outside the borough, rather than those in it?

The reason is that the provision of social housing in Britain is now being mixed up with property speculation. The rules that apply to these 'affordable offers' are that if you are able to pay £3,472 a month, you could end up owning 75% of the apartment after twenty-five years. The offer applies only to people living outside the borough, because those living within it have already managed to find a way to live there. Should those potential tenants/owners moving in from outside later find themselves able to pay an additional £1,047 a month, they could take part fully in the great property casino.[58] As it is, they can now have a small stake in it. But what really underlies the maximum income limit of £77,200? The reason why there is a maximum income limit is because this property was being let by a housing association, which receives government subsidies if it engages with such schemes.

As I was downloading these figures from the website of this particular housing association, I came across the following news item, which at first glance sounds like New York, not the UK: '1 February 2013. News: East Village bidding opens for social rent homes ...'[59] Even getting into social housing can now involve entering an auction. Allocation is no longer based on the original principles of social housing: prioritizing those in greatest need or those who had waited the longest. Privatization has been stretched so far that 'bidding' is required even in social housing. This is a deliberate blurring of the boundaries between the state and the private sector.

There are ways in which the apartheid-like distinction between buying and renting can and should be reduced. People should be able to move far more easily between the two tenures, but not in order to secure a profit. They should buy when it suits them to become their own landlord and to undertake the upkeep of the building. The private rented sector does not have to be synonymous with the profit-making sector, in the way that schooling in private schools is mostly not synonymous with profit-making (most are a form of charity). However, to get to that point will take quite a few changes, many of which are suggested later on in this book. First we need to agree why we need change.

In the private sector, allocation currently has nothing whatsoever to do with need. If you want it, and can afford it, you can have it. That is similar to most private schooling, even when, ostensibly, there are entrance exams (many are not as hard as they make out). The privatization principle is that a purchase can occur regardless of the need you might have for that property.

A few regulatory measures might be in place to try to deter people from being too greedy – capital gains taxation on second, third and fourth properties and so on – but these can often be circumvented by the knowledgeable.[60] Much more than that is needed, including a culture change – but a culture change is possible. The affluent do not send their children to private schools owned by shareholders. Why in the future do we think our children and grandchildren will be willing to purchase property from those who have bought it for so much less? People learn to avoid being ripped off after first having been stung.

Another way is possible. Affordable private renting is possible, but for it to be affordable rent controls are needed. Statistics released during 2012 have shown that well over a quarter of the population of countries as large as Germany, as income equitable as Denmark, the Netherlands and Sweden, and as affluent as Luxembourg and Austria live in privately rented dwellings with no subsidy from the state. Renting can be very pleasurable; in Switzerland almost half (49.9%) of all households rent privately. The top 1% of Swiss earners (including many bankers) take half as much as in the UK, so those with less have proportionately more and can therefore pay market price rent.[61] Housing systems are far from perfect in these countries, and the poor are often still living in substandard housing, but the gaps in living standards between different groups in Britain are far wider than in places like Switzerland, Germany or Denmark.

Take a look at a wider view of the Gleadless Valley in Sheffield. So much that is new and innovative in housing finance is happening in London that it is easy to forget that the reason why housing is so expensive in the capital is that over recent decades more and more people have been encouraged to move to the south. There is now less housing in Sheffield than there used to be. Much housing was demolished a decade ago to prop up the private market. I used to take my eldest son, when he was a toddler, to watch tower blocks in Sheffield being blown up in the early noughties, often quite near this spot. I stopped doing it when he started to say 'tower goes boom' when we passed those that were left. Schemes to build affordable housing in London are partly schemes to squeeze more and more people into that city, while there are cities with huge amounts of green space and buildings requiring renovation not more than a couple of hundred miles away.

It is where income inequalities are higher and private landlords are most unregulated, such as in the UK and the US, that private renting becomes unaffordable; and that is when people become desperate to buy. A very tightly regulated private market, weighted more in favour of the tenant, can be a large part of the ideal solution. Regulation is very hard for individual landlords to oppose after it begins. What can they do: demolish their property in a fit of pique if decent regulations are introduced?

Income inequalities tend to be higher in countries with less regulation over the allocation of housing. It is hard to know what came first: the toleration of rising inequalities or the deregulation that allowed inequalities to rise. In such countries what regulation remains tends to be a one-way process, limiting the contribution of the state to subsidizing just those on insufficient incomes, but not limiting the scope of the rich to profit from the housing market. The map below shows the maximum that the state, in 2013, can contribute to rents across England and Wales.[62] These limits can be imposed, and yet there is little control over what rents landlords can demand, or over how many properties one person can buy, and leave empty, should they wish.[63]

Why, though, do we need much of a private rental market at all? Why not the larger 'property-owning democracy' that we were moving towards before the crash and the huge rise in private renting? In the short term, what makes buying housing more affordable is a low interest rate. By autumn 2012 interest rates were so low in the United States that the 'average on the fifteen-year fixed mortgage, a popular refinancing option, dipped to 2.69%, down from last week's record low of 2.73%'.[64] This was the lowest rate on record, at that time, of all reliable records going back to at least the 1950s. Why, then, are we not seeing more buying and less renting?

Interest rates were forced down by central banks to drop to historic lows in 2008. Across much of the periphery of mainland Europe, and both in the UK and in the US, huge numbers of people had been coerced into borrowing extremely large sums of money. However, the finances of the next potential cohort of home-buyers were on average (by then) in such a poor state, and their ability to put down a deposit had been so diminished by the slump, that lenders became desperate, and the Bank of England, the European Central Bank, the Federal

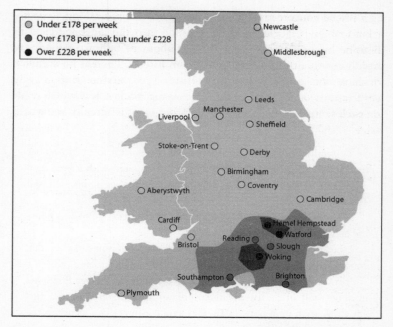

Figure 10. Maximum weekly local housing allowance permitted after April 2013, England and Wales.

Reserve Bank and all the other central banks of rich (and not so rich) nations started to do whatever it took to keep base rates low. For a time, in the UK, this came close to giving money away to the commercial banks that did the lending (at 0.5% or less), and, although the money still has to be repaid, at that interest rate there is not so much urgency to repay.

Because no alternative to free-market mayhem is imagined, interest rates in the UK have to stay low today to prevent the housing crisis turning into a US-style disaster. Ten years ago a deposit to buy a home in the UK was about nine months' average salary; now it is three years'.[65] Banks require far higher deposits, and average salaries have fallen in real terms. With house prices continuing to soar, something had to give, and that something was interest rates. Unless offers of very low rates were continually made to new 'market entrants', the high-priced housing market could not be kept limping along. Recently a kind of desperation has been slipping into the language used to describe housing prices: they are just about to fall; are falling; are rapidly rising; or just about to rise even further. There is no stability. No certainty. As an example, here is just one of the thousands of early 2013 reports on the state of the US housing market. It is worth reading each sentence twice to try to work out what is actually being said here:

> Single-family home prices in the United States slipped in November from a month earlier, but were up 5.5% compared with a year ago, according to the S & P/Case-Shiller housing price index released Tuesday.
>
> The annual increase builds on a string of gains that point to a housing market that is on the mend.
>
> 'Housing is clearly recovering,' David Blitzer, Chairman of the index committee at S & P Dow Jones Indexes, said in a statement.
>
> Prices on a non-adjusted basis slipped 0.1% from October. Prices fell in about half of the twenty metropolitan areas covered by the survey . . . A separate report on Tuesday said consumer confidence in the United States dropped in January to its lowest level in more than a year.[66]

Describing housing prices as 'recovering' while they are still falling shows how familiar financiers have become with prices falling. But, at the same time, in other parts of the United States, financiers talked of a rapid recovery being under way in late 2013. In Britain, house prices are deeply divided. In Kingston upon Hull the price of an average three-bed home was under £70,000 and falling rapidly early on in 2013. During that same year, in Kensington and Chelsea in London, average prices of flats rose above the £1 million barrier, often for just two-bed flats. In one year prices had risen by 13.4%. In 2008 the average price had been £750,000.[67] It is in London where the housing market is overheated to the point of meltdown, but, as if defying the physics, it continues to get hotter and hotter. As it does so, there is no sense of surety over the current direction of travel. On 16 September 2013 some fifty news stories were generated by one press release issued by the property firm Rightmove. Parts of that press release

View of Sheffield city centre, with St Paul's Tower, now the city's tallest building, to the left. The tower consists of private apartments with retail on the ground floor. Outside of London, development has been far more modest, but the future is still far from certain, despite the lack of boom. Here the problem is not impossibly high prices, but too few buyers. This is despite a huge influx of new students to this area of the city in the last decade. The Victorian town hall, built in the last decade of the old Queen's reign, can be seen just to the right. Sheffield Hallam University in the centre, along with the rest of higher education in the city, now brings in more money to the South Yorkshire region than all the combined metal trades. New housing reflects changing times and a belief that people will crowd into city centres again, but, for that to happen, the centres will have to become more affordable and remain affordable; and young people will have to keep on coming to these cities in the north. The cost of housing cannot continue to rise as incomes and benefits fall.

reported falls in central London prices; other parts reported a rise in overall London prices; falls in prices away from London; and a rise nationally. Nobody really knew what to think.

To think about how housing prices might alter in the near future, take a step back and look at the national trends in UK housing prices over the course of the last thirty years (in the graph below). In the UK the 1980s boom lasted from September 1983 to September 1989; the fall bottomed out in December 1992 and prices rose from then onwards, more often in later years, until a peak was reached in November 2002. The period since then has been volatile, now possibly entering its second decade of volatility.

After 2002, prices still rose in the wake of falls, but usually by less than the year before, although the degree of oscillation in the annual and monthly swings is far higher than before 2002, given the growing price volatility. I take the final dotted line further down than others might, suggesting it could, in future, drop below the most recent 2008 minimum. I do this because, as in 1989, I do not think we are yet at the low point to which housing prices could or should fall. If, in 1989, you had said that there would not be as great a fall again in house prices, you would have been wrong. The year 2008 saw a much greater fall.

I could be wrong. Prices may not drop again in the next two decades, at least not in London. Both you and I have no way of knowing what the long-, or medium-, or even short-term trend will be. That is the nature of markets. The housing market may have turned in 2008 and now be on the way up, but with some very dramatic fits and starts. However, if it is, some of the fundamental relationships between average prices and average incomes will have changed forever.

One person who closely follows the UK ratio of house prices to earnings is David (Danny) Blanchflower, now Professor of Economics at Dartmouth College in the United States. In September 2013 he argued that that ratio, still at a high of 4.5 to 1, remained well above its long-term trend.[68] Predicting house prices can only be a very inexact science. But I place most faith in David Blanchflower's assessment that the housing price trend is still downwards in 2013. He is supported by the IMF, which says housing prices in the UK remain too high and could easily drop by a further 10%–15% relative to

Britain's current average salaries, which themselves continued to fall during 2013.[69] The graph below shows the average change in housing price, not the overall price, and incorporates the Blanchflower and IMF assessments in determining how to place the most recent (dashed) trend line.

Because in most years the bars in the graph below have been above the zero horizontal axis, meaning that prices were rising during those quarters of those years, property-owners in Britain tend on paper to be far better off than those who do not own. Of course, this varies very much between different areas. In some parts of the country (where prices have not risen much) property-owners have not seen such increases in their wealth. In other parts the graph is just a mild echo of the huge increases they have experienced in the nominal value of their homes, especially in the most recent years.

What makes an area rich or poor can vary. In the past, being located in the south-west quadrant of a city often made housing more expensive, as the prevailing wind brought clean air more frequently into those neighbourhoods. Today, being located near a transport hub can

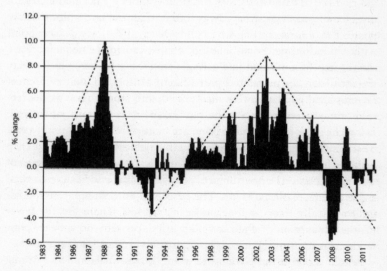

Figure 11. Three-month on three-month housing price change, 1983–2012, UK, and trend lines.

have just as great an impact on an area's affluence. Another determin-
ant of local variations in urban housing prices is a house's position
relative to poor areas. The further away it is, the higher its value tends
to have grown. In more equal countries such as France, Japan or Sweden, where fewer people are either very poor or very rich, living away
from the poor attracts a lower price premium. Housing price inflation
tends to be lower too. Volatility such as that shown above is rarer.
Analysts who do not find growing wealth polarization (in the period
from 2000 up to 2006, just before the crash) to be the major problem
consider volatility as the key unusual aspect of the UK housing market. As researchers from Glasgow University's Department of Urban
Studies concluded in work published in 2010, using data from before
even the most recent and most volatile times: 'Perhaps the most
important aspect of our findings, however, is not the trend (or lack of
it) in housing wealth inequality, nor its cyclical nature, but the enormous amplitude of the cycle.'[70]

In more unequal countries there are fewer areas of mixed housing
tenure: fewer people rent next to where others own. Even in London,
the rich try to live away from the poor – though that might mean a
distance of only two streets away, rather than the two miles that are
possible in a northern English city. However, at the very densest point
within London, where population is most crowded, inequalities are
more often found along just a single street. For instance in Pimlico,
the most densely populated part of central London, that two-street
geographical gap cannot be maintained, and stories such as the one
told immediately below (at the start of the next section), of the rich
living cheek by jowl with the poor, are more common.[71] It really can't
be stressed enough that in more equitable rich countries the social gap
between rich and poor is narrower, not just in terms of money but
also in educational opportunities, in health status and in shared social
space and recreational tastes. The perceived need to separate oneself
geographically from anyone poorer is far less. There are far fewer
people who are very rich to complain about people who are very poor
living next door to them, of whom, of course, there are fewer too.

Britain is one of those countries where 'location' determines housing
price more than any other factor. In Britain, the location of a house away
from the poor and near 'good' schools has recently grown in import-

Original Georgian ceiling laths can be seen in a home set for refurbishment in Nether Edge, Sheffield. You have no way of knowing it, unless you know Sheffield, but Nether Edge is an area where precise location is particularly key in determining property prices. People will talk about the décor of homes, the wonderful 'original features' of the property, but where exactly a house is located within this suburb of the city, nearer to Nick Clegg's constituency, or nearer to the central Sheffield end, will be what determines the price you might pay or the rent you will have to pay to live there. The older university (of the two in Sheffield) and the steep Rivelin Valley mark the other boundaries of posh Sheffield more clearly. Recently the secondary school nearest much of Nether Edge, where this ceiling is, Abbeydale Grange, closed because too few children from this area went to it and so it had entered 'special measures'. Because they did not go, its reputation suffered, but the reputation of the neighbourhood was maintained. Most children in Nether Edge go to higher-ranking comprehensive schools, away from the city centre, further from the poor. Homes in this area are then refurbished rather than demolished. Everything is related to everything else: schools to homes, homes to politics, politics to schools, but, as the great US geographer Waldo Tobler put it, most simply, near things are more related than far.

ance. When estimated statistically the relative effects of these factors are found to be greatest in north-west England, but the absolute gaps are greatest within London, where, in 2012, research conducted (at taxpayers' expense) by Lloyds TSB Private Banking found that a fifth of top state schools within the capital appeared to command a housing premium of over £100,000. The bank's researchers concluded property within the postal district of Henrietta Barnett School in north London had the largest premium, of 91% (£394,282), in comparison with the average house price in neighbouring areas in that part of London.[72]

What happens in London is mirrored in microcosm elsewhere. Throughout Britain there is a local school premium on the price of housing. The premium can be negative, in effect a discount, in the catchment area of schools deemed to be very poor. It is positive when schools are deemed very good, and particularly in areas within walking distance of some of the most expensive private day-schools – schools that only 1% or 2% of all children attend, and that are almost always found in London and the south-east. Thus local schools also manage to affect the inflation of prices in the capital. It is not just that the highest paid jobs are there too.

LONDON

Every city has its rich and poor areas, but London can combine extremes of both in the same streets. When property prices are high enough, only two groups can afford to move in: the rich, and migrants who are prepared to cram several people into each room. In one house on the street where I used to live in Pimlico, migrant workers slept six to a room in bunk beds. In the otherwise identical house next door, a single family rattled about in a gorgeous mansion.

– Neil O'Brien, Director of Policy Exchange, 2012[73]

When it comes to housing, there is nowhere in the world quite like London. Sure, there are other expensive cities, but no other city in the developed world contains such a deep – and growing – chasm between rich and poor, and such comparatively expensive housing for both groups. The extraordinarily high cost of all kinds of housing in London rubs salt into the wounds made by inequality. Even the director of a right-wing free-market think tank (Policy Exchange) complains (as quoted directly above) of no longer being able to live in the centre of the city because he is neither rich enough nor poor enough.

Others have acclimatized to what London has become. They know there is the strange world of Zone 1, where multimillion price tags are now the norm for anything with three or more bedrooms. They know of the horrors of sheds and overcrowding in inner east London. But many Londoners find that these extremes make where they live – make places like Haringey, or Brent, or Epping Forest – appear more normal. Many Londoners say that people appear to be able to 'muddle on' at least for the time being. But to an outsider, especially to someone looking to rent or buy in London for the first time, it does not look like that.

Right now there is growing division within London, division that is reflected across the UK more generally but less acutely. By February 2013 it was reported that the average price of all property in the capital, of any dwelling anywhere in London, had reached £398,000. That is a fortune; and, by that point, it was more than 6% higher than the average that had been reported for February 2012. Remarkably, however, it was after that point when the acceleration really set in. By the early autumn of 2013 the rises for the entire south-east were said to be more than 6% a year. Some suggested that these high prices had 'more to do with the allure of Kensington and Chelsea addresses such as Egerton Crescent – where the average is £8,136,000 – than the fortunes of Barking and Dagenham'.[74] However, prices in Westminster fell by 7.4% in August 2013. Initially that mini-slump was blamed on the summer heatwave.[75] Outside of the core of Zone 1, prices continued to rise, at least then. Even in the cheapest east London borough the cost of an average home by early 2013 had already reached £210,944. The entire south-east England average had by then climbed to £211,092.

London is not the most expensive city in the world to live in – that is Tokyo. But, as incomes are more equitably distributed in Tokyo than they are in the UK, as the transport system works so well there, as crime is so low, and as median wages are higher, living in Tokyo is less stressful. Less stress happens when you worry less about crime, about competing at work in a system that rewards ageing and collegiality over naked ambition, and when people have higher average levels of mental health. Tokyo is the most expensive city because the Japanese people remain among the most prosperous. There is very little poverty in Japan,[76] and because of that, and because the rich take so much less in Japan, there is much greater choice for most people about where, within each Japanese city, they can live. Wherever they live, however, space is at a premium, as it is in any megacity.

There are fifteen cities in the world that are more expensive to live in than London, but (other than Tokyo) most of them are smaller, all have fewer people living in poverty, and all have cheaper accommodation near their centres, if not in their centres. Not one is surrounded by an entire region where the average house price exceeds £200,000, and not one has housing in its cheapest enclave that is as expensive as the housing in Newham or Dagenham (two of London's lowest-priced boroughs). London is also very odd in other ways. It has the greatest concentration, and the largest number, of people living in poverty within Western Europe. And this city in which so many poor people live is also becoming more expensive, both on its own terms and in relation to other places with expensive housing and a high general cost of living. All this is also occurring at a time when median incomes in the UK are falling.[77]

It is the top end of the London market that receives the most attention, but those increases have a profound effect on housing prices across the capital and across the south-east of England. Price rises in Egerton Crescent ripple out to Newham and Dagenham. Type that Kensington street name into the property sales website Zoopla, and the first hit you got in September 2013 was Flat 1 of Nos. 26–7, which sold for £610,000 in March 2002 and which the website now estimates to be worth over £1.5 million. Recently, London's most expensive house was sold for £300 million, while the most expensive flat fetched £65 million.[78] When such excesses are to be found nearby, or only a few miles away, asking 'just' £0.2 million for a modest three-bed home in the East End begins to appear reasonable.

The top London price may well be higher than nearly a third of a billion pounds, because not all sales are recorded through the Land Registry. When individuals masquerade as companies, their property is officially transferred from one company to another, rather than sold. Clearly it is not a company that wishes to live in a flat, but a person or family; but if a company owns it and someone buys the company, the flat has not been sold. It may appear that the point being made here – that a few very rich people hide their purchases of property through companies – is a purely academic one and cannot have that much effect until such behaviour begins to tempt a wider range of people. We are getting closer to such extremes.

The prices in the south-east of the UK are also bolstered by factors other than convenience of location. For some of the world's richest people, London housing often comes with an extra incentive to buy. It is a little like those shops in the tourist areas of the British capital that advertise 'tax-free shopping' for foreign nationals. The London property market sells itself as a bargain to those who are not British, but are in the very top global-wealth bracket. But London is far from a bargain for poorer immigrants, who are often fleeced of the majority of their incomes to live in the worst housing in the capital.

Top prices in London can rise so high because they come at a special discount to purchasers from outside Britain. Overseas sales have soared due to interest from Asia. It is not just the tax breaks, but also sterling that is attractive. In 2013 the *New York Times* explained to its worldwide readership that the current weakness of the British currency has only reinforced price rises, as the pound slumped during 2008, and by 2013 was still worth about 20% less against both the US dollar and a series of other Asian currencies, 'giving Asian purchasers more leverage'.[79] In addition, with non-domiciled status, you can buy in a way that avoids a great deal of tax on your property and on your income. In his 2013 autumn statement the Chancellor proposed to end this loophole by making non-resident owners of property liable for tax on their capital gains made after April 2015; but he did not say how he proposed to collect the tax from people who might not have any address in the UK after they had sold their spare homes here.[80]

There is a concurrent effect of the pound being lower that also influences London and the south-east. British people who own property overseas are finding it costs them more and more to maintain it, to travel to it and to live abroad when they are in it. Overseas property-owners are predominately based in London and the south. However, if their pensions, paid in sterling, do not soon rise in value, many from the UK living in Spain may soon have to return. They will need homes to return to and then even more property in Spain will be empty, while more property will be needed in the UK, especially in the south of England. Building for migrants, including returning migrants, is easier to justify than building for more second homeowners. Elsewhere in southern Europe, in Cyprus, in Greece (especially in Crete) and in Malta, there are many British pensioners now finding it harder to get by on their devalued sterling pension.[81] On 25 June 2013, when the government cut the winter fuel allowance for 100,000 pensioners living in warmer overseas countries on the grounds that they did not need it, they may not have envisaged that this might cause a few extra pensioners to think of returning to the UK, pensioners who would be quite likely to rent and perhaps qualify for housing benefit.

At the very start of this book great store was made of the fact that the value of all residential property in Britain, including all that which is being rented, is estimated at £5.5 trillion, but it was not then pointed out that now almost a quarter of all this money is tied up in London, and that much of the rest of that national wealth is housed (literally) not too far from London. The graphic below makes this clear. The London effect is so great that residential property in the nearby commuter town of Reading is worth more than all of that in the much larger city of Newcastle-upon-Tyne.

The Director of Research at the company that produced the £5.5 trillion figure, Hometrack, explains: 'The housing market's total value is on a scale that dwarfs the commercial property market and is twice the size of the FTSE All-Share equity market. This is why housing is so important economically and as a store of wealth. With the value of outstanding mortgage debt at just over £1 trillion, the analysis shows just how much equity there is in the market.'[82] This imbalance is one reason why there is such an obsession with keeping the housing market overinflated. Some £4.5 trillion of the wealth of people in Brit-

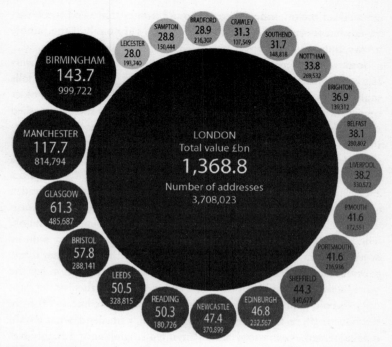

Figure 12. The value of property in Britain by urban area, 2012, total equity (£ billion).

ain, mostly the wealth of a rich minority, relies on property values staying high, and especially on their staying high in London.

In September 2013 the Royal Institute of Chartered Surveyors (RICS) called on the Bank of England and the government to act if house price inflation exceeded 5% annually to prevent another bubble forming, perhaps through encouraging the rationing of mortgages. This particular suggestion was greeted with outrage from some of its own members, business leaders and *The Times* newspaper, representing people who wish to profit more and more from the increases in London, the area being targeted by the RICS.[83] However, when even this organization tries to slow down the madness, you begin to sense that something is seriously going amiss. Surveyors do better the faster the market moves, when there are more homes that need to be surveyed; but they also know that they will do very badly if the bubble grows, bursts and slumps.

Some of the money that has come into London from overseas buyers has been spread around the south-east of England (and, despite the falls in the value of the pound, also over quite a large area of France), as older owners sell up, move out and cash in. Often few questions are asked about where that overseas money was made. A man who profits by setting up a sweat shop in China or India might, years later, wish to buy his daughter a flat in Knightsbridge. She did not really make that money and neither did he. It was made by those who laboured in that sweat shop. However, if workers in India and China secure greater rights and a slightly larger share of income in future, as workers in Europe and North America did before them, there will be less money flowing into London. The capital's top-end estate agents rarely seem to pause to wonder whether the numbers or tastes of the very rich are as robust as they think.

Seen as a safe haven, London remains a favoured location for the world's richest people. But how safe an investment is this former capital of an old imperial empire that now functions more like an offshore tax haven? If you had a large amount of money to spend, what would it take to make you worry about buying a single flat at a highly elevated price in a London street, when spreading it out in diverse investments might be the better option? What conditions would have to prevail, what stories would you have to hear, before you thought twice about all these so-called 'not to be missed' opportunities to buy because prices were due to rise even further?

What if, in late autumn 2013, following the news that non-residents would soon be liable for capital gains tax, the world's super-rich were to look more carefully at what the true value per square metre of London property actually was and then compare it with other places? Or what if they were to look at living conditions not that far away from the most expensive places and wonder just what London may be becoming, given how people are currently housed there today? Do the world's super-rich really need to live near where all the central London office workers also want to congregate, and not that far away from very abject poverty? There are other places to buy.

Housing conditions in poorer parts of the capital have recently

It might look like London, but it is not London. Instead, this image shows a new mixed-use commercial and residential development overlooking a former industrial area to the north of Sheffield city centre. This particular style of London property development is now aped around the world, including within Britain. It would not be hard to imagine banks of computer screens surrounding the concrete pillars within these open-plan offices, were this block to be located within the Square Mile and not a two-hour train journey due north of it. Because of that distance, and despite the supposedly near-frictionless speed with which information can flow, this entire building can now be rented for far less than what a fraction of a single floor would cost in the heart of the British capital. But, despite the low commercial rent, these floors remain empty. Volatility in commercial property prices, lets and occupancy is even greater than in the residential sector. When firms are doing well, they can justify moving to swanky new offices, but when they are doing badly, it is better to sack space than sack people. Far more are then asked to work from home for more of the working week, or to become self-employed and then be contracted back in. Working from home impacts on what space a home needs. Everything is related.

been compared unfavourably with those in Hyderabad in India in comments made to investigative journalists examining how people have been living in the poorer parts of Newham in London in the last two years. One example given was that, during 2012, a family of four with a baby was found in London illegally renting a single room in an unlicensed house currently in multiple-family occupation.[84] The conditions in these homes – problems with the sewage, rubbish, rats, bedbugs, cockroaches, but above all the acute overcrowding – are similar to the rookeries (slums) of the capital that were mostly demolished between fifty years and a hundred years ago.

The London rental market is notoriously expensive. Each room in a multiple-occupancy dwelling in London can earn the landlord £400 a month. Potential tenants might find it slightly cheaper to rent (illegally) a shed in a back garden, at around £350 a month – although such an arrangement usually involves no hot water, barely any heating and mattresses on the floor. If a room is in a part of London that is both poor and hard to get to, it can be rented from as little as £240 a month in a four-room (two up, two down) terrace. If you wish to investigate this world yourself, simply spend a day looking in shop windows in poorer but quite central parts of London at the little cards advertising spaces in the cheapest of former homes. It is not just in inner London where thousands of sheds are now used for housing; the practice has spread as far out as Slough.

Both the most expensive flats in Knightsbridge and the sheds at the bottom of the 'housing ladder' are massively overvalued as places to sleep. No one knows how many sheds in London are currently being let illegally. However, one data company claims it has mapped, in what it claims is a unique new database, all those that could be used for sleeping throughout the whole of Greater London and further out. This database is available for purchase from the GeoInformation Group, which sells itself as a leading supplier of geospatial data and services. The company explained that the release of its new 2013 product, the UKMap® Sheds Base Map, was timed to coincide with a recent initiative set up by the government to tackle the problem of 'Beds in Sheds'. Quite what that initiative is remains unclear. However, it suggests it is 'offering the ideal mapping solution for those who need to accurately identify and act on illegal dwellings'.[85] Where there is a profit to be made, even in stopping others making a profit, no stone is left unturned, and no shed need be overlooked should your local London borough buy this software.

The landlords who rent out the sheds say that they are not forcing anyone to take their accommodation. They are just placing the sheds on the open market. What they're doing is illegal,[86] but they might simply refer to that as 'too much red tape'. This is one of the problems with having such an open market in housing. If it were better controlled, and if the penalty for housing people in sheds was possible imprisonment, I very much suspect landlords would start to behave better and would, for instance, also ensure they always paid their taxes on rental income. When letting is illegal, no tax is paid on that rental income. Encourage people to profit greatly and then, for some, 'bending the rules' is just about being more entrepreneurial.

An adequate number of inspectors with adequate powers are needed. Otherwise landlords will not just let out sheds, but will build substantial illegal two-storey structures the width of their properties' back gardens and rent these out by the room to several families. At present most outbuildings are rented out to single adults or childless couples, but in the district of Slough, some way outside of London, in just one small part of that district, some 211 outbuildings were recently found to have been rented out – and all but one illegally. The local council have estimated that up to 3,000 sheds may be occupied in the district as a whole. In theory the landlords could be fined £200 a day, but so far hardly any have.[87] Clearly they are not afraid. These landlords may not be that rich, but they are aping the attitudes of those much richer than themselves in trying to make a quick buck out of those who are vulnerable to exploitation. They may even feel that they both deserve and need the money, perhaps to help them pay their overinflated mortgage. When people are given a free pass on greed, that greed can trickle down.

The rich – who are concentrated in London – often claim that it is only because of them that the poor can live at all, have jobs created for them, and receive benefits mostly from their taxes and charity from their largesse. One *Times* journalist recently calculated that 'London pays a quarter of all income tax, three times as much as Scotland and more than the north-east, the north-west and Yorkshire and Humberside put together. A quarter of all corporation tax comes from London, more than twice as much as any other region. A quarter of all business rates are raised in London, as is a third of all stamp duty. When all tax receipts are added up, London contributes a fifth of the total and the south-east provides the same again. Despite the regular political pronouncements that the economy will have to be "rebalanced", London is thriving.'[88] Commentators from the north retort that London is thriving at the expense of properties being empty just a few hours' train ride from the capital, property (and people) just as shiny and new, and nearer to open green spaces, but not located quite so near the heart of the money.

The (southern) *Times* journalist's argument could be written another way, and in a way that might help to make the logical fallacy in his case clearer. It is true that the richest 1% of people pay over a quarter of all income tax, and it is because most of them live and work in London that London does too. This will be at least three times as much as the group just below them, the next 1%. From this, do we conclude that the very richest are very worthy – are worth three times more than the second 1%? Or do we conclude that they pay themselves so much (and charge such high rents) that not enough remains for others to be paid sufficiently and for those others to pay a little tax in their turn? This sort of thinking gives rise to coalition government that actually celebrates taking people out of tax because their incomes are so low that they cannot afford to contribute to the common good.

The journalist's argument is scuttled not simply by inequalities between rich and poor, but by inequalities all up and down the income and housing scales. It is because there is so much inequality at the apex that most people in the top 10% in the UK do not see themselves as rich. Own a three-bed house in Slough and you and your family might well be in the top tenth of the country by income, should you collectively bring in, say, £60,000 a year. But that might not quite cover your mortgage payments. You, your partner and your grown-up child might all be working. You may be in the top 5% of people by wealth, given the rising value of your home, but you may still be struggling to get by each month. So what options do you have? You rent out the shed.

But what if we were to evict all the people sleeping in all the sheds in and around the capital? All the people who now can afford to sleep only in sheds? Could the problems be solved by making the poorest go away, by clearing out the sheds like some Latin American government might clear out its *favelas*?

What, in general, will happen, if London continues on its current trajectory and eventually 'relocates' (for which read 'evict') everyone living in normal housing who relies on benefits and who does not pay tax, is that the city's nature will change. I believe that London will become soulless and cruel as a result.[89] The desperate (those below the radar and not receiving welfare benefits) will still rent sheds; they'll just need to ensure they have no heater at all so the infra-red cameras can't spot them.

What is needed is a cultural change away from greed. We need a return to a time when if you wanted a lodger you would put them in your third bedroom, not in the shed. We need a new future too, not just the best of the past. We need fewer people needing lodgers and fewer people desperately wanting to lodge within commuting distance of the most overheated quarter of the economy. The alternative is a dystopia that would quickly come to be seen as normal.

What if London were to continue to boom economically and the rest of the country continue to slump? With even more higher-rate taxpayers, Londoners could soon be paying half of all the tax in the UK. Someone joked to me recently that they might have to build an electric fence around the M25. People in London who were not among the very richest would find it even more difficult to acquire housing with enough space for children; there would be less access to childcare, so it would be harder to maintain two full-time incomes (the carers themselves would be priced out). What it means to be a 'Londoner' would fundamentally change.

The coalition government opposes limits being put on bankers' bonuses by the European Union on the grounds that this might lead to some of the richest leaving London; they want the poor to leave instead. They want those they see as 'unproductive', because they are paid so little for what they do, to make way for more of the richest people in the world. They want the children of the rich to be given more space in the city; and they want the children of the poor to go. But recently bankers' bonuses have fallen, so, again, we have no certainty as to what direction the trajectory of the capital and its surrounds, and by implication a majority of the UK housing market by value, is taking at any particular time. But we do know that if their bonuses rise again, given how many thousands of highly paid bankers there are in London, more jokes will be made about the apparent need for that electric fence. We know that more areas, currently homes to the poor, will be taken over by the rich. But we can also hope that this trend is coming to an end.

In 2013 Bloomberg reported that fewer than half of the luxury homes bought in London during all of 2012 were purchased with cash. This was a rapid fall, down from about two thirds of all luxury property being purchased that way in 2011. (Cash transactions are not just under-the-radar money-laundering exercises or organized crime purchases; they are how the very rich, as well as landlords and developers, often buy property.) That fall in very rich people buying very expensive property with what was, in effect, spare cash was shown to be directly attributable to the banks reining in bonuses.[90] However, despite this fall, in 2012, £3 billion of bankers' bonus money was still spent on housing in London and the wider south-east.[91] That is a huge annual injection of income being turned into wealth. Some of the bonus money is used to buy homes for others to rent, and tenants will soon make up the majority of Londoners as a result of so many more now at the top choosing so recently to try their hand at being a landlord, although often using a letting agency to do all the hands-on work involved.[92]

What might be done to curb the apparent worth of property in the south-east of England rising higher and higher, out of the reach of most except those who will then charge others sky-high rent? Earlier chapters have mentioned introducing rent controls and building more homes for new arrivals. You cannot just build in the north and in Wales and Scotland and hope that people will move there. You need to move key activities out of London, jobs that do not need to be in London. Why continue to squeeze government and so much of the civil service into that city, so many major hospitals, and so many universities? Much was moved out in the past, albeit temporarily, during war-time, and the BBC has recently shown what is possible by establishing large parts of their operations in Salford.

Currently there is no vision of an alternative to growing social and spatial polarization in the UK. To turn around the housing crisis, far more than just a few half-baked policies are needed, especially the coalition policies aimed at underwriting landlords and pushing poorer people out of the south-east. Illegal actions by landlords that deprive people of their homes by evicting them with too little notice, or housing people in sheds that are unfit to live in, need to become serious criminal offences. Actions by landlords such as the immoral continuous pushing out of tenants to bring in new, higher-paying replacements can damage renters' mental and physical health (on which more below, in Chapter 7). Furthermore, spare bedrooms need not be taxed in social housing, as there simply is not enough smaller property to accommodate those who need it. Some will end up in sheds. Just as we still believe (I hope) that no one should have to sleep in a shed, so too we should have other real and realizable aspirations.

There is no good reason why we should not have the long-term aim of every family being able to live in a home with a spare room for a playroom, or for a study, or for visitors. We already have enough bedrooms in Britain for this to be possible (on which more in later chapters). Every single person should be able to have at least an apartment of their own, and not be forced to share with others whom they do not know. Rearranging people to fit better into the stock we already have cannot be done well by authoritarian diktats like the Bedroom Tax; but even the Home Builders Federation of the UK, representing private home-building firms, recognizes that pensioners living in large properties with many empty rooms are currently sitting on (and in) property worth £400 billion. Move families into those large homes, and the pensioners into the flats they vacate, having brought the quality of those flats up to scratch (including insulation and soundproofing), and both households have just one spare bedroom, rather than one having many and the other having no spare space at all. In September 2013 the think-tank Demos published the results of a survey that found that: 'The majority of older people in three-, four- and five-bedroom homes want to downsize.'[93]

Our problems in housing are so great that many different policies are needed to help us to fit better into what we have; to renovate the stock; to build what extra we need; and to finance the changes in a way that does not stoke up fear. People need more rights to be able to stay in their home: to become tenants if they cannot pay the mortgage, but not to have to move if they fall on hard times. That aspiration might create new problems, but a limited version of the right to stay already exists and so, later on in this volume, consideration is given to looking at what extending that right might imply, and how it might have many other currently unforeseen benefits. However, it may take a further slump before a cultural change can take place – before housing can be made solid again, dependable, not a speculation for acquiring wealth, but a place of certainty to sleep in, and to sleep safely in. Asking for housing that won't impoverish you through your monthly rent or mortgage costs is not asking for much; but without a further slump it might be asking for the moon.

6

Slump

Human beings have no choice but to occupy a place in the world, and more often than not develop strong emotional ties to that place, so being displaced by external forces – having that place taken away, given to someone else, or even bulldozed – is among the most appalling of social injustices. Displacement involves the removal of a basic human need (shelter) upon which people depend absolutely – practically, socially, emotionally and psychologically.

– Tom Slater, Geographer, University of Edinburgh[1]

We have more housing in Britain – more homes and more rooms in those homes – than we have ever had before. This is not just in absolute terms, but per family, per person.

It is not that we have been building that many more new homes. We have been building less than half the number it is often claimed that we need.[2] What we have mainly been building is new rooms in or on existing homes. We have been opening up attics and inserting skylights and stairs. We have been putting new rooms on top of garages or building entire new wings. We have been extending homes backwards, sideways, downwards, adding an en suite, a second or third bathroom and, above all else, adding more bedrooms. We have been doing this partly because we thought we needed the room, and partly because we were told that we would easily recoup the cost of these additions in the rising future value of our property – those of us who owned or were buying, that is.

We may well have been wrong about the recouping of the costs of recent extensions. When people look up the supposed value of their property, they assume that is what they will get, but only those who have sold have actually recouped.[3] However, what we have done is to ensure that there is enough property for all who need it, because we have been quietly building all those extensions and loft conversions, and so enlarging what we have, even if we have not been building so many separate new dwellings.

In quietly adding on to existing property, we have also helped to stoke a system in which people try harder and harder to move to where the property is most expensive – where there is the least spare property, but where there are the most job opportunities. However, we are not availing ourselves of every square metre of extra space we own, of all those loft conversions and bedrooms over the garage. We are at the point we build them, but shortly afterwards, when the teenager for whom the bedroom was built turns eighteen, the room is empty because the teenager is off. Half of all young women in England now go to university either at age eighteen or at age nineteen. Some stay at home but many move out. If within our means, we have extended our properties to fit the maximum size of our family, but when that size dwindles we tend not to move on, partly because offspring keep boomeranging back when they can't afford a home of their own, and partly because the longer we wait, the more, we think, we'll make.

We could share out the dwellings we have better, and share out people among regions better. Prices rising higher in the south and falling in the north have coincided with worse living conditions in all parts of the country: more overcrowding in the south and more destitution in the north. If current trends continue, we may well start demolishing property again where demand is lowest. The perceived 'national' housing shortage is, in fact, a regional shortage, part of the growing north/south divide. Everywhere there is vacant housing that needs to be used better. But in certain areas there is a growth of empty housing stock that is partially disguised by very high rates of underoccupancy, rates made possible by how cheap housing away from jobs has become. Or, to put it better, cheap as far as people with 'good' jobs are concerned.

An image from inside a council flat that is being repainted by the new tenant. The flat is in Batemoor, a suburb of Sheffield. Three-bed ex-council houses in Batemoor were on the market for £65,000 in 2013; other (non-ex-council) three-bed terraces were going for £75,000; two-bed semis in the more salubrious corners, £85,000; and a three-bed detached, £100,000 – all this in an average part of an average northern city. Rents here are much lower than the national average too, but how the property is maintained reflects that. If you want something doing, often enough it is best to get on and do it yourself. Your landlord might chuck in the paint, but unless the décor is really beyond the pale, they will not throw in the painters too. Similarly, if you are dismayed by the way housing in general is allocated at the whim of others, you need to take action yourself. Political parties, pressure groups and campaigning organizations can give you ideas, even slogans and websites, but only when people have done it themselves, have taken more control, has better housing been won. No paternalistic patron ever willingly hands over the keys. When things have got better in the past, it has been because they have been made better. When we tolerate what is bad, what we get is bad.

In a society that is growing ever more unequal, a good job has come to be synonymous with one that pays well. This is partly the result of how we finance housing, but the way we finance housing, in many areas, is responsible for the current economic slump. There is also a great risk of current events causing a new slump in future in the newly overheated markets in and around London. This is a concern above and beyond the issue of the extent to which the world's super-rich might be partly to blame for driving up property prices in central London.

Ultimately the question being asked here is whether housing in Britain is really worth the price we are paying for it. This applies both to newly built housing and to all existing housing. It is also worth asking whether, as a whole, some housing has become so expensive because in other places it has become so very cheap – in the places where people do not want to be. The problem is that we have little choice in the matter. If we want to be where the jobs are, we have to pay the price. That price is not just qualified in monetary terms. It also includes quality of life, as increasingly more and more people have to live in a very small space of very low quality.

SMALL ROOMS

Britain's new-build homes are the smallest in Western Europe and many are too small for family life . . .

– Royal Institute of British Architects, 2011[4]

The problem in a place like London, you might think, is the lack of rooms, but you'd be wrong. Even in London there are, as the 2011 census revealed, more rooms than people, many more rooms than people. In fact, though you may find it hard to believe, there are so many rooms in London that there are more rooms that are designated as bedrooms than there are people living in the city. Rooms in new-built property tend to be too small, but rooms in older properties are generally large enough, and most London property is still old. Luckily the Victorians believed that lots of air in our homes was good for us. Unfortunately they also bequeathed us free-market economic theory. However, as discussed above, the free market does not balance supply and demand well when it comes to housing; it usually increases the imbalances that already exist.

Not all rooms are equal. It is not just that some are larger than others; some don't even count as rooms at all. In 1911 the UK census enumerators were instructed to 'count the kitchen as a room, but do not count scullery, landing, lobby, closet, bathroom, nor warehouse, office, shop'.[5] A century later the 2011 census wording proposed a rather less generous definition: 'Do not count bathrooms, toilets, halls or landings or rooms that can only be used for storage such as cupboards. Count all other rooms, for example kitchens, living rooms, utility rooms, bedrooms, studies and conservatories. If two rooms have been converted into one count them as one room.' What constitutes a room may have changed – but, thanks to the decennial censuses, we are still able to put a number on how many rooms exist.

Part of the reason why the British have some of the smallest new housing being built is the national obsession with rooms – in particular, with acquiring a three-bed or four-bed house. In the past, British housing was so overcrowded that the idea of a house of your own became the idyll, the ideal to be acquired. Today rooms are sometimes made smaller to accommodate the prized little strip of garden around a home.[6] Furthermore, because the British price housing based on the number of rooms, rather than the total floor space, a little extra profit can always be made by making rooms in a new property just a fraction smaller. Yet people are getting both fatter and taller, and most of us have much more stuff, at least much more than our parents had. We are also getting better at looking at the total floor-space figure on the floor plans we are considering and not being distracted by the glossy photographs taken with special camera lenses that could make the inside of a goldfish tank appear palatial. While the number of rooms in existence has been increasing in recent years, the amount of floor space and total housing volume has not been keeping pace.

The 2011 census in the UK was the first to count bedrooms; previous

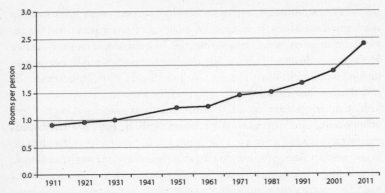

Figure 13. Rooms per person in housing in Britain: census count turned into a ratio, 1911–2011.

censuses did not make separate bedroom counts. Bedrooms were defined as any room intended for use as a bedroom when the property was built, whatever its current use, and any room that had been permanently converted for use as a bedroom, including any room constituting a bedsit. A house with a playroom and a study could easily become a house with two more bedrooms, should the need arise, but they are not counted as bedrooms in the census. Nevertheless it is instructive to look at, how many rooms we use today as bedrooms in Britain.

The 2011 census tells us that there are some 66 million bedrooms in England and Wales for around 55 million people.[7] Just over 21 million people in England and Wales are married or in a civil partnership, and presumably often share a bedroom. So, even if no one else was sharing a bedroom, even if there were no bunk-beds and no cohabiting couples, of these 66 million bedrooms, at least a third (22 million) are empty on any given night. This estimate of empty rooms of course doesn't take into account those rooms that could be bedrooms, but that are not defined as such because they are put to other uses. The vast majority of these empty bedrooms are found in the private sector, mostly in homes owned outright, or in property on which people are currently paying a mortgage that has nearly been redeemed.

The census allows us to know how many bedrooms are empty in each small area, within each tenure group. For example in owned-outright property in Batemoor, Sheffield, we could find out how many spare bedrooms there are and compare those with how many spare bedrooms there are in council houses. But, for all the census's detail, it is the simplest truths on housing that are the most important. Notably, the nearer housing allocation gets to a pure market, the less efficiently rooms are allocated among families and the households they constitute.

In 2011, in Wales, the average number of rooms per household rose to 5.7; and the number of bedrooms, counted for the first time, was found to be 2.8. The census counted, for the 3 million people in Wales, some 7.4 million rooms and 3.5 million bedrooms – or 2.5 rooms per person and 1.2 bedrooms each. If no one shared a bedroom in Wales, that still left at least half a million spare;[8] in fact, given that so many couples do sleep together in the same bed, let alone bedroom, at night, the number of spare empty Welsh bedrooms is probably significantly higher. In England the averages were only a little lower, at 5.4 rooms and 2.7 bedrooms per household. That translated into some 2.4 rooms per person based on a recorded population of 52 million household residents in England having (if evenly spread) 1.2 bedrooms each, with over 11 million spare bedrooms if no one shared a bedroom and probably, in reality, significantly more spare at any one time. In England, in 2011, there were 126 million rooms, of which 63 million were bedrooms for a population of 52 million residents.[9]

Even in London – just in residential housing, where the average household had access to 4.7 rooms and 2.5 bedrooms – there were 1.9 rooms per person and 1.01 bedrooms each, which is to say some 92,000 more bedrooms than people. All these figures are publicly available from the online census records, for every town, city, district and village in the country. The number of rooms and bedrooms per person in Britain has not just been rising, but that rise – as the graph above shows – has recently accelerated. So why do the British have a housing crisis? Why are rents and prices skyrocketing in London? What is going on?

The answer is that, since the census of 1981, the distribution of both housing space and rooms has been becoming progressively more unequal.[10] Since that date, a higher percentage of the extra rooms in houses and flats in Britain has been annexed by families or individuals who already had the most extra rooms to begin with. A family with three or four bedrooms appeared to be more likely to add an extra room to their property than did a family in a smaller home.[11] What is more, smaller households were moving into larger properties; and households that became smaller after their children flew the nest were more likely to stay put in those properties.

Professor Rebecca Tunstall has done more work on the growing mismatch between people and rooms, and the rising inequalities in housing that result, than any other housing expert. Her analysis shows that the last increase in the unequal distribution of rooms in Britain occurred almost a century ago, between the censuses of 1911 and 1921 in Britain. At that point the best-off tenth of households had access to four times as many rooms per person, in comparison with the worst-off tenth. After 1921 this inequality fell constantly over the next sixty years, until the census of 1981, which recorded the greatest-ever level of housing equality. Then, the best-off tenth still had access to three times as many rooms each, in comparison with the worst-off tenth, but housing had never been as equally distributed since censuses first recorded numbers of rooms as well as people.

Professor Tunstall has gone further, suggesting a cause for the trend she has revealed. She noted that the distribution of rooms corresponded very closely with the fall and rise in income inequalities. As the economic gaps between the poorest and richest families in Britain narrowed from 1921 to just before the 1981 census, families in Britain were able to house themselves more and more equitably with each decade that passed. It was not just that more houses were built. The trend occurred even as several waves of immigration resulted in many poorer families turning up at the bottom end of the housing spectrum. What happened was that the new housing that was built was shared out better in each succeeding decade until 1981. Year after year we became better housed – but then, in the early 1980s, everything changed.

At that point, something altered about how money was shared out in Britain and, from then until now, we have become an increasingly

This image is of a former playground at the Park Hill Estate and shows the part of the building yet to be redeveloped. The Park Hill Flats appear in the opening scenes of the film *The Full Monty*. They rise above Sheffield City train station and are now Grade II listed. Most are empty, awaiting redevelopment. The walkways between the flats were built wide enough for a milk float to be driven along them, but now the rooms are viewed as too small. Part of the redevelopment consists of building out into that walkway, to make the rooms just a little larger. But then there is storage space to think of. The lifts may still be large enough to take a milk float up to the top floor, but where do you store whatever you lift up to your small castle in the sky? These flats were built for families. Today the enlarged version of them is being marketed to single people and young couples. What we think of as a decent amount of space increases over time. However, it could come to decrease too, for instance, if these flats were found in the heart of London, and not in Sheffield.

unequal society. There were housing-specific factors, such as the 1980 'right-to-buy' scheme that allowed formerly more efficiently used council housing to be sold at greatly discounted prices to council tenants. Before privatization, if a family left the house it usually became home to the next not-too-well-off (and not that small) family. However, after privatization, the new owners of an ex-council house tended to underoccupy or to resell to even smaller households. The gentrification of former council housing has been widely reported and is partly responsible for the current shortage of accessible housing to many families.

However, the introduction of 'right-to-buy' cannot be said to be the trigger for the increasing inefficiency in our use of housing in Britain; Professor Tunstall measured only a gradual increase between 1981 and 1991. The increase was fastest twenty years later, between 2001 and 2011, when there were the fewest spacious council homes remaining to be privatized. It was not the housing policy that was at fault, but rather the new income distribution that had been created. Income inequalities rose quickly after 1979, reducing flexibility, and rising wealth inequalities followed that upward trend around a decade later, growing from around 1989. Wealth-inequality trends always lag behind income trends.[12]

The table below shows the percentage share of the total sum of money received annually by the richest elements of society in the UK: the very, very, very richest (0.01%); the very, very richest (0.1%); the very richest (1%); and the richest (10%) during the course of the last century.[13] If you want a single underlying explanation of why Britain now has a housing crisis, you need look no further than this table. If income were to be evenly distributed among the population under a situation of complete equality, 0.01% of the population would always get only 0.01% of the income. As it is, by 2009, that best-off fraction of the population was receiving 122 times that amount, a huge proportion and one that they last exceeded over seventy years ago.

What is key is how the percentages of income accruing to the people in these richest percentiles fall over time, until 1981, and then rise again. That trend in growing equality between 1921 and 1981 fol-

Table 1. Share of national income of the best-off fractions in the UK, 1911–2009 (%).

% of all	0.01%	0.10%	1%	10%
1911	4.19	11.1	24.4	47.0
1921	2.90	8.1	20.3	42.0
1931	2.44	7.2	18.3	38.0
1941	1.57	5.0	13.1	35.0
1951	0.85	3.2	10.9	33.0
1961	0.60	2.4	8.6	30.0
1971	0.40	1.7	7.0	29.0
1981	0.36	1.5	6.7	31.0
1991	0.73	3.1	10.3	38.0
2001	1.08	4.5	12.7	39.0
2009	1.22	5.1	13.9	40.0

lows and perhaps helped to influence many other similarly timed trends. For example, it was when we became most equal in income – in the now much maligned 1970s – that we began to care most for the homeless; and it is in the present-day, when we have again become much more unequal in income, that we again find homelessness rising.

Late in 2013 Professor Tunstall updated her figures: she incorporated 2011 census results for the first time. What she found almost perfectly mirrored the rise in income inequality shown in the table of income inequalities above. In 1981 the best-off tenth of households had 3 times as many rooms in their homes, in comparison with the worst-off tenth, rising to about 3.7 times as many by 2001. By 2011 that housing-inequality ratio had risen, at a more rapid rate than *ever* before, to more than 5 times as many rooms per person in the home of each housing-rich person, in comparison with the worst-off tenth. This was now a higher ratio of housing inequality than any that had been measured at any point since at least 1901.[14]

What had New Labour done to accelerate housing inequality so greatly between 2001 and 2011, before the current coalition government had had a chance to increase it even further? It could have been that the trajectory was already in place and the growing inequality was not simply the fault of that government, but New Labour did little to slow its growth.

Two issues should now be looked at as possibly more important than was first thought. First, the introduction of the Local Housing Allowance has meant that housing benefit from 2009 onwards was not paid on the full rent if any bedrooms were deemed spare for a private sector renting family.[15] So this was, in effect, a private renter's Bedroom Tax. Families in privately rented accommodation, therefore, did not move to even slightly larger accommodation, even if that accommodation was cheaper or on offer at the same rent, because their benefits would be docked if they did.

Secondly, it is worth considering the impact of the vast number of one- and two-bed urban flats that were built by developers during this period. There was probably never really the demand for all of them, given their small size, but families who really wanted or needed a three-bed place were buying or renting these smaller flats, as that was all they could afford on the private rental market. Now that we have seen the rising inequality figures, we have some idea of how much of an effect this might have had.[16] The flats were originally aimed at affluent individuals, or especially affluent students, but were not all easily filled. The 2011 census results suggest that they often came to be filled by squeezing in poorer families.

It is, ultimately, the 2011 census that shows us that we cannot build our way out of the disaster of our current housing system. We first have to deal with growing inequality, with how to better share out and look after what we have already got.

A terraced house during refurbishment held under private ownership in Nether Edge, Sheffield. Housing at many levels is simple. You need rooms: they need to be insulated. You need light: it is better if the window is double-glazed. You need heating: radiators are now nearly ubiquitous, but there is a wide variety of ways in which the water in them can be heated. We used to count how many homes lacked hot running water, or an inside toilet, or had no central heating, but we have now got most of those necessities in almost all of our homes. What we most often lack today is space, but only because it has become normal to have a little more space than in the past. You notice the noise from next door more too. In many ways we have never been better housed than today. We have never had better access to toilets and the means to wash within our homes, not just ourselves but also our clothes. We have never had better-heated homes, although more of us are finding it harder to pay to heat them. We have never had as well insulated and roofed homes, never had as little damp as we have today, nor as much electric light; and yet we have also never had as much to validly complain about how expensively we are housed as we have today.

HOUSING FINANCE

Property taxes have become the UK's latest battleground over who should pay – and how much – as the country faces a record budget deficit and the government's austerity programme is forcing cuts in social programs such as disability benefits and aid to families with children. In London in particular, where affluent foreign buyers have kept home prices rising even in the face of the country's first double-dip recession since the 1970s, limits on council taxes have left many lower- and middle-income renters and homeowners paying almost as much as the wealthy, and sometimes more.

– *Bloomberg News*, 25 October, 2012[17]

The news programme on Bloomberg, the US business TV channel begun by the man who became New York Mayor, Michael R. Bloomberg, reported with shock that even the Sultan of Brunei had applied for a 10% discount on his council tax and so saves about £200 a year because the home he owns in London, on 'billionaires' row, is his second or third (or thirty-third) home. Often the very rich object to taxes in principle, and object so strongly that they will apply to be let off an amount that they would never notice. Perhaps it is just so it can be noticed that they have done this? Perhaps they think they pay too much tax overall?

Housing and taxation have a long and vexed history. There are groups, like the US Tea Party, which believe with semi-religious fervour that property is in some way sacred and taxing it is a sin.[18] The UK's current system of local taxation, the council tax, was introduced two decades ago, in 1993, after a widespread series of riots against its predecessor, the Poll Tax, which was a fixed amount to be paid by every adult. The council tax is largely based on property, not people: the greater the value of your house, the more you pay, but only up to a maximum limit. If your house is very valuable, then – however great the value – you pay nothing above the cap, a special concession to the very rich.

The council tax on a property worth £1 million or £10 million is identical. Furthermore, the tax on a property worth £320,000 when it was valued in 1991 is not four times greater than the tax on an £80,000 property; but is only twice as much. You pay proportionately more council tax the lower your tax band. It is simply an unfair tax. Proportionately the council tax is a higher proportion of your wealth per year the less wealth that you have.

Recently changes have been made to the UK council tax to make it even more disproportional, thus taking even more from the very poor. These changes have been dubbed the 'Eric Pickles's Poll Tax', after the Minister for Communities and Local Government, who introduced them. Before the changes were introduced, very low-paid workers were exempt from paying any council tax because this was a sum they simply could not afford to pay. But, as a result of Eric Pickles making that rebate discretionary since April 2013, local councils, under government pressure not to raise anyone else's council tax bill, can now charge some of the poorest households in England, though poorer pensioners remain exempt. The scheme is expected to save the Treasury £500 million a year, and about two million low-income families will be affected.[19] The legal situation is gradually becoming like a return to the Poor Laws, with local worthies listening to your case and deciding your fate at a whim.

In late autumn 2012 a report on these council tax increases for the poorest, carried out for the Conservative London borough council that controls the City of Westminster, explained that 'The size of these amounts in respect of council tax would in many cases be uneconomic to recover, with the costs of collection, including legal recovery costs which fall to the council being higher than the bill, and would in all likelihood have to be written off when the debt is uncollectible.'[20] In other words, local councillors in Pickles's own party believe that the current situation has been made worse by the arrangements that he introduced. This rise in bills will be piled on top of the new Bedroom Tax discussed earlier.

At exactly the same time that the British government was trying to force people in social housing to move if they had one or more 'spare' bedrooms, it also began to do all it could to help the wealthy own housing with as many spare bedrooms as possible. In February

2013 the government announced plans to limit the costs of long-term public or private care in old age to £75,000, in order to protect wealthy individuals' wealth, mostly their housing wealth. The state will pay for their care costs in a residential home, and their property can remain empty at no cost to the individual – including exemption from council tax – until they die, provided that they can still pay the accommodation costs of around £10,000 a year.

The £75,000 spending cap was proposed as an improvement on the present situation, whereby you don't have to sell your home if a relative over sixty (or under if disabled), or your spouse or partner, still lives in your home. The new system also includes a home-care package, but only if your needs are classed as severe or substantial.[21] The potential financial benefits of the proposed changes are revealing. If, for example, your assets, after paying all accommodation costs, are £100,000, it is possible that care costs will take 75% of that, but if you are worth £200,000 they will take only 37.5% of the total – and progressively less the more you have. You may be able to avoid some of these costs altogether by taking out insurance with a private company. The push for this comes, therefore, from owners of more expensive property, from the private companies that will profit from providing the insurance, and from the private companies that will profit from providing the care.

Private companies specializing in risk tend to be owned by very wealthy individuals who aim to profit from our ignorance about what for us are possibly one-off events, such as being too ill to carry on living as we are. The amount you might lose is fixed by government to make it possible for insurance companies to offer attractive-looking policies that are a safe bet for them, because they know the real risks involved. Essentially these are policies that look reasonable to many very low-risk people. If your politics are on the left you might call this a scam; on the right and you could say it allowed 'entrepreneurial zeal'. But hopefully you can see that the situation is both complex and confusing, and hence ripe for profit.

The mixing up of housing with insurance and inheritance, coupled with rising income inequality, has become socially toxic. People hold on to housing they do not need to live in because they want to retain assets to hand on to their children in a world that is clearly becoming more precarious – a world in which it looks more and more as if you need to look out just for yourself and for those you directly care about, ultimately at the expense of others.

It would be better if fair property taxes were paid by the living, before inheritance tax kicks in at death, so that not so much wealth is hoarded, but often the living work hard to avoid tax. Some of the living work so hard, and are so opposed to sharing what they see as their personal wealth, that they will behave in ways that are criminal. Many otherwise law-abiding folk will be prepared to commit fraud to try to avoid taxes, especially on inherited property.

At the lower end of the spectrum of property and inheritance fraud sit the borrowers who are found not to actually exist, or at least not to exist as described to the lender. Below this are numerous smaller frauds, and it is these that the press tends to concentrate on, such as housing benefit scams. At the very lowest level of housing fraud is someone begging for money for a bed for the night or just for a cup of tea, only to use the money they are given to buy a can of beer. However, if I were on the streets, I would ask for money for 'a cup of tea' too, but I'd look for something a little stronger to buy with that money to help me forget my situation.

Higher up the spectrum is claiming housing benefit on your privately rented flat when your real income is higher than declared. Above that is illegally subletting your council home. Above that comes avoiding capital gains tax, say, switching the ownership of a property with a relative. Above that comes using companies and non-dom status to avoid tax. At the very highest end of the housing-fraud spectrum are multibillion-dollar businesses that make very small adjustments to rates that influence trillions of pounds' worth of mortgages.

By summer 2012 it had become evident that the top banks themselves were illegally manipulating the reported average inter-bank lending rate, or Libor, and that at least transactions worth $500 trillion had been adversely affected according to the British regulators.[22] This fraud was committed by bankers based in London. What they have done may not have been strictly housing fraud, but the rates they were illegally influencing affected money principally invested in housing.

A formerly homeless girl takes down the phone number of her new key worker in Sheffield. We rarely connect the growing number of young people living on Britain's streets, or those being housed in hostels and living in squats, with current economic and finance policy. We don't see the connections with an increase in the number of elderly people trying as hard as they can to hang on in there, living in the old family property, rattling around in it and not going into a care home or just into a smaller flat, so that they can maximize the inheritance for their children. However, as they and millions of other older people stay in homes built for larger families, many other people's children cannot settle down as young adults with someone they meet because there are no homes they can afford to rent as a result of the shortage created by the elderly. The elderly, in the main, are not living with so much space because they want to, but because they want to benefit the generation that will come after them. Underlying all this is the far murkier manipulation of finance and housing markets. Manipulating interest rates makes it more expensive to borrow, so inheritances become more vital. Seeing the links all the way down the chain – from the man who fixed the Libor rate yesterday to the girl who has no home today – is far from simple; which is why they have got away with it for so long, and why they will continue to do so until we all become less pliant.

Whether it's £20 of unwarranted housing benefit claimed, £2,000 cash-in-hand to a builder or a £200,000 bonus secured because your Libor guesses were correct (after having manipulated them with your mates), it is still fraud. It is, however, fraud that increases by several orders of magnitude as you move up the spectrum. It would take millions of acts of homeless people all uttering the same lie to equate to a single lie of a single banker awarded a bonus. In the end some of the monies fraudulently raised might be spent on the same thing although in different form: cocaine in the boardrooms, Special Brew on the streets. In this way we are all the same, but when it comes to housing there are barriers between us that are often simply insurmountable.

The homeless are not equal. Just giving everyone the opportunity to be housed, saying that they have the right, should they work hard enough, does not mean that we really are equal in opportunity. If you are not well housed you cannot easily present yourself as available for work. You look a mess. You smell. This is an equality of opportunity that, in the words of Jeremy Waldron, Professor of Law, Jurisprudence and Social Policy (in a landmark paper published in 1991), said was an equality that had no realistic prospect of ever happening.[23] Similarly, if you have to live in the poorest part of town, you are not equally able to compete for work, for education, for a chance.

What is reducing the chances of the homeless, and the badly housed, most is not government's failure to ensure that houses are built, but rather other people's over-consumption of housing. 'Second' homes should be part of the homelessness debate. Empty rooms are not alone in being responsible for others having less access to housing. The more homes that are used as spare homes, the fewer first homes there will be, and the less space there will be for others.

Space, however, is not the only issue. Skyscrapers use up very little ground space, but they too potentially increase homelessness, because the resources used up in building them could be put to better use. It is far more expensive to build a skyscraper than it is to construct the equivalent floor space of normal offices or apartments. So second homes, empty and under-occupied property and skyscrapers are all part of the present housing and building waste. There has never been so much scope to house ourselves both far better and far cheaper than we currently do.

View over Brook Hill in Sheffield, showing social housing at the front and smaller private apartments to the right. In the distance, on a former slag heap, a ski-slope has been built, but it is not a great success. When it comes to skiing, Sheffield is about as far from Davos as it is possible to get. The key decisions that affect how people are housed in Sheffield are now made nowhere near that city. Most of the people who get to influence housing policy do not live in the kinds of housing that their decisions influence each day. Housing ministers and commentators, chief executives of housing organizations and the main financiers of housing, as well as those designing new housing benefit rules, tend to live in very expensive properties. Can you imagine having education policy designed by people who do not use state education for their children and have not gone through it themselves? Or try to imagine the National Health Service being run well by people who do not rely on it, people who know that if they are ill they can afford the most expensive of private treatments that almost no one else can buy. All these basic services become badly managed when run and discussed by people with little knowledge of them and with no personal stake in those services working well.

Early in 2013 the then UK Planning Minister, Nick Boles, and the Chairman of the National Trust, Simon Jenkins, debated housing on national TV.[24] Jenkins suggested that the housing crisis could be solved by building more high-rise flats in cities. Boles retorted that he had been to at least two of Jenkins's homes, and that anyone who had access to more than one home was in no position to tell others that they should live without a garden. The next day Boles gave a speech at the offices of the right-wing think tank Policy Exchange, in which he claimed that the only way forward on housing, for Conservatives, was to deregulate building on green land. The National Trust is a conservation body, so it is little wonder that Jenkins was angry about what Boles was suggesting. The Conservative political party used to believe in conservation, but as it has moved further and further towards free-market ideology, obstacles to making a profit, such as preserving green belts, have come under threat. This creates tension within Conservative circles, as green belts also protect the high property prices of the richer people who tend to live within the belts or have views out towards them. Often what is being protected are the values of second homes – country retreats.

The acquisition of second homes is positively encouraged by the UK taxation system. Second homes often attract a council tax discount of up to 50%, depending on the policy of the local council.[25] By contrast, as we have seen, council tax bills for the very poor are soon set to rise. We are currently finding out more and more of what the coalition government really desires for Britain; but only in dribs and drabs, as journalists and housing analysts with a personal interest discover what UK, or at least English, housing policy really is. It has been disguised because clearly a majority of potential voters do not benefit from it.

The housing policy that emerged during 2013 encouraged a further free-for-all – a kind of survival-of-the-fittest future for housing, in which a few property-owners, including landlords, will become even richer, but most people will end up paying even more for the privilege of buying in the long run, while thinking they are enjoying low interest rates in the short term. The legislation put in place by the current government to deregulate the planning process, to guarantee more bank lending and to penalize poorer households was not even hinted at in any political party's manifesto, nor in the May 2010 coalition agreement document.

Outside of England there are already plans under way to reverse policies that have been brought in without voters getting to have a say. In Scotland, it was announced in autumn 2013 that the Bedroom Tax would be scrapped.[26] These plans were bolstered by the finding that some 50,000 people faced eviction because of the tax, and that hundreds of thousands more were falling into arrears, especially in low-income areas of Scotland.[27] Earlier – as if the fallout from the Bedroom Tax being implemented were not enough – in January 2013, it was revealed by analysts working for the Resolution Foundation think tank that the discretionary council tax rebate referred to above, the one dubbed 'Eric Pickles's Poll Tax', was very unlikely to be given to those in need, as local councils faced such great cuts in other parts of their budgets.

In September 2013 it was said that the government's 'decision to reduce the budget for council tax support by 10% means low-income households face a tax increase of up to £600' a year.[28] Numerous cuts started to kick in during 2013. The example the Resolution Foundation gave was that a single parent who is in employment could see their annual council tax bill rise by over £10 a week after April 2013. Subsequently, if their employment is low paid – and most single parents who work are not well paid – it may be nearly impossible to find that additional £600 a year. Enforced payment of this money, said Westminster Council (referred to above), would be uneconomical. Hopefully Westminster won't even ask for it, but legally they are entitled to try, and other councils appear to be trying. By September 2013 one in three council tenants was already in arrears on their rent, a far higher number than ever recorded before, and rising, because of all these cuts and charges.[29]

Meanwhile, at the luxury end of the housing market, a boom is currently under way in the UK, mimicking trends seen first on the other side of the Atlantic. The largest US luxury home and luxury second-home builder, Toll Brothers, a company that focuses on affluent customers who typically make at least $100,000 a year and (it claims) who have spotless credit records, reported a great increase in orders and forecast higher revenue for the years to come. You often see adverts for this company on the internet, and they are not doing badly: 'We are enjoying the most sustained demand we have experienced in over five years,' Toll's Chief Executive, Douglas C. Yearley Jr, said, when interviewed in 2012.[30]

Douglas C. Yearley Junior's salary in 2011 had been $1 million, plus a further $4.5 million of stock awards, options and other forms of 'compensation', according to company records.[31] Such immensely high salaries and a boom in luxury building, coupled with the continued immiserization of the poorest in society, tend to come before a fall. Financial analysts are increasingly on the lookout for falls, and when the amount of what is called 'quantitative easing' – the printing of virtual money in London and New York – slows, a fall might very well be on the cards.

In the US, the Federal Reserve decided to carry on with its ploy of quantitative easing through to at least winter 2013 because of such fears.[32] What is unpredictable is how the housing market will polarize before the next fall. If a fall is prolonged, it is called a slump. But how can we tell if a slump is coming or is already upon us? One way is to look up into the sky. Slumps, over the course of the last century,

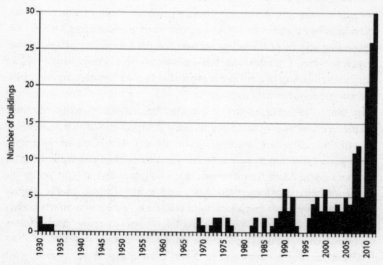

Figure 14. Number of buildings over 256 metres high built per year, worldwide, 1930–2012.

have tended to be accompanied by the concrete results of massive over-exuberance. One form of over-exuberance is the construction of very tall buildings.

Very tall skyscrapers are a good measure of excess: objects we build not necessarily when we need them, but when we are feeling flush enough to afford them. It turns out that, worldwide, as many very tall buildings have been erected in the last three years, 2010 to 2012, as in the previous eighteen. In those twenty-one years combined some 152 buildings over 256 metres tall were built around the globe. Two built earlier were destroyed on 11 September 2001 and are not included in the graph above. The idea to draw this graph came from having recently seen one like it that detailed all new buildings in New York over 70 metres high.

New York's peak building period came not in 2012 but in the early 1930s, just after the 1929 economic crash. A copy of that New York diagram is shown below. It illustrates how, after the excesses of 1930s building – financed and planned for often long before 1929 – came a long period of building calm in New York. A period of calm could be returning again to the United States, but it will depend on legislation, not just economics. As of 2013 house prices in New York are still not moving. They remain just 3.3% above their 2006 average levels. By December 2013, on the other side of America, housing prices in Los Angeles were described as having stayed flat since June.[33] That summer's rumours of a property revival in the US appeared overblown just six months later.[34]

In the 1950s and 1960s, when the US economy was booming, people were sensible and limited the construction of tall buildings. Back then such edifices were still remembered as symbols of the excessive 1920s exuberance. Planners knew skyscrapers were needed not to turn an honest profit, but to impress the suggestible. Later, as potential investors began to forget the past, and in the run-up to the 1970s recession, Americans began to build tall again, with most 1970s buildings reaching their maximum height a few years after the peak of that economic slump. The graph below makes all this very clear.

The same thing happened in New York again in the 1980s, and again in the noughties. Perhaps the current worldwide bubble of high-rise building is an echo of this New York phenomenon. By 2012,

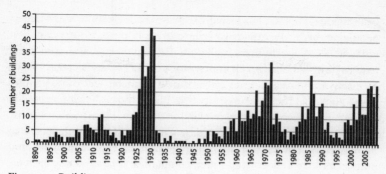

Figure 15. Buildings over 70 metres tall constructed in New York, 1890–2009, by year.

in London, the cranes used to construct tall buildings were more often being taken down than put up. Figures were released in January 2013, after a helicopter crashed into a construction crane working on high-rise near Vauxhall tube station. These revealed that, even as the property boom in the capital continued, at least in terms of apparently rising home values, the number of cranes on London's skyline fell, from 712 in the first half of 2011 to 413 by the first half of 2012.[35]

Cranes finally begin to come down on London's skyline when the building of the showiest commercial and residential property itself begins to slow down. By spring 2013 it was also revealed that, in the light of fewer bonuses, bankers and very wealthy overseas investors were buying and refurbishing a little less residential property in central London than they had been the year before. Then, in August 2013, average prices dropped by over 7% in Westminster, 5% in Camden, 4% in Brent, and 3.5%, and 3% in, respectively, Kensington & Chelsea and Greenwich;[36] while over in Greenwich Village, New York, and in much of the rest of America, prices had not even recovered sufficiently to fall so much again. By 2013, according to one US property speculator, they remained '22% below the 48-year "trend line" [established] between 1951 and 1999'.[37]

It is not just within more provincial towns and cities that power appears to be lacking. Many decisions that affect London and New York are no longer made anywhere near those two cities, at least not by individual families. Increasingly they are made by some of the richest people on earth, who are driving the current boom in housing, at least in those places where there is a boom. (Where there is no boom, there tend to be no super-rich.) Of course some of the key decisions are made precisely in the twin centres of the world financial economy, London and New York. The private equity firm Blackstone is headquartered in Park Avenue, New York; and its London offices are in Berkeley Square. But when a firm like Blackstone starts to buy up homes that used to be bought by families, ordinary people need to begin worrying, and need to look at who is behind such companies. Whose money are they investing?[38]

The clue as to where private equity firms get their cash from is in the words 'private equity'. It is the private money of the extremely rich. So now we need to look at some of the richest people on the planet. It is their behaviour that is currently leading us most forcefully in the direction of what could be a widespread slump.

SUPER-RICH

For the cost of a small family house in Fulham, you could buy a street in Sunderland. For the amount some of the world's wealthiest people are willing to pay to own a home in Kensington, they could also buy a small town if they looked hard enough. London's property prices have gone mad. But it is an insanity which is likely to take its toll on the rest of us.

– Anthony Hilton, business and finance journalist, 2013[39]

Anyone who knows anything about the UK and housing knows that the influx of increasing numbers of international, super-rich individuals into the heart of London is what has driven the continued property boom there, with a substantial ripple effect, convincing more local buyers that property within the M25 is worth as much as they have paid for it. When a home in the centre of London appears to be worth many millions of pounds, it can appear plausible for your home on the edge of London to be valued at many hundreds of thousands of pounds.

The map below shows where prime central London property is to be found, and also who has been finding it. House prices in these areas were reported to have risen by over a third since the 'low point' of March 2009, so that by spring 2012 they were 12% higher than they had been at the height of the previous boom.[40] In the first seven months of 2013 alone they rose another 6%, but in August, as reported above, the first falls were announced. Within days evidence was also published of prices falling in some of the poorer boroughs, partly because council tax is higher the poorer the area![41] However, these falls were ignored by the British press, which, in autumn 2013, preferred to concentrate on hearsay stories that the rich were still flooding in.[42] All it takes to sustain a bubble is over-confidence and hearsay. The more any small falls in housing prices are ignored, the greater the eventual large fall will be.

London prices appeared to be rising up to Christmas 2013, although not in the least and most expensive parts of the capital. Insecurity elsewhere in Europe, especially in Greece and Cyprus, continued to fuel the influx of wealthy foreigners into London and prevented more price falls. The recent rise in prices had been instigated by Russian oligarchs, who in turn were followed by Chinese factory-owners. Next came tax exiles from mainland Europe. But before the Russians there had been others. There have been elite French and other non-English-language schools in London for many years, because for decades much of Europe's elite preferred London to 'home'. So the current boom is built upon a recent history of London as a sanctuary for the super-rich.

The super-rich have had the most effect on London's boom, but are too few in number to be its sole cause. Beneath them the not-quite-so-rich have also been contributing. What the super-rich change the most is the everyday thinking of those just below them, who ape their behaviour in slightly more modest ways. This mind-set cascades down to otherwise normally sensible people, who in turn behave in ways that are simply not rational when looked at with detached eyes.

Take posh sheds – not in prime gardens in Slough, but in prime seaside resorts on the English south coast, remembering that this coast

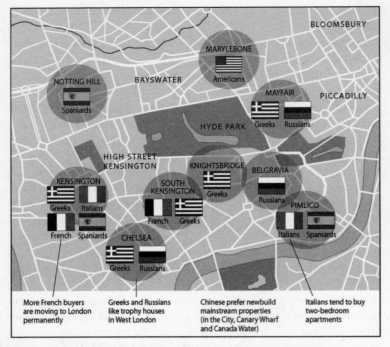

Figure 16. Prime central London property locations and national preferences, 2012.

hardly ever has Mediterranean temperatures or beautiful mountainous vistas. In Britain these sheds by the sea are called beach huts. How much do you think the most pricey beach hut sells for? The answer is more than a sixth of a million pounds, for a one-room building you cannot (by law) sleep in! You may think you need to look to the super-rich to know who is buying beach huts for £170,000, but it is not them. The market is fuelled by people who have made a lot of money, who mimic the buying patterns of billionaires, but by buying huts, not mansions.

A little group of people with more money than sense can now be found in every small town in the south of England, and in many larger towns in the north. Take one particular genuine beach hut, the one that famously sold for £170,000, which is a thirty-minute walk from the nearest road: it turns out that 'It has been bought by a wealthy family from Christchurch, whose children are now grown up.'[43] Christchurch is no Monte Carlo. Such buying patterns, and the oft-repeated stories about them, cause many slightly less opulent people to think that the extremely wealthy, as well as the super-rich, might have a lot more money than they need.

Some time ago that descendant of minor Russian aristocracy, Nick Clegg, suggested a 'mansion tax', a new asset tax on homes worth over £1 million. Others quickly pointed out that there was no need for a new tax to achieve extra revenue generation; adapting the existing council tax bands could work better. Currently each residential property in Britain is taxed according to which of eight price bands, 'A' to 'H', it fell into when valued in 1991. Many new bands might easily be created above band 'H'. In 2005 the National Assembly for Wales added an extra band, band 'I', on property worth over £424,000, but that applies only in Wales. The Deputy Prime Minister could have suggested adding bands 'J' to 'O' to get up to £1 million.[44] However, Clegg wanted a simple newspaper headline.

There is a problem with copying the Welsh and adding extra bands, each £100,000 more than the last. Long before you hit the top property prices you quickly run out of bands if you do this in England. However, there is an alternative. If each council tax band above 'H' (£320,000) were to be doubled – so that band 'I' applied to property worth more than £640,000; 'J' to that valued at over £1,280,000, and so on – homes worth more than £40 million would then fall into band 'O'. In a truly progressive society the associated council tax would double with each successive band above 'H'. A mansion tax is not a bad idea – but it is far better to implement it like this, in increments, so that those with property worth £5 million know they are paying less, proportionately, than the few who own (or are renting) homes valued over £20 million.[45] English society is still a continuum, not just an 'us and them' division. Property taxation needs to be fair and progressive right up to the very top of that continuum. No doubt the odd 'asset rich but income poor' occupant of a $40 million home would be wheeled out to try to illustrate how unfair such a tax would be, but they surely could take in a lodger? Remarkably, no government in England since 1991 has dared to have the bands reassessed, so anyone who has benefited from over-average property price rises has, as yet, paid no extra tax.

Alternatively (or additionally), if Nick Clegg wants a new asset tax, he should look back at the good old Liberal idea of a land value tax. This would be a tax on all land on the basis of what it would fetch in the market, not just on homes on the basis of the price at which they last sold. A land value tax has a particular beauty in that if a land-owner claims his or her land is worth less than its estimate for tax purposes, the government can always offer to buy the land at that price; they can call his or her bluff.

The vast majority of people in Britain would see their council tax bills drop if they were replaced by a land value tax. Few people own very large gardens, let alone grouse moors or office blocks. The land value tax would also revolutionize commercial property taxation. In one step, the nature of our relationship with land, property and hous-ing would change. This may well still be a step too far for the whole of the UK, but it is being considered in neighbouring Ireland as I write, and could be very popular in Scotland, as well as in the north of England, in Wales, and among young adults in the south of Eng-land. In fact, the group who might benefit from opposing such a tax is relatively small; but that small group does have most of our money and land.

If Nick Clegg really wants to look at the possible beneficial effects of progressive taxation, including land taxation, what he needs to do is to look away from his coalition partners, and well away from their disdain for the less well-off. He should turn instead to some of his favourite places, many of the more prosperous countries of Europe. These countries have less income inequality than the UK, and their inhabitants live longer lives, suffer less crime and respect each other more than do the British. One aspect of that degree of respect has been measured in surveys asking how much you might trust a stranger;[46] but mutual respect is also evident in their choice of polit-ical parties. For example, it is still common to have socialist parties on the Continent, and there are far more successful green parties there than in the UK.

In France, following the socialist election victory of June 2012, the very richest people are now set to pay as tax 75% of the annual income they receive above the first £810,000. This represents excess and unneeded monies being diverted to other French citizens with less to spare. But in Britain it would be characterized as a punishment for 'wealth creation'. In Sweden those earning above £200,000 a year pay almost 57% tax on their additional income over that threshold. In Britain it would be suggested that this will hinder the Swedes in the 'global race'. In Denmark the higher tax rate kicks in at an even lower salary point, at the rate of 55% for all income over the first £46,000 a year. This keeps housing prices down in Copenhagen. In Britain the rich would much rather pay less tax and see everyone else pay more in rent or mortgages in order to be housed.

It is not just better asset taxation, council tax and land taxes that could help to keep down housing prices in future. The best-off being taxed more on their surplus incomes – income they simply do not need in order to live well – would keep prices at the top down, as the rich would then have less to spend on housing. Which is better: a multimillionaire buying a home for £2 million, or a multimillionaire paying an extra £1 million in income tax and buying a home costing 'just' £1 million? In the countries where the rich pay more tax, there are usually also more good jobs for ordinary people. 'Wealth creators' may sometimes create jobs, but they are not necessarily the ones you aspire to have.

The rich in Denmark have less to spend, but they live in a country of greater social solidarity as a result. Fewer people need to pay for a car to get to work, because of the better public provision of cycle lanes. In the Netherlands the top rate of tax is 52% on any income received in excess of £46,000 a year. The Dutch are now on average the tallest and most healthy people on earth. In Austria the 50% rate kicks in at incomes over £49,000. Unemployment benefits in Austria are many times higher than those in Britain, and the middle classes in Austria do not fear losing their jobs in the same way as a result. They are freer to take risks and to move between jobs. In Britain to lose your middle-class job without quickly finding another is also to lose your class status, to enter a world you know little about – one that you have learned to fear.

These European countries are far from being socialist utopias. In Denmark, for example, wealth inequalities by one measure[47] remain higher than in the UK – a legacy of a far more unequal past – but those inequalities are currently falling, whereas in Britain they are rising. A large part of the reason why wealth inequalities in Denmark are falling is because income taxes at the top are higher, so the income-rich are left with less after tax. If, therefore, the Danish rich attempt to make additional money out of other people, they get to keep less of it. This ensures a little more salary and bonus restraint at the top.

In Britain the 45% income tax rate does not kick in until incomes exceed £150,000 a year. If you are British, just try explaining how much you get in unemployment benefit (Job Seekers' Allowance), should you lose your job, to an Austrian. It is so little that the Austrians, or the Germans, or the French, or the Belgians, or the Swedes, or the Dutch usually won't believe you. This is because unemployment benefit rates are so much higher in almost all other northern European countries, and good rent controls often not only exist, but are also strictly enforced. There is less need for housing subsidies when low wages are not so dreadfully low and unemployment benefits can be lived on for at least a year, if not two, while searching for another job.

You could argue that lower taxes incentivize people to work harder, as they get to keep more of what they earn; lower taxes also make them less choosy about the employment they do take. But someone could easily counter this by listing all those poorer countries where tax rates are much lower than in Britain, but where the elderly live in abject poverty and much of life is still nasty, brutish and short. It's a simple political choice: embark on a race to the bottom; or tax the rich heavily and avoid widespread poverty as a result. The choice becomes more obvious when the need to reduce our overall consumption levels is also considered – not just to reduce pollution but also so that we are able to live better, less materially driven lives in the future. An unwillingness to address these deeper issues is a large part of what sustains our current housing crisis.

Since the election victory of 2010, Clegg and his Conservative allies have kept on looking for solutions to the housing crisis that would also allow the rich to stay very rich. Clegg's next suggestion was that parents should be allowed to dip into their pension pots to provide their offspring with the down payment on a property. It did not take long for people to point out that this would raise housing prices even further, while creating more potentially impoverished pensioners.

The *Daily Mail* noted how Clegg's plans rapidly began to unravel 'as it became clear that only a small minority of families would be able to take advantage of them. Critics said they were a "gimmick" which would apply only to the well-off, who can afford to risk losing some of the money they have saved to finance their retirement.'[48] When the *Daily Mail* turns against a coalition government doing all it can to try to keep housing prices high, you sense that a fundamental shift in mainstream sentiment may be under way. But this is a shift towards uncertainty and ever more worry, rather than towards a New Jerusalem. So many property-owning/mortgagee voters think they have so much to lose from lower house prices that almost no mainstream politicians are suggesting that it would be good if prices and rents were soon to fall. All they can suggest is that it would be helpful if they were not to rise further.

Other comments on the *Daily Mail* website also helped to explain to Nick Clegg why his idea would not work; and his colleague, Liberal Democrat Simon Hughes, offered some helpful advice too, but in the pages of the *Guardian* (as what he had to say remains anathema to the *Mail*). He pointed out that the average deposit on a home in Britain has now risen to £65,000, while in London it is over £100,000. He said that we had reached the point where it was impossible for most to buy without help from an (often ageing) parent or unspecified 'other benefactor', and that this applied not only to young people but also to the middle aged. And he explained that Britons living in social housing, one fifth of the population, had no chance of ever owning property now, as the door was 'firmly closed on the possibility of future homeownership'.[49] Simon Hughes advocated controlling and reining in the purchase of second homes, but implied that this alone would not be enough to prevent the housing crisis growing deeper and heading further towards disaster.

Something has to give, and the 'unthinkable' is being considered, but, so far, just quietly. During summer 2012 plans were being considered on the right wing of British politics that included the imposition of both capital gains tax and a new annual holding tax (of 2% of the property's value) to be applied to any overseas buyers of English second homes worth £2 million or more. According to the think tank Institute for Public Policy Research, these were 'measures on which the government is currently consulting'.[50] Property consultants began to look for loopholes in the proposed legislation that could apply to 'non-natural persons' whose homes would be used only for 'genuinely commercial activities' rather than for living in.[51] By autumn 2013 the Chancellor had announced that non-doms would be paying capital gains tax on their properties from 2015. On the UK political left, similar thoughts and policies are being bandied about a little less quietly, with the tax including all rich buyers, not just those from overseas. Then, just before Christmas 2013, Ed Miliband promised that Labour would implement a series of more progressive housing policies, should that party gain power in 2015.

What happens if none of these plans is implemented, none comes to any real fruition; or, if they are implemented, loopholes are found? A colleague of mine living in London joked that he and his partner were planning to 'build an electric fence around our house to keep out the riff raff and mansion tax inspectors and keep in our nanny'. 'Good idea,' I said, 'but how are you going to get in food?' I suggested that the Waitrose delivery-van driver would have to be microchipped. 'Eat the poor,' he replied, meaning metaphorically of course, not literally. What I think he really meant was – what else could he do? He had to keep earning as much as he currently earns to keep his head above water in the pool of competition in which he and his partner now find themselves. Any talk of having to pay a mansion tax frightens them. And they are far from right wing.

There are many examples of backsliding on what initially appear to be progressive policy proposals. When the Labour Party version of the mansion tax was finally announced in February 2013 by Ed Miliband, its proposed rate had dropped to 1%. Labour had back-pedalled, I suspect, because too many of their friends, advisers and MPs live in London property valued at well over a million. Despite the reduced proposed levy, London's chattering classes received the news with some dismay. That *Guardian* commentator and multiple-property-owner Simon Jenkins complained: 'By setting the tax at 1%, which is high, Miliband has made sure of a howl of protest from the asset-rich and cash-poor, who will need to find multiples of £5,000 a year for each half million in value above £2 million.'[52] It was interesting, and key to understanding the dilemma we are in, to see that Jenkins thought that

A half-boarded-up home in the Nether Edge suburb of Sheffield. Often it is suggested that any increases in property taxation for the very affluent will lead to some boarding up of homes that they cannot afford to run. However, there are already many large boarded-up properties that are seen as a good investment by their owners because they do not have to pay a high rate of taxation for holding them empty. We need policies that deter vacancy while simultaneously making housing more affordable. Far more progressive taxation is needed to help bring down the supposedly high value of larger homes. We need a devaluation that makes these homes affordable, so that people can live in them as a family or as a large group of young adults. Also, if prices were falling, and not expected to rise again anytime soon, the owner might be keener to get a quick sale. In the photograph above, the upper windows of this property are not boarded, because it is thought that potential squatters would find it too hard to gain access through those windows. Britain has enough homes, but has neither the systems nor the society needed to make good use of its plenty. What's more, if property taxation were to bring down the value of homes in London, how many people living in London might consider living in a house like this in Sheffield? How many people stay in London a year longer than they really want to because their home is making more money than they do through their jobs?

a 1% levy was high. Over at the *Daily Telegraph*, letter-writers with expensive properties also complained. They said that they would find it hard to keep their 'family' homes open to the public, or that the tax would encourage them to 'rip out our improvements and deliberately devalue'.[53] One school of thought suggests that the more they squeal, the nearer you know you're getting to the money.

LENDING SLOWDOWN

> *[When it began in 2007] this self-reinforcing process was, in effect, a massive bank run that caused the shadow banking system to shrivel up, much as the conventional banking system did in the early 1930s.*
>
> – Paul Krugman, economist, 2008[54]

Researching property values and lending trends is not a cheap business. If you request data from the Land Registry for England and Wales on all residential property transactions, you will be told that 'Our charging policy follows Treasury guidelines.' And then you will be told the prices that you will have to pay, should you wish to receive many years' worth of data:

1995–2004 inclusive (11 million records) = £30,000 + VAT
2005–February 2011 inclusive (5 million records) = £49,010 + VAT[55]

Furthermore there is an annual subscription of £2,200 plus VAT. But, even without paying any of this money you can tell that something dramatic has happened just from the sales figures.

From 1995 to 2007 there were, on average, just over 1,136,000 registered property sales a year in England and Wales. Since then there has been a slump in property sales, so they are now averaging just over 643,000 a year. In short, since 2008, the UK housing market has been suffering a slowdown. It shows no sign yet of sustained recovery. The apparent price rises of late summer 2013 were not accompanied by a corresponding large increase in the number of sales. So the average selling prices rose, even while the numbers upon which those averages were based fell or stayed low. Furthermore, the prices being paid by buyers using a mortgage were also found to be *falling* as the overall average purchase prices *rose*; it was the cash buyers who were fuelling the mini-boom of late 2013, and then only to any great extent in London.[56]

All the residential property in Great Britain and Northern Ireland is valued at between £5 trillion and £6 trillion. However, that figure can only be assessed in relation to what Britain itself is worth in economic terms, as an island, as a place to call home. By summer 2012 it had become clear that Britain's annual gross national product, its $2.2 trillion economy, had become dwarfed by the $15 trillion in banking assets that were (in financial theory) housed in the City of London. Roughly half of that $15 trillion was held in the most volatile of asset classes. Those assets existed, if the word 'exist' can have its meaning stretched, in the form of bank-to-bank loans and, even more dangerously, in high-risk derivative securities. In summer 2012, when reporting all these figures, the *New York Times* suggested that 'the worry is that what was once an asset has become a liability, with the City becoming, in effect, too big to regulate'.[57] For the UK as a whole, with turnover not picking up, it was dawning on a few of those overseas investors who read the *New York Times* that there was as yet no sign of a gradual return to business as usual. This may explain part of the August 2013 slump better than 'the warm weather' does![58] It may also explain the Prime Minister's desperate announcement in September 2013 that 'help-to-buy' would be brought forward and introduced within the week. The UK property market of 1995 to 2007, when nearly 15 million properties changed hands, is history.

When prices rise rapidly, a slump always occurs eventually, because someone is taking more than they need, a little 'extra'. In the case of a casino, it is the supposed cost to the 'house' of providing a gambling venue that is used to justify that extra. In the case of housing, it is greedy property speculators, together with colluding banks, that demand short- and medium-term 'interest', who add to the cost of borrowing. This can make gambling on housing not worthwhile for the vast majority of people, people who have to borrow such great sums in order to buy. It is when sufficient numbers of potential buyers think that it would be foolish to risk all that they have that a slump comes.

Just as it is impossible to know with any certainty when a new slump might start, so too it is very hard to know when a slump will come to an end. Just as with violent earthquakes, we can recognize the circumstances in which price slumps are more likely to occur, and the places where they are more likely to happen, but we cannot know precisely when they will strike. If markets were more predictable, if they tended to replicate past behaviour very simply, their patterns could be exploited for great future profit. Analysts like to pretend they can do such things, and some may even believe that they can, but most learn that they can't.

When it comes to gambling, there will always be a few winners, and some of them will claim it was their 'system' that helped them to gamble successfully. Some argue that the financial crisis of 2008 was caused by top bankers' lack of skill, and hence by their inadequate betting systems. This would be despite those bankers having been assessed by the market as being worth extraordinary salaries and bonuses. People who believe that bankers' salaries are justified are forced to blame the 2008 crash on 'excessive government regulations'. Others suggest that the crisis would have occurred anyway, as all the bankers were really engaged in was a sophisticated form of gambling that was destined to eventually fail, just as all Ponzi schemes must eventually fail.

Trying to recognize a sign of the slump to come in the housing market, as with any other market, is like trying to guess where a roulette ball will land as it clatters around the wheel. It is tempting to try, but ultimately futile. It is better to wait until it falls into the zero slot before declaring that the table is to be cleared, but we cannot resist speculating (in the US roulette wheels now have two zero slots, making the chances of losing out there even higher). One possibility is that the current slump will be followed by a further slump. In the case of the UK this is, at the very least, worth considering.

In January 2013 it was reported that rents in England and Wales had begun to fall – not just in a few peripheral areas but overall – and that rental arrears had worsened, with some £326 million late or unpaid rents being recorded across these two countries, the highest level since the previous maxima of January 2012.[59] And then rent arrears rose even further as half (yes half!) the families hit by the Bedroom Tax were added to the roles of new debtors.[60] Rents had even begun to fall in London and the south-east of England. Yet this was hardly a case of slump following slump, for rents had been rising rapidly after the volume of home sales halved. People had voted with their feet: unable to afford a mortgage, they had decided to rent instead. For most, that was not much of a decision. They had no effective 'market choice'. Just as most of those who must pay the Bedroom Tax have few options when it comes to securing a smaller property, so most of the rest of us have very few options when it comes to buying a property.

Over the calendar year 2012 London recorded the largest annual rise in average rents (6.3%), followed by the south-east, where rents were recorded as being 3.9% higher than the previous December.[61] However, in the East Midlands and Wales, rents had already been falling for a year by 2013; and across the whole of England and Wales estimates of the total rent arrears in the private sector were found to have grown to their highest level since August 2012, with total arrears of £326 million in January 2013, up sharply from a total £241 million recorded just two months earlier. These January arrears now represented '10.1% of all the rent that was due across England and Wales, while November's arrears represented 7.4% of all rent'.[62]

Thus, even in a country where housing prices have been falling in many areas outside of London, many people can't afford to pay rents at their current levels, let alone at even higher ones. Salaries and wages away from London have been falling even faster than housing prices. Within and around London, rents have been rising faster than salaries and wages. But nowhere have rents fallen by as much as benefits have been cut. Realizable demand – households wanting a new home that can also afford one – is dropping; even in the south-east more and more people cannot put up enough money for what they need.

Couples who have split up continue to live in the same home, even sleep in the same bed. Grown-up children do not leave the nest. New migrants do not stay in the kinds of numbers that would really help to energize the economy; many who do arrive quickly leave again, because the housing is so poor. More new migrants replace those who choose not to settle. The orthodox story that is told is of immigrants 'swamping' the south, supposedly immune to the high cost of living there; but orthodox stories are often based more on the accepted myths of our times than on reality. Look back to when immigrants were last so often blamed for making life worse in Britain: in the early 1970s, when there was also a housing price spike.

Orthodox economists suggest that housing crises are rare and are often preceded by other economic shocks, but recent analysis has found that in the last major world financial storm to have occurred prior to 2008, that of the early 1970s, a housing crisis preceded later economic troubles: 'Conventional wisdom has it that only the oil price hike in the fall of 1973 mattered. But it turned out that the property crash preceded the oil price hike by six months or more, and the recession was well under way by the fall.'[63] In an analysis carried out since the 2008 crash, Professor David Harvey of City University, New York, has re-evaluated what occurred in 1973 and suggested that it was problems with growing housing debt that mattered more than oil. He also found that, working back in time, a similar story can be told of the 1929 crash, which was preceded by a fall in the valuations of real estate securities, with the result that buyers' loans became unsecured. In Florida the apparent value of building permits had increased eightyfold in the six years between 1919 and 1925, and US house prices rose fivefold during those same turbulent few years – all this prior to the 1929 crash. People at the time talked of migrants and immigrants as a cause of the problems, when, in hindsight, it is clear that they were not.

A slump can come at any time, or not for years. When I was first typing these words I read, in February 2013, that the People's Bank of China had just been reported to have injected 450 billion yuan (US $72 billion) into money markets. Apparently 'it was the largest-ever one-day liquidity action conducted by the central bank.'[64] The reason given was to steady nerves, as so many people had withdrawn money to buy gifts for the Chinese New Year. But why was so much more needed for this New Year than for the previous one? Whatever the event that caused that slump, it will almost certainly not be New Year gifting. There is always a next slump, but its real trigger will probably not be obvious at the time.

In November 2012, as I was at first pulling together material for this book, I read that 'According to the estate agent Knight Frank, the price of prime residential property in London has increased by 49% since March 2009 – five times more than the UK as a whole.'[65] Like many others, I wondered then whether London could be becoming, financially, a separate country – or whether this could be yet another bubble. The latter has more of a precedent. Well-informed commentators writing about that time thought a new slump likely, but the canny ones never say when it will hit; they just keep repeating that eventually it will. For example, David Blanchflower, the best-known former member of the Bank of England monetary policy committee, said in January 2013 that 'My guess would be that nominal house prices will have to fall by a further 15% or so.' As always, he did not say when that fall would take place.[66]

High housing prices in the UK are maintained by the feeling that paying rent is like throwing money away. This feeling is generated by two realities. First, the amount of rent that most people pay far exceeds the value of the service they are paying for. Largely unregulated landlords try their hardest to maximize their incomes and to minimize the expenditure they 'lose' on maintaining the properties they let. If they did not do this, faced with competition from the more unscrupulous majority, they would have lower financial resources to fall back on in times when it is harder to get tenants and they would be more likely to have to sell up and leave the business. Thus rent control is needed to bring down rents, to deter the landlords most interested in making a profit and most intent on offering a bad service. Such controls would in turn bring down housing prices, resulting in more people buying when they needed to and fewer looking to rent unless they wanted to.

Second, ever-rising housing prices can make renting feel like throwing money down the drain. People ask why pay rent when, if you instead pay a mortgage, you could eventually own a property worth a small fortune. One answer is that if housing prices fall, that small fortune could turn, with added negative equity, into a large debt. Where house prices continued to fall in the north of England and in Wales and Scotland during 2013, they did so partly because people who could buy carried on renting, as they did not want to purchase an asset that was shrinking in value.

In contrast with much of the north, housing prices in southern England are rising rapidly as I type (in late 2013), building up (at some point) towards a slump or a crash. This surge in just-about-realizable demand is principally because, as currently constituted in the UK, free market private renting encourages people and businesses to be or to become bad private landlords, not just through charging rent that is too high, but also by not offering terms that are secure enough. People renting social housing now also face a growing insecurity of tenure. Government can suddenly change the rules at will, making people face fines and, ultimately, eviction. Renting in general feels increasingly insecure. As Duncan Bowie of the University of Westminster (located at various sites in the heart of London) succinctly explains, the 'private rented sector is in effect deregulated. There are no rent controls; no minimum security of tenure, and statutory regulation of minimum standards is limited to houses in multiple occupation . . . [and] is largely ineffective.'[67]

Paying more for housing means less is available for all other commitments. The number of babies being born worldwide is currently slowing at its fastest-ever rate. In richer countries people partly blame housing costs for having fewer children. In the densest cities in poorer Asia, and not just in China, where it has been mandatory, one baby per couple is now the norm.[68] What each generation spends most of its money on changes over time. Our grandparents spent far more on their food than on housing; our parents often spent more on cars than on housing. We, however, spend more on housing than on anything else. Our children may – on average – spend more on education unless they can stop that particular bubble from forming, but that is a subject for a future book.

Mortgage-lenders use people's worries about paying even higher rents in the future, and the carrot of the prospective wealth, to entice them to take out very large loans. They don't point out that, even at low interest rates, borrowers will often have to pay back at least twice the value of the loan before they actually own the property outright. Most borrowers in the UK and the US have little idea what total sum they will or did end up paying back, because interest rates so often dramatically rise and fall over the twenty-five- or thirty-year lifetime of a typical mortgage. They also have little idea of what the final value of the property they are buying will be. But people tend to be optimistic.

In researching this book, I have talked to dozens of journalists and housing analysts about what they thought might happen to UK interest rates in the near future. A large group thought those rates would not rise at all, or, if they did, by just a fraction in the coming years. Almost all were middle aged. Almost all lived in London. And almost all had many years of mortgage payments ahead. Hardly any of these commentators rented. They needed interest rates to remain low. Thus, there is a group-think operating in housing today that is understandable but dangerous. It prevails at the very top of the supposed pyramid of understanding, among experts, who then help to maintain an optimism about the future of housing throughout society. Rarely are commentators asked to seriously consider the actual probabilities.

In the same way that people don't consider (if in a partnership) that their marriage or other arrangement may break up – although the likelihood of that has never been higher – they often don't consider, when buying property, that one of the two jobs needed to pay the mortgage might disappear; that they may need or want to move earlier than they currently anticipate; that they are liable for all the repairs and upkeep on the property; or that they can fall ill. People are made to worry about what might happen if they were to die, but not about all those much more likely unfortunate events that can happen to them. The likelihood of death during the life of a mortgage is low, but lenders still make life insurance mandatory when a mortgage is taken out. The original meaning of the word 'mortgage' in French is 'death contract'. Other forms of insurance, such as insurance if you become too sick to work, are not mandatory. Struggling borrowers can make more money for the lender if they fall into arrears and have to pay penalties. And recently lenders have mis-sold payment protection insurance on a massive scale – which then further deters borrowers from insuring themselves against illness or an accident curtailing their income.

Lenders often justify lending at a profit, and trying to maximize that profit, by suggesting that charging at interest rates well above the base rate allows them to reward savers. However, the gap between the rates at which banks lend and the interest rates that they offer to savers shows how much they cream off. Just compare what they offer today. As I type, a ten-year fixed-rate mortgage costs about 4% a year on the high street, with a fee of £1,500 to apply. Simultaneously the bank offering this rewards its savers with a rate well below 1%, a rate that is below inflation.

Lenders also suggest that much of the profit that banks make goes to shareholders, many of which are pension companies; banks are therefore indirectly financing our pensions. But most people do not have a private pension, and pension provision is incredibly inequitable. For most people, the greatest wealth inequalities of all are to be found between different groups of pensioners. All the justifications for keeping the status quo ultimately make sense only for the very few at the top.

If you are poorly housed in middle age, you are also more likely to be poorly housed as a pensioner. The graph below shows how, in Britain, the number of properties on which loans are being granted remains at half the peak of 2007, while remortgaging became four times less common after 2009 than it was before 2008.[69] Remortgaging is raising a further debt based on the supposedly growing value of your home. When homes don't grow in value, remortgaging becomes harder, but even in the south-east of England, where houses have apparently risen greatly in worth, banks are less and less willing to lend more: they clearly think property prices might well be overvalued by at least 20%. That is why the Chancellor stepped in to guarantee that 20% in his March 2013 budget.

The fall in mortgage borrowing shown in the graph below is not due to a sudden increase in thrift among the population. It was initially mainly the result of governments having curtailed bank lending since 2008, to stop the banks building up a debt mountain that government would then have to underwrite (as happened in Ireland). This fall in lending largely explains the slump in buying detailed above. Many people would still like to buy their 'next' home, but have no possibility of raising the deposit and the other start-up costs required. Hence George Osborne's new 'help-to-buy' initiative in his March 2013 budget, guaranteeing loans on all property to cover falls of up to 20% of their current value – the value that the banks believe isn't there. If the value was there, the banks would lend the money

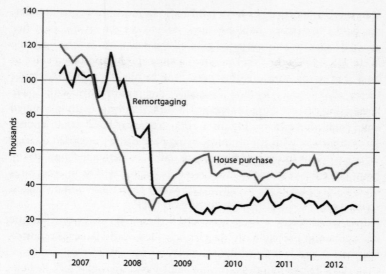

Figure 17. Monthly approvals of loans secured on dwellings in the UK, 2007–12.

without the need for those guarantees. The government is covering the risk to the bank, not the risk to the buyer. The buyer is being encouraged to take a huge risk, one even banks think is foolhardy.

In the US the fall in mortgage-lending since its peak has been even more precipitous. In 2005 mortgage-lending reached a peak: over a trillion more US dollars were lent than were paid back that year. But then lending fell like a stone with the crash in 2008, recovered slightly in 2011, and fell again in 2012. When you look at mortgage-lending in the US it is clear that the effects of the crash are ongoing. There was a rise in lending up to March 2013 that looked impressive at first glance, at 38%, but, because lending had fallen so much, this amounted to only an additional million or so new mortgages in a year. Most of the rise was due to remortgaging, as people were finding it harder to get by on so little money. Furthermore, black and Hispanic borrowers who asked for some of this new money were much more likely to be denied it, in comparison with white or Asian applicants.[70] So if it was a recovery, it was a recovery only for a favoured few.

In the US, mortgagors have paid back so much, in aggregate, that the banks' mortgage liabilities have fallen in each of the past five years, despite the enormous value of all the new loans still being made in the US. This is the first time such a situation has occurred since at least the 1970s, and possibly ever. One result of this is that other forms of consumer lending, especially credit-card borrowing, have been rising rapidly. Non-mortgage US total domestic lending reached a net peak of over $117 billion in total credit-card and other lending (in comparison with the amounts being paid off) by the third quarter of 2012.[71] This unsecured borrowing had become higher than at any point since the year 2000, and it is still rising today. The interest rates on unsecured loans are usually much higher than those on mortgages, so even more money then has to be paid back.

It is worth being a little wary of all these debt estimates, despite their apparent precision. In March 2009 the Federal Reserve reported that banks had lent $35 billion less on mortgages, in the year 2006, than those banks had thought they had! Furthermore, the Fed's published figure on mortgage-lending for 2008 was initially 37% adrift.[72] These discrepancies, of billions, are somewhat understandable, but it

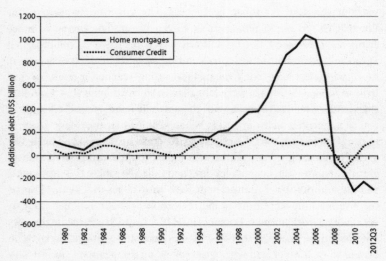

Figure 18. Additional debt added annually by sector, United States, 1979–2012.

would be wrong to assume that the Federal Reserve has a clinically accurate grasp of current events, or even that the banks reporting to it also concurrently knew the exact state of their own mortgage books. The current fall (shown opposite) could be found, in future, to be far sharper, to be going deeper, than what is depicted here.

The vast bulk of the US mortgage debt mountain, lent between the years 2000 and 2007 – some $6 trillion – remains unpaid. Much may never be repaid, but US banks have been recouping more than they have lent every year since 2008, although only because they have been prevented from lending yet more on housing by the US authorities. They would lend far more if they knew the authorities were prepared to underwrite whatever they lent. It is mostly only because US regulation has been a little more lax on other forms of consumer credit, such as affects those credit cards, that lending has been able to grow again in the US. In 2013 those reports of rising mortgage-lending referred to above were mostly for remortgaging. If banks can't lend – especially on new property and to finance home moves – they cannot profit; but if they cannot recoup almost all that they lend, they also fail.

In the UK we need to learn from the US, and not mimic it so much. So many of our major banks were in the grip of US institutions by the early 2000s that we almost blindly followed US financial policy – in some areas, to our detriment. For example, the US does have more property taxes than the UK, but we didn't choose to copy any of those and revise our out-of-date and very unfair council tax system. However, what happens in many states in the US at least shows that greater property taxation is possible, if only to get more currently unused property into use. In New Hampshire, where total taxation is lower than in forty-three other US states, property taxes are, on average, about $2,424 when calculated per *person* per year. The same tax is charged on a home used by one person as it is on a similar-sized dwelling containing six people.[73] Greater taxation is therefore levied on a person living in an underused property, on second homes, on holiday homes and on empty commercial property. This happens in much of the US already, and in the UK it would encourage those in possession of such property to put it to use and not let it remain empty.

In the UK, making the council tax system more progressive is entirely possible. As outlined above, it could be done by extending the bands to cover properties worth many tens of millions of pounds. Such a reform would be a stepping stone towards a proper land value tax, and is just one of many ways to deal with the volatility, the inequity and the disparity of the UK property market. It could also help to reduce rents for the vast majority who live in modest properties, because when property values fall it is harder to justify charging such high rents.

The introduction of a fair land and housing tax, rising to far above the current mansion tax threshold, might help to reduce speculation, and also help to control the rises in property values in London, thereby mitigating the size of the property bubble and hopefully cushion the impact of that bubble when it bursts. However, to enact any new policy we have to stop believing that what will be will be, and that we are powerless to intervene.

7

Speculation

Rightmove said home prices will increase 6% this year instead of the 4% it previously estimated ... Nationally, values were up 4.5% this month from a year earlier, while prices in London were 8.2% higher, [but] asking prices fell by 7.4% on the month in the City of Westminster. They declined by 5% in Camden and by 3.3% in Kensington & Chelsea. The average asking price in the UK is 245,495 pounds ($389,300).

– *Bloomberg News*, September 2013[1]

Just before the small 1989 crash in the UK housing market, and in an uncanny echo of late 2013, house price estimates were rising rapidly nationally, but the rise had stalled in London. Then, as if out of nowhere, prices began to fall. First they fell in the centre of the capital, in autumn 1988. I know because, in the early 1990s, as part of my PhD studies, with data from the largest two building societies, I mapped prices in 10,000 wards for every year of the 1980s. I used a new mapping technique that involved the generation of very detailed area cartograms, which let you see all those individual statistics together on one page. I could see the fluctuations in prices in different areas, like an estate agent with knowledge of his or her particular patch, but I could see them for every neighbourhood in every town and in every rural area across the whole country. I was no longer looking at a list of figures, but at an actual picture. To describe that picture with a few statistics would have been similar to describing a painting as having an average colour of red.

The housing price picture is never uniform: there are local exceptions and regional exceptions. The regional exceptions do not neatly fit any administrative areas. I got to be the first person to see dark spots gather on the maps of housing price changes up to 1989. I was able to see, in great detail, the geographical progress of a housing market crash. Negative equity spread like an epidemic across the country, slowly, then very quickly and often unpredictably. Few places were spared. Recovery was gradual. Later I mapped the data for 1993. In 25% of wards, 25% to 50% of people who had bought with a mortgage between 1988 and 1991 were in negative equity; in a further 12% of wards it was over 50%. And with the new computer-generated cartograms I could see where each of those wards was. By then, although most were in the south, there were still scatterings in the north, Scotland and Wales.

Back in the 1980s and 1990s only a few people could monitor local house price changes across the whole of Britain.[2] Today far more people have access to the data. But, in January 2013, just nine months before tripling its forecast of the coming national rise to 6%, the property experts at Rightmove had suggested they would be only 2%.[3] In early summer Rightmove increased its estimate of annual housing inflation to 4%, in autumn to 6% and then in December 2013 they increased it again, to 8%[4]. Speculation is rife, the forecasts are unreliable and actual housing prices fluctuate.

The same is happening in the US today, and it is not only the forecasts that fluctuate wildly but also the reporting of them. On 24 September 2013 the *Financial Times* titled its story on the release of one set of figures 'Pace of US house price rises slows as mortgage rates climb'.[5] The BBC had reported the same data the same day under the headline 'US house prices in biggest annual rise for seven years'.[6] By December 2013 the *Los Angeles Times* by-line read: 'November's median of $385,000 has been about the same since June. Sales slump'.[7]

At the heart of the housing crisis, as with the situation more broadly, is speculation. The problem ranges from those who seek to make a quick buck by lending in the short term, to people who are desperate for help to pay the rent or make a mortgage payment, through to those who seek to make a profit in the long term, more slowly and steadily – all out of our basic need to be housed.

Similar sorts of speculation had occurred previously in Britain, most recently when credit became more easily available after the sudden deregulation of financial markets on 27 October 1986: the 'Big Bang'. After that people began once more to fall behind on debt repayments in ways that had not been seen since the 1930s; enough time had passed for the lessons of the 1930s to have been unlearned. In other European countries governments were more careful. But in Britain, where there was a desire to be economically 'great' again, such caution was viewed as timidity. Similarly, in the US, which was struggling to maintain its economic greatness, the old rules were relaxed from the early 1980s onwards to allow short-term profits to be maximized.

Earlier in this book the housing turmoil of the 1930s and 1970s was described, and it was suggested that we could learn from remembering those times. It was also suggested that perhaps we can be forgiven for forgetting them, given how long ago those crises were, but most older adults should be able to remember the 1980s and the period since then. In Britain the 1980s ended with that small housing market crash, but we took little note of it at the time other than to see it as a few too many people trying to buy when prices were too high, often in an attempt to save a little tax by purchasing before September 1989. After that date only one member of a couple could claim Mortgage Interest Relief at Source (MIRAS) on their tax. That particular subsidy was ended entirely in April 2000. However, in hindsight the rush to get in before Multiple Mortgage Tax Relief ended was not the prime cause of the over-exuberance of 1988. Rather, it was the availability of new money to borrow in the late 1980s that was mostly to blame. Worryingly we have more new money than ever available now, but this time it is underwritten by the government. If you were trying to set up the market for a great fall, you could hardly do better than this.

In the nineties and noughties, increased financial speculation and the creation of more and more new money by banks[8] led to ever greater lending, rapidly rising prices and rents, increased indebtedness, more arrears and a rise in defaulting. Mass defaulting on mortgage payments was curtailed only by a dramatic reduction in base lending rates. This was done to try to keep the show on the road in the hope that somehow there would be a return to the new normal. But what we have been living with since has been far from normal: housing insecurity has increased, and governments have been creating new money through quantitative easing. We know this can't carry on for long, our general sense of security has fallen, and collectively even our health has begun to suffer in ways that can now be measured. But the worse it gets, the more they entice us to borrow.

Ultimately speculation in housing is wrong, because it harms human health. It unnecessarily increases rents and prices. Living in fear over whether you will be able to pay the rent, or keep up the mortgage payments, slowly hacks away at your sense of being part of society, makes you increasingly anxious and harms your well-being. Worrying that the care home you are living in as an elderly pensioner is about to go bust because the landlord has increased the rent is to worry about homelessness. Old alternatives to renting become necessary again as rising homelessness is suffered by the young: the frequency of squatting rises; millions more end up sleeping on friends' sofas for a week, or two, or more. But for those with children, and for those who are older, direct action such as squatting (or indirect action such as sofa-surfing) is less of an option, and many people get into greater and greater debt.

DEBT AND ARREARS

It's shocking to think that so many families will be starting the New Year with a huge weight hanging over them, trapped in a daily struggle to keep their home. Payday loans may seem like a quick fix, but the huge interest charges mean things can quickly spiral out of control.

– Campbell Robb, Shelter's Chief Executive, 2013[9]

In Britain, Margaret Thatcher's first government put the country into long-term debt by allowing, even encouraging, export manufacturing industries to fail: shipyards, coal mines, steel plants and car factories.

Instead her government used the profits made from exporting oil to cut taxes, especially to financiers. Exporting oil took little manufacturing skill; it was not that 'hi-tech'. Thatcher's government could have used the money to support manufacturing instead of tax breaks, as was done in mainland Europe; but some large manufacturing and extraction industries were heavily unionized and the unions were Thatcher's enemy number one. Governments in other European countries did not take such an antagonistic approach to industry, nor did they give so many tax breaks to financial services and the potential customers of those services. Banking in the UK became part of the 'financial industries', as if bankers were somehow industrious, as if money were hacked out of rock.

In several other European countries many old industries evolved into new, cleaner and younger businesses. But in the UK, as a result of Thatcher's deindustrialization, 'Britain last ran a current-account surplus in 1983 and has been in deficit since then, borrowing money from countries like China and selling commercial assets to foreigners.'[10] The huge rise in debt in Britain since the 1980s is also directly linked to the decisions taken then and to the growing social inequality that resulted. Bankers got relatively richer; workers became relatively poorer. The proportion of GDP going to wages fell and that to profits rose. Falling in between that growing gap, many people got into more and more debt to try to maintain their position on a ladder of income and wealth whose gradient was becoming progressively steeper – harder to climb and easier to slip down.

It is because of the Thatcher economic 'revolution' that paying for housing for young adults in Britain is like trying to run faster and faster on a hamster wheel. With Thatcher's deregulation, a wider spread of people were permitted to take out home loans on more expensive properties. Because of this, a new phenomenon began in the 1980s: large numbers of people getting into arrears on their mortgages. That had been quite rare before Mrs Thatcher's government took charge.[11] But more and more thought that they had to speculate to accumulate, and that the most expensive properties would rise the most in value. The temptation to borrow more than you could reasonably afford was often too much. Then prices rose as the result and it became necessary to borrow just a little bit more again, especially in many areas of the south. People started to have doubts about the doubts attached to borrowing. 'Don't be a skinflint', they would say. This is what you have to do.

As one of Thatcher's contemporaries put it shortly after her death: 'She created today's housing crisis, she produced the banking crisis, she created the benefits crisis ... Every real problem we face today is the legacy of the fact she was fundamentally wrong.'[12] However, it would grossly overstate her individual abilities to suggest she did all these things alone. She had help, and she followed the guidance of her like-minded colleagues and the teachings of a few older men who had a theory that promoting individual selfishness would, overall, increase the common good. They got a chance to test that theory, and it was that idea – Thatcherism, promoting selfishness above the common good – which turned out to be wrong.

To be in arrears means to be behind in your mortgage payments. A high level of arrears is not necessarily a sign of woe. When housing prices are rising, buyers being late with their payments is often seen as less of a problem. They and their lenders know that the value of the homes is going up and that the buyers' share of the equity in the properties is growing. Some may view a few months' arrears as a form of secured borrowing, cheaper than using credit cards, although they would usually do better to make a formal agreement with their lender to extend their mortgage rather than incurring penalty fees; but, even if they don't make such a formal agreement, they will often still do better in comparison with taking out other unsecured loans.

Debt got out of hand in the UK almost as soon as financial deregulation began in 1986, so that by 1989 there was that small housing market crash. Many younger buyers with only small deposits got into negative equity in the late 1980s and very early 1990s, when prices fell. They were left either with a debt that could not be covered by selling their home, or were unable to remortgage to cover any new debts, including mortgage arrears.

In the aftermath of the crash, the proportion of properties being repossessed by the banks rose rapidly, to nearly 1% of all the dwellings that the banks had on their books. That 1% being repossessed in a year was a very large share of all properties. It represented a significant proportion of all properties changing hands at any one time and resulted in parts of the market being flooded with properties being sold off at auction. That in turn reduced prices further.

Once prices had fallen slightly, in 1989, for many people their arrears began to rise rapidly too, and when prices are falling, rising arrears are far more problematic as far as lenders are concerned. People who would normally have sold their home at a profit if they could not make the payments, and then bought a cheaper one, or who would have remortgaged to borrow more in hard times, could not. Unlike now, at that time it was usually only after a few months' worth of arrears had been recorded that proceedings to repossess were begun. But as the value of dwellings diminished following the 1989 housing price falls and negative equity rose, lenders became increasingly reluctant to take over properties, to repossess them. So, by 1995, up to 4% of all UK mortgages were in arrears of 2.5% or more of the outstanding mortgage balance. But our collective memory-spans appear to be getting shorter when it comes to the dangers of housing speculation, and by 2005 we had largely forgotten that housing crash.

Speculation works only because our memories can be so very poor, but is it really possible that they are getting poorer with time? The 1930s had become a distant memory by the 1980s. The lesson of the early 1990s was also quickly forgotten in the 'boom' years of the noughties. Our collective memory does appear to be becoming shorter and shorter, as do the gaps of time between boom and bust. Perhaps that is because more people than ever before are making money out of housing, and most of them do not want us to think about the possibilities of failure.

I remember the 1989 housing market falls only because I made so many maps of the geography of the market crash during my postgraduate studies. I worry about history repeating itself now because my first research job was to study the effects on people and neighbourhoods of negative equity.[13] Most people will have forgotten, and anyone under forty today is too young to remember. As prices rose and jobs returned, the level of arrears fell, so that by 2004 under 1% of all mortgages repayments were in arrears – which meant that more than 99% of all borrowers were up to date with their monthly payments! Yet in 2008 arrears jumped to 2%, falling again only as the historically low interest rates brought them under control.[14]

What will happen in the next few years can only be guessed at – but we can at least guess with the benefit of hindsight. The banks appear to have some hindsight, which is why they will not lend large mortgages to people on not very high salaries, or without a large deposit, unless the government guarantees that any losses the bank makes after repossessing and reselling any property are reduced by up to 20% of the original purchase price. In practice this means most likely reducing the potential bank losses to zero.

Any increase in interest rates, unemployment, or any future fall in housing prices, is likely to see arrears and then repossessions rise very much more quickly than the official forecasts currently predict. These short-term forecasts are shown in the graph below. Those dots stretching into 2015 in the Bank of England's report have been put there to reassure. No one who knows the history of housing sees them as

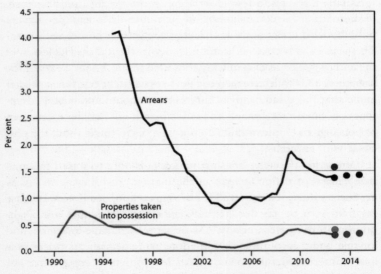

Figure 19. United Kingdom mortgage arrears and possession rates, 1990–2015. Council of Mortgage Lenders' projections for end of 2012 are also shown.

reliable. The Bank of England used to put wide confidence limits around its future projections. It now tends not to show error bars of uncertainty for fear of causing fear. It also now tends not to project very far ahead, as the few dots in the graph opposite indicate, limiting its horizons to avoid the risk of being proved very wrong very quickly. On the roller-coaster we are currently riding, nobody knows what will be around the corner. We really haven't been here before.

In early 2013 money for lending was still drying up, and banks were becoming more and more intent on getting back their monies. They told hundreds of thousands of people holding interest-only mortgages that should they want to alter any of their arrangements, they would need to convert their mortgages into repayment ones. This will increase those borrowers' mortgage payments – and, presumably for some, their arrears. Then government stepped in with the March 2013 budget: more mortgages were to be underwritten in the near-future, so more could be offered, but interest-only mortgages would no longer be offered.

As volatility rises, a few months can seem like an age in finance. Back in 2012, one commentator on the website 'Moneysupermarket. com' reported how the cheaper mortgage deals in the UK were coming to an end. She found that by November 2012 there were only 211 interest-only deals available from 27 lenders. A year earlier there had been 485 such offers available from 42 lenders. But she also found that there had been no fall in the offers of interest-only mortgages on 'buy-to-let' homes, on loans to landlords, 'as these deals are not classed as "residential"'.[15] Just how long current 'business as usual' will remain usual, and landlords will still be allowed to borrow at current low interest rates without also having to repay, remains another open question. In September 2013 the West Bromwich Building Society increased its rates for existing landlord customers, causing great anger, as the landlords had thought those rates were fixed.[16] As detailed above, government also underwrites the banks when lending to them, again encouraging speculation, until suddenly an event like a hike in interest rates dampens enthusiasm. Because housing prices are still so high in comparison with wages, most families continue to find it very hard to pay the mortgage on a newly purchased home, even at low interest rates. To avoid arrears – or more likely to avoid that third or fourth missed mortgage payment that might start repossession proceedings – people are entering into even riskier forms of borrowing. By the end of 2012 almost a million people in the UK had used a payday loan to cover their rent or mortgage; a further 2.8 million used an unauthorized overdraft; some 7.8 million were struggling to pay for their housing, of which 1.4 million were slowly (or quickly) falling behind with their payments.[17] The result is an inevitable rise in repossessions. As Janet Hunter put it in spring 2013, on behalf of the Housing Rights Service, 'increasing numbers of families are losing their homes. We are struggling to cope with this and unfortunately we cannot see the situation improving for some considerable time.'[18]

While some are making fortunes, others go to the wall.

First, families fail to make that one mortgage payment. The next month it is harder. There are suddenly two payments to make, and the reason why the first was missed has not gone away. Things have become even worse than they were the month before, while the stress of being in arrears will not have helped. Then comes the third month, and people ask their family for help. In the fourth month they ask friends. They say that they have a problem with the boiler, need petrol for the car, but the friends can guess. And they worry what those friends must think of them. But this current spate of problems did not start in the UK.

As mentioned earlier,[19] in the US, being in arrears on your mortgage payment is called 'mortgage delinquency'. For European readers it can be a shock the first time they see such language being used (although some Credit Unions now do use it). For Europeans, delinquency means anti-social and usually criminal behaviour, most often associated with juveniles, a 'stage' some teenagers go through – but also a word generally thought unhelpful to use nowadays.

The point at which mortgage-lenders decide to foreclose on a mortgage in arrears is entirely up to them. All along, they were the legal owners of the property you might have thought was yours. They held the deeds. When the housing market is depressed, lenders are loath to begin proceedings, as they might then end up with a vacant property on their hands, and one that is declining even faster in value than it was when occupied. In the US, when the housing market collapsed in

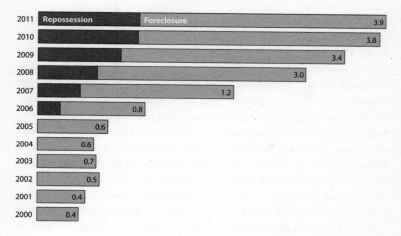

Figure 20. Repossessions and foreclosures in the United States, 2000–2011 (millions).

the wake of the 2008 crisis, the annual increase in foreclosures stalled abruptly, but arrears spiralled upwards. As Figure 2 of this book illustrated (p. 25), the average number of days to complete a foreclosure in the US nearly tripled in the US nationwide, from about four months in 2007 to nearly a year by 2011.

In the US the legal processes involved in a lender foreclosing on a loan and actually repossessing the home are separated. In the UK this is not the case – at least, not yet. Here the gap in time between repossession being granted by a court and the date of eviction is usually brief. But if the UK were to replicate recent trends in the US, with banks morphing into landlords when housing prices fall, the language of housing in Britain would ultimately change. This might not be a bad outcome overall, as long as banks were forced to be good landlords, or to subcontract to housing associations with good track records.

For instance, in areas where prices have already been falling for several years and are well below their 2007 peak, British banks could begin to repossess homes where the mortgage is in arrears, but then come to some arrangement with the occupiers of those homes to convert their ownership into a form of 'tenancy'. The mortgage rescue scheme (on which more below) was the first manifestation of this idea in the UK. Banks don't want to become landlords – it is not as profitable as lending – but circumstances mean that they might be forced into such an arrangement. And, if they begin such arrangements for some customers, why should others not also have the option? Why should banks be allowed to repossess when the value of the home has risen and they can make good their liability, but not allow the family to remain as paying tenants? It doesn't seem fair. In a world made fairer, the rent on a property would be lower than the mortgage. In both the US and the UK that was once the case.

The research body that released the figures shown in the figure above recorded 1.15 million homes being repossessed in the US in 2011.[20] This was the estimate based on what it knew by the end of 2012. In the UK, Shelter suggested that almost 200,000 families were at risk of losing their homes by September 2012,[21] which is not a dissimilar proportion to that found in North America, given the relative populations of the US and the UK. Shelter also found that, despite property prices still rising in London, it was within that city – especially within the poorer East End – that the risk of losing their home was greatest for mortgagors. The same, by the way, had been true back in 1989. By Christmas 2012, some 2.7% of families in the boroughs of Barking and Dagenham were affected; 2.6% in Newham; 2.2% in Haringey, Hackney and Southwark. Unemployment was the most likely immediate cause. If these figures sound low, remember that they are annual: it will often be happening to different sets of families the next year, and the year after that.

To extrapolate: if families with more insecure finances are not replaced by more financially secure in-comers, then, were current trends to continue and current laws remain in force, over half of all families in a borough like Barking and Dagenham might be facing eviction at some point over a twenty-year period. That is a long-term disaster, not a short-term crisis. Depression then follows the normalization of crisis. In Spain the disaster has already begun. In the five years following 2007, foreclosure proceedings began on some 420,000 mortgaged properties in that country. What is more, a majority of those actions resulted in the physical eviction of the family living in that property. Most people did not make themselves voluntarily homeless. They did not walk out.

By spring 2013 over 500 Spanish families were being evicted from their homes every day. One family, who had already paid $98,000 (€71,500, £60,000) of a $323,000 mortgage at the point they defaulted, then received a demand for an additional $405,000 after their home had been repossessed, because the bank had continued to add interest to their debt. García Lamarca, a researcher based at the University of Manchester, has documented how similar actions have not only led to hundreds of thousands of families now having no place to live in Spain, but also to their being (in theory) in debt for the rest of their lives. At the same time, she estimates that '20% of Spain's total housing – 5.6 million homes – remains unoccupied.'[22] However, people in Spain will be in life-time debt only for as long as they put up with the politicians that have sanctioned such debt, and their homes will remain unoccupied only for as long as the clamour to use them is presented as unreasonable. Informed politicians from all over Europe now look at Spain and worry about what can happen in housing. Some also look for inspiration in dealing with what might soon happen in their own countries.

British politicians and those in charge of the UK financial watchdogs during the years 2010 to 2013 reassured themselves that what happened in Spain will not happen here by looking at the quarterly pattern of repossessions and noting no great rise. However, as one insider explained it to me, on condition of anonymity, the decision to repossess is a timing decision by the lender; and currently we have as much of a problem as we had in the early 1990s, when many people were evicted. The difference is that now far more families are affected, and the debt per family tends to be of a lesser size. This, as far as lenders are concerned, means that it's not yet worthwhile taking any action against most individual families who are behind with their payments.

The position, and therefore the statistics, can become clouded when lenders appoint 'receivers of rent' in 'buy-to-let' cases: this allows them to take over ownership of the property from a landlord but avoids a repossession order being made (as no one is being evicted when the tenants stay in place); the foreclosure, as a result, does not appear in the Council of Mortgage Lenders' repossession statistics. The landlords still lose the property, but their tenants do not immediately lose their home.[23] However, in all these situations the occupants remain in fear that as soon as the bank thinks it can make a profit on the sale, it will serve notice that the tenancy is to end. Such cases are considered contracts coming to an end, and so also fail to figure in repossession statistics.

Reassurance is dangerous in the current climate. Some within the UK government are aware that the crisis could be worsening, but they vacillate between concern over a growing bubble and the fear of an imminent crash. They look around the UK and wonder how on earth prices and rents in the south-east can rise, given what else they see. Much nearer than Spain is Ireland, which was hit by a property disaster in 2008. The leading social research institute there found that the crash had affected every aspect of social and economic life, in both urban and rural communities. It left in its wake mass property vacancy as well as renewed mass emigration. There are hundreds of unfinished estates, thousands of empty offices, dozens of ghost retail parks and, above all else, 'a topography of broken lives, shattered dreams, terminal indebtedness, and, for some, chronic stress, anxiety, depression, and even suicide'.[24] It is hardly surprising those in power in the UK are so reluctant to talk of the possibility of a bubble leading to a crash.

If the housing crisis does worsen, the repercussions will be far wider than many currently realize. We know this from studies undertaken in the US, which acts as the model for what ensues when you allow market forces to reign supreme. When housing fails, what follows is a decline in human health, even for those not immediately affected.

Research by Janet Currie of Princeton University and Erdal Tekin of Georgia State University, published in 2011, found that, among those who lived in a neighbourhood where there was a sudden rise in property foreclosures and evictions, there were statistically significant increases in urgent unscheduled hospital visits, almost all by members of families not themselves actually being evicted. This included an increase in visits for preventable conditions; people were looking after their health less, so ended up making more frequent emergency visits to hospital. The people of the neighbourhood were becoming more worried and more ill through worry, or were less able to look after their health. These researchers also found that the estimated effects could not be accounted for by any increase in unemployment in the area; nor were they that closely correlated with declines in housing prices, or rising out-migration, or people switching from out-patient providers to hospitals. Their study was thorough.[25] They were sure that it was the actual foreclosures and the fear they engendered that were literally putting people in hospital.

In Britain the provisional death counts for England for 2012 became available in mid-January 2013. That count showed a total of 465,290 deaths, an increase of 11,966 (or 2.6%) on the equivalent 52 weeks of 2011. A conscientious researcher who works in public health reported on the mounting death toll and explained that this 2.6% increase is the biggest proportional increase in deaths that we have seen in the past seventeen years.[26] Most of the additional mortality was among elderly women, and it was not, as far as we yet know, due to an epidemic or the weather. The researcher's employer, Public Health England, later distanced itself from this finding, suggesting that you could make an informed guess that the rise in mortality might be due to influenza, but it did not report the results of tests for any new strains; nor did it explain why current vaccination programmes might not be working so well any longer. Many observers did not find this reassurance convincing,[27] particularly as it chose to stop its employee from highlighting the weekly death reports from August 2013, which would allow others to check what was occurring.[28]

In time, an analysis of where and when the 2012 UK mortality rise occurred will probably reveal a link to increasing insecurity in housing, including within communal care homes, which were rocked both by several scandals that year and by one very large private care-home provider, Southern Cross Healthcare, going bust because its annual rental bill had become unaffordable. The majority of residents in care homes are elderly women. The fear of losing a room in a care home can damage health, but, because younger deaths tend to be more newsworthy, the rise in elderly deaths was, at first, ignored. Later, when it was suggested that the deaths might be due to the flu, that explanation was ridiculed by two of the UK's leading epidemiologists – Dr David Stuckler and Professor Martin McKee;[29] interpretations vary depending on what model is being used, but there is evidence that incidents of flu were unusually low in the UK at this time.[30] Despite levels of flu being low, reports of falling life expectancy among the elderly began to circulate in the UK by the winter of 2013.[31] These are the first recorded falls since the 1930s.[32]

Financial crises are now known to have extremely rapid as well as long-lasting effects on health. Over 10,000 suicides were caused in 1998 alone by the Asian financial crisis of that year.[33] In fact the initial turmoil of a crisis and the insecurity it brings can cause suicide rates to rise before any actual rise in unemployment. This rapid rise in anxiety, associated with the fear of becoming jobless, was recorded in both 2008 and around the time of the 1929 crash.[34] And during both periods the rise did not quickly abate.

During 2013 it was reported that calls to the Spanish equivalent of the Samaritans concerning suicide had risen by 30% over the course of the previous year, and that suicide had become the leading non-disease cause of death in Spain. By 2012 the figures were nine Spaniards killing themselves a day, and almost 200 suicide attempts being made a day.[35]

Many of these suicides and suicide attempts will be influenced by concern over housing. In Spain the finance system is now causing more deaths than road-traffic accidents. Shocks to our personal sense of security can be very hard to bear. Shelter makes us physically secure; having a home in which to reside and to meet with friends and family helps keep us mentally secure. We now know that insecurity over housing – simply the fear that you and your family may lose the roof over your heads – can badly affect both your mental and physical health.

Another half-boarded-up home and garage in the affluent Nether Edge suburb of Sheffield. This is a fine solid property. It contains enough rooms to house more than one family well; yet even the garage has had to be secured for fear of vandalism. It is also a property in a relatively affluent area of the city, but not the most affluent. Its current state illustrates that it is not just in the worst-off neighbourhoods where people suffer when the housing market becomes volatile. We do not appear to know what to do when prices fall, as they have in this part of Sheffield. Often we board up homes, hoping that what we thought were the good times will return and that someone, from somewhere, will take out an even bigger debt than we did, just to give them the right to live in them. At some point our systems of financing housing will have to change. They will have to come to rely less on younger generations paying ever more money for the right to shelter than we did. When that point arrives, property like this will still exist. All the sewers that serve housing like this will still be there. Homes will not have disappeared. But working out what we need to do to get the boarding taken off, the insides renovated and homes like this reoccupied is the conundrum.

HEALTH AND EVICTION

... when inequality becomes large enough, the very rich no longer live in the same society as everyone else ... the gap between the rich and the rest is such a threat to our health.

– Angus Deaton, Professor of Economics, Princeton, 2012[36]

On 9 January 2013 the US Institute of Medicine released a report that clearly showed that the US population of every social stratum has worse health than those in comparable developed countries such as Germany, Japan, Spain, Italy or France.[37] The superficial reasons given for why people have poorer health in the US were adverse birth outcomes, more injuries, more homicides, more infectious diseases, more drug-related cases of premature mortality, more obesity, more diabetes, and a greater prevalence of heart disease and chronic lung disease. However, the underlying reasons behind the Institute of Health's suggestion for all these outcomes were not greater laziness, risk-taking or fecklessness in the US, but were the more adverse social and economic conditions found there, the greater poverty and the wider inequality, and the fact that such 'a stressful environment may promote substance abuse, physical illness, criminal behaviour, and family violence'.[38] Having little or no welfare state to fall back on means that, when housing and other costs increase, visits to the doctor have to be curtailed.

The Institute of Medicine Report's authors linked high US asthma rates to unhealthy housing; yet this was a minor phenomenon in comparison with the mental distress being caused by rapidly rising housing and financial insecurity. Proportionately far more Americans are, quite rationally, in fear of losing their homes than are people in any other rich country on earth. Even after Greece's cataclysmic financial crash, fewer people were homeless in Greece in comparison with the US. Greece has a very long way to go to get to the situation in the US, where so many people sleep in cars and sleep rough. In Greece many evictions of debtors don't occur because of new laws brought in to protect people during the crisis.[39] Few in the US would consider laws protecting residents in that way a possibility. Most do not know of the greater rights enjoyed by many Europeans, or of how tenants in Japan cannot easily have their rents increased or be made to leave a property when they don't wish to.[40]

At the extreme of the relationship between poor health and bad housing are the findings that bank-lending decisions in Chicago led to high or even rising homicide rates in particular neighbourhoods of that lakeside city. María Veléz, Assistant Professor in the University of New Mexico, studied lending records and found that people living in black and Latino communities were less likely to be allowed to take out loans in comparison with people living in areas that were predominately white. She also found that African-American areas had five times (and Latino neighbourhoods two times) as many homicides as white neighbourhoods. She then ran a predictive model, which suggested that it was the insecurity of housing that led to this: 'holding all other variables constant . . . [We find] that black and Latino neighborhoods would experience fewer homicides if more financial capital were infused into these neighborhoods. These findings suggest that neighborhoods are shaped profoundly by the decisions of external economic actors.'[41] In other words, rising insecurity in housing can lead to a measurable deterioration in the local social environment, and it has been shown that this directly raises the homicide rate. It was mostly in those housing blocks where people were the victims of racism in lending practices that the violence was worse. There are many similar findings to these, and many of these findings date from before the crash, from before the situation in so many neighbourhoods became much more dire.

Evidence concerning the crash and the general stress it has brought in its wake is still being gathered. The one set of international comparisons that has been put together, by David Stuckler of the University of Oxford and Sanjay Basu of Stanford University, suggests that, where austerity has been greater, the resulting general social harm and damage to physical and mental health is also worse.[42]

There are more and more signs of public health being damaged in Britain by current austerity cuts – and not just through possible higher mortality rates among the very elderly, or more suicides at the extreme.

Our overall levels of mental health and our sense of well-being have suffered, and that has affected our general health. We already know that self-reported levels of good health in the UK have been deteriorating. In early 2013 the UK's Office of National Statistics announced that the proportion of adults reporting their general health to be very good had fallen from 40% in 2009 to 34% by 2011.[43]

When a whole group of people has been harmed by some event, if they can find someone to blame for the harm, they have the option of going to court to seek recompense. Particular groups can claim particular grievances from having suffered harm and distress through how they were treated. As yet we have not had any class-action law suits concerning mortgage mis-selling in the UK, although groups of landlords are threatening to take banks and building societies that have increased their interest rates to court. Their slogan to try to drum up support is: 'Your wealth is at risk if you choose to ignore this message!'[44]

Again, it is instructive to look across the Atlantic for clues as to what might be happening. In July 2012 Wells Fargo, the largest mortgage-lender in the US, agreed to pay a minimum of $175 million 'to settle accusations that its independent brokers discriminated against black and Hispanic borrowers during the housing boom'.[45] That is a huge sum of money to hand over in compensation, and from just one lender. The times may be changing as to what behaviour the courts and the people, and some of their politicians, are willing to put up with from bankers; but, then again, perhaps not. After all, in many respects, it appears to be business as usual in the banking sector. However, the amount of fines has been rising in recent years, and in September 2013 Barclays Bank was ordered to pay back £100 million in interest charges that turned out to be illegal. The bank tried to hide this fact within a much larger document; thankfully a few slightly more radical outlets, and then newspapers, gave that story prominence.[46]

Newspapers, which are often almost reverential in their treatment of financial institutions and their misdemeanours, often appear to offer very little sympathy to individuals who are down on their luck, even when purporting to care. For example, newspaper stories on the growing phenomenon of squatting in your own home often try to give a glimpse into the human side of these statistics, but the effect of these stories can be to detract from the weight of the numbers. What they need to do is both to say how many millions of people have been affected and to delve into the full depths of sadness, fear and despair that can result when people can no longer pay for their shelter.[47]

Journalists are not normally reticent about being ghoulish, so why not spell out just how bad so many people's mental health has become? Families are allowed to stay in their homes only when it is in the direct financial interests of the lenders not to evict them. Corporate lenders care about suicides only because life insurers won't pay up on 'deliberate' deaths, thus depriving the lenders of their repayments.

It would help if occupiers knew they had access to more bargaining tools. A home that is occupied retains what value it might have far longer than one that is abandoned. The occupying family act as unpaid security guards, cleaners and caretakers. The mortgage company may then reduce the loan to a level the family can pay, but, if the occupiers are out of work or in low-paid work, they may have enough money only for food and not for a reduced mortgage payment.

In the US today the mortgage company will often pay for buildings insurance when the family cannot. But they will hardly be prepared to pay for food or give the caretaker any wage. You might retort 'why should they?' The answer is that, if they are retaining the right to evict at any time, the residents are effectively becoming their employees, their caretakers. However, it is only the building they value, not the people.[48] And its value depends on how it is kept up, and on how the neighbourhood it is in is kept up – an empty house devalues the whole area.

Boarded-up empty property on a street can easily raise the average negative equity for other families living in homes on that same street. Nearby property prices fall. Evictions also contribute directly to rising homelessness, which, if visible, also further devalues a neighbourhood. Having your neighbours sleeping by your gutter does not make your home look good. You may think this applies only to the US, but in Britain, as more homeless hostels and probation hostels are shut, more people who do lose their homes will find themselves roofless. In the city of Bristol, in autumn 2013, some 150 people were threatened with losing their homeless hostel beds as enhanced austerity cuts were imposed.[49]

NEGATIVE EQUITY

People do not want to be confronted with the sight of the homeless – it is uncomfortable for the well-off to be reminded of the human price that is paid for a social structure like theirs – and they are willing to deprive those people of their last opportunity to sleep in order to protect themselves from this discomfort.

– Jeremy Waldron, 1991[50]

If you have ever wondered why interests rates have remained so low for so long in the UK, consider this. Keeping up the value of the neighbourhood presents something of a dilemma to lenders. When borrowers fall behind on their payments if, for example, interest rates rise, the usual action is to evict them; but if millions of borrowers fall behind, what then do you do? In the UK, government tries to avoid the dilemma by urging the Bank of England not to raise rates. Banks and building societies then tend to follow suit and take their cut by charging their customers much more than the base rate, but not as much as they otherwise would.

In the US, interest rates did not need to rise to bring on a crisis: property values and wages both falling had a similar effect. This is why Vickee Adams, a spokeswoman in the home mortgage division of the US bank Wells Fargo, stressed in 2012 that the bank was keen to support 'folks remaining in their homes – there is a benefit to keeping a community with residents'.[51] And this is where we began this housing disaster story: by introducing the implications of the growth in inequality in the US at the start of this book (pp. 24–5).

Bankers in the US letting some people live free in former homes gives us one possible scenario for what might happen if and when interest rates in the UK rise and/or housing prices fall. You might ask: why don't Wells Fargo and other banks simply turn their defaulting customers into tenants and charge them a rent? A good explanation is that they did not charge rent and become landlords the last time there was a housing finance crisis, in the 1930s, and Wells Fargo survived that. This is made clearer by a comment posted online in response to the news story in which Vickee was quoted. The comment was made by 'Bob', and it is not easy to forget once you have read it. It succinctly tells us what we should most remember about the past, and it is admirably terse in explaining where we might be tomorrow in countries like the US and the UK:

> When I was seven years old my parents picked a house out of a booklet provided by a title company and bought it. They found the previous owners (mortgagees), who had long since defaulted on their mortgage, living there. It was a great hardship for the occupants to leave; they had no place to go. My parents had to have them evicted in order to move in. Many years later, I found the booklet and realized that about 20% of the homes in the town were listed and many of my school classmates belonged to 'squatter' families. It obviously benefited the banks and title companies to let people squat rather than let the properties fall into ruin and there was always the chance that they could repurchase their former homes. That was 1939. That is now.
>
> – Bob, Boonsboro, Maryland, 2012[52]

When I first worked in housing in the early 1990s, it was negative equity that I studied: where it occurred, who was affected, how those unsecured debts then altered other aspects of the lives of those affected, like voting and health.[53] One newspaper story keeps on coming back to me today as I analyse this current crisis. That story was about a couple discussing their negative equity: the woman was called Janet, I think, and the man might have been called Tim. They didn't look very happy; they had recently split up. Janet was holding a cup of tea and looking miserable in the photograph accompanying the story. They had to stay in the house they had bought, to continue living with each other, with someone they no longer loved, because of the early 1990s UK housing crisis.

Today it is no longer whole houses that are being shared by people who have split up, but just one bedroom. This is despite our having more beds than ever before, per person. And it is not just couples who have split up who are doing this. Very poor immigrant tenants talk of hot-bedding – two or three people using the same bed but sleeping in it at different times of the day and night. But a general sense of housing being in crisis might begin to be better appreciated when it's not just the very poor who have to share a bed when they'd rather not do so. The story that follows was told in the UK in 2013; twenty years on, the couple are called Adela and Tanek, not Janet and Tim. Here is the situation as Adela describes it:

> It was a difficult decision and a terrible step backwards, but eventually we decided we had no choice but for me to move back into the family home . . . We get on well as friends but this situation is terribly awkward and very wrong. We want to get on with our lives and meet new people but we're stuck together. We can't afford a second bed and have nowhere to put one anyway. We don't have a sofa we can sleep on and we don't want the children to have to share their room with one of us.[54]

In the early 1990s I had to constantly explain what negative equity was if I wanted to write about that new phenomenon. It was a new phrase then; it even featured as a new 'word of the year' in one review of the year's news. Today few people interested in housing do not know that negative equity is the difference between the outstanding mortgage owed and a home's current value. Equity becomes 'negative' when a property's value drops to less than the debt secured on it – meaning that the potential owner is paying back to the bank more than their property is worth, on top of the interest.

In the US 'nearly 16 million US homeowners, or 31.4% of all homeowners with a mortgage, were financially under water in 2012. They owed $1.2 trillion more than the value of their homes.'[55] As I write, figures for 2013 have yet to be released, but we know that remortgaging in the US is on the increase again, as reported above, so positive equity is being drawn down. In a response to persistent negative equity, the city of Richmond, California, voted, on 11 September 2013, to use the power of eminent domain (similar to compulsory purchase orders in the UK) to 'become the first in the nation to acquire mortgages with negative equity in a bid to keep local residents in their homes'.[56]

Negative equity can be set up from the start by corrupt lenders. A data analyst in the US has used housing transaction data to determine whether the initial survey, or 'appraisal', of a property done on behalf of the lender deliberately inflated its value. This puts the buyer into instant negative equity. If current property valuations are being made at levels that are unattainable or unsustainable, in parts of Britain this could be happening now.

The data analyst's company, Triaxx, identified loans that might have been inflated by comparing every sale to fifty sales of similarly sized property sold at the same time.[57] The analyst estimated that for one lender alone, ResCap,[58] 'phoney appraisals' resulted in $1.29 billion more being lent than should have been. One example was of a mortgage issued in November 2006 on a home in Miami. This was for the purchase of a 1,036-square-foot single-family residence (a very small home for America). The appraisal was that the property was worth $495,000 and it allowed a $396,000 mortgage to be issued, at 'a relatively conservative 80% loan-to-value ratio'.

However, what appeared to be an 80% loan can easily turn out not to have been a loan at that lending proportion at all. Analysing ten similar sales made around the time of this loan, Triaxx suggested that the property in question was actually worth about $279,000 – so the $396,000 mortgage represented a 142% loan-to-value borrowing ratio. Triaxx's report added, drily, that the value of the home in question might possibly have been justified had it contained gold-plated bathroom fixtures and diamond-encrusted appliances. Of course, the Triaxx technique to check for fraudulent valuing only works if the majority of lenders are not also inflating their surveys. It is when fraud becomes the norm – when almost every surveyor says all homes are worth more than the asking prices a year ago, at the same time as average wages are falling – that we should realize we cannot go on like this.

Could house prices soon rise greatly again and free mortgagors trapped by negative equity in the US, across much of Europe and elsewhere in the rich world? Many think not in the near future, but all it takes is for a little general inflation to take place and housing price inflation will free those currently trapped. Such a rise might help people in debt, but it would not make housing more affordable, unless housing prices did not rise by as much as wages and salaries. In November 2012 reporters at the *Wall Street Journal* suggested that a tipping point had been passed in the UK. They drew the following graph. It may look to be only of marginal relevance here, but when eventually one of those upward blips becomes a trend, everything that is currently stable in housing changes.

Ten months later, in August 2013, the Consumer Price Index (CPI) remained at 2.7%, so if October 2012 was a turning point, nothing has turned very much yet; although the Retail Price Index (RPI) did rise from 3.1% in July 2013 to 3.3% by August, just twenty-eight days later.[59] The RPI includes the cost of mortgage payments; the CPI does not. Housing is once again becoming more expensive in the UK, rapidly so in autumn 2013, but the ability to pay for it is not rising.

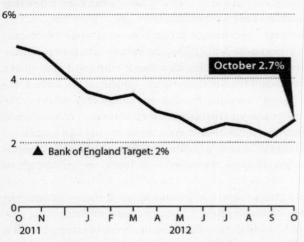

Rising Again
U.K.'s annual inflation rate measured by year-to-year change in CPI

Figure 21. *Wall Street Journal* depiction of UK inflation trends, October 2011 to October 2012.

There are many other signs that inflation might soon rise. In late February 2013 the UK lost its AAA credit rating. The last time that occurred, back in the 1970s, inflation became high and then rose further. Rising inflation has the beneficial effect for households in negative equity of releasing them from their debt, but it also tends to make central bankers believe that interest rates should be increased too, to dampen any further rise (as people then have less spare money to spend); otherwise inflation keeps on rising and rising and eventually another bubble is formed.

Neither rapidly falling nor rising housing prices will help us all, in aggregate, in future. They will help some people, but not others. What this book argues is that more housing rights are needed, as is a slow change in attitude, until we again see housing as shelter, as the buildings around which communities grow, not as retirement nest-eggs. Slowly falling housing prices and rents would rebalance the economy. Benefits need to rise faster than wages, wages faster than salaries, salaries faster than housing prices, and rents need to rise slowest of all, if at all. Describing the path we should take to get to this situation, which I attempt to do in the next chapter, is far harder than describing the ideal situation we need to aspire to; but first we have to know that the alternative of future staggeringly unaffordable housing is frightening enough to make the effort worthwhile.

In Ireland there are countless neighbourhoods that are now characterized by mass negative equity: 'For residents in these estates, they are living with the stress of an uncertain future with regards to works being completed, massive negative equity (in excess of 60% from peak), and a lack of a sense of place and community.'[60] Negative equity at current Irish levels requires price rises in many areas of 60% simply to remove the unsecured part of the debt. An inflation rate of 2.7% achieves that only with a continuous eighteen years of uninterrupted price rises. Thus, if the value of housing in many areas of Ireland were to rise by the current rate of UK inflation, in a generation it would again be worth what families paid for it in 2008. But why should that happen?

In March 2013, the Irish government went back to its major creditor, the EU, to ask for more money and longer repayment terms. In December 2013 it officially escaped the direct control of international creditors, although the Troika will return to inspect the country's books twice a year for many years to come.[61] As Alan Barrett, head of the Economic Analysis Division at Ireland's Economic and Social Research Institute, put it in a considerable understatement, Ireland in early 2013 was in 'a fairly unstable situation'.[62] A day later it was reported that property was still selling at auction in Ireland for *less than a fifth* of its peak price.[63] Even before that 'eminent domain' reaction in Richmond, California, the government in Ireland, through the National Asset Management Agency (NAMA), created in late 2009, had begun to convert empty former private homes into homes that could be used for rent through housing associations. Some 4,000 were announced in 2013, but that is only a tiny fraction of the 96,000 that need to be converted.[64] Unfortunately the Irish are also looking to sell off part of that rental portfolio to invest-ment funds,[65] claiming they are struggling to drum up enough interest from potential not-for-profit landlords.[66] Transfers to not-for-profit landlords is the kind of action that is still being demanded in Europe's other most housing-downturn-affected country, Spain, where elected officials have been talking about the need for fundamental change and for extending compulsory purchasing powers for many months now:

> Utopias aren't chimeras; they are the most noble dreams that people have. The dream of equality; the dream that housing should belong to everyone, because you are a person, and not a piece of merchandise to be speculated with; the dream that natural resources – for instance energy – shouldn't be in the service of multinationals, but in the service of the people. All those dreams are the dreams we'd like to turn into realities.
>
> – Juan Manuel Sánchez Gordillo, the Mayor of
> Marinaleda, 2012[67]

You might think that Marinaleda is an exceptional case, and that Gordillo's pronouncement isn't typical of Spanish officialdom. And you would be right. But when you look at what has happened in Ireland since that Spanish mayor spoke, you might also think he was just a little ahead of his time. All around Europe the underlying circumstances continue to change. In Greece average property prices are now falling to levels below half of their 2008 peak, below what in 2012 was thought to be their floor price.[68] Under these circumstances what was once impossible becomes possible in many parts of Europe, just as the seizing of land and property for the public good has now become possible in Richmond, California.

When Juan Gordillo, the Mayor of that small town in rural Andalusia, led farm labourers into supermarkets to expropriate basic living supplies, he explained to the television cameras that a better world was possible, just one small step, or theft, at a time. When it comes to providing housing, a better world is more easily possible. In contrast to taking food off supermarket shelves, or supplying energy, housing does not need to be stolen, only more equitably distributed. It can be made to belong to everyone just a little bit more than it currently does by extending rights, by saying that everyone has the right to be housed. Governments could transfer empty privately owned property into social housing, and those who are hoarding in a time of austerity could be cajoled, taxed or otherwise persuaded out of such behaviour.

As they now chant at demonstrations in Spain, 'No people without houses, no houses without people',[69] which is fitting in the country with the largest number of empty homes and also home to Europe's largest slum shanty town, Cañada Real Galiana.[70] There is no necessity in Europe to see shanty towns grow, but they will grow if we fail to share out better what we have, or at least share as well as we used to. As yet there are no similar shanty towns or slums in the UK, but there could be in future, as housing values skyrocket in some places and nose-dive in others.

Most people want to stay in their homes, but some who have split up (or who are suffering domestic violence and should split up) desperately want to leave. The major problem for people with negative equity comes when they want to move. They can't sell – but imagine a scenario in which they could sell their property to their lender and become tenants with a new landlord. Then they could leave. The 'right-to-stay', the right to become a tenant in the home you are already living in, would – ironically, given its title – also give home-buyers with negative equity the option to leave. It is the counterbalance to the 'right-to-buy', and it already exists in legislation in the UK for households with children or other vulnerable persons; it is just not yet well enough implemented.

The 'right-to-stay' is the right to stay in your home when adverse economic circumstances mean you would be better off becoming, in effect, a tenant. It has much wider implications for the housing market in the UK if it is ever extended. It is the missing link in UK housing legislation between mortgage-buyers and tenants. Tenants in social housing have the 'right-to-buy', the right to become mortgage-buyers; so why should people who have a mortgage not have the reverse right – the right to become tenants? In the US, lawyers acting on behalf of bankers who currently own property in negative equity are trying to block current plans there to make this possible: 'which they say relies on them swallowing losses'.[71] Not everyone wins when residents gain more rights. Such rights are only won and extended during times of great turmoil, but we may well be approaching such turmoil again now, across the entire rich world.

A portent of what could come was first seen in Greece during the summer of 2010, when a law was passed allowing mortgage-holders to remain in their property when they have negative equity and can no longer afford to keep up their payments. What is more, this law also gives them a long-term way out of financial purgatory. It enables borrowers to avoid foreclosure on their primary residence if they commit to pay back a portion of their remaining mortgage debts at an average mortgage rate over at most twenty years for amounts of up to 85% of their home's current market value – significantly not the value of the property when the mortgage was secured. This gives the residents equity of at least 15% of the new value, and the banks have to swallow the losses.[72]

All around – in Italy, Spain, Portugal, Ireland, Iceland and even in the private property capital of the US – change is afoot. Some change is vocal and direct; some is more cautious; much is pragmatic; and almost all of it is too little too late – but the model of the last thirty-three years of banks profiteering from people's struggles just to be able to stay in their home when things become adverse is now under widespread threat. The denial of profits to the banks is the possibility that has emerged from the crisis.

The law rescuing mortgage-holders in Greece was brought in by the then Economy Minister, Louka Katseli. It does not apply to the most expensive properties, so the wealthy are not protected; moreover, borrowers have to show that they have no other assets with which to repay their debts. Only the main home is protected and then only if its value is under €150,000 for the unmarried, and under €300,000 for married couples.

Contrast the extension of housing rights in crisis-stricken Greece with the timidity of the UK government, which, during 2012, sought to give mortgage-holders the additional right to build small extensions to the backs of their (bank's) property without planning permission;[73] and which tried and failed in that same year to encourage more people to become mortgage-holders by promoting the 'right-to-buy'. In the UK many people do not have a right to shelter, and those that do can still be given inappropriate shelter. People have the right to get into debt in order to buy, to build, to extend or just to spend, but not the right to stay in their homes and to be protected from the vagaries of the market. Perversely, the more people are prepared to take on additional debt the better the economy is said to be – rising debt and spending are often taken as a sign of consumer confidence, which helps the market economy. The government often seems more willing to protect the banks from market forces than its own people, even though individuals cannot be expected to understand these forces as well as the banks.

Unsurprisingly the high-profile 2012 'right-to-buy' relaunch had minimal take-up. Some 5,697 people in twenty-five local authorities expressed a desire to buy their council house. However, only 233 have done so because less than 5% of those who were interested were earning enough money.[74] Almost everyone who has the financial wherewithal to buy in the UK has already bought. More people need to be able to sell – especially those who are finding it hard to keep up their mortgage payments. In theory people can sell and stay put as tenants in the UK under existing laws, but the current coalition government has no enthusiasm for promoting or extending these laws. People currently have the right to sell the home they are buying back to their lender or to have it passed on to a housing association. In England this is called the Mortgage Rescue Scheme (MRS); there are similar schemes in Wales and Scotland; while a full mortgage rescue scheme was proposed for Northern Ireland in 2010 but has not yet been implemented.[75]

The current UK 'right-to-stay' is in fact a 'right-to-sell': the ownership of your home can be passed from your bank to a new landlord, even when you own only a small part or none of it. These schemes were proposed during the previous government's term in office but were not developed enough when New Labour was in power. Take-up was not insignificant, but it was not celebrated. Perhaps this was because becoming a tenant again in the UK is seen as a source of shame. Perhaps the word 'rescue' does not help. All these current schemes appear not to be favoured by the current UK government and their Unionist allies in Northern Ireland, but all remain on the statute book, ready to be used should the crisis deepen to disaster, should interest rates need to rise rapidly, and should it become essential to avoid the mass eviction of families who can no longer pay their mortgage.[76]

The coalition government might wish to see the absolute private property rights of banking corporations defended, but it has no plans at present to reverse the 'right-to-sell' legislation. It might know that this is indefensible in the current climate, and so it allows local authorities to continue to use the legislation. In the city of Sheffield over a hundred MRSs were completed between 2010 and 2012. This was done by transferring ownership to housing associations. However, experts on housing in that city suggest that the numbers were so low because the amounts allowed under the new housing benefit caps are often not enough to pay the rent.

The cuts in housing benefit can prevent those who can no longer pay the mortgage from being 'rescued' and turned into tenants. It is not fecklessness but almost always loss of employment, reduction in contracted hours, illness or separation that causes families to become at risk of losing their home. Local housing experts in Sheffield claim that the existing schemes are not enough. There also needs to be more responsible lending with robust landlord regulation, as well as more advice and help with budgeting and money management.[77] But services such as the Citizens Advice Bureaus have been savagely cut just at the time they are most needed. That service began to be decimated in April 2011.[78]

We are currently in the middle of a fight over the philosophy and legality of the right to be housed, the right to advice and the right not to be ripped off. The 'right-to-stay' – to sell the home you are in to a social or even to a private landlord, but to continue to occupy it as a tenant – would work only if tenancy conditions in the UK became more palatable. If it becomes necessary for even more families to rent, rather than to borrow and buy, and if families currently locked into mortgages are to regard a switch to renting as acceptable and not as a retrograde step, there will have to be a reform of tenants' rights. Many of the rights that tenants enjoyed in the past in the UK have been lost, but below is a list of what is currently the practice in other (similar) countries to show what the range of workable options is.

Table 2. Notable private rental practices in other countries.

Country	Purpose	Practice
Ireland	Tenant security	Four years' security of tenure after initial year
Sweden	Tenant security	Offers indefinite leases
Hong Kong	Tenant security	Offers two-year leases
Netherlands	Landlord finance	Depreciation allowance
France	Landlord finance	Offsetting rental losses against other income - 'negative gearing' - makes investment more appealing
US	Single ownership	Blocks of rental properties under single ownership, making properties easier to manage and portfolios easier to assemble
Switzerland	Rent regulation	Rent ceilings, regularly adjusted by officials, that may not be exceeded for affordable properties
Denmark	Rent regulation	Sets an officially determined rate by which rents are allowed to increase for new tenancies and has local rent control boards
Austria	Rent regulation	Only permits mid-tenancy rent rises in line with Consumer Price Index inflation
Finland	Rent regulation	Bans landlords from passing on costs to cover maintenance
Belgium	Rent regulation	Allows landlords to increase rents to make improvements to property
Germany	Tenant control	Landlords rent out a 'shell' that tenants can then decorate themselves
Spain	Social-private	A public institution (Sociedad Pública de Alquiler) has been created to provide guaranteed rental schemes for tenants and landlords in order to encourage the development of the rental sector

Imagine if the UK had many of those rights enjoyed by tenants in all those other countries listed above. Imagine if you had the 'right-to-stay' as long as you lived in your rented home, as long as you paid the rent. What about rent staying fixed for at least two years or even for five years, at which time you could renegotiate? Imagine if the rent could not simply be increased at the whim of your landlord but was set by a local board, perhaps exactly like Local Housing Allowances for housing benefit are set. Why isn't the allowance the maximum rent? That is no more odd than having a minimum wage to prevent exploit-ation. We won that minimum wage only in 1997. How long before we win a maximum rent? But please don't stop imagining just yet.

Imagine if there were minimum-quality standards that ensured housing for rent had qualities that most people would be willing to put up with, and not just 'low quality for the poor'. You might say that landlords could not afford to provide all this. But, if that were the case, they would then have to sell their property cheaply to a devel-oper family that could do it up, and prices would fall. For some reason landlords are able to do all this in much of the rest of (at least northern) Europe. Perhaps it is because house prices there are lower, when they rise they climb more slowly, and negative equity then becomes rarer. High-quality rental accommodation may by itself be keeping house prices down. Of course, less profit is made out of housing in almost all of the rest of Europe; someone loses. But the main motivation for pro-viding good health services, good education and good-quality housing should never be profit.

There is currently a battle taking place over housing policy in the UK. On one side are those arguing for progressive change; these are advocates ranging from groups wishing to increase rights for squat-ters, to think tanks producing options such as those shown in the table above,[79] to political parties less inclined to kowtow to bankers. Opposing them are people who see their purpose as protecting the property interests of a rich minority. This group wants to see more squatters imprisoned because they see squatters as the thin edge of a wedge in the battle for more housing rights. They don't want 'easy options' for the homeless. If the rich minority wins, then, instead of greater rights and a more efficient rationing of our current housing stock, we'll get increased homelessness.

HOMELESSNESS

[From today] councils will be able to discharge their duties to homeless people with the offer of a suitable twelve-month tenancy with a private landlord, and homeless families will now end up in short-term private lets.

— Shelter, 9 November 2012[80]

The date 9 November 2012 marked a watershed. It was when we lost one of the most significant of those housing rights that had been won in the 1960s and strengthened through 1970s political agitation after people watched *Cathy come home* on the BBC, the 1966 film showing a young mother as she traipsed from private let to the streets, to destitution and despair. Measures in the Localism Act of 2011 meant that from that day, 9 November, just seven weeks before Christmas 2012, local councils were no longer legally required to offer homeless families and vulnerable people a secure home managed by them or by a housing association landlord. Instead, they could put the newly homeless straight into the hands of a private landlord, whose main goal was to profit from their homelessness. In the coalition government's words, before 9 November 2012, 'under the previous rules, people who became homeless were able to refuse offers of accommodation in the private rented sector, and insist that they should be housed in expensive temporary accommodation until a long-term social home becomes available.'[81] The 2011 Act also made it possible to rent out council houses on only short-term lets.

In Britain, youth homelessness last rose when housing benefit payments for homeless sixteen- and seventeen-year-olds were made illegal by Margaret Thatcher's government in the very early 1980s. David Cameron would like to reduce young people's housing rights even further. If he gets his way, almost all those aged under twenty-five won't qualify for any housing benefits if homeless.[82] They will get no support at all and have to stay with family or live on the streets. Already people aged under thirty-five can be allocated only enough

housing benefit to allow them to live in a room in shared accommodation, sharing some or all of a kitchen, bathroom, toilet and living
room with strangers. If they fall out with other residents, they can
then easily become homeless. And, once homeless, if they don't have
a child or are otherwise very vulnerable, the authorities have no
responsibility for them, other than to ensure that they are not easy to
see on the streets. This is the UK in 2014, but where did the thinking
that this was OK come from?

Go back twenty-five years, to 1989, and across to the US, once the
results of an earlier mini-housing-crisis spreading across the country
had become a bit more normalized in people's perceptions. It was
reported that New Yorkers had begun to grow tired of confronting
homeless people every day. They met them on the subway, and then at
the mainline train stations; they were stepping over them at the
entrances to supermarkets and even on the doorsteps of their own
apartment buildings. The then Advocacy Director for the Coalition
for the Homeless, Keith Summa, explained that 'People are tired of
stepping over bodies.' And Lynette Thompson, a Transit Authority
official who was at that time overseeing the outreach programme for
the homeless in the subways, said that during 1989 there had been a
marked change in the tone of letters she was receiving from subway
riders. 'At the beginning of last year, the tenor of those letters was
"Please do something to help the homeless." But since August and
September, they've been saying: "Just get them out. I don't care. Just
get them out." '[83]

I first saw hundreds of homeless people when I visited San Francisco in the early 1990s. Even though I was carrying out research into
housing I was shocked, but the Americans around me had become
used to the situation and stepped over the live bodies. Thus what
began in the States has spread to Britain. In both cases what came first
were the government polices making it harder to secure a home, then
the mass homelessness, then the acceptance of mass homelessness. In
the States the Reagan government of 1980–88 began legislation early.
By 1989, when George Bush Senior became President, the Republi-
cans had succeeded in creating a blame-the-victim sea-change in
public opinion. The Thatcher government took a little longer to secure
the policies that would result in so many more young people living on

the streets, but eventually Thatcher's protégés managed to create the same sea-change in thinking: namely that those who have fallen on hard times have only themselves to blame.

Once people become immune to mass homelessness, the only time the homeless are treated well is in the immediate aftermath of an earthquake or similar disaster, when many decently housed people become homeless as well. But when homelessness becomes common among a minority and little is done to alleviate it, the homeless begin to be blamed for their own plight. Yet many of us seem to be unaware of quite how close to the possibility of homelessness we are.

A quarter of all employed people in Scotland are only one monthly pay cheque away from becoming homeless. If a parent lost their job, most two-parent families with children in Scotland, and almost all lone-parent families with children (some 56% of all families in total), could pay the rent for only the next three months. By Christmas 2012, about 1% of this number, or over 5,300 children, were already being housed with their families in emergency homeless accommodation.[84]

It is not lack of housing that is causing homelessness to affect children in the UK. Politically there is a lack of will to tackle the private rented sector, including hotels and B&Bs profiting out of the homeless. In London, where there are still more bedrooms than people, it can cost councils in the heart of the capital up to £350 a night to put a family up in expensive hotel accommodation that is completely unsuitable as emergency accommodation.[85] Yet the reduction in the availability of homes in the social housing sector, and the 9 November 2012 change in legislation, give councils no option but the private sector when it comes to rehousing those on low incomes, including the newly made homeless.

The majority of landlords just want their high rents paid and the property kept in good order, but the impact of many of the current changes, including the sporadic and badly implemented introduction of Universal Credit, means that all councils will soon no longer be able to facilitate direct payments of housing benefit monies to landlords. The gap between rents and benefits is growing, just as the gap between house prices and wages is growing. All this is very confusing for tenants, just as mortgages are very confusing for buyers (including landlords, who do not read the small print and find that their tracker mortgages no longer track the base rate). The state welfare rules are complex and constantly changing. For example, housing benefit is now set on the 30th percentile, rather than the 50th, of assessments of local rents, and is to be uprated using CPI rather than RPI.[86] But how many people know what the differences between those two indexes are, let alone what the acronyms stand for? All of this makes it harder to house people who are poorer, and more people then end up homeless.

Underlying all the recent changes to law and regulation appears to be a coalition government desire that the private sector in England should be able to make more money out of the homeless. In 2012 two unnamed 'private providers' were awarded contracts by the Greater London Authority, currently controlled by Conservative Mayor Boris Johnson. The contracts could be worth as much as £5 million in the short term. They are designed to allow those private companies to tackle what is termed 'entrenched rough sleepers'. 'Entrenched' is defined as people who have been recorded as persistently sleeping rough in the capital over the course of the last two years: some 831 such homeless people were identified in 2011 and 2012. These are seen as the 'hard core' of the estimated 5,678 people sleeping rough at some point in London in the financial year 2011/12. The organization encouraging all this, liaising between the local authority and the suppliers, is a rather shadowy group called Social Finance.[87]

The two private providers who have been awarded the contracts to clear the homeless from London's streets will be rewarded for their 'investment' if five criteria are achieved: first, a 'core outcome' – a reduction in the total number of recorded rough sleepers; secondly, a reduction in the number of individuals who are seen to be sleeping rough over a succession of quarters; thirdly, a confirmed sustainment of tenancy in a non-hostel setting;[88] fourthly, a confirmed, 'successful' reconnection to a country in which the individual 'enjoys' local connections (a euphemism for what may be deportation); and, fifthly, a decrease in the average number of A&E episodes per person per year. All this is defined as 'progress', although these targets look as if they are concerned more with the cosmetic appearance of London than with the plight of the homeless.

These guideline targets appear on the website of Social Finance, whose board members include hedge fund managers.[89] Social Finance isn't one of the two private providers; it is a private broker between government and the providers. It helps the government to remain at arm's length from the action, shields it from any blame – a necessary precaution, should those private providers, motivated by profit and under pressure to achieve financially rewarding targets, be tempted to resort to means that voluntary organizations might regard as unethical.

The companies involved (which are hard to identify, possibly due to commercial confidentiality) would no doubt stress how ethical they are; and yet, reading all the details, it is hard not to speculate that the number of individuals bedding down on the streets will be reduced by harassing the homeless – by forcing them to find places where they are not seen as they are sleeping, within multi-storey car parks, for instance, or under canal bridges. 'A sustained tenancy in a non-hostel setting' could be in the worst of Rachman-style bedsits, with no support or socialization. A 'confirmed reconnection to another country' sounds not dissimilar to the National Front's suggestion of offering people from the Caribbean a one-way flight 'home' in the 1970s. A decrease in A&E episodes might be achieved by directing an ill homeless person to another, non-A&E – and possibly less suitable – facility. Were the death rate – high anyway for rough sleepers, who have an average life expectancy of dying in their forties[90] – to increase, a fall in their numbers might be achieved. Not necessarily good outcomes, unless you think a dead rough sleeper is better than one who is breathing. At times the efforts to remove rough sleepers and the techniques used to estimate their numbers are worryingly reminiscent of the bad science of badger culling, which was being tendered for at the same time.

The number of rough sleepers in the UK rose by almost 25% in just the twelve months to autumn 2011. Material now taught to children in schools in Britain explains that every year some 75,000 children in the UK will wake up homeless on Christmas morning. A further 1.6 million British children live in housing that is overcrowded, temporary or run-down. The 2011 census revealed that the proportion of homes rented privately containing children has soared by 69% since 2001. Other surveys find that currently some 44% of British people believe their children won't be able to afford to buy their own home. All these facts are being taught to children in schools in Britain today. What must they think of their parents?[91] What the children are not told is that if housing rights are not improved, and mortgage defaulters are not given some security of tenure, all these numbers will inevitably rise. Perhaps they will start to work this out for themselves?

Those people made homeless with children at least still have a limited right to be housed, as a family, by a local authority, although now only in a one-year let in what is often the most shoddy local private accommodation. But increasingly that right is being ignored. Local authorities try to pass the buck to each other, to pass the family on to another area, but when that is no longer possible the homeless family is often placed in what is supposed to be temporary B&B accommodation. Cynically, in June 2013, the government asked local councils with some of the 760 families who had been in B&B for over six weeks by June 2013 to take part in a bidding auction for funds to rehouse them.[92] Thousands more are in B&B at any one time, but for less than six weeks.

Homes often become security for small businesses. In February 2013 a London family of four – a mother with three children – were being housed in a single room. Only a few weeks earlier they had been living in a five-bedroom house, but then the husband's business went bust and the family were made homeless to pay his debts. She and the children were moved to a different B&B every fortnight for two months. It cost the council almost £1,000 a week to provide one room in Lambeth for them. As the mother explained: 'There's no place to cook, no fridge, no wi-fi, no washing machine, no place to put our things. The whole place ends up smelling.'[93] The children also did not really know where they were or what was happening, because they were kept moving between one temporary accommodation and another.

The report from which this story was drawn revealed that the number of families being housed illegally – that is, for more than six weeks – in such accommodation has risen ninefold since 2010. From May 2010, when the coalition government took office, up until 2012 there was a rise in the number of families in such dire straits of almost 1,000%! In 2013 it was revealed that the number of families living in B&B in London had soared again to over 2,000. The homeless charity Crisis directly blamed government cuts for the rise.[94]

There are too few statistics kept on homelessness; and the government is keeping track of fewer groups of people all the time. In England the Department for Communities and Local Government doesn't count the number of single adults asking for its help other than those who have recently been in care. It no longer counts those who come for help who were in the Armed Forces, or sleeping in night shelters or hostels. Nor does it try to estimate the numbers that are sofa-surfing. By contrast, in December 2012, the devolved Scottish parliament extended its homelessness legislation, so that anyone finding themselves homeless through no fault of their own was entitled to settled accommodation.[95] This was so uncontroversial there that it had been passed unanimously by the Scottish parliament.

There is a perception that recent rough sleeping increases in London are mostly connected with arrivals from Eastern Europe; that this homelessness is the result of a specific sets of circumstances. But there are no statistics to suggest that this is the case, whereas there are numerous well-researched claims to show that one British family with children is becoming homeless every fifteen minutes and that, if the current increase were to continue, by 2015 over 10,000 families with children will be homeless in England.[96] But by 2015 we may not know if this has occurred, given how the statistical services we rely upon are currently being so readily disbanded.

No department is more enthusiastic in cutting statistics than Eric Pickles's Department for Communities and Local Government, the department responsible for housing. The National Housing Federation explains that 'Beyond the six-week mark, no data is collected on length of stays in B&Bs. This means we do not know how long families are really spending in this type of accommodation.'[97] This apparent lack of interest in such information might appear to sit oddly with Pickles's frequent pronouncements that he cares deeply, and with his personal role as a trustee of the homeless charity Brentwood Foyer, which had forty bed spaces in March 1999.[98] Brentwood Foyer was still looking after young single homeless people aged over sixteen and under twenty-four in 2012.[99] It would be worth asking Pickles what he knows of the outcomes of the hundreds of young people who must have passed through its doors, staying between six months and two years, since 1999.

Shelter has issued a 'classroom kit' to help teachers give lessons about homelessness and the issues surrounding it. For example, children are asked to imagine they are different people in a national debate on housing. One suggestion is to imagine that you are an environmentalist:

> You are against the new development. You are unhappy about the added traffic the new development could bring to local roads, and you wonder whether the new homes will be as carbon neutral as they could be? You are worried that new developments are concreting over Britain's greenbelt and that areas of brownbelt, which can be valuable urban wildernesses, are being lost too. You think that it might be better to restore old houses than build new ones.[100]

There is potentially great significance in the development of this classroom kit and similar initiatives. If young people today are taught the reality of just how badly housed many of their peers are, or how badly housed they are in comparison with most of the children living in the rest of Europe, this could prove to be one of the ways in which our culture on housing can be changed for the generations to come. A child finds it hard to imagine ever having to pay for a home, but it is the children of today who will be most affected by the changes being made by the coalition government, and their children in turn.

Housing prices in Britain are high partly because so few people have so much control over so many buildings. As the proportion of people who are tenants increases, so too will the power of landlords. And those landlords can see an ever-growing market for the bedrooms they have to rent out. As Shelter's classroom kit explains: 'England's population is projected to increase by 10 million between 2010 and 2035 and be nearly 18 million higher by 2061.' Most of that increase will be the children born to today's children. A large part of the rest will be their grandparents and parents living longer; a smaller part will be more immigration; but all of this is additional foreseen profit for landlords.

Shelter's classroom kit for schoolteachers continues by explaining that the government's latest household projections have indicated that there is an accelerating pressure for new housing, suggesting that an additional 5.1 million new households are expected between 2011 and 2031. This will be considerably more than the number added over the two previous twenty-year periods: 3.6 million more households between 1991 and 2011 and 3.2 million more between 1971 and 1991. What the kit doesn't say, however, is that we have built more rooms than we have gained people during both those previous two twenty-year periods; the charity concentrates on dwelling numbers, not dwelling size.

The Shelter classroom kit next gives teachers details of the growth occurring disproportionately in the south-eastern corner of England: 'with the London, south-east and east regions accounting for over half (52%) of the 2010–35 population increase despite comprising only 30% of England's area'.[101] If schoolchildren can be expected to cope with these issues, and such figures, why is there not a wider debate among their parents? Perhaps it needs to be set as adult homework? The current expected level of population increase will require more house-building – but not so very much more if we use what we have in better ways.[102]

So let's explore some areas in which we might be able to use what we already have more efficiently. One good place to start is with squatters and how they might help us to get empty property, including commercial property, into residential use.

SQUATTING AND REFURBISHMENT

What the squatting dispute boils down to is a split between those who consider private property to be sacred, and those who would prioritize the right to shelter. Few people would happily forfeit a second home to squatters, but nor does it feel morally justifiable for a nation to have an estimated 930,000 empty homes while people sleep on the streets.

– Steve Rose, journalist, 2012[103]

People don't simply accept being made homeless. Many become resigned to it, but others do something about it. If you are homeless and no organization will house you adequately, you may have to house yourself in empty properties – to squat. Almost all squatting involves an empty property that is not being used. It is a rather more effective method of using genuinely empty rooms than the Bedroom Tax. But, while the UK government often talks about people doing things on their own initiative, squatting is one initiative it detests. So, since 2012, it has criminalized what had been, until very recently, only a civil offence.

While the UK government justifies the Bedroom Tax with the excuse that money must be saved by filling every last bedroom in social housing, it nonetheless manages to find a lot of money to attack squatters. Campaigners 'have calculated the cost of criminalizing squatting to be projected to cost upwards of £790 million over a five-year period following introduction of the legislation in 2012'.[104] The money could be better spent.

It is true that squatting can cause great problems. Sometimes, of course, squatters can be ill-behaved or even destructive, but rarely do squatters wish to put themselves or their homes in peril in such a way. Squatting is by its nature precarious – and squatters often feel they have no option but to squat.

The first squatter to be imprisoned under the new law was Alex Haigh. Alex had moved from Plymouth to London in search of work. Just twenty-one years old and living with two others in a vacant housing association property, he was arrested, tried and sentenced to twelve weeks in gaol in September 2012. He would have been young enough to be housed in the dormitory of the Brentwood Foyer, the charity that Eric Pickles is a trustee of, had there been a spare bed there at that time. But he would have had no choice about his roommates, and likely nowhere nearby where he could find good work. Squatting is entrepreneurial; there is a little more freedom to choose your friends and to live near places where you can be enterprising.

When 21-year-old Alex was imprisoned, a Ministry of Justice spokesperson is reported by the BBC to have said: 'For too long squatters have been playing the justice system and have caused homeowners untold misery in eviction, repair and clean-up costs.'[105] What the spokesperson did not even hint at is that there are good reasons why people like Alex prefer the risks of squatting to the alternative of offers from the likes of Pickles's 'foyer' charity. The Ministry of Justice looked only at the costs for the owner of a vacant property, at those clean-up costs, and not at the costs of insecurity for squatters. The Ministry of Justice has a very narrow view of justice. Almost all squatted buildings are empty properties bought for investment purposes; and most are vacant commercial premises.

A wider view of justice would add the misery of the squatters to those clean-up costs; and, at an extreme, the feelings of suicide brought about by eviction. A wider view of justice would consider the despair you get when you are trapped by debt and negative equity in a property you wish you had never been fooled into buying. It would take into account how a 21-year-old might feel about being placed in a dormitory for the homeless out of town where there is no work and little hope. If necessary, all these social evils could have a monetary value attached to them to help people who find it hard to understand feelings to develop a better sense of justice.

There is a growing body of nasty right-wing opinion that opposes what it calls a more lavish system of 'social housing' on the basis that it creates an incentive for indolence. Such rhetoric is a modern-day version of the Victorian regressive who believed that hunger was a far more effective weapon than the overseer's whip in encouraging workers to toil. Those who today are against the homeless being decently housed are not so ideologically different from their predecessors who opposed health care, including the 1930s eugenicists who believed a national health service would only help the weak to survive and breed.

Everyone should be able to benefit from the quiet enjoyment of a home, free from noise, from harassment and from fear. But among the rich, the far right sees the quiet enjoyment of their property, no matter how big their property might be, as being a similar basic right. That enjoyment extends to their wealth, their homes and their land, and to the right to grow their legacy ever larger. However, as they cannot live in all their homes at the same time, they leave a lot of property empty, and what should be a real home for a real family becomes just empty property gathering dust.

The concept of households having the right to the quiet enjoyment of their home was introduced to try to protect tenants from being harassed by landlords and loan sharks; its purpose was not to provide a covenant for the protection of the rich. Just as freedom of speech does not give you the right to shout 'fire' in a crowded theatre, so the quiet enjoyment of your home does not give you the right to keep property empty at the expense of other families.

It is a renewed conception of the apparent sanctity of private property that is, perhaps, the real impulse behind the new anti-squatting laws. That would certainly explain why the new laws are failing so dramatically. In April 2013 more than two dozen lawyers revealed that not one conviction under the new squatting laws had protected owner-occupiers; instead 'the effect . . . has been to facilitate keeping properties empty, despite the current housing crisis.'[106] Why would a government change the law to keep buildings empty?

At any one time between 20,000 to 50,000 people in the UK squat, almost all in abandoned buildings, and only very rarely in one that someone else actually wants to live in. By definition it is hard to be more precise than that; squatters tend not to be a group well covered in surveys or by a census. But we do know that they number around just 0.1% of the population of the UK, or perhaps even less. Worldwide, a tenth of all people squat, a rate that is one hundred times higher than that in the UK. Most of the poor world is far more inequitable than the UK. And the more inequality there is, the higher becomes the proportion of people who have to squat. It is only in a just society that the squatting rate can fall to zero.

People squat because the alternatives are worse – be they the Eric Pickles's type of 'foyer' charity or the private sector profit-making equivalent. The current government wants to criminalize squatting even further, extending the legislation to allow the police to arrest and imprison people who are sleeping in abandoned commercial buildings and old barns and other out-buildings. Yet such a crackdown will prove economically unviable. The more people they force out of squatting, the more they force into emergency homelessness accommodation or the cheapest of rooms in the private rental market, or on to the street, which will make things worse for everyone.

An example often helps, and hundreds of thousands of people worldwide were shown what is going wrong today in Britain when Bloomberg reported on what just one planning officer was finding in one London borough in 2012. Christine Lyons is the Chief Planning Enforcer of the London borough of Newham. What she described to

Bloomberg's reporters in the summer of 2012 evoked scenes reminiscent of Victorian England. She showed them illegally run properties occupied by tenants who were crammed into what that TV channel described as slum-like conditions, with entire families living in single dirty rooms and in those garden sheds. As the channel crudely put it: 'Surveying the stinking toilet and fly-infested kitchen are all in a day's work for Christine.'[107] This was hardly a great advert for London.

Why do people put up with these conditions, and why do Londoners as a whole allow their city to contain such housing misery? The international viewers of Bloomberg might have wondered what is going on in the UK. Perhaps those paying rent to live in such squalor are too afraid to squat elsewhere. One man in the report on Christine's work found that what he thought was a cupboard in the kitchen next to the fridge turned out to be the place someone was renting to sleep. The house was licensed for five to sleep in, but it turned out that there were twelve occupants. The landlord was fined – but how long before another twelve desperate tenants move in?

Squatting generally involves a less cramped existence than the bottom end of the private rented market or a full-up homeless shelter; squatting is also more affordable and freer in many other senses. You are free of the expense of renting, free to choose where you live and how you live there. Squatters often renovate the empty properties they occupy. Why wouldn't they? There clearly is a need for that renovation, but there should be no need for so many to squat. There is enough housing for all, even in a crowded island like Britain, even in the heart of London (where it really cannot be repeated enough that there are still more bedrooms than people). What we lack is a housing policy that is collective, not individualistic.

The incentive to look after just our own interests can be great. If you are a mortgage-payer hoping to sell in future, you may think: don't do up the home, just paint over the cracks and sell it at a profit. If you are a landlord, you may think of asking your tenants for another £10 a week. They can't really afford it, but you'll get an extra night's skiing for that extra £520 you gain a year. You get an extra £3,120 if you put up the rent when you have six tenants sleeping in the house! Similarly, if you are a tenant living in a society promoting more and more individualism, you might well think of illegally subletting your housing association flat. Everyone else is on the fiddle – why not you? Ultimately it is thinking as an individual and then being frustrated with your life, with the idea that you have too little, which bolsters all these attitudes, including, at the extreme, the thought: why not give the bloke sleeping rough a kicking when you've had a drink? He's scum. Contempt gets into the very language we use; when we talk about some people as taxpayers, and others as living on welfare, we grow contemptuous. And contempt so easily breeds more contempt.

8

Solutions

The prime minister urged people to 'trust' the Bank of England, which has been given an enhanced role in monitoring the effect of the ['help-to-buy'] scheme on prices ... Mr Cameron also used his Andrew Marr interview to stress that there would be no 'mansion tax' if he was prime minister after the next election, making it clear that this would be a so-called 'red line' – a point he would refuse to concede – in coalition negotiations.

– BBC News, September 2013[1]

Sometimes it is tempting to suggest that policymakers should simply look at what the current Prime Minister is suggesting and do the opposite. But progressive politics often moves slowly, and, just when you think there is no hope, it materializes. When better solutions are implemented, often at first you hardly recognize them, they have been so watered down. Then you say that they are not enough. Next you change what it was you were demanding. You keep on fighting. But eventually, one day, you look back and suddenly realize how far you have come. That is how changes have been won elsewhere; it is how they were won in the past. It is how the consensus becomes something else, often imperceptibly slowly; it is how progress is made.

THE RIGHT NOT TO BE RIPPED OFF

*... the past was better. For the future to be better, we need to
break with an economic model that no longer works.*

– Paul Mason, BBC Economics Editor, 2012[2]

The crisis of housing is part of a wider crisis. Those who currently
benefit from the crisis have more financial control over politicians
than those who lose. In the UK, a recent investigation found that
banks, insurers, hedge funds and private equity firms pay an estimated
annual £15.8 million to thirty-eight public affairs consultancies
(including several public relations firms) to lobby the government on
their behalf. On top of that spending, currently one in six members of
the House of Lords benefits personally from direct financial links with
financial services firms. A majority of the members of the committee
of the House of Lords that scrutinizes the budget are also 'paid by
finance firms'.[3] None of this is called corruption because these lords
declare these interests, as if the declaration actually absolves them.

In total the British financial services industry is estimated to spend
£92 million a year lobbying both policymakers and so-called market
regulators to act in their favour rather than in the favour of ordinary
citizens and consumers, or of residents, families and households.[4] In
future children will be taught about how unelected men in the pay of
banks sat in a chamber of the houses of parliament and acted to protect a few rich vested interests; but as yet that information has not
reached any 'classroom kit'.

Part of the underlying reason for our current housing crisis is the
toleration of endemic corruption in our legislature and legal and
financial systems. What allowed that corruption to increase were the
problems associated with the growing inadequacies of our old housing systems, mostly set up around a century ago: state housing,
building society-funded housing, charity-provided housing. State
housing has been 'residualized' and is now reserved only for those
perceived as failures; building societies have mostly been privatized.

Charitable housing associations now more often behave as if motivated by profit than by charitable concern; often this transformation is called putting them on a 'sound financial footing'.

Financing the buying of a house through a mortgage is increasingly risky for many people, given that the nature of work is becoming increasingly precarious. The state is no longer seen as providing a safety-net for all, only a selected few, the deserving, so social housing is stigmatized. In eras when the rich take more, even charities can become less charitable, a little more mean-spirited, a little more pejorative, describing their actions as philanthropy rather than as campaigning. They help the poor to budget better instead of working harder against the injustice of their poverty. I have watched this happen over the course of my lifetime, and this occurs even when, and perhaps because, those with the most have ever more to 'give'.

Currently, across the developing world, people are buying fewer homes, staying in their current homes for longer, borrowing less if they can, slowly paying back debts – and, in so doing, deflating the economy. Many of these trends read like good signs, but they don't reflate an economy dependent on ever-growing consumption. When people are pessimistic, their behaviour alters; they do budget better without having to be told. Four years after the current crisis began, in April 2012, some 28% of residents in Great Britain stated that they thought their personal financial situation would get worse over the next six months and only 22% thought that their situation would get better. For the majority, their financial situation deteriorated.[5]

Think about what else goes wrong when housing goes wrong. How hard is it to recruit schoolteachers in a city where the prices and rents are astronomical? How easy is it to get people to move into areas where the housing is so cheap that they suspect something is going wrong with the local economy? Housing costs the least in the places that need the most help, the places that most need people with disposable income. But, for some perverse economic reason, low housing prices are not seen as attractive. Migrants from outside the UK, and young migrants within the country, tend to go to where housing costs the most, to London more than anywhere else. But migrants come only when it is worth coming, when there is money to pay for jobs to be done, when they plan to earn rather than to spend.

Mervyn King, the former Governor of the Bank of England, explained that 'most of the huge debts accumulated by banks could be tied to the huge bonuses executives received as reward for their lending.'[6] Those huge bonuses and the impression they gave – that bankers were simply on a personal mission to enrich themselves – created great mistrust. That mistrust of the banks, the main mortgage-lenders, now clearly reaches right to the top, to Bank of England governors. The laws are being changed at a European level to try to better control the bankers' activities, and hopefully the activities of many others who try to profit by inserting themselves between a home and its occupant. However, the UK government is trying to prevent those changes (in Brussels) to allow bankers to take as much money in bonuses as they like.[7]

Interestingly, in Scotland, the following fees are now unlawful when charged for people trying to rent a home: fees for carrying out credit checks; fees for carrying out reference checks; charges for checking and preparing an inventory of items in a property; any administration charge to renew an existing tenancy; any non-refundable 'holding fees' or similar payment as an inducement to grant a tenancy; charges for arranging duplicate copies of the lease; a payment to transfer formally a tenancy to someone else (known as an 'assignment'); and the provision of overpriced furniture – including the sale of furniture to a tenant for an excessive price. In Westminster, many would describe that as too much regulation, unlike in Holyrood.

In 2012 Shelter Scotland launched a campaign to encourage private sector tenants to take their letting agents to court to win back monies they had been wrongly charged. One tenant, Rachel Ryan, said of her search for a home: 'We eventually found a flat that we liked and decided to arrange a viewing. The agent that showed us around, answered our questions about the rent, deposit, and when we could move in, but the one thing he failed to mention before we paid the £250 non-refundable "holding fee" was that we would also be asked to pay £175 in agency fees and £35 VAT.'[8] That meant that as well as paying two months' rent in advance – which came to £1,275 – Rachel and her partner had to pay £460 in one lump sum to the agent if they wanted to secure the flat. Rachel contacted Shelter for advice and secured a refund of all the illegal charges. In total Shelter Scotland helped seventy-three people start proceedings that allowed them to reclaim over £11,400 in the first twenty-four hours of their website's operation.[9]

That was spring 2012. By the November of that year there had been a 43% increase in calls to the charity's helpline, and Shelter Scotland declared that 'So far, more than a quarter of a million pounds in claims have been made.'[10] All this was achieved by just two Shelter Scotland workers. That is an annual take from unscrupulous landlords of over £125,000 each. If you ever think nothing can change, look to Scotland and to this work. However, real success would be for the Shelter website to no longer be needed. Perhaps letting agents should be prosecuted for theft and fraud when they commit it? They might then start to police themselves.

It is not impossible to imagine a day when, to be well housed, we no longer rely on the actions of charities, even ones as laudable as Shelter or Crisis, both set up a few days after the first broadcast of the BBC television play *Cathy come home*, in 1966. But currently that day does seem rather a long way off, given the current UK policy direction and the continued reliance of our economy on an overheated housing market. It need not be like this. We no longer depend on charities to provide health care. People no longer go to the charity hospital. Such hospitals were almost all nationalized in 1948.

The recent increase in private provision within the NHS is a step backwards, but in housing, for most people in Britain (who do not rely on social housing) we never took the step forward that was needed in the first place. Implicit in that step is the idea that all should be well housed and no one should profit greatly out of housing. If you think that aspiration fanciful, the most obvious correlate is how not relying on charity funding has largely transformed education in Britain; the schools that claim charity status today are mostly charities for the rich. And hardly any private firm currently profits much from delivering education, although sadly more and more are trying to turn that sector into a money-spinner. Housing, health and education are all essentials, but hardly any of us can become experts in their consumption; that is because our personal involvement is largely through one-off events, with choice greatly limited by circumstance. We need a diversity of provision, but we also need protection from those who would profit by having some inside knowledge, vested interests and fewer scruples than most.

Lansdowne flats with the Leverton Gardens tower blocks behind, in the Sharrow neighbourhood of Sheffield. Housing has always been the difficult third sector of state provision in Britain. The 1944 Education Act ensured that free secondary education would become available to all, as also occurs in the US. The 1948 implementation of the National Health Service ensured the same for health care, which was a policy not followed in America. When it comes to housing, and more in line with the US, government in Britain is increasingly confining itself to the direct provision of homes only for the very worst-off, with the result that state housing is now seen as housing for the poor. Greater state influence in housing need not mean more state housing. It could include curtailing the undue profit that is made from private housing, controlling the extent of capital gains that can be made, including selling on flats like these – flats that may have been bought under 'right-to-buy'. More state control could also mean more control of the rents that are charged to the private tenants of what was once state housing. It could include a shift from building social housing units to the nationalization of some private housing under various 'right-to-sell' schemes, all at the instigation of the current residents. Whatever does happen in future will not replicate what has occurred in the past: how we become better housed is up for debate. But the fact that we do need to be better housed should be obvious to all.

Currently in the UK progress in education and health seems to be in reverse gear, moving gradually away from non-profit provision, as has been the case in housing for some time. When we were last as economically unequal as we are today, enough people acted so that hardly anyone in the population had to rely on charity. The steps taken were many, and often each alone appeared insignificant; they ranged from striking to improve pay to voting out corrupt MPs. Less obvious political actions can be important. There was a growing general distaste of greed from the 1930s through to the 1970s. People commented more and more openly on unfairness and campaigned for greater equality: between men and women; between landlord and tenant; and between rich and poor.

Back when so much of the provision of housing was not an entitlement – when no one would have envisaged B&Bs being used for homeless families – back in 1921, it was possible for the academic Richard Tawney to write that 'No one has forgotten the opposition offered in the name of the rights of property to factory legislation, to housing reform . . . Even to this day . . . an English urban landlord can cramp or distort the development of a whole city by withholding land except at fancy prices, English municipalities are without adequate powers of compulsory purchase.'[11]

The great challenge we face today is that many people have forgotten – or have never been told – that not so long ago we were a much more equal society. Councils would, for instance, force the purchase of property from private landlords at the low price of its actual worth and demand the demolition of the slums.

You can get rid of filth. If only we remembered that, our political parties, charities and newspapers would not now be so feeble in promoting housing rights. It is because we have forgotten what can be achieved that housing charities have become increasingly essential. Once more churches and charities are being relied upon to provide soup kitchens to feed hundreds of thousands of people in the UK at least for part of the year, now each and every year.[12]

The diagram below was produced by a charity established to fight poverty in Africa but that now also focuses on where it began: in Britain. We have become less able to look after ourselves. We have been taken for a ride and need to realize that it is time to become less stupid.

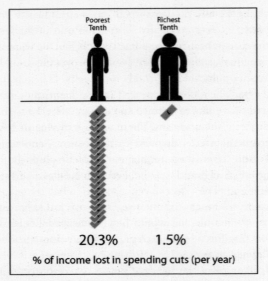

Figure 22. The effect of spending cuts on people in Britain, 2010–16.

THE RIGHT NOT TO BE STUPID

For our workers in the big cities, freedom of movement is the first condition of their existence, and landownership could only be a hindrance to them. Give them their own houses, chain them once again to the soil and you break their power of resistance to the wage cutting of the factory-owners. The individual worker might be able to sell his house on occasion, but during a big strike or a general industrial crisis all the houses belonging to the affected workers would have to come on to the market for sale and would therefore find no purchasers or be sold off far below their cost price.

– Friedrich Engels, 1872[13]

Most people find it hard to imagine great social change. The world in which a single industry can dominate a city is ending, but the world in which a 'general industrial crisis' can harm the 'market' value of all property is with us as never before. Look to Cyprus and the run on its banks in 2013, look to Greece, to Italy, Spain, Portugal, over to parts of France, to all of Ireland, up to Iceland, across to the US and to Detroit – and of course the UK.

At the heart of the housing crisis are those theories that housing is best allocated by a market open to speculation. Shelter then becomes the cornerstone of the economy, the main sink of wealth and savings. More money is invested in homes, less in business, and certainly less is trusted to the government, either in tax or through the buying of government bonds. The best-off believe their homes will earn them a luxury retirement. They don't even consider what the state pension might be; for them it is pocket money. The worst-off know that if they do not strive, they could easily lose their home. Being made homeless, apparently, is the threat that drives the market. Homelessness is the stick; wealth is the carrot.

Markets work as efficient distributors of resources only when people can opt out of them, when customers can say they want 'none of the above'. But in housing markets, even if people can no longer afford to pay the market rate, whether in rent or through a mortgage, they still need to be housed. They can't 'choose' to go without a home. Consequently they are open to exploitation. Look to more equitable countries, where the housing market works much better, where there are fewer homeless people and cheaper homes. Look to Scandinavia, Japan, the Netherlands, Austria and Germany for countries where housing might be far from perfect, but where better provision is made for the majority.[14]

At particular times housing and politics can become a heady mix of enthusiasm and goodwill. In Britain, in the 1950s and 1960s, successive housing ministers promised to construct hundreds of thousands more homes a year than their predecessors. Both before the First World War and after the 1970s, housing became the Cinderella policy, the one that never quite got to the budgetary ball. It featured neither in the many lists of past achievements nor in manifesto desires. Not even an administration with real social ambition was much committed to housing, and few politicians vied to hold the portfolio.

When times get really bad, far-right parties rear their nasty head and claim that council homes should go first (and hence almost only) to people whose parents or grandparents were born locally. This is an attempt to bringing back an aspect of the Poor Laws, where relief was given only to the best-behaved locals of the parish. By autumn 2013 it was not the remnants of the fascist British National Party but the more mainstream UK Independence Party that was advocating that only 'locals' who had family nearby should qualify for social housing.[15] Sadly, at times the Labour Party has toyed with similar policies – 'British jobs' for 'British workers' rather than 'British homes' for 'British families' – but near enough to cause worry, although thankfully Labour still knows that racism remains more unpopular than immigration.[16]

One of the most vocal supporters of the last Labour government, Polly Toynbee, explains that 'we remember all that Labour did best: an NHS immeasurably improved, 20% more pupils with five good GCSEs, many more at university or in further education, minimum wage, right to roam, civil partnerships, 3,500 Sure Starts.'[17] But, in summing up the supposed triumphs, she says nothing about whether the nation was better housed after thirteen years of that Labour government. It was; there was a huge 'decent homes' renovation programme completed both well on time and on budget; but that was not news. It did not even become news when the programme was quietly ditched in 2010.[18]

When housing rose up the news agenda, as the crisis worsened between 2012 and 2013, Toynbee looked back at New Labour's record. Despite normally being a cheerleader for Labour, she concluded that, despite the renovation programme, when it came to housing and the financial crisis in the UK, 'Labour is just as much to blame. Gigantic bubbles inflated house prices to such a degree that Shelter estimates a chicken would now cost £51 if food prices had risen as fast over recent decades.'[19] There is no need for house prices to have risen so far and so fast, but it does look as if it was a conscious decision on the part of the last Labour government not to try to rein in the price rises. It would not have been necessary for that government to have built more housing in order to bring the prices down.

Rather, it 'just' needed a sustained programme of renovation of existing stock, curbs on rent rises and policies to prevent speculation, including beefing up their policy to prevent so many empty properties being left empty for long.

In contemporary Britain, instead of any government plans for refurbishment and renovation, rumours of speculative new green belt building abound. It has been suggested that 100,000 homes could be built on green belt land east of Birmingham. This would in the process create the UK's largest conurbation, stretching some forty miles from Coventry up through to the north of Wolverhampton. That there might be such a plan was recently denied by the government – but it was, nevertheless, revealed in a speech by Andrew McNaughton, the Chief Engineer on the proposed high-speed rail line HS2, which is to run from London to Birmingham.

When it became evident that, under new laws passed by the coalition, developers would be permitted to build on green belt, David Cameron tried to distance himself from any such schemes: 'he was brought up in the "beautiful village" of Peasemore in Berkshire, where he learned to ride as a youngster.'[20] The implication is that this country-reared son of a stockbroker would not countenance such building. However, his government has passed the planning laws that will allow it.

It is not impossible to imagine a chasm opening up between the Conservatives – who claim that they will conserve the green belt even while relaxing planning law – and Labour politicians, who say they will encourage much more new home-building but with greater state control. In his September 2013 conference speech Ed Miliband pledged that Labour would ensure that private builders built at least 200,000 homes a year, every year, up to 2020, a million in total in five years, if they should gain power in 2015.[21] He said there would be a renewed New Towns programme; that towns would be permitted to grow out of their (often Labour-controlled) boundaries and into the (often Conservative-controlled) surrounding countryside; that developers who did not use their land-banks would lose them; and that he would work to put a commission in place before 2015 to make all this happen shortly after a Labour election win. Labour's autumn

2013 plan sounded inspiring, but in fact (once the years of slump are factored in) it is just a return to normal building levels, and it doesn't begin to address the issues of inequality in housing. What Labour's new housing policy would ensure is a stabilization of the situation: enough homes to cope with recent immigration, but no redistribution of our existing stock, to help us all fit better into what we already have.

Ed Miliband is the son of immigrants. He perhaps has a better grasp than the country-reared son of a stockbroker as to why most people need just one decent home, and how prejudice can lead them to not even get that. But what Miliband is not yet willing to do is to take on those who have a vested interest in thwarting a more equitable distribution of housing.

In two of the richest, but also most inequitable, of rich countries in the world, politicians on the centre-left promise more but deliver less. In the US, the President is the grandson of a man who was imprisoned by the British.[22] Unlike his grandfather, he is no revolutionary, but Obama does scare some bankers, a little. In May 2009 Barack Obama told the CEOs of America's largest banks: 'My administration is the only thing between you and the pitchforks.'[23] He then promised beleaguered American mortgagors he would rescue them, but reneged on that promise for three quarters of those whom he had pledged to help. He had kept the pitchforks away but he had also prevented the US from turning towards a fairer future for housing.

As the *New York Times*, a paper normally sympathetic to the Democrats, revealed: 'Mr Obama said in Arizona a few weeks after taking office that the government would help "as many as three to four million homeowners to modify the terms of their mortgages to avoid foreclosure".' As of May [2012], 4.3 million people had applied for aid, but only one million had received government-sponsored modifications, according to the most recent data. About a third of those turned away lost their homes, were facing foreclosure or had filed for bankruptcy.[24] All this, however, was much more than the coalition government in the UK was prepared to do, and more than Labour has yet promised to do.

Labour promises to boost new housing start numbers (building homes) from 100,000 to 200,000 a year, but not to protect families from future foreclosure. The first serious assessment of Labour's Mortgage Rescue Scheme (its experimental 'right-to-stay' policy) found that 2,600 households had been helped to avoid repossession and homelessness, but at a cost of in excess of £240 million. The original plan had been to help 6,000 households for only £205 million. As the head of the National Audit Office put it, in May 2011, when commenting on the Department for Communities and Local Government's overall record: 'The Department made assumptions about the level of demand for the Mortgage Rescue Scheme and made the wrong call. There was more need than expected for more expensive support and less for the relatively low cost rescue option.'[25] The National Audit Office said that as a result the scheme was bad value for money. What they didn't point out is that if the banks had been given less compensation, it could have been very good value for money indeed.

The coalition government made cuts to the Mortgage Rescue Scheme and scrapped other schemes once it came to office. The scheme had prevented an even greater rise in homelessness, and its implementation also meant that many households that did not in the end take it up instead got good advice;[26] but by 2012 it was clear that demand for 'mortgage rescue' was not growing. With interest rates falling to sometimes as low as 2%, fewer households were getting into trouble with their mortgage payments. But such low interest rates meant that the selling price of housing in many areas had not fallen further. So now newly forming households are unable to buy, and there is a continued slowing of the market and a growing fear of the inevitable eventual impact of future interest rate rises.

The sole concession to the conundrum we are now in, and the centrepiece of the government's March 2013 budget, which has been discussed already in detail much earlier in this book, was to try to shore up the housing market. That shoring up has, among other things, made it cheaper to buy second homes, with £12 billion pledged for the underwriting of a large part of many, if not most, new mortgages for seven years.[27] All this does is to maintain high housing prices, thus preventing new mortgagors from buying starter homes from households that have grown larger and that need to move up and out. The most expensive schemes start in 2014. Many commentators believe that the real aim is to delay any crash until after the General Election, scheduled for spring 2015.

A more radical opposition party would advocate changing policy to show what would still be possible when the money runs out. As has been said earlier, many empty properties can be brought back into use. Squatters do this, and criminalizing them is counterproductive. Compulsory purchase of persistently empty properties may well be needed, as Ed Miliband now admits, but it will actually have to be carried out often enough for attitudes to change, not just threatened. We know this because, as mentioned in the chapters above, New Labour put a law on the books that allowed a building to be purchased after it had stood vacant for six months, but only when this could be justified and there was no alternative. That law was hardly used at all. As a result of the underuse, when the coalition government made the law less effective in November 2012 – by extending the period any residential building can lie empty, with no action even being proposed, to two years – hardly anyone noticed.[28] They were acting in the interests of landlords and multiple-property owners in lengthening the period to two years, but few people knew, because New Labour, throughout its thirteen years in power, had neither explained how valuable the old law could be nor had it utilized its potential.

For any property that has been empty for two years, an Empty Building Management Order can be made. People being homeless or shockingly housed nearby are adequate justifications. However, although it would be good to get the time period back down to six months before action can be taken, it is not the legality that is really stalling progress towards converting more empty buildings into homes; instead it is a lack of political will. The threat of compulsory purchase, enacted enough times to be believed, would be a huge 'incentive' for the owners of empty property not to leave that property empty. Converting empty buildings into residential property during a commercial property market slump is a cheap solution. It can be made even cheaper if a future government declares that the amount of compensation property-owners will receive will be based on its value when it was vacated, with a further reduction depending on how long it had remained unoccupied.

Many commercial properties are empty: office blocks not being used, workshops mothballed, and shops boarded up. Conversion to residential dwellings could renew the high streets that the out-of-town superstores and the internet have decimated. It would not be easy – each residential property needs its own front door, not a door into a shop – but it is possible. Complaints are always made about change and some people would lose out. The complaints would come from every sector, and some would be unexpected. For example, artists will complain that they cannot find cheap commercial property to rent as studios, places in which to create their art. A few already do when housing schemes like this are proposed. But shelter is more important than studios.

A more utopic vision of the future would see us make space for both studios and homes, for both work spaces and rooms for recreation. Much land from the continued decay of old industry remains to be freed up across the rich world. More and more brownfield sites are becoming available. In Britain they are mostly in the north, where the hill-walking is better and the air cleaner too. More and more jobs are done from home, on the internet, or at the very least do not require a mile and a half of flat land, such as used to be required by a steel mill. As our work requires each of us, on average, to have less space to work in, more space is freed up to house us all. So why does none of this happen? Why are we becoming more and more crammed into the south-east of England? Why are the new Rachman landlords not demonized? Why can we not fix housing as we fixed it before? Is it because we need collective action, but have lost the will to act collectively during recent decades, decades in which individual 'aspiration' has triumphed?

Local voluntary models work painfully slowly, if they work at all. The East London Community Land Trust, the first of its kind in the UK to try to build homes for local people, run by local people, is still stumbling along years after its inception in 2007; its latest news (in February 2013) is a message from the year before, saying 'You are cordially invited to our community-led design weekend to help design and build the UK's first-ever urban Community Land Trust!'[29]

Acting locally on housing only gets you so far, and it does not get you there very fast. It was acting collectively nationally that achieved rent control in the past. That began with the Rent Restriction Act of 1915 and the Housing (Homeless Persons) Act of 1977, just part of a long list that can be drawn up to show that housing in the past was improved mostly through collective action.[30] Acts of parliament to restore and improve old rights, to change the law on tenure, on capital gains and on council tax, are one way forward, but a new age requires more than just new laws; it requires a different kind of thinking.

People need to stop thinking of decent housing as something only a few deserve, and realize that it is something we all need. In almost all rich countries we have never had as much housing available as we have now. Never has our financial model for allocating that housing been more obviously wanting than it is now.

Post for tenants past and present is left in the hallway of a Georgian house, now divided into six flats, in Nether Edge, Sheffield. Someone has been stacking the post ever so neatly. Someone cares about how the entrance to their home looks and is willing to spend the time needed to keep it tidy. They might do it because they begrudge their neighbours' tardy attitude to dealing with their bills, but they know that if they did not act, no one else would tidy up. It is easier to act in a collective way when you can see the immediate impact of your actions, and it takes only a few people to act collectively for everyone's environment to be improved. The alternative to collective action is a mess. In this case the post would all be in a pile, and each tenant would have to sort through that pile, making it more of a mess. They would have to do this whenever they wanted to see if they had received a letter. We are painfully aware of our personal influence on others (and what they think of us) when we worry about not barging ahead in a queue, or not taking more than our fair amount of space on the bus or train, not putting luggage on a seat when people are standing. But when actions are less visible – if people don't know that you are responsible for that empty home or shop, or they believe you when you say that you cannot afford to sell at a lower price – once what you are doing becomes less obvious, it is easier to be selfish.

CONCLUSIONS

The stagnation of the living standards of the majority is not at all unrelated to the success at the top; in effect, those at the very top are plundering the poor and the middle classes . . . the market is at risk because extreme differences of power make a mockery of the voluntary nature of market transactions. The political system is at risk because plutocracy gradually replaces democracy.

– from a review of Joseph Stiglitz's work by
Angus Deaton, 2013[31]

In housing, volatility increases as inequality increases. When the distinguished economist Angus Deaton spoke of the stagnation of living standards that most citizens of the US have been experiencing for nigh on a generation, he was describing how what was once a solid certainty – that most people in the world's richest country would do well and be housed adequately throughout their lifetime – has melted into thin air following the 2008 crash. Growing inequality has induced even greater volatility and caused the market to fail.

Volatility is ultimately the reason why even those not bothered by the idea of increasing inequality should be bothered. You may think you are doing fine – you own a home and it is worth a lot – but its value is being propped up by a government desperate for your vote, a government that appoints members to its national bank's advisory board who will ensure that interest rates are kept at historically unprecedented lows. Low interest rates cannot last forever. If fast money can find somewhere better to go in the globe, it will go there, and the quantitative easing that makes such low rates possible cannot last forever. Everything depends on confidence in the market – so the more volatile the market, the sooner it will crash.

A boring market, with fewer second- and third-home buyers, becomes a safer, slower market. A rental market where rents are both lower and less variable, because tenants have more similar incomes, leads to improved conditions of tenure in place of a few better-off tenants renting swanky apartments. When inequality rises, most people become ever more dismayed by what they are getting for their money. Discontent becomes rife. Joseph Stiglitz has found that, in the US, plutocracy is already replacing democracy. A plutocracy is a society both ruled and dominated by a tiny minority of its wealthiest citizens. And we are in danger of plutocracy spreading to Europe.

By 2013 it was revealed that up to a third of all council homes that had been purchased under the 'right-to-buy' had been sold on to just a few rich landlords. Take, for instance, Ian Gow, who was the minister who presided over the introduction of Thatcher's 'right-to-buy' scheme. His son is now a housing tycoon, owning more than forty ex-council flats in one London estate alone. As one commentator remarked, 'You couldn't make it up. The family of one of the Tory ministers who oversaw "right-to-buy" ends up owning swathes of ex-council homes.'[32] If American plutocracy spreads to Europe, it will enter through the UK first. But there are many signs to suggest that this will not happen.

As they often do, events may be moving faster than policy. In Ireland a new tax is being introduced on property, one that increases in line with the value of that property. While not strictly a land value tax, its effect may well be similar in terms of acting as a brake on future rising housing prices. Unsurprisingly, the most vocal opposition to the tax has been from the wealthy residents of those parts of Dublin where prices remain highest. Of course, there are many slightly less affluent areas in Dublin the rich could move to if they wished to reduce their tax liability, and a huge number of empty properties from which to choose. It is not the threat of being unable to afford a home that worries them; it is the possibility that they may not be able to keep all their wealth in a land where so many have lost all that they had. Great inequality engenders a great fear of sharing.

The new Irish property tax has embarrassed the UK Treasury, which claimed that imposing a similar tax in Britain would be too costly. A land registry would be necessary to administer any property tax, and the UK already possesses a mostly complete one. Ireland does not have one at all, and yet 'the Irish revenue commissioners put the cost of setting up the system at €25.9 million for 2013 with an additional initial IT outlay of €9 million, the majority of which will be attributed to the development of the property register.'[33] This is much less than 3% of all the money that, it is predicted, the tax will raise. If the British could match the Irish, given that much of the work of registering property has already been completed, the cost of administering a new land value tax could be less than 1% of all monies raised. It is not as if there is no precedent for such a tax: the US has one. If they can make it work there, we can make it work here. In certain US states, various small land value taxes already exist. When a land value tax is in place, it becomes financially far less profitable to sit on unused land and homes. Indeed, it has often been claimed that one of the quickest ways to improve a country's infrastructure or to generate jobs is to introduce such a tax. The US land value tax is widely credited with having cured the 1930s slump.[34] A land value tax is in the interests of the vast majority, but the wealthy don't view all people as equal.

In Britain the journalist Kevin Cahill calculated that, in 2002, 69% of the land was in the hands of 0.6% of the population. Government statistics show that since then the concentration has intensified. Between 2005 and 2011 the number of landholdings in England had fallen by 10%, while the average size of holdings had risen by 12%. This could be one of the fastest consolidations of ownership since the Highland Clearances.[35] The British have enough land and housing; it is just that increasingly most of it is owned by a smaller and smaller elite.

A crisis is inevitable if the richest 1% are allowed to continue to obtain an ever-greater share of the national wealth. The rich have to hold that share in one form of investment or another. It could be in shares, or in gold, but it need not be in land. The fundamental problem with the rich is their wealth and the consequent effects of their ownership of such a great share of the things we all need. But better to let them hoard gold than land and physical property.

We need to remember that housing is a special kind of good – a social good – which brings with it wider benefits. In this it is like education and health. It is better for all of us if others are also well housed, well educated and healthy. The similarities do not end there. Housing is also not something that you tend to be a repeat consumer of, not if things go well. Completely free markets work well only with goods that you buy often, so that you can learn from your purchasing mistakes. People do not want to move home many times in their lives, but they can feel they have no alternative. This volatile environment is precisely what the housing market of the past few decades has encouraged.

You cannot be a well-informed consumer of housing unless you are a landlord or other housing agent. The unfettered market does not work well in allocating housing, because levels of knowledge are so unevenly distributed and there is no sane way of balancing out such knowledge – not unless you want everyone to become like an estate agent in their understanding of housing markets. You might use a search engine to show you all the property available in your area to rent or to buy, but do you know how often sales, once agreed, fall through? What is the average rent in some streets? Is it normal to be asked to put down six months of rent as a deposit? And why is the mortgage broker so keen for you to take out one particular product – does she get a kick-back? Housing is becoming harder and harder to secure and to understand.

What is clear is that the housing market will not be made more equitable through voluntary action on the part of the most interested parties. We need to help the rich to learn to control themselves. As a first step we should at the very least be enacting policies such as that suggested in 2012 by researchers from the Institute for Public Policy Research: levying a land value tax on, at a minimum, all currently undeveloped developable land that is worth above £2 million in value. This would swiftly encourage new building and raise funds for the government for housing investment.[36]

A land value tax is evolution, not revolution. It is now being proposed by some of the most serious of commentators. It is being introduced in places like Ireland with the blessing of not-too-radical international economists. The existing UK council tax is a very crude and inefficient form of it. Many have called for a better land value tax, but only a worsening of the current housing crisis is likely to waken up the wider public to the need for it.

Taxation may be just a part of any solution, but it is fundamentally necessary for two reasons. First, it can discourage excessive land and property holding by a very few. Secondly, in raising funds from those who have the most to give, it helps to house those who most need help. Wealth is redistributed.

Among rich nations, wealth inequalities are lowest in Japan, Spain, Italy, Finland and Australia. Next come New Zealand and the Netherlands, then Portugal, Germany and Canada. Only after these ten countries are passed over do we get to the UK (more unequal in wealth than all of them). There are three large rich countries that have greater wealth inequality than the UK: France, Denmark and the US. The order of countries changes if income inequalities are used to rank them instead of wealth inequalities. Going by income, both France and Denmark are much more equitable places to live in than the UK. Part of the reason why France and Denmark have such an uneven distribution of wealth is because of their openness to poorer immigrants who arrive with so very little; this, and the legacy of slavery, accounts for wealth inequalities in the US. The sons and daughters of slaves inherit no wealth, which disadvantages generations of their descendants.

In both France and Denmark inequalities in income are lower than average for OECD states, despite higher wealth inequalities. The academic paper that first reported these statistics also showed far higher correlations between wealth inequality and premature mortality than between income inequality and poor health.[37] Where income inequalities are currently highest, wealth inequalities will grow most in future. Where income inequalities are lowest, wealth inequalities may already be falling.

I would advocate gradually reforming council tax into 'a national land and property value tax'; also extending mortgage controls to prevent lending getting out of hand; and introducing a more effective safety-net for mortgagors – that 'right-to-sell' and become a tenant, should you find you are unable to pay the mortgage. The already established 'right-to-stay' laws, which are currently used very little and then only through the recently much muted Mortgage Rescue Scheme, could be enhanced into a 'right-to-sell' that could actually make a difference.[38]

Mortgage controls may sound scary and imply great levels of state intervention, but great state intervention is currently required to sustain, promote and expand the uncontrolled mortgage market in the UK. Simply pulling back on the bank guarantees would help to create a more controlled market. In the US the similar loan-aid programme has been found to have aided banks far more than home-buyers, to the tune of $12 billion by 2012, with the money mostly going to J. P. Morgan and Wells Fargo;[39] it too could be fruitfully curtailed. The UK's own £12 billion guarantee went ahead early in October 2013; and, in the end, if the market were to fall and the guarantees had to be drawn on, the money would also go mostly to a couple of the big banks, while the mortgagors who could not keep up their payments would be left in dire straits. If the market doesn't fall, the banks win anyway. It is grossly irresponsible of the UK government to gift a 'win-win' situation to the banks.

Although the 'help-to-buy' scheme has been described as the equivalent of a rich dad giving his children money to help with their deposit, it is not. No one gives the mortgagor any money; instead they have to take out a bigger mortgage. The scheme is better characterized as a rich dad, the government, going to the bank manager and giving him or her a financial inducement to approve a mortgage that the bank manager considered risky, the risk being the likelihood of the mortgagor getting into arrears. There is, however, another risk that does not immediately affect the bank. The Chancellor, George Osborne, thinks the scheme could support up to £130 billion of new mortgages, with government liability expected to be no more than £12 billion. If this happens, excessive house price inflation is inevitable, making the situation worse for future buyers and creating a market at ever greater risk of crashing.

If interest rates were to increase, property values would fall but there would be large-scale defaulting on mortgage payments. There would also be the rent increases imposed by landlords to cover their own increased mortgage payments. Consequently a way would have to be found to avoid mass evictions and the accompanying misery and dereliction of poorer areas, which would be hardest hit. But no solution comes for free. Monies will need to be raised. If the private sector is to be deterred from instigating any further increase in evictions, the 'right-to-stay' will need to be funded. The most secure way to raise money is by taxing the property and the land of those with more than they need – wealth which of course cannot be moved or hidden away in offshore locations.

One of the most favoured estate agents of the very richest investors has already tried to pour cold water on the idea of introducing high land taxes, including the mansion tax now proposed by both Labour and the Liberal Democrats. In Labour's version an annual levy of 1% would be placed on homes worth over £2 million, raising £2 billion a year. The estate agent Savills said it would raise only half that amount, but it has a great vested interest in trying to prevent the imposition of land taxes. Housing developers are similarly opposed to these proposed interventions, but, as Ed Miliband pointed out in December 2013, the four largest saw their profits soar by 557% by the end of that year.[40] Many are beginning to tire of the rich telling them that there is no alternative.[41]

This book has been concerned with why it is that the activity and dignity and freedom of millions of people in Britain, and hundreds of millions of people around the world, are at stake because they cannot get secure access to decent housing.[42] Or, to put it more as a politician might, these are people who are not free to be who they could be, to do what they could do, to hold up their heads and live without fear of debt, to live where it would be reasonable to live. These people could be you. They are the majority. In economically unequal countries it is not that poorer or just average people do not work hard enough or try to save enough; it is that we have allowed a few to become too rich, with the result that most of us find it very hard to find suitable places to live in at all. Because of actions by the rich – such as buying property for investment purposes and turning 1970s flats back into giant 1920s-style townhouses – housing becomes more and more of a struggle for each successive generation in the UK.

In countries such as the Netherlands and Denmark housing is far better allocated, and this allocation is getting better over time. These countries are not dissimilar to the UK, yet, as the numerous examples given in the pages above have shown, in much of mainland Europe housing is better shared out. This is not just because these are more equitable societies. Denmark even has a more uneven distribution of wealth than the UK, as discussed above, but respectively 15% and 10% of the households in these two countries receive state benefits towards their rent, in comparison with 18% in the UK, which is still a proportion far greater than that in most OECD countries.[43] Both countries control rents far better than the UK does, as well as dampening down house prices.[44] As a result people are far freer to choose where they live in the Netherlands and Denmark – nearer their places of work, for example.

The way we organize our housing influences many other aspects of our lives, including our preferred way of getting to work and hence how far from work we live. Cycling was mentioned in Chapter 6 of this book (p. 221). In the UK only 2% of all journeys are undertaken on a bike. This compares with 27% in the Netherlands and 18% in Denmark. In an increasing number of European towns more than 50% of all journeys are made by bike.[45] To get adults and children cycling, you need people to be able to live near enough to where they work to be able to give up the car. You need sensible housing policies for that. In Japan, car use has been falling for over two decades, and this is not unrelated to the fact that housing is far more mixed there than it is in Britain:[46] smaller properties are built next to larger ones, and it is normal (even if officially still illegal) to cycle slowly on pavements. There are also very few very poor or very rich enclaves. People can live nearer their work.

Public transport and other public policies are more easily improved when housing policy is improved. By contrast, the more individualist is the housing policy that a country adopts, the more individualist its transport becomes. Allow urban sprawl and an increasingly inefficient 'free' market begins to dominate, which forces many people to live a long way from where they are employed. More and more people will come to rely on cars to get them to almost any destination – to school, to the local shops, and not just to work. And the more people rely on cars, the more segregated each residential neighbourhood becomes. Make renting attractive and affordable, dampen the expectation of speculative gains on buying property, and poorer areas rise in attractiveness, while places that were mainly popular because they were expensive become both less popular and less expensive. Left alone, the market fails to move towards such equilibrium.

Housing shows how markets can fail – and a failure in this area matters more than in almost any other area of our lives. That is because we need housing every day, all of us, all the time. And we appear to be forgetting that. For instance, just over fifty years ago, the major problems facing housing in Britain in the Penguin Special on the subject (released in 1962) included ensuring kitchens were built with 'room in them for people to sit down to meals comfortably'.[47] Housing issues back then were being addressed more efficiently and practically; we were moving in the right direction. The questions were about what to improve next. We were not preoccupied by old problems that were becoming much worse.

How housing issues have changed from being so practical and inclusive in their aims to being so divisive can be hard to grasp. But if you believe that there must be a better way, the good news is that you are not alone. The largest continuous International Social Survey Programme undertaken worldwide has found that most adults in rich countries do think that people should be decently housed and that their governments have a duty to ensure such a situation. For the British, there is a particular reason why hope is warranted. Past advocacy for better housing has left a lasting mark on our collective conscious, as revealed by our answers in those international surveys. Because of this, future campaigning starts from a higher threshold. In comparison with sixteen other affluent democracies for which there is data – Australia, Canada, Denmark, Finland, France, Germany, Ireland, Japan, the Netherlands, New Zealand, Norway, Portugal, Spain, Sweden, Switzerland and the US – in 2012 the British were 'significantly more likely to believe the government has a responsibility to "provide decent housing for those who can't afford it" . . . More than 85% of British respondents supported the government's responsibility for housing.'[48] This is in comparison with 'only' 77% of adults in the US who believe government should be involved in housing. But even there less than a quarter of the population believe that how we are housed is nobody's business but the individual's. Over three quarters believe government – all of us acting collectively – is responsible. That argument is already won. The next argument is what government must do, as we come to realize that what we have been doing for decades no longer works.

Recently, a former US cabinet secretary asked his mentor from college, who had been born in the 1930s,[49] what hope there might be of most Americans coming to see that they were going down the wrong path; the older man answered: 'Yes, and they're starting to understand that ... And beginning to see that the distinction between the middle class and poor is disappearing. Many who were in the middle have fallen into poverty; many more will do so.'[50] He went on to explain that, for decades, those at the top had tried to convince the middle class that their economic enemies were ethnic minorities and the poor. But now that old divide-and-conquer strategy is starting to fail. And as it fails, he suggested, it will be possible to create a powerful political coalition of the poor and the middle classes. Soon America will be a majority of minorities. Women are gaining more and more economic power. He could see a lot of reasons for hope. But he was old enough to remember the last time US society was made more equitable.

The former cabinet secretary countered that the 400 richest Americans are now wealthier than the bottom 150 million Americans put together and that they have more political influence than ever. The older man replied: 'Just you wait.'

We have already built enough homes. We have more bedrooms than we have ever had before. But a few have been taking far more than their fair share, increasingly so ever since 1980; and very recently they have been taking far more again with each year that has passed since the crash. Many at the very top of society have been harming the rest: in evicting the poorest from their homes, in penalizing people far more cramped than they are for having a spare room, in impoverishing the middle earners through high rent and mortgages, in damaging the chances of those in the top tenth (but not the top 1% of society) by enticing them to borrow more. The vested interests in British housing are currently stoking up the embers of the last crash to create a new crisis. But a crisis is as good a time as any to get our house in order.

What we are currently seeing is not a conflict between old and young, but a new real and dangerous historical trend. A whole generation has now grown up in an economy based on monopolistic markets and the myth that these are somehow free markets. The cuts and, for most, a recession without an end in sight drives people apart as they struggle not to be left behind. In these circumstances everyone – rich and poor – is afflicted with contagious insecurity, mistrust and a growing fear of the future.

It matters who provides goods or services, and under what conditions. It is no good saying that it doesn't as long as customers are satisfied. It is wrong to assume that tax is a penalty rather than a subscription to society. We are currently in a vicious cycle where the less solidarity you have, the less you want. But humans contain within them an innate desire for large-group cohesion. It's why we chant in crowds and feel happy at festivals. We developed the impulse a long time ago in order to survive. All the modern threats we face could, if described accurately and addressed carefully, drive us to rediscover this desire to work better together. If the threat to our housing and our children's chances of being well housed is realized as optional, rather than inevitable, then there is hope.[51]

Many suggestions have been made in the chapters of this book about what policies could be done better. To end, I take ten of these and list them, not in any particular order. There is nothing exhaustive about the list that follows, but any single policy on its own, unless introduced in an era when attitudes are changing, is unlikely to have a great effect. Our housing will be made more solid through a conjunction of new policies, not through any single one. But we need lists of options to think about. So here is mine:

1. Extend the current council tax bands up to band 'Z' with a view to transforming the tax into a fairer national land and property tax.

2. Enhance the existing 'right-to-stay' into a 'right-to-sell', giving mortgagors the right to become tenants rather than face eviction.

3. Second homes, holiday homes and empty commercial property need to be included in a fairer property tax system to discourage waste.

4. Spare bedrooms should not be taxed. Every family should be able to live in a home with a spare room for visitors. We already have enough rooms. Every single adult who wants their own space should have it.

5. An enhanced home-building programme will be needed if more people come into the UK than leave, as has been the case in recent years.

6. Benefits are now so low that they must soon rise faster than wages, which must rise faster than salaries – all of which must rise faster than home prices. Rents need to stay still, if not fall. All these are out of balance.

7. Greater income and wealth equality would be improved by the reintroduction of rent controls, which would also reduce housing benefit bills massively. The already calculated Local Housing Allowances could be used to set the maximum fair rent in an area.

8. Squatting and all other acts that are done purely to seek shelter and not to steal items for profit should again be a civil, not a criminal, offence. Squatting is a symptom of a problem, not the problem.

9. Illegal actions by landlords and bankers that deprive people of their home and shelter should become criminal, rather than civil, offences.

10. We have to recognize that housing is central to environmental sustainability. When we build, we need to build for the very long term.

Of all of these suggestions the first and last may be the most important. Recently the mildly conservative Institute for Fiscal Studies came out in favour of better land value taxation when it concluded that current taxation of land and property is inefficient and inequitable.[52] The rich will not hoard land and buildings if they are taxed heavily for doing so. But, as the taxes are set as a proportion of current value, and as their introduction will reduce that value, they might well fall over time, because the land values themselves will fall due to the tax. Such a tax would probably be introduced gradually, but even knowing that more was to come would influence prices downwards. The money could be put to good use in ensuring all are well housed, but also housed in a way that considers both the future and the environment as if they mattered. We cannot simply build again as fast as possible. Most homes survive for far longer than most people. Good housing stands for many generations. Housing should be about the long term, about provision, not profit.

Should you have got to this point and still remain to be convinced that there is a serious problem to be addressed, a housing crisis requiring very different answers to those which are usually proffered, you certainly are a magnanimous reader, or perhaps one willing to countenance views very different from your own. To try to finally convince you that all is far from solid when it comes to housing in Britain, I'll leave the penultimate words to the Dublin-based writer Julian Mercille. In an exhaustive study of how the housing bubble in Ireland grew so large, he concluded that so many people apparently showed so little concern for the future because 'prior to the bubble's collapse, the media made little mention of it, remained vague about it or tried to refute claims that it even existed, thus sustaining it.'[53]

While first writing the last words of this book, in May 2013, I watched how muted was the reaction to the downgrading of Co-operative Bank stocks, which were suddenly knocked down six levels to junk status. This news was mainly confined to the specialist financial press.[54] Revisiting those words in the autumn of 2013, I wonder why there was not more shock when it was announced that 6,700 landlords would be having their interest rates greatly increased without warning by the West Bromwich Building Society (which found a note in the small print allowing them to do this). It got a footnote in the broadsheets and even a mention on the BBC,[55] but why not more coverage? No doubt here will presently be another event and, as always, I'm left thinking, if not now, then soon.

If the housing crisis must worsen before we can believe in it, our scope for action will be limited. Property that has become devalued, because it was not built in the 'right' places, will be unnecessarily and wantonly demolished; the health of many will have been irreparably harmed; financial systems, having forced great debt upon people that will never be fully repaid, will have sunk further into the mire; more people will have been taught that looking after their own interests is all they can do and that they will get by only at the expense of others.

The sooner we act, the easier it will be. The last time we faced a crisis as deep as our present predicament the mass unemployment and eventual war that followed changed the course of history. We have forgotten so much of what we learned then, but in 1930, a year after the great crash, a prediction was made for the world in a century's time. It remains a prediction that could still come to pass unless we heed its warning and the solution implied within it:

> Of course there will still be many people with intense, unsatisfied purposiveness who will blindly pursue wealth – unless they can find some plausible substitute. But the rest of us will no longer be under any obligation to applaud and encourage them.
>
> – John Maynard Keynes, 1930[56]

Desisting from applauding or encouraging those who would blindly pursue wealth turned out, in the long run, not to be enough. Thus we find ourselves again in the quandary that Keynes identified, a lifetime after he wrote those words. There will always be people who are greedy, but there will come a time when we properly recognize this to be a problem, when we look at the relations between us more soberly than we do now, and when we are compelled to act on what we more clearly see. Another prophecy was made a lifetime before Keynes was writing. It gave this book its title, and it has yet to come to pass:

> All that is solid melts into air, all that is holy is profaned, and man is at last compelled to face with sober senses, his real conditions of life, and his relations with his kind.
>
> – Karl Marx and Friedrich Engels, 1848[57]

In January 2014 the *Financial Times* released an analysis showing that over the course of just the last five years the equity of mortgage holders in Britain had fallen by £169 billion, while that of landlords had risen by a massive £245 billion.[58] There is no surer sign of a housing crisis turning into a disaster than this.

Afterword: Housing Chaos

Homelessness is rising. Fewer people are able to secure social housing and less and less money is being spent on the upkeep of that stock. Private landlords spend less doing up their properties while house prices rapidly rise out of the reach of most people in most areas. But it could become worse. In the US an extra million children became homeless between 2006 and 2013. The highest ever US rate of child homelessness was reported in the run up to Christmas 2014.[1]

Fewer and fewer people are able to get a mortgage. In the UK stricter tests have been introduced to try to prevent banks and building societies lending as recklessly as they did before. There have been repeated warnings to borrowers that at some point interest rates will have to rise. Up is the only direction in which they can go.

At least a third of mortgagees would struggle if interest rates were to rise by just a couple of percentage points.[2] The further house prices in the South of England climb the greater that proportion will grow as new entrants become more stretched. People who are a safe bet at one point in time can easily lose their jobs, split up or become ill. Add a slight rise in mortgage interest rates and anyone already struggling to pay the bills quickly gets into arrears.

Prices have risen because the government has been trying to get them to rise. At the end of 2014 the campaigning organization 'Priced Out' calculated that the government-sponsored new-build Help to Buy programme had helped raise average prices by £46,000 in 18 months – or 27% – resulting in an additional 258,000 renters being priced-out of buying a home as compared to the 31,000 buyers helped by the scheme. Some three and a half million people who would have normally been able to buy a home are now trapped in private renting.[3]

Private renting in the UK is generally appalling as there is so little regulation. We have become used to such low quality service that we consider poor quality as normal quality. In November 2014 the House of Commons Library reported that 213,000 private tenants had been evicted in the last year after asking for basic repairs to be carried out. A further half a million tenants did not dare to complain about any faults due to fear of eviction. A majority of landlords, some 56%, say they have evicted tenants.[4]

By July 2014 it had become clear that a third of all privately rented property was being rented out in poor condition; that tenure was both the most expensive and lowest-quality sector of housing in the UK. It was also growing rapidly, passing the 4 million households level in 2014, having overtaking social renting in 2013.

When the *Financial Times* (*FT*) confronted the landlords with the facts, the National Landlords Association said that

> . . . the rented sector continues to mature into a functioning and positive market that is serving renters well [and] costs in the sector have remained static . . .

The *FT* then pointed out that private sector rents take up 40% of tenants' gross income according to the annual English Housing Survey. For those who own their homes, the figure is 20%, while social tenants paid 30%.[5] In 2014 landlords were laughing all the way to the bank.[6]

In October 2014, just three months after the *FT* report, rents in the private sector were revealed to have risen to a new all-time-high of £770 a month for the average property in England, £1162 in London.[7] A month earlier they had been £761 a month. A year of such rises would result in a 15% price hike in rents.[8] Even without that, rents are rising faster than inflation, while tenants' wages still lag behind it.

In November 2014 Citizens' Advice published figures showing that there had been a 20% rise in households seeking help over eviction, even among those up to date with their rent payments. Two in five of these households had dependent children. They also revealed that London renters are three times as likely to report problems with vermin than are tenants elsewhere in the UK.[9]

At some point landlords can't or won't be allowed to squeeze yet more out of their tenants in higher rents. The housing benefit bill will have to be cut. People won't take jobs in London if the wages won't pay the rent. It will most probably be social forces rather than market forces that bring about the end of escalation. The lobby in favour of a change in the law to extend tenancies to three or five years, rather than two months, is growing and represents millions of people. In contrast, private landlords are a small group who attract less and less sympathy during hard times.

Almost two hundred years ago, in his *On the Principles of Political Economy and Taxation*, the Economist David Ricardo argued that, in the long term, economic growth would disproportionately benefit landlords.[10] That view fell out of favour but modern day economists are finding that the landlord advantage appears to be true again today; suggesting that without intervention we are looking at an enormous property bubble being driven by rapidly rising land prices forced up as landlords and investors speculate wildly.[11]

In the autumn of 2014 there was little sign of a slowdown in the UK housing market. There were plenty of *warnings* of a slowdown, but very little evidence of prices falling. By September prices fell slightly in most regions, but they usually do in that month. In London prices had risen by a remarkable 18.4% in just one year.[12] That annual percentage increase had itself been rising all year; but no one can tell you what it will be by the time the paperback edition of this book is published. It could crash; it could grow even higher; it is unlikely to remain the same.

On 23 October 2014 shares in the London-based estate agents, Foxtons, fell by 20% in just a matter of hours. They fell because Foxtons said that they did not expect to make as much money next year as they had in 2014. Many investors wondered whether this might be signaling the start of a wider property crash. Annual price rises of 21% were now being reported in London. Four years of such housing inflation and prices would more than double. Everyone in the business knows it has to come to an end, they just don't know when.[13] Rumours abounded that the housing bubble in China had burst but, rather than learn from the experience, the Chinese and many other investors began looking even more earnestly for what they thought was a safe haven in London.

Journalists write about 'luxury' flats being built across the capital. By these they mean flats that might look great in brochures being sold at prices that could never be supported by rents, in areas where no infrastructure has been built to support the new local communities. Those building the flats are only concerned with selling them on to the next wealthy overseas investors who, in turn, are concerned only with doing the same again in a year or so, until someone is stuck holding the unsellable 'asset'.

But what happens when the bubble bursts? Over-stretched landlords with too many new mortgages will go to the wall, many investors will be burnt, but new private landlords entering the market may simply buy up more property cheaply, out-bidding potential first time buyers, since landlords are offered better mortgage terms.

The *Telegraph* newspaper now regularly reports on the woes of the young upper-middle-classes unable to rent a property with a living room. In one story a public relations account manager shares a home with an accountant, a filmmaker, a barrister, a solicitor and an advertising executive. All six of these otherwise well-off people have to share with each other, and only have a kitchen as communal space. Even with promotions and pay rises these young adults should expect to be living in cramped accommodation for some time. London's population is set to rise by a million in the next few years.[14]

The estate agent Savills predicts that between 2014 and 2019 across England and Wales the number of households privately renting will increase by 1.2 million, owner-occupiers will fall by 200,000 and social renters fall by 50,000. Half the fall in owner-occupiers is predicted to take place in London. Private landlords are predicted to buy the equivalent of all the new build flats and homes in London, and a further 100,000 currently mortgaged or owned homes, and some 10,000 currently social rented properties.[15]

Looking forward, the Joseph Rowntree Foundation extrapolates and suggests that by 2040 private rents will rise by more than twice as much as incomes, resulting in a majority of future private renters in England living in poverty. Social renting, currently the tenure of one in seven people, will house only 10% of the population by 2040. It will be even worse if 220,000 homes a year are not built by the 2030s and if another £20 billion a year is not spent on housing benefits as more poorly paid families come to rely on the state. All of this is just if current trends continue, not following a further downturn.[16] In the last six years, two thirds of all new housing benefit claimants have been middle-income-earners.[17]

How do politicians react? The Conservatives keep inflating the bubble, most recently by announcing that upon reaching retirement age pensioners can purchase property with their pension pots rather than take an annuity. Only the most affluent pensioners will be able to do this but the policy was presented as if it would apply to all. The Tories need house prices to rise until at least the day before the general election of May

2015. If they win an outright majority, the Tories propose to end the building of what little social housing is now constructed by abolishing the 20% levies local councils are allowed to charge on new developments for new roads, schools and affordable housing provision.[18]

Nick Clegg did not mention housing in his speech at the 2014 Liberal party conference, although he did claim that his party would build ten garden cities by incentivizing local communities to ask for building around their homes by offering them an express train service.[19]

Labour published the Lyons review, which suggested changing the law so that local councils should have real powers to ensure that if land has been allocated for development in a plan, it is actually delivered, including the ability to levy a charge where delivery has not occurred (and there is no good reason for the failure). The review also proposes the possibility of Compulsory Purchase Orders being applied to acquire land at close to existing use value – in other words at agricultural prices.

However, building 200,000 new homes a year will not lead to Utopia, unless they are in the right places, owned and rented out the right way. At some point someone has to acknowledge that the reason we have to build more homes is due to immigration. Immigration we are lucky to benefit from. 'Lucky' because it is conditions out of the UK's control, such as a favourable time zone, the spread of the internet and the spread of the English language, which draws so many young, productive and daring people in.

With net immigration comes a necessity to build. Without building new homes people can be held to ransom. When held to ransom they strike out in all directions, including blaming immigrants. But it is not immigrants that are the problem – it is the 'investors'. Economist Aditya Chakrabortty found the appropriate analogy:

> I can think of one other aspect of everyday life where this has happened recently: food. Over the past 10 years, wheat and other staples have become a financial asset class, to be speculated in by Goldman Sachs and Barclays. The result has been misery and even starvation for the poor of the Third World. For the poor of London, the financialisation of property spells homelessness.[20]

In London at the end of 2014 the New Era housing estate was fighting for its life. The estate is in Hoxton where 'investors' have recently been making millions buying and selling homes. The Conservative MP Richard Benyon had been persuaded not to buy the flats in partnership with the US private equity company Westbrook partners and evict the tenants, despite the potential boost to his £110 million family fortune through charging 'market rents'. This turnaround was achieved by public petition where 300,000 people registered their disapproval. The authors of the petition then turned to try to influence Westbrook partners not to raise the rents and in effect evict the tenants, when Westbrook took over as the new sole landlords.[21]

Private landlords, of which Westbrook is just one among many, have bought up so much formally owner-occupied and social-rented property that their wealth will have grown by £109.5bn in the year to April 2015. This is due to the rising value of their existing property and the increases in the rents they charge. The total value of all landlords' property holdings in Britain will exceed £1 trillion by mid-year 2015, with 41% of that amount being in London.[22]

Outside London there are still a few areas where house prices are lower than in 2008, where private rents have collapsed and homes may have to be demolished, and where living conditions are rapidly declining not due to overcrowding but under-use. By October 2014 it took 3.5 average homes in the North East of England to buy one modest home in London, four years earlier that divide had been 2.5 times. By late 2014 the estate agent Frank Knight was predicting that the gap would only grow wider.[23]

In his December 2014 autumn statement George Osborne announced an £800 million cut to stamp duty on the purchase of properties. All his previous budgets had concentrated on measures designed to raise housing prices and the cost of housing, committing more spending or guarantees in this area than any other. George was determined that prices should increase, at least up until election day 2015, and for far longer than that if more and more people are forced to rent.[24]

Only the well-off will be able to buy a home in future. Most people will have to rent and enrich a landlord. Just under 80% of people think it is harder to buy a home now than it was a generation ago, even in the hardest times of the recent past. Over 80% of people think the main political parties won't deal with the problem effectively.[25] This is what chaos looks like.

Notes

I CRISIS

1. The 61% figure comes from J. Heartfield, *Let's build! Why we need five million new homes in the next ten years*, London: Audacity, 2012. http://www.audacity.org/research.htm

2. P. Collinson, 'House prices: guide to property hotspots', *Guardian*, 30 March 2012. http://www.guardian.co.uk/money/2012/mar/30/house-prices-guide-property-hotspots#

3. R. Lynch, 'UK "value" falls by £94 billion', *Independent*, 2 August 2010. http://www.independent.co.uk/news/uk/home-news/uk-value-falls-by-pound94-billion-2041594.html. On the annual cost of the NHS, then around £105 billion, see: http://www.kingsfund.org.uk/projects/general-election-2010/faqs#budget

4. S. Carrera and J. Beaumont, 'Income and wealth', *Social trends*, No. 41, Table 5. http://www.ons.gov.uk/ons/rel/social-trends-rd/social-trends/social-trends-41/index.html

5. M. Easton, BBC, 'Housing crisis deepens', *BBC News*, 12 June 2012. http://www.bbc.co.uk/news/uk-18416365

6. R. Ramesh, 'Sharp drop in new affordable homes under coalition, council data shows', *Guardian*, 10 February 2013. http://www.guardian.co.uk/society/2013/feb/10/sharp-drop-new-affordable-homes

7. HP Sauce, 'Cunning stunts', *Private Eye*, 23 August–5 September 2013, No. 1,347, p. 9.

8. S. Hawkins and J. Bingham, 'End of the Thatcher property revolution', *Telegraph*, 28 June 2013. http://www.telegraph.co.uk/news/politics/10149480/End-of-the-Thatcher-property-revolution.html

9. T. Ross, 'David Cameron: my mortgage plan for struggling families', *Telegraph*, 27 September 2013. http://www.telegraph.co.uk/news/politics/david-cameron/10342014/David-Cameron-My-mortgage-plan-for-struggling-families.html

10. https://www.gov.uk/government/news/montague-plan-offers-boost-to-private-rented-sector

11. ITN, 'Demand for homes doubles the rate houses are built', *ITV News*, 23 August 2012. http://www.itv.com/news/update/2012-08-23/report-offers-blueprint-to-expand-private-rented-sector/

12. P. Thomas and H. Brennan, 'Osborne unveils £130 billion MIG scheme and £3.5 billion of shared equity loans', *Money Marketing Newspaper*, 20 March 2013. http://www.moneymarketing.co.uk/home/budget-2013/budget-13-osborne-unveils-130bn-mig-scheme-and-35bn-of-shared-equity-loans/1068076.article

13. C. Fincher, 'Government fleshes out contested mortgage guarantee scheme', Reuters, 23 July 2013. http://uk.reuters.com/article/2013/07/23/uk-mortgage-guarantee-idUKLNE96M00820130723

14. M. d'Ancona, 'David Cameron: a Prime Minister in a hurry', *Telegraph*, 28 September 2013. http://www.telegraph.co.uk/news/politics/david-cameron/10341422/David-Cameron-a-Prime-Minister-in-a-hurry.html

15. L. Elliott, 'George Osborne's "help-to-buy" scheme "a moronic policy"', *Guardian*, 4 June 2013. http://www.theguardian.com/business/2013/jun/04/george-osborne-help-to-buy-moronic

16. A. Withnall, 'Tories bring forward "help-to-buy": young Britons to get 95% mortgages next week', *Independent*, 29 September 2013. http://www.independent.co.uk/news/uk/home-news/tories-bring-forward-help-to-buy-young-britons-to-get-95-mortgages-next-week-8847350.html

17. In Scotland a very limited form of the scheme will run, only supporting mortgages on new-build property and then only those worth less than £400,000: BBC, 'Scottish "help-to-buy" scheme unveiled', *BBC News Scotland*, 27 September 2013. http://www.bbc.co.uk/news/uk-scotland-scotland-business-24297003

18. R. Ramesh, 'Extra 10,000 working people a month reliant on housing benefit, says report', *Guardian*, 22 October 2012. http://www.theguardian.com/society/2012/oct/22/working-people-housing-benefit-report

19. G. Peev, 'Working families on housing benefit soar: number of applications rising by 10,000 every month', *Daily Mail*, 22 October 2012. http://www.dailymail.co.uk/news/article-2221111/Working-families-housing-benefit-soar-Number-applications-rising-10-000-month.html

20. D. Bartlett, 'Why does the UK subsidize landlords so much?', *Liverpool Daily Post*, 28 January 2013. http://blogs.liverpooldailypost.co.uk/dalestreetblues/2013/01/why-does-the-uk-subsidise-land.html

21. Ramesh, 'Extra 10,000 working people a month reliant on housing benefit'.

22. D. Johnson, 'Rent controls: should they be reintroduced?', *Guardian* housing network blog, 5 August 2013. http://www.theguardian.com/housing-network/2013/aug/05/rent-control-debate

23. Communities and Local Government Committee, 'Supplementary written evidence submitted by Shelter', February 2013, posted online 16 July. http://www.publications.parliament.uk/pa/cm201314/cmselect/cmcomloc/50/50ii06.htm

24. P. Inman, 'Bovis reports boost in half-year profits as sales rise 18% with prices up 6%', *Guardian*, 20 August 2012. http://www.theguardian.com/business/2012/aug/20/housebuilder-bovis-boosts-half-year-profits

25. J. Titcomb, 'Barclays chief warns of housing bubble', *Telegraph*, 11 September 2013. http://www.telegraph.co.uk/finance/newsbysector/constructionandproperty/10301510/Barclays-chief-warns-of-housing-bubble.html

26. N. Klein, *The Shock Doctrine: the rise of Disaster Capitalism*, London: Picador, 2008.

27. Attempts to sideline the poor in the US show the price of such failure: 'In poor black neighborhoods, eviction is to women what incarceration is to men: a typical but severely consequential occurrence contributing to the reproduction of urban poverty.' M. Desmond, 'Eviction and the reproduction of urban poverty', *American Journal of Sociology*, Vol. 118, No. 1 (2012), pp. 88–133.

28. R. Frank, 'Falling behind: how rising inequality harms the middle class', lecture presented to the seventh Aaron Wildavsky Forum for Public Policy, Richard and Rhoda Goldman School of Public Policy, University of California at Berkeley, 18–19 October 2001. The book based on the lecture was published by the University of California Press on 9 July 2007.

29. R. Frank, 'Positional goods and keeping up with the Joneses', Young Foundation and Smith Institute joint seminar, No. 11 Downing Street, September 2006, reply by Oliver James. http://youngfoundation.org/publications/positional-goods-new-inequalities-and-the-importance-of-relative-position/

30. T. Walker, 'Society: the only way is Finland', *Independent*, 23 May 2012. http://www.independent.co.uk/news/uk/politics/society-the-only-way-is-finland-7778796.html

31. D. Dorling, *Fair play: a reader on social justice*, Bristol: Policy Press, 2012, Table 44.1, p. 349.

32. S. Pizzigati, *The rich don't always win: the forgotten triumph over plutocracy that created the American middle class, 1900–1970*, New York: Seven Stories Press, 2012.

33. 'Delinquency' is a US term for people in mortgage arrears. See section below concerning repossessions, in Chapter 7 by Figure 20, page 249.

34. Again, to see how bad the situation can become, look to the US, where: 'Overall, the government's priorities remain in the wrong place – it continues to spend the majority of its housing subsidies on those who need it least.' L. Cattell, et al., *We call these projects home*, New York: Right to the City Alliance, 2010, p. 53. http://www.righttothecity.org/index. php/resources/reports/item/61-we-call-these-projects-home

35. G. Oliver, 'Claim: "Draconian rules preventing firms from building homes"', *Oxford Mail*, 21 September 2013. http://www.oxfordmail.co.uk/news/10669374.Claim_____Draconian_rules_preventing_firms_from_building_homes___/?ref=rc

2 PLANNING

1. M. Stephens, 'Tackling housing market volatility in the UK', Joseph Rowntree Foundation, research report, 16 May 2012. http://www.jrf. org.uk/publications/tackling-housing-market-volatility-uk

2. Shelter, 'Building more homes' campaign, website accessed August 2013. http://england.shelter.org.uk/campaigns/why_we_campaign/building_more_homes

3. E. Twinch and N. Duxbury, 'Cable calls for massive house-building programme', 'Inside Housing' website, 25 September 2012. http://www. insidehousing.co.uk/development/cable-calls-for-massive-house-building-programme/6523911.article

4. C. Hope, 'David Cameron backs Nick Boles over house-building plans', *Telegraph*, 5 December 2012. http://www.telegraph.co.uk/earth/hands-off-our-land/9724371/David-Cameron-backs-Nick-Boles-over-house-building-plans.html

5. D. Dorling, 'Fairness and the changing fortunes of people in Britain', *Journal of the Royal Statistical Society (A)*, Vol. 176, No. 1 (2013), pp. 97–128. http://www.dannydorling.org/?page_id=3597

6. G. Speight, 'The lending frenzy of the 1930s', presentation made at the Ashmolean, Oxford, 2010. http://winton.ashmus.ox.ac.uk/PastSeminars/Michaelmas2010/Colloquium/Presentation%20Slides/Speight.pdf

7. F. Alvaredo, et al., 'The top 1% in international and historical perspective', National Bureau of Economic Research Working Paper No. 19075, May 2013. http://www.nber.org/papers/w19075

8. H. Glennerster, 'Why was a wealth tax for the UK abandoned? Lessons for the policy process and tackling wealth inequality', *Journal of Social*

Policy, Vol. 41, No. 2 (2012), pp. 233–49. Page 4 of free online version: http://eprints.lse.ac.uk/42582/1/Why_was_a_wealth_tax_for_the_UK_abandoned_(lsero).pdf

9. R. Tunstall, 'What should we worry about when we worry about housing problems?', inaugural lecture, University of York, 2012, Table 2. http://www.york.ac.uk/chp/news/2012/inaugural/

10. Ibid. These figures come from the same Table 2: if an absolute space poverty line is used, that can also be seen to be growing from 1991 to 2001, by which time over 11% were poorly housed. No 2011 figures had yet been calculated to continue the times series at the time of writing this chapter, but some are included in Chapter 6 below (see Figure 13) and what they reveal is a dramatic rise in housing inequality.

11. D. Dorling, *The no-nonsense guide to equality*, Oxford: New Internationalist, 2012.

12. Figures for median age at death are normally higher than life expectancy because infant deaths reduce the mean. Office for National Statistics, 'Mortality in England and Wales: average life span', 17 December 2012. http://www.ons.gov.uk/ons/dcp171776_292196.pdf

13. N. Cohen, 'A coalition of the complacent', *Spectator*, 7 January 2013. http://blogs.spectator.co.uk/nick-cohen/2013/01/a-coalition-of-the-complacent/

14. Office for National Statistics, 'Births by area of usual residence of mother, England and Wales, 2011', press release, 31 October 2012. http://www.ons.gov.uk/ons/rel/vsob1/births-by-area-of-usual-residence-of-mother--england-and-wales/2011/index.html

15. D. Dorling, *The population of the UK*, London: Sage, 2012 (second edition), Chapter 2.

16. London Councils (the lobbying body of London's 32 borough councils and the City of London), 'London's school place shortage', 2013. http://www.londoncouncils.gov.uk/policylobbying/children/schools/primaryschools.htm

17. M. Pember Reeves, *Round about a pound a week*, London: Virago, 1913; 1979 reprint, p. 35.

18. House of Commons Library, 'A century of change: trends in UK statistics since 1900', House of Commons Library Research Paper No. 99/111, United Kingdom Parliament, 21 December 1999. http://www.parliament.uk/documents/commons/lib/research/rp99/rp99-111.pdf (page 12)/

19. C. Jones, 'Bank of England's Mark Carney seeks to win over guidance sceptics', *Financial Times*, 29 August 2013. http://www.ft.com/cms/s/0/bec5124e-0fd6-11e3-a258-00144feabdc0.html

20. See A. Haldane, S. Millard and V. Saporta (eds.), *The future of payment systems*, London: Routledge International Studies in Money and Banking No. 43, 2007, Chapter 10 by George Speight.

21. G. Speight, 'The lending frenzy of the 1930s'.

22. T. Powley, 'UK government faces pressure to drop "help-to-buy" mortgage scheme', *Financial Times*, 13 August 2013. http://www.ft.com/cms/s/0/43c4f0b2-035d-11e3-b871-00144feab7de.html

23. B. Green, 'England's housing stock grows slower than the population for the first time in decades', blog entry for Building.co.uk, 30 June 2011.http://brickonomics.building.co.uk/2011/06/england's-housing-stock-grows-slower-than-the-population-for-the-first-time-in-decades/

24. National Housing Federation, 'Parents feel the strain as grown-up kids remain living at home', press release, 6 September 2013. http://www.housing.org.uk/media/press-releases/parents-feel-the-strain-as-grown-up-kids-remain-living-at-home

25. N. Crafts, 'Delivering growth while reducing deficits: lessons from the 1930s', Centreforum policy paper, 2011. http://www.centreforum.org/assets/pubs/delivering-growth-while-reducing-deficits.pdf

26. T. Leunig, 'We need to learn from the 1930s: in the 1930s, Britain's economy grew thanks to low interest rates and house-building', *Telegraph*, 25 April 2012. http://www.telegraph.co.uk/news/politics/9226679/We-need-to-learn-from-the-1930s.html

27. L. Samy, '"The paradox of success": the effect of growth, competition and managerial self-interest on building society risk-taking and market structure, *c.* 1880–1939', Discussion Papers in Economic and Social History No. 86, January 2011, University of Oxford, Figure 14. http://www.nuff.ox.ac.uk/economics/history/Paper86/Samy86.pdf

28. T. Greenham, head of Finance and Business at the New Economics Foundation, speaking on *The Today Programme*, BBC Radio 4, 19 December 2012. http://news.bbc.co.uk/today/hi/today/newsid_9779000/9779870.stm

29. G. Eaton, 'Cameron's tax return isn't enough', *New Statesman*, 11 April 2012. http://www.newstatesman.com/blogs/staggers/2012/04/cameron-tax referring to *The Times*: http://www.timesonline.co.uk/tol/news/politics/article6267193.ece?token=null&offset=84&page=8 (first accessed by this author when it was not hidden behind a paywall, on 15 July 2009).

30. Department for Communities and Local Government, 'Live tables on dwelling stock (including vacants). Table 101: by tenure, United Kingdom (historical series)', 21 May 2013. https://www.gov.uk/government/statistical-data-sets/live-tables-on-dwelling-stock-including-vacants

31. T. Shepperson, 'The Rent Act 1977 in context', 'Landlord-Law' website blog, 19 July 2011. http://www.landlordlawblog.co.uk/2011/07/19/the-rent-act-1977-in-context/

32. G. Horsfield, *Family spending: a report on the 2010 living costs and food survey*, London: Office of National Statistics, 2012, p. 13. http://www.ons.gov.uk/ons/rel/family-spending/family-spending/family-spending-2011-edition/index.html

33. Again, see M. Pember Reeves, *Round about a pound a week*, p. 35.

34. P. K. Piff, et al., 'Higher social class predicts increased unethical behaviour', *Proceedings of the National Academy of the United States*, published online 27 February 2013. http://www.pnas.org/content/early/2012/02/21/1118373109.full.pdf+html

35. A. Mani, et al., 'Poverty impedes cognitive function', *Science*, Vol. 341, No. 976 (2013). http://www.sciencemag.org/content/341/6149/976.full.pdf

36. D. Dorling, 'Mean machine: structural inequality makes social inequality seem natural', *New Internationalist*, Issue 433 (2012). http://newint.org/features/special/2010/06/01/structural-inequality/

37. M. Bennett-Smith, 'Niall Ferguson: Keynesian economics flawed because Keynes was gay, childless', *Huffington Post*, 4 May 2013. http://www.huffingtonpost.com/2013/05/04/niall-ferguson-keynesian-economics-gay-childless_n_3215427.html

38. M. Gongloff, 'Niall Ferguson re-apologizes for dumb Keynes statements, makes more dumb statements', *Huffington Post*, 5 August 2013. http://www.huffingtonpost.com/2013/05/08/niall-ferguson-apologizes-keynes_n_3238940.html

39. O. Wilde, 'The soul of man under socialism', London: privately printed, 1891. http://www.marxists.org/reference/archive/wilde-oscar/soul-man/

40. Ibid.

41. G. Fraser, 'A debate over whether decent housing is a basic human right is long overdue', *Guardian*, 5 July 2013. http://www.guardian.co.uk/commentisfree/belief/2013/jul/05/debate-decent-housing-human-right

42. At the New York University School of Law and, in Britain, successor to Isaiah Berlin and Gerald Cohen as the Chichele Professor of Social and Political Theory at All Souls College, Oxford University.

43. Jeremy Waldron, then Professor, Jurisprudence and Social Policy Program, Boalt Hall School of Law, Berkeley, University of California: J. Waldron, 'Homelessness and the issue of freedom', *UCLA Law Review*, Vol. 39 (December 1991), pp. 295–324. http://faculty.washington.edu/pembina/all_articles/Waldron%201991.pdf

3 FOUNDATIONS

1. ITN, 'Young people locked out of housing market', *ITV News*, 13 June 2012.http://www.itv.com/news/calendar/2012-06-13/young-people-locked-out-of-housing-market/

2. L. Bourke, 'How to leave property to your grandchildren', 'City Wire' website money blog, 19 September 2012. http://citywire.co.uk/money/how-to-leave-property-to-your-grandchildren/a619412

3. Ibid.

4. J. Hills and H. Glennerster, 'Why the left needs to take wealth seriously again', *Juncture*, Vol. 20, No. 1 (2013), pp. 72–9. http://onlinelibrary.wiley.com/doi/10.1111/j.2050-5876.2013.00730.x/pdf

5. D. Dorling, et al., *The great divide: an analysis of housing inequality*, London: Shelter, 2005. http://www.dannydorling.org/?page_id=460

6. J. Bingham, 'Two million elderly planning to sell home', *Telegraph*, 21 August 2013. http://www.telegraph.co.uk/property/propertynews/10255271/Two-million-elderly-planning-to-sell-home.html

7. J. Hills and H. Glennerster, 'Why the left needs to take wealth seriously again', p. 74.

8. E. Howker and S. Malik, *Jilted generation: how Britain has bankrupted its youth*, London: Icon Books, 2010.

9. D. Willetts, *The pinch: how the baby boomers took their children's future – and why they should give it back*, London: Atlantic Books, 2010.

10. J. Mercier, 'Greed is good. Now it's legal', 'Sanlam Private Investments' website blog, 8 August 2013. http://www.spi.sanlam.co.uk/investment-thinking/investment-blog/greed-good-now-its-legal/

11. The world's best-off 1% include all of the best-off 10% in the UK and US; because only a minority of this group are also holiday or second-home owners, most do not see themselves as wealthy. See the graph in B. Sutcliffe, 'The world distribution of gross national income', *Environment and Planning A*, Vol. 41, No. 4 (2009), p. 764. http://www.envplan.com/abstract.cgi?id=a4227

12. N. Blackmore, 'Home-buyers in London need £64,000 deposit', *Telegraph*, 28 August 2013. http://www.telegraph.co.uk/finance/personalfinance/borrowing/mortgages/10271969/Home-buyers-in-London-need-64000-deposit.html

13. R. Wilkinson and K. Pickett, *The spirit level: why equality is better for everyone*, London: Penguin, 2010. Note this is the second edition with a changed subtitle, because even the very richest do better when all are more equal.

14. D. Staunton, Noam Chomsky interview: 'The public can make a difference – and in more democratic societies, a lot of difference', *Irish Times*, 1 April 2013. http://www.irishtimes.com/news/world/noam-chomsky-interview-the-public-can-make-a-difference-and-in-more-democratic-societies-a-lot-of-difference-1.1344852

15. TUC Scotland (2010), 'Myth number 7: the UK's deficit was caused by high government spending', report, 2010. http://www.thereisabetterway.org/top-myths-about-the-crisis/the-uk-s-deficit-was-caused-by-high-government-spending

16. Office for National Statistics, 'Public sector finances, March', released 23 April 2013. http://www.ons.gov.uk/ons/dcp171778_306382.pdf

17. S. P. Chan and M. Oliver, 'Budget 2013: Britain's debt and deficit', *Telegraph*, 20 March 2013. http://www.telegraph.co.uk/finance/budget/9932748/Budget-2013-Britains-debt-and-deficit.html

18. BBC, 'UK loses top AAA credit rating for first time since 1978', *BBC Business News*, 22 February 2013. http://www.bbc.co.uk/news/business-21554311

19. C. Keena, 'Sean Dunne bankruptcy in contrast with position of small borrowers: if you want debt forgiveness, you need to have enormous debts', *Irish Times*, 3 April 2013. http://www.irishtimes.com/business/sectors/financial-services/sean-dunne-bankruptcy-in-contrast-with-position-of-small-borrowers-1.1346903

20. H. Spencer, *Social statics; or, the conditions essential to human happiness specified, and the first of them developed*, London: John Chapman, 1851.

21. US Department of Labor, *One hundred years of US consumer spending: data for the nation*, New York City, and Boston: Office of Publications and Special Studies, 2006. http://www.bls.gov/opub/uscs/

22. Income inequality in the US is higher today than at any time since 1917. E. Saez, 'Striking it richer: the evolution of top incomes in the United States', working paper, University of California, Berkeley, Figure 2, updated with 2012 preliminary estimates. http://elsa.berkeley.edu/~saez/saez-UStopincomes-2012.pdf

23. M. Easton, 'Rent "unaffordable" for low-income families in third of UK', *BBC News*, 15 July 2013. http://www.bbc.co.uk/news/business-23273448

24. That is more square feet of housing per person when it comes to UK and US measurements, square metres elsewhere. Possibly just after the Black Death we had more. For an estimate of the global housing stock see data at 'Worldmapper' website. http://www.worldmapper.org/display.php?selected=194

25. BBC, 'Social housing waiting lists rise in England', *BBC News*, 15 January 2011. http://www.bbc.co.uk/news/uk-12198429

26. In Essex: J. Melley, 'Social housing: Essex has thousands on waiting lists', *BBCNews*, 26 January 2013. http://www.bbc.co.uk/news/uk-england-essex-21202473

27. K. Reeve and E. Batty, 'The hidden truth about homelessness', report for Crisis and CRESR, May 2011. http://www.crisis.org.uk/data/files/publications/HiddenTruthAboutHomelessness_web.pdf

28. That 240,000 figure may be an overestimate made from assuming 38% of street homeless people rather than all homeless people have squatted. However, as an estimate of all those who have ever squatted, and given how many did as children with their families after the Second World War, I think it is reasonable. For the sources see: K. Reeve, 'Squatting: a homelessness issue, an evidence review', report published by Crisis and CRESR, October 2011. http://www.crisis.org.uk/publications-search. php?fullitem=327

29. A. Grice, 'Numbers of homeless people in UK up by 17 per cent', *Independent*, 9 September 2011. http://www.independent.co.uk/news/uk/politics/numbers-of-homeless-people-in-uk-up-by-17-per-cent-2351644. html

30. A. McGibbon, 'If we want the government to take housing seriously, a national tenants' union is the first step', *Independent*, 18 February 2013. http://www.independent.co.uk/voices/comment/if-we-want-the-government-to-take-housing-seriously-a-national-tenants-union-is-the-first-step-8500068.html

31. Empty Homes Agency, 'Statistical archives of the Empty Homes Agency', June 2011. http://emptyhomes.test-host.net/wp-content/uploads/2011/06/amended-stats-08-09-1.pdf

32. There is also a vibrant positive squatting movement growing again across Europe but it tends to be for the young and childless. http://sqek. squat.net/; and, in particular, Squatting Europe Kollective, *Squatting in Europe: radical spaces, urban struggles*, New York: Minor Compositions, 2013. http://sqek.squat.net/wp-content/uploads/2013/03/sqek-book.pdf

33. D. Henke and R. Evans, 'The many homes of Michael Meacher', *Guardian*, 20 January 2001. http://www.theguardian.com/uk/2001/jan/20/politics.labour

34. B. Obama, quoted and recorded in K. Q. Seelye and K. Bennett, 'Obama counts McCain's houses', political comment blog of the *New York Times*, 21 August 2008. http://thecaucus.blogs.nytimes.com/2008/08/21/obama-counts-mccains-houses/

35. The true number may be higher. D. M. Halbfinger, 'The McCain proper-ties', *New York Times*, 23 August 2008. http://www.nytimes.com/ref/us/politics/mccain-properties.html?ref=politics

36. J. Steenhuysen, 'US life expectancy falls slightly in 2008: CDC', Reuters press release, 9 December 2009. http://www.reuters.com/article/2010/12/09/us-life-expectancy-idUSTRE6B86K720101209 See section 'Health and eviction' below as to how housing is becoming more connected to health.

37. D. Dorling, *Unequal health: the scandal of our times*, Bristol: Policy Press, 2013.

38. L. Berman, 'Death (certificates) took holiday in wake of bankruptcy fil-ing', *Detroit News*, 29 August 2013. http://www.detroitnews.com/article/20130829/METRO01/308290046

39. The old phrase attributed to Francis Bacon in 1625 comes to mind: 'Money is like muck, no good unless it is spread.' For the modern-day equivalents of this truism, see the 'Equality Trust' website. http://www.equalitytrust.org.uk/research/education and http://www.equalitytrust.org.uk/research/mental-health

40. Child Welfare Information Gateway, *How many children were adopted in 2007 and 2008?*, Washington, DC: US Department of Health and Human Services, Children's Bureau, September 2011. https://www.childwelfare.gov/pubs/adopted0708.pdf

41. BBC, 'Half of the world's prison population of about nine million is held in the US, China or Russia', *BBC News*, report, 2013. http://news.bbc.co.uk/1/shared/spl/hi/uk/06/prisons/html/nn2page1.stm

42. Justice Policy Institute, *The punishing decade: prison and jail estimates at the millennium*, Washington, DC: Justice Policy Institute, 2000. http://www.justicepolicy.org/images/upload/00-05_rep_punishingdecade_ac.pdf

43. *Guardian*, 'Housing crisis: home economics', editorial, 2 September 2012. http://www.guardian.co.uk/commentisfree/2012/sep/02/housing-crisis-home-economics-editorial

44. Royal Institute of Chartered Surveyors, 'Royal Institute of Chartered Surveyors/ Ci Portuguese housing market survey: lettings sector shows first signs of weakness', press release, November 2012. http://www.rics.org/Global/Portuguese-Housing-Market-Survey-November-2012.pdf

45. G. Tremlett, 'More than a quarter of Spanish workforce are jobless', *Guardian*, 24 January 2013. http://www.theguardian.com/world/2013/jan/24/quarter-spanish-workforce-jobless

46. RTÉ, 'Fitch expects further 20% drop in Irish house prices', *RTÉ News*, 9 January 2013. http://www.rte.ie/news/2013/0108/361799-fitch-sees-further-20-drop-in-irish-house-prices/

47. S. Binge, 'Still no bottom for Spanish house prices', *Property Show Rooms*, online magazine, 17 September 2013. http://www.property-showrooms.com/spain/property/news/still-no-bottom-for-spanish-house-prices_312902.html

48. Colm McCarthy, describing the response to a news item on Irish TV on 2 October 2008, quoted in M. Lewis, *Boomerang: the meltdown tour*, London: Allen Lane, 2011, p. 98.

49. M. Lewis, 'When Irish eyes are crying', *Vanity Fair*, March 2011. http://www.vanityfair.com/business/features/2011/03/michael-lewis-ireland-201103.print

50. J. Smyth, 'Ireland. Bleak houses: the country faces a mortgage crisis that could trigger mass evictions and jeopardise stability', *Financial Times*, 29 April 2013. http://www.ft.com/cms/s/0/f5d742a8-a3a1-11e2-ac00-00144feabdco.html

51. S. Garrett, 'Australians warned of Irish-style housing crash', *Irish Times*, 2 September 2013. http://www.irishtimes.com/business/sectors/commercial-property/australians-warned-of-irish-style-housing-crash-1.1512560

52. P. Geoghegan, 'Rebuilding Iceland', *Sunday Business Post*, 22 May 2011. http://www.petergeoghegan.com/?p=462

53. P. Eavis, 'Ireland plans bold measures to lift housing', *New York Times*, 9 October 2012, p. A1 (New York edition). http://dealbook.nytimes.com/2012/10/08/ireland-mortgage-bill-aims-to-aid-owners-and-jump-start-economy/

54. J. Smyth, 'Ireland acts on unsustainable mortgages', *Financial Times*, 13 March 2013. http://www.ft.com/cms/s/0/fc299d74-8bfd-11e2-b001-00144feabdco.html

55. R. Burtenshaw and A. Robinson, David Harvey interview: 'The importance of post-capitalist imagination', *Red Pepper* magazine, August 2013.http://www.redpepper.org.uk/david-harvey-interview-the-importance-of-postcapitalist-imagination/

56. R. Kitchin, S. O'Callaghan and J. Gleeson, 'Unfinished estates in post-Celtic Tiger Ireland', Northern Ireland Statistics and Research Agency Working Paper No. 67, 2012, p. 13. http://ebookbrowse.com/nirsa-working-paper-67-unfinished-estates-in-post-celtic-tiger-ireland-pdf-d312024595

57. P. Geoghegan, 'Icelandic myths', *London Review of Books*, 25 June 2012.http://www.lrb.co.uk/blog/2012/06/25/peter-geoghegan/icelandic-myths/

58. HM Treasury, *Report under Section 2 of the Loans to Ireland Act 2010*:

1 October 2012 to 31 March 2013, London: Her Majesty's Treasury, 2013.https://www.gov.uk/government/publications/bilateral-loan-to-ireland

59. D. O'Donovan, 'Property crash "over" as Moody's insists market at bottom', *Irish Independent*, 14 November 2013. http://www.independent.ie/irish-news/property-crash-over-as-moodys-insists-market-at-bottom-29753716.html

60. J. Mackintosh, 'Europe's house price bubbles: Iceland, Ireland and Spain updated', *Financial Times*, 'Long Short' blog, 13 March 2013. http://blogs.ft.com/ft-long-short/2013/03/13/europes-house-price-bubbles-iceland-ireland-and-spain-updated/

61. S. Lyall, 'A bruised Iceland heals amid Europe's malaise', *New York Times*, 7 July 2012. http://www.nytimes.com/2012/07/08/world/europe/icelands-economy-is-mending-amid-europes-malaise.html?_r=1

62. Only three countries in Europe are more equitable than Germany, according to their 90:10 income inequality ratios: Sweden, Norway and Finland. Housing markets were far more likely to get into crisis in countries with high income inequalities. See D. Dorling, *Injustice: why social inequality persists*, Bristol: Policy Press, 2010, p. 323, n. 37.

63. R. Rayasam, '"Cement gold": German property market soars amid euro crisis', *Der Spiegel*, 22 June 2012. http://www.spiegel.de/international/germany/german-real-estate-market-soars-amid-euro-crisis-a-838437.html

64. C. Bryant, 'Germany's gold standard jobs record masks hidden flaws', *Financial Times*, 2 September 2013. http://www.ft.com/cms/s/0/0bf80e46-0fc2-11e3-99e0-00144feabdc0.html

65. O. Hatherley, 'A terrace house for £1 or £250 million – Britain's bizarre housing crisis', *Guardian*, 24 April 2013. http://www.theguardian.com/commentisfree/2013/apr/24/terraced-house-250m-housing-crisis

66. N. Blechner, 'Droht in Deutschland eine Immobilienblase?' ('Is Germany threatened by real estate bubble?'), *ARD.de News,* 15 January 2013. http://boerse.ard.de/performance-und-rendite/vorsorge/droht-in-deutschland-eine-immobilienblase100.html

67. Land Registry, 'House price index, July', released 29 August 2013. http://www.landregistry.gov.uk/__data/assets/pdf_file/0010/54001/HPIReport20130822.pdf

68. I. Birrell, 'The housing crisis: a nightmare caused by our sanctified suburban dreams', *Guardian*, 20 August 2012. http://www.guardian.co.uk/commentisfree/2012/aug/20/planning-housing

69. Royal Institute of Chartered Surveyors, 'New RICS commission into

the UK housing crisis', RICS press release, 7 February 2013. http://www.rics.org/uk/knowledge/news-insight/press-releases/new-rics-housing-commission-calls-for-evidence/

70. S. Nolan, 'Britain faces slowest housing market recovery on record with some property prices not set to peak again until 2021', *Daily Mail*, 6 January 2013. http://www.dailymail.co.uk/news/article-2257916/Britain-faces-slowest-housing-market-recovery-record-property-prices-set-peak-2021.html

71. H. Brennan, '"Help-to-buy" could spark 30% surge in house prices', *Money Marketing*, 7 May 2013. http://www.moneymarketing.co.uk/news-and-analysis/mortgages/help-to-buy-could-spark-30-surge-in-house-prices/1070754.article

72. Royal Institute of British Architects, '2013 budget: a missed opportunity on affordable housing and green growth', RIBA press release, 20 March 2013. http://www.architecture.com/NewsAndPress/News/RIBANews/News/2013/2013BudgetAmissedopportunityonaffordablehousingandgreengrowth.aspx

73. HP Sauce, 'George Osborne's £15.5 billion "help-to-buy"', *Private Eye*, No. 1337 (5 April 2013), p. 9.

74. L. Chiswick, '"FirstBuy": flawed, and such small portions – a government initiative to reignite the housing market offers a lifeline to builders but little for buyers', 'City Wire' website money blog, 22 June 2011. http://citywire.co.uk/money/firstbuy-flawed-and-such-small-portions/a502558

75. A. Jones, 'Company behind the new Notts. campus goes bust', *Nottingham Tab Student Newspaper*, 1 April 2013. http://nottingham.tab.co.uk/2013/04/01/opal-goes-bust/

76. A. Jupp, 'Thirteen Opal companies fall into administration', *Manchester Evening News*, 13 March 2013. http://www.manchestereveningnews.co.uk/business/property/further-13-companies-within-manchester-1741874

77. BBC, 'UK wages decline among worst in Europe', *Business News*, 11 August 2013. http://www.bbc.co.uk/news/business-23655605

78. H. Wilson, 'Nearly 2,500 British bankers paid over €1 million, says EU regulator', *Telegraph*, 15 July 2013. http://www.telegraph.co.uk/finance/newsbysector/banksandfinance/10180313/Nearly-2500-British-bankers-paid-over-1m-says-EU-regulator.html

79. B. Brady, 'Labour revives plan to protect private tenants', *Independent*, 13 January 2013. http://www.independent.co.uk/news/uk/politics/labour-revives-plan-to-protect-private-tenants-8449404.html

4 BUILDING

1. H. Rifkind, 'Why we should fear the new housing bubble', *Spectator*, 17 August 2013. http://www.spectator.co.uk/columnists/hugo-rifkind/8993311/why-we-should-fear-the-new-housing-bubble/

2. J. Rickards, 'Repeal of Glass–Steagall caused the financial crisis', *US News*, 27 August 2012. http://www.usnews.com/opinion/blogs/economic-intelligence/2012/08/27/repeal-of-glass-steagall-caused-the-financial-crisis

3. L. Adelman, 'Racial preferences for whites: the houses that racism built', *San Francisco Chronicle*, 29 June 2003, quoted on Slide 23 of S. Carlson, 'A history of homelessness in America: homelessness 101', two-day workshop. http://mesh-mn.org/workshops-events/homelessness-101/ Relying greatly in turn on Ken Kusmer's *Down and out, on the road: the homeless in American history*, Oxford: OUP, 2002.

4. A. Smithers, *The road to recovery – how and why economic policy must change*, Chichester: Wiley, 2013.

5. M. West, 'Capital losses: the interactive map that shows the London boroughs where house prices are actually FALLING', *Daily Mail*, 17 September 2013. http://www.thisismoney.co.uk/money/mortgageshome/article-2423620/The-London-boroughs-house-prices-falling-just-like-rest-country.html

6. A. Hull and G. Cooke, 'Together at home: a new strategy for housing', Institute for Public Policy Research, report, 21 June 2012, p. 53. http://www.ippr.org/publication/55/9279/together-at-home-a-new-strategy-for-housing

7. L. Boyce, 'OECD reveals the world's cheapest and most overvalued property markets', *Daily Mail*, 'This is Money' website, 1 June 2013. http://www.thisismoney.co.uk/money/mortgageshome/article-2333944/Property-prices-Britain-31-high-says-OECD.html

8. P. Wintour, 'We need to build houses on a third more land, says planning minister', *Guardian*, 27 November 2012. http://www.guardian.co.uk/society/2012/nov/27/housebuilding-needs-more-open-land

9. W. Hurst, 'Labour fires warning over land "hoarding"', *Building Magazine*, 21 June 2013. http://www.building.co.uk/news/labour-fires-warning-over-land-hoarding/5056698.article

10. L. Mark, 'Bovis Homes boss slams land hoarding claims as "nonsense"', *Architects' Journal*, 21 August 2013. http://www.architectsjournal.co.uk/news/bovis-homes-boss-slams-land-hoarding-claims-as-nonsense/8652223.article

11. Staff reporter, 'Who owns Britain: top UK landowners', *County Life*, 11 November 2010. http://www.countrylife.co.uk/countryside/article/506868/Who-owns-Britain-Top-UK-landowners.html

12. W. Johnson, 'UK migration falls by a quarter as student and foreign worker numbers fall', *Telegraph*, 29 November 2012. http://www.telegraph.co.uk/news/uknews/immigration/9711047/UK-migration-falls-by-a-quarter-as-student-and-foreign-worker-numbers-fall.html

13. Outside of Sydney! Note housing prices are high in the UK because wealth inequalities are high. In other countries with far less housing available per person, prices are often lower.

14. A. Hill, 'Woman, 81, left to starve after immigration raid on care company', *Guardian*, 9 May 2013. http://www.guardian.co.uk/society/2013/may/09/woman-left-to-starve-raid-care-company

15. C. Blackhurst, 'Lib Dems in fresh row over "racist leaflet"', *Independent*, 11 November 1993. http://www.independent.co.uk/news/uk/lib-dems-in-fresh-row-over-racist-leaflet-1503514.html

16. W. Johnson, 'Curbing mass immigration could bring down house prices, Theresa May says', *Telegraph*, 12 December 2012. http://www.telegraph.co.uk/news/uknews/immigration/9739590/Curbing-mass-immigration-could-bring-down-house-prices-Theresa-May-says.html

17. R. Syal, 'Boris Johnson criticizes Theresa May over immigration claim', *Observer*, 16 December 2012. http://www.guardian.co.uk/politics/2012/dec/16/boris-johnson-theresa-may-immigration

18. All these figures come from Table 209 of a government statistical data set as accessed on 17 January 2013 from: https://www.gov.uk/government/statistical-data-sets/live-tables-on-house-building

19. See Chapter 6 of this book for details of what the latest census reveals about both the numbers of rooms and bedrooms in residential housing in Britain in 2011 and how rooms per person have increased.

20. T. Lloyd, 'Let councils build – and borrow', *Shelter*, policy blog, 13 March 2013. http://blog.shelter.org.uk/2013/03/let-councils-build-and-borrow/

21. P. Collinson, 'Equity release is not the solution for older people who need extra cash', *Guardian*, 16 March 2013. http://www.guardian.co.uk/money/blog/2013/mar/16/equity-release-older-people-cash

22. E. Klinenberg, 'I want to be alone: the rise and rise of solo-living', *Guardian*, 30 March 2012. http://www.guardian.co.uk/lifeandstyle/2012/mar/30/the-rise-of-solo-living.

23. D. Dorling, *Population 10 billion*, London: Constable, 2013, p. 229.

24. Personal communications with Alex Fenton, referring in turn to the

estimates made of required stock repairs in the English Housing Survey. See also the 1984 work of A. Curtis, 'The great British housing disaster'. http://www.youtube.com/user/AdamCurtisFilms/videos

25. Oxfam, *The perfect storm: economic stagnation, the rising cost of living, public spending cuts and the impact on UK poverty*, Oxford: Oxfam, 2012.poverty,http://policy-practice.oxfam.org.uk/publications/the-perfect-storm-economic-stagnation-the-rising-cost-of-living-public-spending-228591

26. Rightmove, 'Summer selling challenge', July Index, 2012. http://www.rightmove.co.uk/news/house-price-index/july-2012

27. H. Osborne, and J. Treanor, 'Mortgage lending stalls over six-month period', *Guardian*, 25 March 2013. http://www.guardian.co.uk/money/2013/mar/25/mortgage-lending-stalls-six-months-bba

28. Although estate agents put the fall down to rising stamp duty; see R. Neate, 'Foreign buyers behind half of £2 million-plus home sales in London', *Guardian*, 6 May 2013. http://www.guardian.co.uk/business/2013/may/06/foreign-buyers-luxury-home-sales-london

29. H. Jones, 'Average two-bed prime London property to hit £1 million', 'Introducer Today' website. http://www.introducertoday.co.uk/news_features/average-two-bed-prime-london-property-to-hit-C2A31-million?tickertape=yes

30. Statutory Instrument No. 2,625, 'Housing, England: The Housing (Empty Dwelling Management Orders) (Prescribed Period of Time and Additional Prescribed Requirements) (England) (Amendment) Order 2012', made 17 October 2012; laid before parliament 23 October 2012; came into force 15 November 2012. http://www.legislation.gov.uk/uksi/2012/2625/pdfs/uksi_20122625_en.pdf

31. N. Duxbury, 'PM to be warned – cut green levies and you will increase bills for poor', 'Inside Housing' website, 25 October 2013. http://www.insidehousing.co.uk/eco/pm-to-be-warned-cut-green-levies-and-you-will-increase-bills-for-poor/6529212.article

32. Shelter, personal communication – with researchers of the charity attempting to estimate the number, London, June 2013. As yet no policy document has been published giving an actual estimate.

33. A. Fenton, 'Housing benefit reform and the spatial segregation of low-income households in London', report, University of Cambridge (Alex is now based at the London School of Economics); an online copy of the report is here: http://www.cchpr.landecon.cam.ac.uk/outputs/detail.asp?OutputID=240 See also A. Fenton, et al., 'Public housing, commodification, and rights to the city: the US and England compared',

Cities, Vol. 35 (2013), pp. 373–8. http://dx.doi.org/10.1016/j.cities.2012.10.004

34. For a brief history of similar attacks see T. Slater, 'Grieving for a lost home, revisited: the Bedroom Tax and displacement', University of Edinburgh, School of Geosciences blog entry, 23 September 2013. http://www.geos.ed.ac.uk/homes/tslater/bedroomtax.html

35. B. Thomas and D. Dorling, *Identity in Britain: a cradle-to-grave atlas*, Bristol: Policy Press, 2007. http://www.dannydorling.org/?page_id=1467

36. London Borough of Hammersmith and Fulham, cabinet briefing, 23 April 2012, p. 141. http://image.guardian.co.uk/sys-files/Guardian/documents/2012/05/02/hamm.pdf

37. R. Ford, 'Knee-jerk Islamaphobia: why Trevor Kavanagh is wrong about British Muslims', *New Statesman*, 21 January 2013. http://www.newstatesman.com/politics/2013/01/knee-jerk-islamophobia-why-trevor-kavanagh-wrong-about-british-muslims

38. HomeOwners Alliance, 'The death of a dream: the crisis in home-ownership in the UK', report, 2012, p. 10. http://hoa.org.uk/campaigns/publications-2/the-death-of-a-dream-the-crisis-of-homeownership-in-the-uk/

39. D. Leigh, H. Frayman and J. Ball, 'Revealed: the real identities behind Britain's secret property deals', *Guardian*, 26 November 2012. http://www.guardian.co.uk/uk/2012/nov/26/indentities-behind-secret-property-deals

40. R. Brooks, *The great tax robbery: how Britain became a tax haven for fat cats and big business*, London: Oneworld Publications, 2013, p. 161 of typescript.

41. J. Ball, 'Secret film shows how buyers of luxury London homes can avoid millions in tax', *Guardian*, 16 December 2012. http://www.guardian.co.uk/uk/2012/dec/16/london-property-tax-avoidance-offshore

42. O. Wainwright, 'Billionaires' basements: the luxury bunkers making holes in London streets', *Guardian*, 9 November 2012. http://www.guardian.co.uk/artanddesign/2012/nov/09/billionaires-basements-london-houses-architecture

43. And the old and the poor are pushed out and off. For a vivid account see B. Dumbleton, *Help us, somebody: the demolition of the elderly*, London: The London Press, 2006.

44. BBC, 'High street vacancies still stubbornly high, says report', *BBC Business News*, 10 September 2013. http://www.bbc.co.uk/news/business-24025297

45. G. Lynn and E. Davey, 'London letting agents "refuse black tenants"', *BBC News London*, 14 October 2013. http://www.bbc.co.uk/news/uk-england-london-24372509

46. J. Bingham, 'White groups facing unspoken racism in UK, says Doreen Lawrence', *Telegraph*, 19 February 2013. http://www.telegraph.co.uk/education/educationnews/9880562/White-groups-facing-unspoken-racism-in-UK-says-Doreen-Lawrence.html

47. S. Beasor, 'Housing benefit and welfare reform: impact of the proposed changes on black and minority ethnic communities', Better Housing Briefing Paper No. 18, Race Equality Foundation, April 2011. http://www.better-housing.org.uk/briefings/housing-benefit-and-welfare-reform-impact-proposed-changes-black-and-minority-ethnic-commu

48. S. Swinford, 'UN report criticizing Bedroom Tax is "absolute disgrace" says Grant Shapps', *Telegraph*, 11 September 2013. http://www.telegraph.co.uk/news/politics/10301297/UN-report-criticising-bedroom-tax-is-absolute-disgrace-says-Grant-Shapps.html

49. Rolling it out to all areas by the end of September 2013: Department of Work and Pensions, 'Benefit cap: final stage starts', press release issued under the policy heading of 'Simplifying the welfare system and making sure work pays', 12 August 2013. https://www.gov.uk/government/news/benefit-cap-final-stage-starts

50. BBC, 'Boris Johnson criticized for "Kosovo" benefits remark', *BBC News*, 28 October 2010. http://www.bbc.co.uk/news/uk-politics-11640219

51. A. Gentleman, 'Squeezed out: London landlords evict tenants hit by housing benefit cap', *Guardian*, 24 April 2010. http://www.guardian.co.uk/society/2012/apr/24/london-landlords-housing-benefit-cap

52. There is sadly a long precedent for doing nothing in the face of obvious unfairness. In housing history see P. Marcuse, 'Gentrification, abandonment and displacement: connections, causes and policy responses in New York City', *Journal of Urban and Contemporary Law*, Vol. 28 (1985), pp. 195–240.

53. R. Ramesh, 'Camden Council plans to move 761 poor families from London', *Guardian*, 13 February 2013. http://www.guardian.co.uk/uk/2013/feb/13/london-council-relocation-benefits-cap

54. P. Butler and B. Ferguson, 'Homeless families to be expelled from London by councils', *Guardian*, 4 November 2012, including a record 1,448 comments from members of the public on the website. http://www.guardian.co.uk/society/2012/nov/04/london-boroughs-housing-families-outside-capital

55. N. Cohen, 'Dumping the poor: Nick Cohen unravels the homes-for-votes scandal engulfing Dame Shirley Porter', *Independent*, 16 January 1994. http://www.independent.co.uk/news/uk/dumping-the-poor-nick-cohen-unravels-the-homesforvotes-scandal-engulfing-dame-shirley-porter-and-reveals-that-her-successors-on-westminster-council-are-still-1407226.html

56. M. Macdonald, 'Local elections: favourable verdict on homes-for-votes', *Independent*, 7 May 1994. http://www.independent.co.uk/news/uk/local-elections-favourable-verdict-on-homesforvotes-1434137.html

57. R. Kay, 'Untold tale of Dame Shirley Porter's scandal', *Daily Mail*, 1 September 2009. http://www.dailymail.co.uk/debate/article-1210385/RICHARD-KAY-Untold-tale-Dame-Shirley-Porters-scandal.html

58. J. Dromey, opposition housing spokesman, quoted in R. Ramesh, 'London councils face questions for housing families outside the capital', *Guardian*, 3 December 2012. http://www.guardian.co.uk/society/2012/dec/03/london-councils-housing-families-outside-capital

59. C. Hartman, *City for sale: the transformation of San Francisco*, Berkeley: University of California Press, 2002.

60. J. Silver-Greenberg, 'ACLU sues Morgan Stanley over mortgage loans', *New York Times*, 15 October 2012. http://www.nytimes.com/2012/10/15/business/aclu-to-sue-morgan-stanley-over-mortgage-loans.html

61. B. Thomas and D. Dorling, *Identity in Britain: a cradle-to-grave atlas*, Bristol: Policy Press, 2007 (see chapters on the elderly, maps of tenure of people aged over sixty-five in London).

62. Thomas and Dorling as above, but now look at the chapter on children and the maps on their ethnicity. Some can be viewed for free here: http://www.dannydorling.org/books/identity/

63. In England and Wales in 1911: 'Domestic service is still the main occupation for working women, employing 1,345,358'. http://www.hastingspress.co.uk/history/1914bluebook.htm

64. B. Roberts, 'Boris Johnson race-row fury: David Cameron was blasted after refusing to condemn Boris Johnson for calling black children "piccaninnies"', *Daily Mirror*, 10 December 2007. http://www.mirror.co.uk/news/uk-news/boris-johnson-race-row-fury-527310

65. D. Dorling, 'Migration: a long-run perspective', Institute for Public Policy Research, paper, 2009. http://www.ippr.org/publication/55/1688/migration-a-long-run-perspective

5 BUYING

1. F. Islam, 'Home ownership: how the property dream turned into a nightmare', *Observer*, 18 August 2013. http://www.theguardian.com/books/2013/aug/18/default-line-extract-faisal-islam-housing

2. Oxfam, *The perfect storm: economic stagnation, the rising cost of living, public spending cuts, and the impact on UK poverty*, Oxford: Oxfam,2012,p.41.http://policy-practice.oxfam.org.uk/publications/the-perfect-storm-economic-stagnation-the-rising-cost-of-living-public-spending-228591

3. D. Clapham, et al., 'Housing options and solutions for young people', Joseph Rowntree Foundation report, June 2012. http://www.jrf.org.uk/publications/housing-options-solutions-young-people

4. Ibid., p. 43.

5. J. Rankin, 'Prudential invests in "Generation Rent" in £100 million deal', *Guardian*, 3 April 2013. http://www.guardian.co.uk/business/2013/apr/03/prudential-invests-generation-rent-100m-deal

6. G. White, 'Prudential boss Tijane Thiam's pay soars to £7.8 million, despite FSA censure', *Telegraph*, 5 April 2013. http://www.telegraph.co.uk/finance/newsbysector/banksandfinance/insurance/9974069/Prudential-boss-Tijane-Thiams-pay-soars-to-7.8m-despite-FSA-censure.html

7. D. Clapham, et al., 'Housing options', p. 45.

8. M. Sergeant, 'Housing: the Grant Shapps v Jack Dromey row deconstructed', *BBC News*, 13 June 2012. http://www.bbc.co.uk/news/uk-politics-18415715

9. R. Ramesh, 'UK housing shortage turning under-thirties into "Generation Rent"', *Guardian*, 13 June 2012. http://www.guardian.co.uk/society/2012/jun/13/generation-rent-uk-housing-shortage

10. 'The impact of welfare reform on housing associations', *HouseMark News*, Issue 612 (2013). http://www.housemark.co.uk/Newsletter.nsf/1/33BD59ABE761608780257B01003AEDA3?OpenDocument

11. A. Hull and G. Cooke, 'Together at home: a new strategy for housing', Institute for Public Policy Research, report, 21 June 2012, p. 53. http://www.ippr.org/publication/55/9279/together-at-home-a-new-strategy-for-housing

12. D. Dorling, *The No-nonsense guide to equality*, Oxford: New Internationalist, 2012.

13. 'January 2012 night count' (633,782 people), National Alliance to End Homelessness (NAEH), 2013. http://www.endhomelessness.org/pages/faqs and http://www.naeh.org/

14. See the 'Chartered Institute of Housing' website. http://www.cihhousing.com/ as accessed January 2013. By September 2013 it was already advertising the 2014 conference (24–6 June if interested)!

15. For quotes on the 2013 conference see: http://www.cihhousing.com/page.cfm/Link=63, and for photographs of the Capita and Kier stands, and fetching images of John Prescott and Michael Heseltine, see the photogallery: http://www.cihhousing.com/page.cfm/Action=photoGallery/

16. S. Hodkinson, 'How the Conservatives ruined social housing', *Independent*, 1 October 2012. http://www.independent.co.uk/voices/comment/how-the-conservatives-ruined-social-housing-8192726.html

17. P. Toynbee, 'How to turn a housing crisis into a homeless catastrophe', *Guardian*, 18 February 2013. http://www.guardian.co.uk/commentisfree/2013/feb/18/housing-crisis-bedroom-tax-failure-to-build

18. L. Simpson, 'More segregation or more mixing?', Economic and Social Research Council Centre on Dynamics of Ethnicity, report, December 2012. http://www.ethnicity.ac.uk/census/869_CCSR_Bulletin_More_segregation_or_more_mixing_v7NW.pdf

19. N. Ledwith, 'Spare bedroom tax on unoccupied council house rooms could force pensioners to move into smaller homes', *Daily Mail*, 18 February 2013. http://www.dailymail.co.uk/news/article-2280358/Spare-bedroom-tax-force-pensioners-smaller-homes.html#

20. P. Butler, 'Foster carers with more than one child will still face Bedroom Tax', *Guardian*, 14 March 2013. http://www.guardian.co.uk/society/2013/mar/14/foster-carers-bedroom-benefits-cut

21. A spare room is often needed, for instance, due to uncontrolled shouting at night, not just to store equipment such as a wheelchair; or because extra space by the side of a bed is required for other equipment.

22. National Housing Federation, 'Bedroom Tax' webpage. http://www.housing.org.uk/ policy/welfare_reform/%E2%80%98under-occupation%E2%80%99_penalty.aspx

23. I had better keep his identity anonymous in case the Metropolitan Housing Association gets upset.

24. C. Brown, 'Lords fear Bedroom Tax will hurt disabled tenants', 'Inside Housing' website, 17 October 2012. http://www.insidehousing.co.uk/tenancies/lords-fear-bedroom-tax-will-hurt-disabled-tenants/6524235.article

25. D. Long, 'Pretty vacant? How policies on underoccupation will hit northern tenants', *Guardian*, housing network blog, 3 October 2011. http://www.guardian.co.uk/housing-network/2011/oct/03/pretty-vacant-under-occupation-northern-tenants

26. The pseudonym being Clare Belz of North Staffordshire. http://www.
theguardian.com/housing-network/2011/oct/03/pretty-vacant-under-
occupation-nothern-tenants#start-of-comments

27. J. Harris, 'The spare bedroom tax: a mess of contradiction and impos-
sibility', *Guardian*, 25 January 2013.· http://www.guardian.co.uk/
society/2013/jan/25/spare-bedroom-tax-contradiction-impossibility

28. E. Lester, 'Social housing spare rooms a luxury – welfare minister', *BBC
News*, 6 June 2012. http://www.bbc.co.uk/news/uk-politics-13671653

29. K. Mudie, 'Loads of room to talk! Bedroom Tax Tory Lord Freud lives
in eight-bedroom country mansion', *Mirror*, 19 January 2013. http://
www.mirror.co.uk/news/uk-news/bedroom-tax-tory-lord-freud-1545677

30. E. Budd, 'Having a baby to get a council house? Not in 2012',
'Mumsnet' website, 2012. http://www.mumsnet.com/Talk/am_i_being_
unreasonable/a1568974-Having-a-baby-to-get-a-council-house

31. Observation by Lyne Lees Hollen, made in 1990, quoted in K. C. Martin, *Hard and unreal advice: mothers, social science and the Victorian
poverty experts*, New York: Palgrave, 2008, p. 55.

32. Shelter, '"Generation Rent" families double in ten years', press release, 1
July 2013. http://england.shelter.org.uk/news/july_2013/generation_rent_
families_double_in_10_years

33. P. Hetherington, 'England's housing crisis is being ignored by politicians', *Guardian*, 8 January 2013. http://www.guardian.co.uk/society/
2013/jan/08/england-housing-crisis-ignored-politicians

34. Barclays, 'Buying beats renting by almost £200,000 over a lifetime',
press release, 18 June 2012. http://www.personal.barclays.co.uk/BRC1/
jsp/brccontrol?site=pfs&task=homefreeopenplanwealth&value=18997

35. B. Appelbaum, 'Family net worth drops to level of early 1990s', *New
York Times*, 11 June 2012. http://www.nytimes.com/2012/06/12/business/
economy/family-net-worth-drops-to-level-of-early-90s-fed-says.html?_r=2

36. D. Blanchflower and A. J. Oswald, 'Does high homeownership impair
the labour market?', Economics Department working paper, University
of Warwick, May 2013. http://www.andrewoswald.com/docs/finalmay-
HomeOwnershipUnemBlanchflowerOswald2013.pdf

37. S. Nolan, '"A nation of estate agents": property sector jobs soar as
Vince Cable warns of dangers of a new housing bubble', *Daily Mail*,
12 September 2013. http://www.dailymail.co.uk/news/article-2418402/
Property-sector-employment-soars-Vince-Cable-warns-George-Osborne-
dangers-new-housing-bubble.html

38. P. Aldrick, 'Estate agent hiring boom helps drive jobs growth', *Telegraph*, 11 September 2013. http://www.telegraph.co.uk/finance/jobs/
10301646/Estate-agent-hiring-boom-helps-drive-jobs-growth.html

39. F. S. Fitzgerald, *Tales of the Jazz Age*, New York: Charles Scribner's Sons, 1922. http://fitzgerald.narod.ru/crackup/056e-eho.htm

40. Office for National Statistics, 'Middle income households, 1977–2011/12', London: Office for National Statistics, 2 December 2013. http://www.ons.gov.uk/ons/dcp171776_341133.pdf

41. D. Alexander and M. Prisk, 'Next steps for £10 billion housing guarantees', 'GOV.UK' website, 1 February 2013. https://www.gov.uk/government/news/next-steps-for-10-billion-housing-guarantees

42. D. Orr, 'Home truths 2012: England', National Housing Federation, report, 22 October 2012. http://www.housing.org.uk/media/home_truths/home_truths_2012_england.aspx

43. Staff reporter, 'British tenants "face highest rents in Western Europe"', *Telegraph*, 28 June 2013. http://www.telegraph.co.uk/finance/personal-finance/7858800/British-tenants-face-highest-rents-in-western-Europe.html

44. N. King, 'UK homeownership falls to lowest level since 1988', *Guardian*, 16 November 2012. http://www.guardian.co.uk/money/2012/nov/16/home-ownership-lowest-since-1988

45. LSL Property Services, 'Rents reach record high in September', report, 18 October 2013. http://www.lslps.co.uk/documents/buy_to_let_index_sep13.pdf

46. T. Cavero and P. Krisnah, *A cautionary tale: the true cost of austerity and inequality in Europe*, Oxford: Oxfam, 2013. http://policy-practice.oxfam.org.uk/publications/a-cautionary-tale-the-true-cost-of-austerity-and-inequality-in-europe-301384

47. Louis Boyson, 1931, quoted in W. N. Goetzmann and F. Newman, 'Securitization in the 1920s', National Bureau of Economic Research Working Paper No. 15650, January 2010. http://www.nber.org/papers/w15650

48. D. Harvey, *Rebel cities*, London: Verso, 2012.

49. As I write, figures from Scotland have yet to be released. For England and Wales see T. Smith, 'What did the census feeding frenzy tell us about housing?', *Guardian*, 2 January 2013. http://www.guardian.co.uk/housing-network/2013/jan/02/social-housing-census-data-2011

50. R. Lynch, 'Unemployment falls with rise in part-time workers', *Independent*, 14 July 2013. http://www.independent.co.uk/news/uk/home-news/unemployment-falls-with-rise-in-parttime-workers-2026252.html

51. K. Gulliver, '"All in it together?" Measuring the impact of austerity, housing strategy and welfare changes on vulnerable groups in social

housing', Human City Institute Bulletin No. 10, March 2012. http://www.humancity.org.uk/publications.htm

52. Ibid.

53. M. Seamark, 'Raquel Rolnik: a dabbler in witchcraft who offered an animal sacrifice to Marx', *Daily Mail*, 12 September 2013. http://www.dailymail.co.uk/news/article-2418204/Raquel-Rolnik-A-dabbler-witchcraft-offered-animal-sacrifice-Marx.html

54. Oxfam, *The perfect storm*.

55. Office for National Statistics, 'The effects of taxes and benefits on household income, 2011/12', statistical bulletin, 2013. http://www.ons.gov.uk/ons/dcp171778_317365.pdf

56. B. Mason, 'Britain: children's charity finds risk of "social apartheid"', 'World Socialist' website, 9 September 2013. http://www.wsws.org/en/articles/2013/09/09/pove-s09.html

57. B. Marshall, 'The housing economy: boom, bust and consumer sentiment', Ipsos MORI Social Research Institute, May 2012, p. 12. http://www.ipsos-mori.com/_emails/sri/understandingsociety/may2012/mobile/no4.html. A year after making the statement above Ben Marshall revealed more poll findings, suggesting that 'the further you travel away from Britain, the better Britain looks': 'How does the world view Britain?', *Union Jack*, 19 January 2013, p. 1. http://www.unionjacknews.com/articles/how-does-the-world-view-britain/. Part of the reason Britain looks better from a distance is because – from a distance – you're not paying to live here.

58. All details were at this 'First Steps' website as of 8 January 2013. http://www.firststepslondon.org/property-details.asp?PropId=7501

59. D. Binns, 'People on housing waiting list in Waltham Forest can now apply to live at Olympic Park', *Epping Guardian*, 31 January 2013. http://www.guardian-series.co.uk/news/10198108.People_on_housing_waiting_list_can_now_apply_to_live_at_Olympic_Park/

60. Although in his autumn statement of 2013 the Chancellor announced measures to make such circumventing a little harder than it had been, but still not impossible. He reduced the period in which you were allowed to claim a home was your main residence, even if you were renting it out, to eighteen months after you stated that you had last lived in it. Landlords who evict every year and claim to move in for a month before renting out again would still be able to avoid capital gains tax and, no doubt, there are less troublesome ways than that, but none that are good for the tenants.

61. Eurostat, 'Housing statistics: data from October 2012', 'European Commission' website, 2012. http://epp.eurostat.ec.europa.eu/statistics_explained/index.php/Housing_statistics

62. R. Ramesh, 'Camden Council plans to move 761 poor families from London', *Guardian*, 13 February 2013. http://www.guardian.co.uk/uk/2013/feb/13/london-council-relocation-benefits-cap

63. Now for as long as two years with no threat of any action being taken by local government – see the reference to the relevant legislation, Statutory Instrument 2625 of 2012, which is given in Chapter 4 of this volume, p. 111 above.

64. Associated Press, 'Mortgage rates fall to a record low', *New York Times*, 4 October 2012. http://www.nytimes.com/2012/10/05/business/mortgage-rates-fall-to-a-record-low.html

65. D. Orr, 'Home truths 2012'.

66. Reuters, 'Home prices up 5.5% from a year ago', *New York Times*, 29 January 2013. http://www.nytimes.com/2013/01/30/business/home-prices-up-5-5-from-a-year-ago.html

67. P. Collinson, 'House prices creep up over 2012', *Guardian*, 29 January 2013. http://www.guardian.co.uk/money/2013/jan/29/house-prices-creep-up-2012-land-registry

68. D. Blanchflower, 'House prices are booming again but the bust that's bound to follow will cost us dear: a rise in rates would inevitably cause an immediate and deep house price crash', *Independent*, 1 September 2013. http://www.independent.co.uk/voices/comment/house-prices-are-booming-again-but-the-bust-thats-bound-to-follow-will-cost-us-dear-8793316.html

69. See quote from David (Danny) Blanchflower in the section below titled 'Lending Slowdown', p. 231. And also A. Monaghan, 'Debt crisis: UK housing slump will deepen, warns IMF', *Telegraph*, 19 July 2012. http://www.telegraph.co.uk/finance/financialcrisis/9413200/Debt-crisis-UK-housing-slump-will-deepen-warns-IMF.html

70. E. J. Levin and G. Pyce, 'The dynamics of spatial inequality in UK housing wealth', Department of Urban Studies discussion paper, University of Glasgow, p. 19. http://www.academia.edu/775502/The_dynamics_of_spatial_inequality_in_UK_housing_wealth_Housing_Policy_Debate_Vol._21_No._1_January_2011_99-132

71. See the leading quote at the start of the section immediately below, 'London', p. 176.

72. Lloyds TSB Private Banking, '£34,000 extra to live near England's top state schools', press release, 10 September 2012, reported in a wide variety of media. http://www.propertyreporter.co.uk/view.asp?ID=10154

73. N. O'Brien, 'Another country: London's separateness from the rest of Britain becomes more pronounced every year', *Spectator*, 14 April 2012. http://www.spectator.co.uk/features/7779258/another-country/

74. A. Ashworth, 'Is a tectonic shift moving Newcastle to the Midlands?', *Sunday Times*, 15 February 2013. http://www.thetimes.co.uk/tto/life/property/article3688460.ece

75. J. Mathew, 'UK house prices fall in September amid heatwave', *International Business Times*, 16 September 2013. http://www.ibtimes.co.uk/articles/506331/20130916/rightmove-uk-house-price-forecast-london.htm

76. Although what there is can be acute, including homelessness in blue-coloured tent cities, but ordered homeless in a country with about half the flat land of England and more than twice the population.

77. J. Waterson, 'Tokyo tops cost of living table – but London rises to sixteenth place', 'City A. M.' website, 5 February 2013. http://www.cityam.com/latest-news/tokyo-tops-cost-living-table-london-rises-16th-place

78. J. Grainger, 'Superhomes – in a league of their own', *Ripon Gazette*, 12 February 2013. http://www.ripongazette.co.uk/lifestyle/home-garden/property-news/superhomes-in-a-league-of-their-own-1-5350104

79. B. Wassener, 'Builders travel to Asia to court buyers for new London homes', *New York Times*, 14 February 2013. http://www.nytimes.com/2013/02/15/greathomesanddestinations/15iht-property15.html

80. D. Dorling, 'Britain's autumn statement: the butterfly effect?', *Economist* blog, 7 December 2013. http://www.dannydorling.org/?page_id=3893

81. Meanwhile, those parts of southern Europe tend to have very low birth rates and might benefit, in the long term, if that housing currently used by pensioners from the north of Europe instead housed young families from further south and east, from just outside of Europe. A similar case can be made for so much of the housing built in Ireland and currently lying unused as young adults leave that island and the population ages.

82. Richard Donnell, quoted in P. Collinson, 'House prices: guide to property hotspots', *Guardian*, 30 March 2012. http://www.guardian.co.uk/money/2012/mar/30/house-prices-guide-property-hotspots#

83. D. Hipwell, 'Outrage greets RICS' call for action to limit house price inflation', *The Times*, 14 September 2013. http://www.thetimes.co.uk/tto/business/economics/article3868899.ece

84. A. Gentleman, 'The woman who lives in a shed: how London landlords are cashing in', *Guardian*, 9 May 2012. http://www.guardian.co.uk/society/2012/may/09/london-landlords-desperate-tenants

85. GeoInformation Group, 'New Shed Base Mapping', press release sent to the author, 12 March 2013. http://www.geoinformationgroup.co.uk/uncategorized/new-shed-base-mapping#more-4544

86. No 'outhouse' can be used to house people without the permission of the respective council. See Ealing Council's advice, accessed December 2013. http://www.ealing.gov.uk/info/100007/housing/1385/illegal_outhouses

87. Staff reporter, 'Beds in sheds programme uncovers more than 200 suspected properties', *Slough Observer*, 26 June 2013. http://www.sloughobserver.co.uk/news/roundup/articles/2013/06/26/90679-beds-in-sheds-programme-uncovers-more-than-200-suspected

88. P. Collins, 'Leave London and you'll find fantasy island', *Sunday Times*, 15 February 2013. http://www.thetimes.co.uk/tto/opinion/columnists/philipcollins/article3688788.ece

89. As I have stated publicly before: D. Dorling, 'Letter: Boris is right to fight housing cuts', *London Evening Standard*, 1 November 2010, p. 47. http://www.dannydorling.org/?page_id=1927

90. C. Spillane, 'Bonus cuts leave less cash for London luxury-home purchases', *Bloomberg News*, 28 February 2013. http://www.bloomberg.com/news/2013-02-28/london-luxury-home-cash-purchases-plunge-on-lower-bonus-payments.html

91. According to Lucian Cook, Director of Residential Research at Savills, quoted in B. Barrow, 'A tale of two nations: rise in value of a London flat enough to buy a house in the north', *Daily Mail*, 1 March 2013. http://www.dailymail.co.uk/news/article-2286269/Rise-value-London-flat-buy-house-North.html

92. C. Whitehead, et al., *Housing in transition: understanding the dynamics of tenure change*, London, Resolution Foundation, 8 June 2012.

93. A. Harrison, 'Help elderly downsize housing, says Demos', *BBC News* (Education and Family), 12 September 2013. http://www.bbc.co.uk/news/education-24050607

6 SLUMP

1. T. Slater, 'Grieving for a lost home, revisited: the "Bedroom Tax" and displacement', University of Edinburgh, School of Geosciences blog entry, 23 September 2013. http://www.geos.ed.ac.uk/homes/tslater/bedroomtax.html

2. A. Morton, 'How to tackle Britain's NIMBYs and end crisis in new house-building', 'City A.M.' website, 9 September 2013. http://www.cityam.com/article/1378688019/how-tackle-britain-s-nimbys-and-end-crisis-new-house-building

3. We can now find out in an instant how much our property is worth on 'Zoopla' or 'Rightmove', the twin oligopolies of the online UK property world. It is surprising so many surveyors stay in business, given these 'tools'. Maybe in the same way that the advent of school league tables caused parents to move towards the areas with supposedly better schools,

these online tools now steer buyers towards areas where they think they should fit in, areas of the city within their precise price bracket.

4. J. Joyce, '"Shoebox homes" become the UK norm', *BBC News*, 14 September 2011. http://www.bbc.co.uk/news/uk-14916580

5. R. Tunstall, 'What should we worry about when we worry about housing problems?', inaugural lecture, University of York, 2012. http://www.slideshare.net/djgb500/inaug-slides-final

6. Which it is to keen gardeners, but they are a minority in many areas. You can tell from the gardens. Many people imagine that they will be more interested in gardening than they turn out to be upon buying a home with a garden. Many others without a garden long for one and would use it well.

7. In case you are wondering about the million-plus people who do not live in households in England and Wales. Beds and bedrooms in communal establishments, halls of residence, prisons, hospitals, care homes and hotels are not counted here. All these ratios are for the 'household population'.

8. These figures are only for people living in flats and houses and are found in the 2011 census tables KS101EW and KS403EW: rooms 7,425,253; bedrooms, 3,647,493; household residents 3,011,182.

9. Ibid.: rooms 126,176,638; bedrooms 63,088,319; household residents 52,059,931.

10. As Professor Rebecca Tunstall explained in her inaugural lecture as the new Director for the Centre for Housing in York; see note 5 above.

11. We have to say 'appeared' because the census records only those present in a home at the time it is taken, not those who might have decided to extend that home, sell it and move on.

12. D. Dorling, ' Underclass, overclass, ruling class, supernova class' in A. Walker, A. Sinfield and C. Walker (eds.), *Fighting poverty, inequality and injustice*, Bristol: Poverty Press, 2011, Chapter 8. http://www.danny dorling.org/?page_id=2446.

13. Redrawn from D. Dorling, 'Fairness and the changing fortunes of people in Britain', *Journal of the Royal Statistical Society (A)*, Vol. 176, No. 1 (2013), pp. 97-128. http://www.dannydorling.org/?page_id=3597

14. R. Tunstall, 'Relative housing inequality: The decline and return of housing space inequality in England and Wales, 1911-2011', personal communication (Figure 6).

15. Intriguingly, as of September 2013, the 'Wikipedia' entry on this reads exactly as if it were edited by civil servants, not by independent members of the public; but it does give the correct dates of introduction even if it is a little disingenuous about 'underoccupying their home' (you can of

course edit this source). http://en.wikipedia.org/wiki/Local_Housing_
Allowance#Bedroom_Requirement

16. B. Thomas, personal correspondence with Bethan Thomas, who kindly
suggested these reasons at a time when she thought she was not thinking clearly, but at least far more clearly than me!

17. C, Spillane and N. Callanan, 'Sultan's tax discount on London house
shows law favours rich', *Bloomberg News*, 25 October 2012; also
reported in the *Independent*. http://www.independent.co.uk/news/uk/
home-news/sultans-tax-discount-on-london-house-shows-law-favours-
rich-8229543.html

18. They tend not to overlap greatly with those who see taxation as the
price you pay for civilization. The nearest organization in Britain to the
Tea Party is the Tax Payers' Alliance, a group that appears to be funded
by a tiny number of people who avidly dislike paying taxes.

19. R. Ramesh, 'Local authorities expect half of poor residents to refuse to
pay council tax', *Guardian*, 15 October 2012. http://www.guardian.
co.uk/money/2012/oct/15/local-authorities-residents-council-tax [note
the estimate of two million comes from dividing £500 million by £5 and
52 weeks in a year].

20. C. Brown, 'London council to make up council tax benefit loss', 'Inside
Housing' website, 1 November 2012. http://www.insidehousing.co.uk/
care/london-council-to-make-up-council-tax-benefit-loss/6524474.article

21. N. Triggle, 'What the cap on care costs doesn't do', *BBC Health News*,
11 February 2013. http://www.bbc.co.uk/news/health-21411148

22. G. Morgenson, 'The British, at least, are getting tough', *New York
Times*, 7 July 2012. http://www.nytimes.com/2012/07/08/business/
barclays-case-opens-a-window-on-wall-st-fair-game.html

23. J. Waldron, 'Homelessness and the issue of freedom', *UCLA Law
Review*, Vol. 39 (1991), p. 322. http://faculty.washington.edu/pembina/
all_articles/Waldron%201991.pdf

24. G. Esler, 'Can locals be persuaded to back new housing in their area?',
Newsnight, 9 January 2013. http://www.bbc.co.uk/programmes/b01psky9

25. It used to be a minimum 10% discount but now some local councils
have no discount to try to reduce the amount of property that is empty,
such as in Gwynedd, in Wales. Others, such as County Durham, plan to
increase the council tax on second and holiday homes substantially to
avoid cuts elsewhere. In Camden they will soon be 'charging council tax
at 150% for properties empty for two years or more. In total there are
more than 7,000 empty and second homes in the borough.' Source: M.
Katz, 'Rebuild the tax base to fund services', letter, *Guardian*, 13 March

2013.http://www.guardian.co.uk/money/2013/mar/12/rebuild-tax-base-fund-services

26. G. Eaton, 'Labour will soon pledge to scrap the Bedroom Tax, says Scottish welfare spokesman', *New Statesman*, 14 September 2013. http://www.newstatesman.com/politics/2013/09/labour-will-soon-pledge-scrap-bedroom-tax-says-scottish-welfare-spokesman

27. False Economy, 'Our research in the *Independent*: Bedroom Tax – 50,000 people face eviction', 'False Economy' website blog, 18 September 2013.http://falseeconomy.org.uk/blog/our-research-in-the-independent-bedroom-tax-50000-people-face-eviction

28. M. Pennycook, 'The coalition's welfare cuts mean a dramatic rise in council tax for the poorest', 31 January 2013. http://www.resolution-foundation.org/blog/2013/Jan/31/coalitions-welfare-cuts-mean-dramatic-rise-council/ also published in the *New Statesman*.

29. Z. Conway, 'One in three "behind on rent" since housing benefit changes', *BBC Business News*, 19 September 2013. http://www.bbc.co.uk/news/business-24149763

30. Reuters, 'Luxury home-builder reports a revenue gain of 41%', *New York Times*, 22 August 2012. http://www.nytimes.com/2012/08/23/business/toll-brothers-reports-revenue-gain-of-41.html

31. Also a board member at *Forbes* since June 2010: http://www.forbes.com/profile/douglas-yearley/

32. BBC, 'What is quantitative easing?', *BBC Business News*, 7 March 2013. http://www.bbc.co.uk/news/business-15198789

33. Staff reporter, 'Home prices in region stay flat', *Los Angeles Times*, 17 December 2013, p. B1.

34. S. Fleming, 'Record property prices boost US confidence', *The Times*, 31July2013.http://www.thetimes.co.uk/tto/business/industries/construction-property/article3829959.ece

35. G. Topham, 'Helicopter crash: strict rules govern London airspace', *Guardian*, 16 January 2013. http://www.guardian.co.uk/uk/2013/jan/16/helicopter-crash-strict-rules

36. S. Hamilton, 'Rightmove raises UK house price forecast after summer lull', *Bloomberg News*, 16 September 2013. http://www.bloomberg.com/news/2013-09-15/rightmove-raises-u-k-house-price-forecast-after-summer-lull.html

37. W. D. Cohen, 'Why Wall Street loves houses again', *Atlantic*, 19 September 2013.http://www.theatlantic.com/magazine/archive/2013/10/why-wall-street-loves-houses-again/309454/

38. Ibid.

39. A. Hilton, 'The super-rich are pushing workers out of the capital', *Evening Standard*, 4 February 2013. http://www.standard.co.uk/comment/comment/anthony-hilton-the-superrich-are-pushing-workers-out-of-the-capital-8480115.html

40. J. Kollewe and R. Neate, 'London property offers stable investment for wealthy Europeans', *Guardian*, 1 June 2012. http://www.guardian.co.uk/uk/2012/jun/01/london-property-stable-investment-europeans

41. M. West, 'Capital losses: the interactive map that shows the London boroughs where house prices are actually FALLING', *Daily Mail*, 18 September 2013. http://www.thisismoney.co.uk/money/mortgages home/article-2423620/The-London-boroughs-house-prices-falling-just-like-rest-country.html

42. M. Brignall and H. Osbourne, 'London property boom leaves super-rich scratching around for a new pad', *Guardian*, 20 September 2013. http://www.theguardian.com/business/2013/sep/20/london-property-boom-super-prime-market

43. Staff reporter, 'Britain's most expensive beach hut sells for £170,000', *Telegraph*, 18 June 2012. http://www.telegraph.co.uk/news/newstopics/howaboutthat/9340653/Britains-most-expensive-beach-hut-sells-for-170000.html

44. Going up in increments of £100,000 at a time, but had his speech writer been quicker he could have called it the 'J2O policy' and added some quip about this particular brand of juice being good for you.

45. D. Dorling, 'Council tax A to Z', letter, *London Evening Standard*, 24 September 2012. http://www.yppuk.org/2012/09/readers-letter-of-day.html

46. R. Wilkinson and K. Pickett, *The spirit level: why equality is better for everyone*, London: Penguin, 2010.

47. N. Nowatzki, 'Wealth inequality and health: a political economy perspective', *International Journal of Health Services*, Vol. 42, No. 3 (2012), pp. 403–24.

48. T. Shipman and J. Salmon, 'Mortgages from the Bank of Nan and Granddad: Nick Clegg reveals plan for pension pots to help younger generation get on the first rung of the housing ladder', *Daily Mail*, 23 September 2012, story updated 24 September. http://www.dailymail.co.uk/news/article-2207367/Lib-Dem-conference-Nick-Clegg-reveals-plan-pension-pots-help-younger-generation-rung-housing-ladder.htm

49. S. Hughes, 'Hands off our homes: from London to the Lake District, the wealthy are buying properties they rarely use. Councils need powers to prevent this', *Guardian*, 24 September 2012. http://www.guardian.co.uk/commentisfree/2012/sep/24/homes-for-living-in

50. A. Hull and G. Cooke, 'Together at home: a new strategy for housing', Institute for Public Policy Research, report, 21 June 2012, p. 2. http://www.ippr.org/publication/55/9279/together-at-home-a-new-strategy-for-housing

51. Estate Office, 'New tax break for overseas property investors', 'London Property Consultants' website, 21 January 2013. http://www.estate-office.com/news/new-tax-break-for-overseas-uk-property-investors-254.htm

52. S. Jenkins, 'The detail of Ed Miliband's mansion tax is daft', *Guardian*, 15 February 2013. http://www.guardian.co.uk/commentisfree/2013/feb/15/ed-miliband-mansion-tax

53. Simon Wood, Rupert Fast and Nicole Sochor, letters, *Telegraph*, 20 February 2013. http://www.telegraph.co.uk/comment/letters/9881083/Ed-Milibands-mansion-tax-policy-threatens-Britains-historic-homes.html

54. P. Krugman, *The return of depression economics and the crisis of 2008*, London: Penguin, 2008, p. 171.

55. Bethan Thomas and I were originally quoted higher figures than these, but over time the prices drop. http://data.gov.uk/forum/general-discussion/property-price-paid-data-for-£50k

56. E. Hammond, J. K. Allen and C. Jones, 'London fuels record growth in UK house prices', *Financial Times*, 17 September 2013. http://www.ft.com/cms/s/0/0d15ebae-1f8f-11e3-8861-00144feab7de.html

57. *New York Times* News Service, 'London's financial center a hub to scandal of late', 'The Ledger' website, 13 July 2012. http://www.theledger.com/article/20120713/NEWS/120719712?p=1&tc=pg

58. 'A heatwave caused house prices to tumble in September as buyers and sellers were distracted from the housing market by the weather, according to property website "Rightmove".' I. Silvera, 'Rents soar to eleven-year high despite house-price dip', *International Business Times*, 23 September 2013. http://www.ibtimes.co.uk/articles/508315/20130923/house-prices-rents-buy-mortgage-london-barnard.htm

59. ITN, 'More people struggling to pay rent as arrears grow', *ITV News*, 18 January 2013. http://www.itv.com/news/update/2013-01-18/more-people-struggling-to-pay-rent-as-arrears-grow/

60. ITN, 'Bedroom Tax blamed for forcing families into arrears', *ITV News*, 19 September 2013. http://www.itv.com/news/central/update/2013-09-19/bedroom-tax-forcing-families-into-rent-arrears/

61. According to LSL Property Services, better known through its subsidiaries: several chartered surveyor businesses; and the estate agents Your Move and Reeds Rains. The report was published in numerous places, including on 17 February at http://www.mortgagestrategy.co.uk/housing-market/

rents-rise-in-january-for-first-time/1046371.article. Perhaps by complete coincidence the same company reported a 6.3% rise in London housing prices just over six months later. http://www.ftadviser.com/2013/09/04/ mortgages/mortgage-data/ftb-market-is-bubbling-nicely-lsl-property-ul TofnIX54WPSeQ41HEwYM/article.html

62. D. Newman, 'Tenants feel the festive pinch despite rental reprieve', LSL Property Services, report, 18 January 2013. http://www.lslps.co.uk/ documents/buy_to_let_index_dec12.pdf

63. D. Harvey, *Rebel cities*, London: Verso, 2012, p. 32.

64. Staff reporter, 'Business this week', *Economist*, 9 February 2013. http:// www.economist.com/news/world-week/21571489-business-week

65. D. Leigh, H. Frayman and J. Ball, 'Revealed: the real identities behind Britain's secret property deals', *Guardian*, 26 November 2012. http://www. guardian.co.uk/uk/2012/nov/26/indentities-behind-secret-property-deals

66. He has made this prediction many times; in 2013 it was first reported in S. O'Connor and C. Giles, 'House prices seen as still too high', *Financial Times*, 1 January 2013. http://www.ft.com/cms/s/0/416dca4c-5407-11e2-bb50-00144feab49a.html#axzz2LrMKpJ2I

67. D. Bowie, 'Tackling squalour: the pivotal role of social housing', Class: Centre for Labour and Social Studies, policy paper, 2013. http://classon line.org.uk/pubs/item/tackling-squalor

68. D. Dorling, *Population 10 billion*, London: Constable, 2013.

69. Bank of England, 'Trends in lending: seasonally adjusted net of cancellations', January 2013. http://www.bankofengland.co.uk/publications/ Documents/other/monetary/trendsjanuary13.pdf

70. M. Chadbourn, 'US mortgage-lending up 38%, racial disparities persist', Reuters, 18 September 2013. http://www.reuters.com/article/2013/09/ 18/us-usa-housing-idUSBRE9880X120130918

71. The source of the figures used here is the Federal Reserve spreadsheet 'D.2: credit market borrowing', found at: www.federalreserve.gov/ releases/Z1/Current/, latest figures January 2013.

72. On how the latest figures released by the Federal Reserve compare with what it knew in 2009 or how much borrowing was taken out in 2006, compare their latest estimates of 2006 with those used in Figure 23, p. 293, of D. Dorling, *Injustice: why social inequality persists*, Bristol: Policy Press, 2010.

73. Staff reporter, 'New Hampshire has the third-highest property tax in the country', *New Hampshire Telegraph*, 23 July 2012. http://www.politifact. com/new-hampshire/statements/2012/jul/23/jackie-cilley/no-income-or-sales-tax-new-hampshire-does-rely-hea/

7 SPECULATION

1. S. Hamilton, 'Rightmove raises UK house price forecast after summer lull', *Bloomberg News*, 16 September 2013. http://www.bloomberg.com/news/2013-09-15/rightmove-raises-u-k-house-price-forecast-after-summer-lull.html

2. Twenty years later I published some of those maps in D. Dorling, *The visualization of social spatial structure*, Chichester: Wiley, 2012. If you are interested in what the anatomy of a crash looks like, see: http://www.dannydorling.org/books/visualisation/Homepage.html; and see Figures 5.12 and 5.13 here: http://www.dannydorling.org/books/visualisation/Graphics/Pages/Figures.html

3. R. Neate, 'Rightmove triples its estimate for housing price rises', *Guardian*, 16 September 2013. http://www.theguardian.com/politics/2013/sep/16/rightmove-triples-estimate-house-price-increase

4. K. Allen, 'House prices could rise by 8% next year, says Rightmove', *Guardian*, 16 December 2013.

5. A. Raval, 'Pace of US house price rises slows as mortgage rates climb', *Financial Times*, 24 September 2013. http://www.ft.com/cms/s/0/9ade322a-251b-11e3-9b22-00144feab7de.html#axzz2ftukXFmB

6. BBC, 'US house prices in biggest annual rise for seven years', *BBC Business News*, 24 September 2013. http://www.bbc.co.uk/news/business-24225746

7. A. Khouri, 'Home prices in region stay flat', *Los Angeles Times*, p. B1, 17 December 2013.

8. D. Graeber, *Debt: the first 5,000 years*, New York: Melville House Publishing, 2013 edition.

9. Shelter, '1.4 million Britons falling behind with the rent or mortgage', press release, 4 January 2013. http://england.shelter.org.uk/news/january_2013/1.4_million_britons_falling_behind_with_the_rent_or_mortgage

10. L. Jansen, 'Britain will be Third World economy by 2014', *CNBC News*, reporting on Larry Elliott and Dan Atkinson's *Going south: why Britain will have a Third World economy by 2014*, London: Palgrave Macmillan, 2012. http://www.cnbc.com/id/49568596/Britain_Will_Be_Third_World_Economy_by_2014_Authors

11. R. Burrows and J. Ford, 'Self-employment and homeownership after the enterprise culture', *Work, Employment and Society*, Vol. 12, No. 1 (1998), pp. 97–119; and J. Ford, 'Casual work and owner occupation', *Work, Employment and Society*, Vol. 3, No. 1 (1989), pp. 29–48.

12. Ken Livingston, former Mayor of London, quoted by O. Wright, 'Anger on the left: anxious Labour mainstream moves to distance itself from hardliners' celebrations after Margaret Thatcher's death', *Independent*, 9 April 2013. http://www.independent.co.uk/news/uk/politics/anger-on-the-left-anxious-labour-mainstream-moves-to-distance-itself-from-hardliners-celebrations-after-margaret-thatchers-death-8565095.html

13. This was when I was under the supervision of Tony Champion and his colleagues. Tony kindly agreed to comment on an earlier draft of this book. I had last worked with him over two decades earlier. On some of that earlier work, see: D. Dorling and J. Cornford, 'The distribution of negative equity in 1993', report to the Lords Commissioners of H. M. Treasury; later published (with help from Chris Gentle) as C. Gentle, D. Dorling and J. Cornford, 'Negative equity in 1990s Britain', *Urban Studies*, Vol. 31, No. 2 (1994), pp. 181–99.

14. Bank of England, *Trends in lending, January 2013*, London: Bank of England, 2013. http://www.bankofengland.co.uk/publications/Documents/other/monetary/trendsjanuary13.pdf

15. L. Howard, 'Days are numbered for interest-only mortgages', 'Moneysupermarket.com' website blog, 30 November 2012. http://www.moneysupermarket.com/c/news/days-are-numbered-for-interest-only-mortgages/0015487/

16. Press Association, 'West Bromwich Building Society hits "buy-to-let" borrowers with 2% rate hike', *Dundee Courier*, 23 September 2013. http://www.thecourier.co.uk/business/news/west-bromwich-building-society-hits-buy-to-let-borrowers-with-2-rate-hike-1.134093

17. Shelter, '1.4 million Britons falling behind with the rent or mortgage'.

18. From the Housing Rights Service in Northern Ireland, where negative equity is worse: UTV, 'Home repossessions at critical level', web video report, 19 February 2013. http://www.u.tv/News/NI-home-repossessions-at-critical-level/ Elsewhere in the UK the rates of repossession were going down at the same time, but that may be temporary.

19. And as explained in more detail in the 'Home Truths' section in Chapter 3 of this volume, p. 68.

20. Statistic Brain, 'Home foreclosures statistics'. http://www.statisticbrain.com/home-foreclosure-statistics/ Relying in turn on data released by RealtyTrac, the Federal Reserve and Equifax, 15 October 2012.

21. Shelter, 'Eviction risk hotspots revealed', press release, 14 December 2012. http://england.shelter.org.uk/news/previous_years/2012/december_2012/eviction_risk_hotspots_revealed

22. G. Lamarca, 'Resisting evictions Spanish style', *New Internationalist*,

April 2013. http://newint.org/features/2013/04/01/sparks-from-the-spanish-crucible/

23. My source wishes to remain anonymous because financial and housing analysts within government and its numerous agencies live in fear of being seen as responsible for sparking a crash. As a result they issue no serious warnings, and the potential bonfire of hopes, dreams and unsustainable lending models grows larger.

24. R. Kitchin, et al., 'Placing neoliberalism: the rise and fall of Ireland's Celtic Tiger', *Environment and Planning (A)*, Vol. 44 (2012), pp. 1,302-26.

25. J. Currie and E. Tekin, 'Is there a link between foreclosure and health?', National Bureau of Economic Research Working Paper No. 17310, 2011. http://ideas.repec.org/p/nbr/nberwo/17310.html

26. Anonymous personal communication, 2013: from the senior public health analyst who had been highlighting the figures, all of which are in the public domain. In July 2013 the *Health Service Journal* posted the report here: http://www.hsj.co.uk/Journals/2013/07/23/u/j/e/Weekly-and-monthly-provisional-figures-on-deaths-registered-in-England-and-Wales--16th-July.doc.

27. Public Health England, 'Excess winter mortality 2012-13', 15 August 2013. https://www.gov.uk/government/uploads/system/uploads/attachment_data/file/229819/Excess_winter_mortality_2012.pdf

28. 'PHE [Public Health England] has also published a letter from its chief knowledge officer about the decision to stop the weekly reports which highlighted the issue.' A. McLellan, 'PHE publishes report on excess winter deaths', *Health Service Journal*, 15 August 2013. http://www.hsj.co.uk/news/hsj-live/hsj-live-150813-phe-publishes-report-on-excess-winter-deaths/5062297.article#.Uj1fStIqjzY. Then, in what was described as a unrelated development, Office for National Statistics suggested not producing the weekly series at all to save between £10,000 and £50,000 a year in costs. http://www.ons.gov.uk/ons/about-ons/get-involved/consultations/consultations/statistical-products-2013/index.html

29. D. Stuckler and M. McKee, 'Why are death rates rising in people aged over eighty-five?', 'Better Health for All' website blog of the Faculty of Public Health, 23 August 2013. http://betterhealthforall.org/2013/08/23/why-are-death-rates-rising-in-people-aged-over-85/

30. The UK was one of only two countries reporting the lowest level of flu intensity during the 2012/13 season across all of Europe. This makes the suggestion that the rising mortality in the UK is due to flu very dubious: European Centre for Disease Prevention and Control, 'Influenza in Europe:

season 2012/13', 2013. http://ecdc.europa.eu/en/healthtopics/seasonal_influenza/PublishingImages/influenza-europe-weekly-infographic.jpg

31. Institute of Financial Accountants, 'Life expectancy at retirement falls for men and women', 'Professional Adviser (IFA)' website, quoting Richard Willets, 6 November 2013. http://www.ifaonline.co.uk/ifaonline/news/2305397/life-expectancy-at-retirement-falls-for-men-and-women. See also:http://www.ons.gov.uk/ons/rel/subnational-health2/excess-winter-mortality-in-england-and-wales/2012-13--provisional--and-2011-12-final-/stb-ewm-12-13.html#tab-Final-EWM-in-2011-12-by-underlying-cause-of-death

32. D. Dorling, 'In place of fear: narrowing health inequalities', think piece, CLASS: Centre for Labour and Social Studies, 21 May 2013. http://www.dannydorling.org/?page_id=3711

33. S-S Change, et al., 'Was the economic crisis 1997–1998 responsible for rising suicide rates in East/South-east Asia? A time-trend analysis for Japan, Hong Kong, South Korea, Taiwan, Singapore and Thailand', Social Science and Medicine, Vol. 68, No. 7 (2009), pp. 1,322–31.

34. D. Stuckler, et al., 'Banking crises and mortality during the Great Depression: evidence from US urban populations, 1927–1939', Journal of Epidemiology and Community Health, published online 24 March 2011. doi:10.1136/jech.2010.121376. D. Stuckler, et al., 'Effects of the 2008 recession on health: a first look at European data', Lancet, 9 July 2011 online: 378(9786):124–5. doi: 10.1016/S0140-6736(11)61079-9.

35. S. Burgen, 'Spanish helpline reports rise in number of callers considering suicide', Guardian, 5 September 2013. http://www.theguardian.com/world/2013/sep/05/spanish-helpline-rise-callers-considering-suicide

36. A. Deaton, 'What's wrong with inequality? Review of Joseph Stiglitz, The price of inequality', Lancet, Vol. 381, No. 9,864 (2 February 2013), p. 362. http://www.thelancet.com/journals/lancet/article/PIIS0140-6736(13)-60154-3/fulltext

37. Institute of Health Medicine, US health in international perspective: shorter lives, poorer health, Washington: National Academy of Sciences, 2013. http://www.iom.edu/Reports/2013/US-Health-in-International-Perspective-Shorter-Lives-Poorer-Health.aspx

38. Ibid., p. 5.

39. On evictions see: Neoskosmos, 'Greece passes law to help debt-stricken households', report, 3 August 2010. http://neoskosmos.com/news/en/Greece-debt-relief-bill-papandreau-katseli. And also see: http://www.protothema.gr/economy/article/?aid=75847 (in Greek but can be automatically translated).

40. Professor Tomoki Nakaya, Rismumeikan University, Kyoto, Japan, personal communication, 22 December 2013. See also Z. Ward, 'Good news for renters in Japan: security deposits, key money on the demise', *Japan Today*, 30 March 2012. http://www.japantoday.com/category/opinions/view/good-news-for-renters-in-japan-security-deposits-key-money-on-the-demise

41. M. B. Veléz, 'Banks and the racial patterning of homicide: a study of Chicago neighborhoods', *International Journal of Conflict and Violence*, Vol. 3, No. 2 (2009), pp. 154–71. http://www.ijcv.org/index.php/ijcv/article/viewArticle/3

42. D. Stuckler and S. Basu, *The body economic: why austerity kills*, London: Allen Lane, 2013.

43. Office for National Statistics, 'General lifestyle survey', 2013. See Table 7.1, 'Self-perception of general health No. 1: 2005 to 2011'. http://www.ons.gov.uk/ons/rel/ghs/general-lifestyle-survey/2011/index.html

44. See: http://www.property118.com/help-us-to-protect-your-tracker-margins/43709/, as accessed 26 September 2013.

45. C. Savage, 'Wells Fargo will settle mortgage bias charges', *New York Times*, 12 July 2012. http://www.nytimes.com/2012/07/13/business/wells-fargo-to-settle-mortgage-discrimination-charges.html

46. G. Hiscott, 'Barclays to refund 300,000 customers after blunder', *Daily Mirror*, 17 September 2013. http://www.mirror.co.uk/money/city-news/barclays-refund-300000-customers-after-2280151#ixzz2fX6xT1xl

47. In the section 'Recent inequality', pp. 24–6, S. Saulny, 'When living in limbo avoids living on the street', *New York Times*, 3 March 2012. http://www.nytimes.com/2012/03/04/us/when-living-in-limbo-avoids-living-on-the-street.html?ref=us&_r=1&

48. Mortgage companies are the financial services equivalent of the Neutron Bomb, that atomic weapon designed to remove people but leave the property they lived in standing to be reused.

49. S. Morris, 'Vulnerable people facing eviction after council cuts support for hostel residents', *Guardian*, 25 September 2013. http://www.theguardian.com/society/2013/sep/25/vulnerable-people-facing-eviction-bristol-hostels

50. J. Waldron, 'Homelessness and the issue of freedom', *UCLA Law Review*, Vol. 39 (1991), pp. 295–324. http://faculty.washington.edu/pembina/all_articles/Waldron%201991.pdf

51. Quoted in S. Saulny, 'when living in limbo'. Note as well that, as the largest lender, Wells Fargo is also the largest US bank when all are ranked by market capitalization.

52. 'Bob', comment in response to above story by Saulny, 4 March 2012, Boonsboro.

53. If you are interested in that era, the resulting papers can be found on the web if you search for their titles: D. Dorling, 'The negative equity map of Britain', *Area*, Vol. 26, No. 4 (1994), pp. 327–42; D. Dorling and J. Cornford, 'Who has negative equity? How house-price falls in Britain have hit different groups of buyers', *Housing Studies*, Vol. 10, No. 2 (1995), pp. 151–78; C. Pattie, D. Dorling and R. Johnston, 'A debt-owning democracy: the political impact of housing market recession at the British general election of 1992', *Urban Studies*, Vol. 32, No. 8 (1995), pp. 1,293–315; G. Davey Smith and D. Dorling, 'I'm all right, John: voting patterns and mortality in England and Wales, 1981–92', *British Medical Journal*, Vol. 313 (1996), pp. 1573–7.

54. A. Hill, 'Trapped: the former couples who can't afford to move on', *Guardian*, 20 November 2012. http://www.guardian.co.uk/society/2012/nov/20/trapped-couples-partners-relationships

55. R. Whelan, 'Negative equity more widespread than previously thought, report says', *Wall Street Journal*, 24 May 2012. http://blogs.wsj.com/developments/2012/05/24/negative-equity-more-widespread-than-previously-thought-report-says/

56. J. Christie, 'California city backs plan to seize negative equity mortgages', Reuters, 11 September 2013. http://www.reuters.com/article/2013/09/11/us-richmond-eminentdomain-idUSBRE98A0FN20130911

57. G. Morgenson, 'How to find weeds in a mortgage pool', *New York Times*, 8 September 2012. http://www.nytimes.com/2012/09/09/business/how-to-find-weeds-in-a-mortgage-pool-fair-game.html

58. The saga is ongoing: 'ResCap is likely to end its bankruptcy this month after winning court approval of a liquidation plan that resolves more than $100 billion in potential lawsuits.' See C. Dolmetsch and C. Smythe, 'ResCap affiliate sues UBS, SunTrust over mortgage securities', *Bloomberg Business Week*, 17 December 2013. http://www.businessweek.com/news/2013-12-17/rescap-affiliate-sues-ubs-suntrust-over-mortgage-securities-1

59. Office for National Statistics, 'Consumer price inflation, August 2013', press release, 17 September 2013. http://www.ons.gov.uk/ons/rel/cpi/consumer-price-indices/august-2013/index.html

60. R. Kitchin, S. O'Callaghan, S. and J. Gleeson, 'Unfinished estates in Post-Celtic Tiger Ireland', Northern Ireland Statistics and Research Agency Working Paper No. 67, 2012, p. 10. http://ebookbrowse.com/nirsa-working-paper-67-unfinished-estates-in-post-celtic-tiger-ireland-pdf-d312024595

61. D. Coleman, 'Ireland prepares to say bye bye to Troika as Finance Minister Michael Noonan warns: this must never happen again', *Irish Mirror*, 13 December 2013. http://www.irishmirror.ie/news/irish-news/politics/country-exits-troika-rule-finance-2924434

62. S. Castle, 'Ireland seeks easing of its debt terms', *New York Times*, 1 March 2013. http://www.nytimes.com/2013/03/02/business/global/ireland-seeks-easing-of-its-debt-terms.html

63. Staff reporter, 'Bargain hunters splash out €13.7 million at property auction', *Irish Independent*, 2 March 2013. http://www.independent.ie/irish-news/bargain-hunters-splash-out-137m-at-property-auction-29104233.html#

64. T. O'Brien, 'NAMA offers 4,000 homes for social housing', *Irish Times*, 18 September 2013. http://www.irishtimes.com/news/ireland/irish-news/nama-offers-4-000-homes-for-social-housing-1.1531855

65. D. O'Donovan, 'NAMA sale of 10,000 apartments to shake up the housing market', *Irish Independent*, 26 September 2013. http://www.independent.ie/irish-news/nama-sale-of-10000-apartments-to-shake-up-the-housing-market-29611569.html

66. D. O'Donovan, 'Focus Ireland rejected offer of properties, reveals NAMA', *Irish Independent*, 1 December 2013. http://www.independent.ie/business/irish/focus-ireland-rejected-offer-of-properties-reveals-nama-29798406.html

67. Which continues: 'First, in the place where we live, with the knowledge that we're surrounded by capitalism everywhere; and later, in Andalusia, and the world.' See: Anticap, 'Protest of the day', 20 August 2012. http://anticap.wordpress.com/2012/08/20/protest-of-the-day-142/

68. Staff reporter, 'Greek housing market remains extremely depressed', *United Press International*, 14 September 2013. http://www.upi.com/Business_News/2013/09/14/Greek-housing-market-remains-extremely-depressed/UPI-20891379183674/

69. *Ni gente sin casa, ni casas sin gente.* D. Stelfox, 'How the Corrala movement is occupying Spain', *Guardian*, 4 March 2013. http://www.guardian.co.uk/world/2013/mar/04/corrala-movement-occupying-spain

70. A. Fotheringham, 'In Spain's heart, a slum to shame Europe', *Independent*, 27 November 2011. http://www.independent.co.uk/news/world/europe/in-spains-heart-a-slum-to-shame-europe-6268652.html

71. J. Christie, 'California city backs plan to seize negative equity mortgages'.

72. Referred to in the section on heath and eviction above; see note 39 on the report by Neoskosmos.

73. Department for Communities and Local Government, 'Streamlining information requirements for planning applications', press release,

27 December 2012. https://www.gov.uk/government/consultations/streamlining-information-requirements-for-planning-applications

74. L. Hanley, 'Living in limbo under failed housing renewal plans', *Guardian*, 21 September 2012. http://www.guardian.co.uk/commentisfree/2012/sep/21/housing-renewal-plans-fail-living-limbo

75. It was Democratic Unionist Party minister Nelson McCausland who stalled on implementation. If you are interested in why, have a look at the 22 June 2013 entry of his blog, where he appears more interested in parading past Catholic churches than housing: http://theministerspen.blogspot.co.uk/

76. See D. Dorling, 'Housing and identity: how place makes race', Better Housing Briefing Paper No. 17, Race Equality Foundation, March 2011. http://www.better-housing.org.uk/briefings/housing-and-identity-how-place-makes-race; and especially if you are interested in the arguments for how such plans would reduce racism in housing. I first debated this when giving the Lord Pitt Memorial Lecture on these proposals in March 2011 as the crisis was deepening and it was becoming clear that non-white Londoners were being proportionately more disadvantaged. See: http://www.raceequalityfoundation.org.uk/training/events/lord-pitt-memorial-lecture-how-place-makes-race

77. C. Shephard, personal communication, Sheffield, 2013.

78. When it was cut by a further 10%, and so was able to help fewer people than the year before, despite the demand for money advice and housing advice growing: Citizens Advice Bureau, 'Cuts in CAB funding leaving thousands with nowhere to turn for help', 6 September 2011. http://www.citizensadvice.org.uk/index/pressoffice/press_index/press_20110906.htm

79. A. Hull and G. Cooke, 'Together at home: a new strategy for housing', Institute for Public Policy Research, report, 21 June 2012, p. 53. http://www.ippr.org/publication/55/9279/together-at-home-a-new-strategy-for-housing

80. D. Garvie, 'A return to revolving-door homelessness?', 'Shelter' website policyblog, 9 November 2012. http://blog.shelter.org.uk/2012/11/a-return-to-revolving-door-homelessness/

81. Department for Communities and Local Government, *A plain English guide to the Localism Act*, London: Department for Communities and Local Government, November 2011. https://www.gov.uk/government/uploads/system/uploads/attachment_data/file/5959/1896534.pdf

82. C. Brown, 'PM confirms age limit plan for housing benefit', 'Inside Housing' website, 10 October 2012. http://www.insidehousing.co.uk/ihstory.aspx?storycode=6524142

83. J. Waldron, 'Homelessness and the issue of freedom', p. 313, quoting from 'Doors closing as mood on the homeless sours', *New York Times*, 18 November 1989.

84. Shelter, 'One in four is just a pay cheque away from homelessness', press release, 18 December 2012. http://scotland shelter.org.uk/news/december_2012/one_in_four_are_just_a_pay_check_away_from_homelessness

85. K. Mercer, 'Homeless Westminster families in four-star hotels', *BBC News*, 7 February 2013. http://www.bbc.co.uk/news/uk-england-london-21362391

86. In other words it is based on what the rents for the very worst housing in an area tend to be and not on the median home, and uprating will not include the housing element of inflation! C. Shephard, personal communication, Sheffield, 2013.

87. For details see http://www.socialfinance.org.uk/ and click 'About us' to find out which hedge fund managers are board members. I have to admit here to being suspicious. It may be because a business model is being used that such exact figures are included in the 'Social Finance' website. The number 5,678 estimate for people sleeping rough just quoted does look like someone tapping consecutive keys on the keyboard, and it is hard to get at the methodology.

88. It is not clear how many individual rough sleepers have to become tenants for providers to be rewarded, for how long they will have to remain tenants, or what quality of home they should live in.

89. Social Finance, 'Improving outcomes for London's homeless', report, accessed 29 January 2013. http://www.socialfinance.org.uk/homelessness. However, as of September 2013, that report has been removed from their website. As for the organization itself, Toby Eccles, its Development Director, claims that it is 'interested in aligning the social with the financial rather than finding a clever wheeze for making money. We are incentivized to work with the complicated and with those willing to change.' A. Travis, 'Will social impact bonds solve society's most intractable problems?', *Guardian*, 6 October 2010. http://www.guardian.co.uk/society/2010/oct/06/social-impact-bonds-intractable-societal-problems. Sceptics remain unconvinced.

90. B. Thomas, 'Homelessness kills: an analysis of the mortality of homeless people in early twenty-first century England', Crisis, report, 2012. http://www.crisis.org.uk/publications-search.php?fullitem=371 or at: http://sasi.group.shef.ac.uk/publications/reports/Crisis_2012.pdf

91. E. Drabble, 'Should we build more homes?', Shelter, *Guardian* Teacher Network, 13 December 2012. http://teachers.guardian.co.uk/teacher-resources/11697/Should-we-build-more-homes-By-Shelter

92. Department for Communities and Local Government, 'Mark Prisk challenges councils to find stable homes for families', press release, 7 June 2013.https://www.gov.uk/government/news/mark-prisk-challenges-councils-to-find-stable-homes-for-families

93. Mother of three quoted in R. Ramesh, 'Illegal use of B&Bs to house homeless soars by 800%', *Guardian*, 18 February 2013. http://www.guardian.co.uk/society/2013/feb/18/illegal-use-bandbs-house-homeless

94. Staff reporter, 'Half of all homeless families forced to live in bed and breakfasts are in London', *Evening Standard*, 5 September 2013. http://www.standard.co.uk/news/london/half-of-all-homeless-families-forced-to-live-in-bed-and-breakfasts-are-in-london-8800303.html

95. BBC, 'New rights for the homeless come into force', *BBC Scotland Politics*,30December2012.http://www.bbc.co.uk/news/uk-scotland-scotland-politics-20870160

96. Staff writers, 'Number of families living in B&Bs at ten-year high in England', 'Ekklesia' website, 19 September 2013. http://www.ekklesia.co.uk/node/19086

97. L. Barker, 'Homeless bound? Homelessness in London, the south-east and east of England', National Housing Federation, report, 13 November 2012, p. 7. http://www.housing.org.uk/publications/find_a_publication/general/homeless_bound.aspx

98. Details on Pickles's departmental webpages and also to be found at Chindits House, Chindits Lane, Brentwood, Essex CM14 5LF. http://www.foyer.net/level3.asp?level3id=71

99. For more details of this story, search around on the web a little using Eric Pickles's name and see: http://www.brentwoodweeklynews.co.uk/news/9965532.Homeless_shelter_evacuated_after_chemical_scare/?ref=rss

100. E. Drabble, 'Should we build more homes?'.

101. T. Champion and J. Goddard, 'The containment of urban England', chapter in a forthcoming book celebrating the life and work of Peter Hall, personal correspondence.

102. For real ambition in Britain, consider what has been achieved by the Low Impact Living Affordable Community (LILAC) in Leeds, where the first residents who designed their own new green housing moved in during spring 2013. http://www.lilac.coop/, but see also p. 302.

103. S. Rose, 'Squatters are not home stealers', *Guardian*, 3 December 2012. http://www.guardian.co.uk/society/2012/dec/03/squatters-criminalised-not-home-stealers

104. H. Wilcox, 'Criminalizing squatting – privatizing empty space', 'New Left Project' website, 13 September 2012. http://www.newleftproject. org/index.php/site/article_comments/criminalising_squatting_privatising_ empty_space

105. BBC, 'Jailed squatter Alex Haigh's mother calls for leniency', *BBC News*, 28 September 2012. http://www.bbc.co.uk/news/uk-england-london-19759056

106. A. Arden, 'Anti-squatting law should be repealed', letter, *Guardian*, 25March2013.http://www.guardian.co.uk/society/2013/mar/25/squatting-law-should-be-repealed

107. S. Clark and C. Spillane, 'East End has thousands in illegal squalor near Olympics', *Bloomberg News*, 26 July 2012. http://www.bloomberg. com/news/2012-07-25/east-end-has-thousands-in-illegal-squalor-near-olympics.html

8 SOLUTIONS

1. BBC, 'David Cameron brings forward "help-to-buy" scheme', *BBC News and Politics*, 29 September 2013. http://www.bbc.co.uk/news/uk-politics-24319583

2. P. Mason, 'The graduates of 2012 will survive only in the cracks of our economy: uniquely, this cohort can expect to grow up poorer than their parents', *Guardian*, 1 July 2012. http://www.guardian.co.uk/commentisfree/2012/jul/01/graduates-2012-survive-in-cracks-economy? The quotation continues: 'For the graduate without a future is a human expression of an economic problem: the West's model is broken. It cannot deliver enough high-value work for its highly educated workforce. Yet the essential commodity – a degree – now costs so much that it will take decades of low-remunerated work to pay for it.' Paul Mason now works for UK television's Channel 4.

3. N. Mathiason, M. Newman, M. McClenaghan, 'Revealed: the £93 million City lobby machine', 'The Bureau of Investigative Journalism' website,2012.http://www.thebureauinvestigates.com/2012/07/09/revealed-the-93m-city-lobby-machine/

4. Ibid. That £92 million figure is estimated by the Bureau of Investigative Journalists.

5. Office for National Statistics, 'Average income falls in the last year', press release, 20 September 2012. http://www.ons.gov.uk/ons/dcp29904_279770.pdf See also the following website which gives a graph for 2001 to

2012 for employees: http://www.ons.gov.uk/ons/rel/regional-trends/
regional-economic-analysis/changes-in-real-earnings-in-the-uk-and-london-
2002-to-2012/art-changes-in-real-earnings-in-the-uk-and-london-
2002-to-2012.html#tab-2–Changes-in-earnings-of-employees-in-the-UK-and-its-
regions--2002-12

6. P. Inman, 'How Mervyn King finally got Bob Diamond', *Guardian*,
10 July 2012. http://www.guardian.co.uk/business/2012/jul/10/how-
mervyn-king-got-bob-diamond?

7. J. Quinn, 'Chancellor files legal challenge to EU cap on bank bonuses',
Telegraph, 25 September 2013. http://www.telegraph.co.uk/finance/
newsbysector/banksandfinance/10333831/Chancellor-files-legal-challenge-
to-EU-cap-on-bank-bonuses.html

8. Shelter Scotland, 'Letting agent fees are unlawful in Scotland', reclaim-
ing form, 2012. http://www.reclaimyourfees.com/

9. G. Brown, 'Parliament fails to accommodate growing housing problem', *Guardian*, 10 May 2012. http://www.guardian.co.uk/society/2012/
may/10/parliament-accommodate-growing-housing-problem

10. Shelter Scotland, 'Digital award for "Reclaim your fees"', press release,
29 November 2012. http://scotland.shelter.org.uk/news/november_2012/
digital_award_for_reclaim_your_fees

11. R. H. Tawney, *The acquisitive society*, London: Collins, 1961 reprint
of 1921 edition, p. 26.

12. Oxfam, *The perfect storm: economic stagnation, the rising cost of living, public spending cuts and the impact on UK poverty*, Oxford:
Oxfam, 2012, p. 24. poverty, http://policy-practice.oxfam.org.uk/
publications/the-perfect-storm-economic-stagnation-the-rising-cost-of-
living-public-spending-228591

13. F. Engels, 'The housing question. Part II: how the bourgeoisie solves the
housing question', *Der Volksstaat*, 1872, § I. http://www.marxists.org/
archive/marx/works/1872/housing-question/ch02.htm

14. J. von Brühl, 'Why the Germans rent instead of buy', *Süeddeutsche*,
10 April 2013. http://www.sueddeutsche.de/geld/immobilien-warum-
die-deutschen-mieten-statt-kaufen-1.1645266. Note that in Japan the
homeless are highly visible but make up only 2 people per 10,000,
whereas the UK has 'one of the highest levels of homelessness in Europe
with more than 4 people per 1,000 estimated to be homeless', more
than twenty times as many as in Japan. Many sources can be found
but the easiest to use is: http://www.homelessworldcup.org/content/
homelessness-statistics (as of Sept. 2013)

15. R. Syal, 'UKIP to give priority to council house applicants with parents

born locally', *Guardian*, 19 September 2013. http://www.theguardian.com/politics/2013/sep/19/ukip-council-house-parents-local

16. R. Behr, 'Westminster may dabble in xenophobia, but the reality is that racism isn't popular', *New Statesman*, 15 August 2013. http://www.newstatesman.com/politics/2013/08/westminster-may-dabble-xenophobia-reality-racism-isn%E2%80%99t-popular

17. P. Toynbee, 'Tony Blair: godfather of realpolitik – and Murdoch's daughter', *Guardian*, 28 May 2012. http://www.guardian.co.uk/commentisfree/2012/may/28/tony-blair-rupert-murdoch-leveson

18. National Audit Office, 'The decent homes programme', report, 21 January 2010. http://www.nao.org.uk/report/the-decent-homes-programme/

19. P. Toynbee, 'How to turn a housing crisis into a homeless catastrophe', *Guardian*, 18 February 2013. http://www.guardian.co.uk/commentisfree/2013/feb/18/housing-crisis-bedroom-tax-failure-to-build

20. That article also revealed that apparently the Prime Minister enjoys feeding lambs and growing vegetables. I don't think he's into renovating houses. He also tends not to threaten bankers. As of September 2013, he is opposing a proposed European ban on excessive bankers' bonuses. See I. Oakeshott, 'Country Dave champions the green belt', *Sunday Times*, 25 March 2012. http://www.thesundaytimes.co.uk/sto/news/Politics/article1001939.ece

21. A. Grice, 'Labour Party Conference: Labour "will build 200,000 homes a year by 2020", says Ed Miliband', *Independent*, 24 September 2013. http://www.independent.co.uk/news/uk/politics/labour-party-conference-labour-will-build-200000-homes-a-year-by-2020-says-ed-miliband-8835593.html

22. B. Macintyre and P. Orengoh, 'Beatings and abuse made Barack Obama's grandfather loathe the British', *The Times*, 3 December 2008. http://web.archive.org/web/20090120210653/http://www.timesonline.co.uk/tol/news/world/africa/article5276010.ece

23. Staff reporter, 'Obama to bank CEOs: "My administration is the only thing between you and the pitchforks"', *Huffington Post*, 4 May 2009. http://www.huffingtonpost.com/2009/04/03/obama-to-bank-ceos-my-adm_n_182896.html

24. B. Appelbaum, 'Cautious moves on foreclosures haunting Obama', *New York Times*, 19 August 2012. http://www.nytimes.com/2012/08/20/business/economy/slow-response-to-housing-crisis-now-weighs-on-obama.html

25. National Audit Office, 'The Mortgage Rescue Scheme', report, 25 May 2011. http://www.nao.org.uk/report/the-mortgage-rescue-scheme/

26. J. Birch, 'Rescue call', 'Inside Housing' website, 25 May 2011. http://www.insidehousing.co.uk/blogs/rescue-call/6515707.blog

27. Staff reporter, 'Osborne's "help-to-buy" scheme could be used for second homes', *Yorkshire Post*, 22 March 2013. http://www.yorkshirepost.co.uk/news/at-a-glance/general-news/osborne-s-help-to-buy-scheme-could-be-used-for-second-homes-1-5519958

28. A reference to the legislation, Statutory Instrument 2625 of 2012, is given in the section titled 'Renovations and reality' in Chapter 4, note 30, p. 335.

29. Community Land Trust, 'Community-led design weekend announced!', latest news article, 5 December 2012, as read in April 2013. http://www.eastlondonclt.co.uk/#/latest-news/4571131363

30. A. McGibbon, 'If we want the government to take housing seriously, a national tenants union is the first step', *Independent*, 18 February 2013. http://www.independent.co.uk/voices/comment/if-we-want-the-government-to-take-housing-seriously-a-national-tenants-union-is-the-first-step-8500068.html

31. A. Deaton, 'What's wrong with inequality? Review of Joseph Stiglitz, *The price of inequality*', *Lancet*, Vol. 381, No. 9,864 (2 February 2013),p.362.http://www.thelancet.com/journals/lancet/article/PIIS0140-6736(13)60154-3/fulltext

32. N. Sommerlad, 'Great Tory housing shame: third of ex-council homes now owned by rich landlords', *Daily Mirror*, 5 March 2013. http://www.mirror.co.uk/news/uk-news/right-to-buy-housing-shame-third-ex-council-1743338

33. P. Inman, 'Irish property tax penalizes Dublin residents, warn critics', *Guardian*, 27 January 2013. http://www.guardian.co.uk/world/2013/jan/27/irish-property-penalise-dublin-residents

34. P. Inman, 'Could we build a better future on a land value tax?', *Guardian*, 16 September 2012. http://www.guardian.co.uk/society/2012/sep/16/'right-to-buy'-tax-revamp

35. G. Monbiot, 'The resurgent aristocracy', 'George Monbiot' website, 4 June 2012. http://www.monbiot.com/2012/06/04/the-resurgent-aristocracy/

36. A. Hull and G. Cooke, 'Together at home: a new strategy for housing', Institute for Public Policy Research, report, 21 June 2012, p. 53. http://www.ippr.org/publication/55/9279/together-at-home-a-new-strategy-for-housing

37. N. Nowatzki, 'Wealth inequality and health: a political economy perspective', *International Journal of Health Services*, Vol. 42, No. 3 (2012), pp. 403–24. http://www.ncbi.nlm.nih.gov/pubmed/22993961

38. The various schemes currently in place are listed here: D. Dorling, 'Housing and identity: how place makes race', Better Housing Briefing Paper No. 17, Race Equality Foundation, March 2011. http://www.dannydorling.org/?page_id=582

39. Staff reporter, 'Home loan aid programme enriches banks', *Microsoft News*, 2012. http://money.msn.com/home-loans/article.aspx?post=8255a2a0-c7d0-4e6a-8e52-88f153566447

40. P. Wintour, 'Ed Miliband promises drive to double rate of housebuilding', *Guardian*, 16 December 2013. http://www.theguardian.com/politics/2013/dec/15/ed-miliband-housebuilding-labour-councils-developers

41. G. Parker, 'Miliband plans mansion tax', *Financial Times*, 'Politics and Policy', 14 February 2013. http://www.ft.com/cms/s/0/1a71aa26-7694-11e2-ac91-00144feabdc0.html#axzz2L5NrbYKa

42. J. Waldron, 'Homelessness and the issue of freedom', *UCLA Law Review*, Vol. 39 (1991), p. 322. http://faculty.washington.edu/pembina/all_articles/Waldron%201991.pdf. The passage I am paraphrasing reads 'what we are dealing with here is not just "the problem of homelessness", but a million or more persons whose activity and dignity and freedom are at stake.' Back in 1991, it was a million in the US, now it is hundreds of millions who are precariously housed across the rich world, whose parents did not know such fear, but whose children are growing up to think their homes are not secure.

43. A. Hull and G. Cooke, 'Together at home: a new strategy for housing', p. 53.

44. Which the control of rent itself achieves (see Table 2, p. 271 above).

45. All Party Parliamentary Cycling Group, 'Britain cycling inquiry', House of Commons, press release, 18 February 2013. http://allpartycycling.org/inquiry/

46. D. Ballas, et al., 'Income inequalities in Japan and the UK: a comparative study of two island economies', *Journal of Social Policy and Society*, March 2013, pp. 1–15. http://www.dannydorling.org/?page_id=3648

47. S. Alderson, *Britain in the sixties. Housing: a Penguin Special*, Middlesex: Penguin Books, 1962.

48. D. Bradly, 'Latent coalitions for egalitarianism may be dormant in Britain, but they are a sleeping giant', 'British Politics and Policy' website blog, June 2012. http://blogs.lse.ac.uk/politicsandpolicy/archives/24150

49. The younger man was Robert Reich, the current Chancellor's Professor of Public Policy at the University of California at Berkeley. He was formerly Secretary of Labor in the 1990s under Clinton.

50. R. Reich, 'The poor and the middle class will save America yet',

30 August 2013. Conversation with an old friend posted at: http://www.alternet.org/visions/poor-and-middle-class-will-save-america-yet

51. S. Kraemer, personal correspondence, 9 March 2013 – containing yet another letter that a newspaper failed to print but that needs to be read, paraphrased here with permission.

52. S. Mirrlees, et al., *Tax by design*, Oxford: Oxford University Press, 2011, p. 481. http://www.ifs.org.uk/mirrleesReview/design

53. J. Mercille, 'The role of the media in sustaining Ireland's housing bubble', *New Political Economy*, 2013, DOI:10.1080/13563467.2013.779652. A summary can be found at: http://www.social-europe.eu/2013/04/the-role-of-the-media-in-propping-up-irelands-housing-bubble/

54. S. Donnelian, 'Co-op downgrade stokes more bail-in fears', *International Financing Review*, 13 May 2013. http://www.ifre.com/co-op-downgrade-stokes-more-bail-in-fears/21085245.article

55. BBC, 'Landlords with West Bromwich face tracker mortgage rise', *BBC Business News*, 23 September 2013. http://www.bbc.co.uk/news/business-24203736

56. J. M. Keynes, 'Economic possibilities for our grandchildren', *Essays in persuasion*, New York: W. W. Norton & Co., 1963, pp. 358–73. http://www.econ.yale.edu/smith/econ116a/keynes1.pdf

57. K. Marx and F. Engels, *Manifesto of the Communist Party*, 1948 printing of the English 1888 edition. http://www.gutenberg.org/cache/epub/61/pg61.html

58. K. Allen, personal communication on 'cash buyers versus mortgages, the Savills analysis', 16 January 2014, published as K. Allen, 'Home buyers left behind in Britain's two-speed housing market', *Financial Times*, 18 January 2014, http://www.ft.com/cms/s/0/ea516116-7f92-11e3-94d2-00144feabdco.html#axzz2qh9TosM5.

AFTERWORD: HOUSING CHAOS

1. P. Foster and J. Gurdon, 'American children facing record levels of homelessness', *Telegraph*, 18 November 2014. http://www.telegraph.co.uk/news/worldnews/northamerica/usa/11236544/American-children-facing-record-levels-of-homelessness.html

2. The *Daily Mail*'s report of this mistakenly called mortgagees 'home-owners', as if they owned their home outright having paid a mortgage off: L. Boyce, (2014) 'A third of homeowners would struggle if interest rates rose by 2% – and only a handful have prepared for higher costs', *Daily Mail*, 10 November 2014. http://www.thisismoney.co.uk/money/

mortgageshome/article-2828375/A-homeowners-struggle-rates-rose-2.
html

3. Priced Out: 'The Priced Out index: 3,496,000 Priced Out', London:
Website, accessed November 2014, http://www.pricedout.org.uk/the_
pricedout_index

4. W. Wilson, 'Retaliatory eviction (England), Standard Note: SN07015',
London: Housing of Commons Library, Page 6 for the 56% figure from
the Landlord's own lobbying body! (2014) http://www.parliament.uk/
briefing-papers/SN07015.pdf

5. K. Allen, 'UK private sector tenants have highest rents and poorest
housing', *Financial Times*, 23 July 2014, http://www.ft.com/cms/s/0/
2dfbc3ee-1259-11e4-93a5-00144feabdc0.html#axzz3Ju8tqTvo

6. Rent doesn't all go on the landlord's mortgage and upkeep costs. £770
a month pays the interest only on a £200,000 mortgage at 4.6%, £1162
a month covers the costs of a £300,000 mortgage. The longer ago the
landlord bought the property, the smaller their mortgage will be and the
greater their profit. However, many landlords have been relying on rising prices to make them bigger profits.

7. N. Wain, 'Private rents soar to inflation-busting record high of
£770 in October', *Daily Mail*, 21 November 2014, http://www.
thisismoney.co.uk/money/mortgageshome/article-2842732/Private-rents-
soar-inflation-busting-record-high-770-October-tenants-finances-stabilise.
html

8. $1-(770/761)^{12}= 15.2\%$. Annual rises to August 2014 had been 2.4%
but they accelerated in September 2014 (see above). Press Association,
'Rents rise to all-time average high of £761 a month in August', *Guardian*, 19 September 2014. http://www.theguardian.com/money/2014/
sep/19/rents-rise-all-time-average-high-august-uk

9. T. McVeigh, 'Revenge evictions: "An electrician said our shower was
unsafe. The landlord's response was to evict us"', *Observer*, 23 November 2024. http://www.theguardian.com/money/2014/nov/23/revenge-
evictions-landlord-evict-us

10. Some five hundred years ago, in 1516, in his philosophical tract *Utopia*,
Thomas More suggested the solution to ensuring good housing for all
would be that 'At every ten years' end they shift their houses by lots.
They cultivate their gardens with great care, so that they have both
vines, fruits, herbs, and flowers in them; and all is so well ordered and
so finely kept that I never saw gardens anywhere that were both so
fruitful and so beautiful as theirs.'

11. K. Knoll, M. Schularick, T. Steger, 'Home prices since 1870: No price

like home', London: Centre for Economic Policy Research (CEPR), 1 November 2014, http://www.voxeu.org/article/home-prices-1870

12. Land Registry, 'September 2014 Market Trend Data', London: Land Registry, 28 October 2014, https://www.gov.uk/government/news/september-2014-market-trend-data

13. D. Roland, 'Foxtons hit by "sharp slowdown" in London housing market, *Telegraph*, 23 October 2014. http://www.telegraph.co.uk/finance/newsbysector/constructionandproperty/11181672/Foxtons-hit-by-sharp-slowdown-in-London-housing-market.html

14. A. White, 'Young Londoners forced to eat on the landing and hang out on the stairs', *Telegraph*, 19 November 2014. http://www.telegraph.co.uk/finance/newsbysector/constructionandproperty/11239064/Young-Londoners-forced-to-eat-on-the-landing-and-hang-out-on-the-stairs.html

15. Savills Annual Housing Seminar Slides, 17 November 2014, partly reported as 'Private rental home numbers to rise 1.2 million in five years as home ownership among the under 35s falls to one in six households' 6 November 2014.http://www.savills.co.uk/_news/article/55328/183957-0/11/2014/private-rental-home-numbers-to-rise-1.2-million-in-five-years-as-home-ownership-among-the-under-35s-falls-to-one-in-six-households

16. M. Stephens *et al.* 'What Will The Housing Market Look Like in 2040?', York: Joseph Rowntree Foundation, 17 November 2014, (see page 7 in particular).http://www.jrf.org.uk/publications/what-will-housing-market-look-2040

17. An extra 350,000 households earning between £20,000 and £30,000 a year, according to National Housing Federation research. J. Sherman, 'Families on £30,000 drive rise in house benefit claims', *The Times*, 2 October 2014. http://www.thetimes.co.uk/tto/news/politics/article4223998.ece

18. D. Stott, 'We need a "long-term housing plan" from the Conservatives', London: Priced Out Press Release, 27 September 2014, http://www.pricedout.org.uk/long_term_housing_plan_conservatives?utm_campaign=party_conferenc&utm_medium=email&utm_source=pricedout

19. T. Revell, 'Nick Clegg promises ten garden cities to battle housing shortage', *Blue and Green Tomorrow*, 7 October 2014. http://blueandgreentomorrow.com/2014/10/07/nick-clegg-promises-ten-garden-cities-to-battle-housing-shortage/

20. A. Chakrabortty, 'New Era estate scandal: families at the mercy of international speculators', *Guardian*, 19 November 2014. http://www.theguardian.com/society/2014/nov/19/new-era-estate-scandal-london-families-international-speculators

21. L. Garrett, B. Watt, 'Keep rents at a rate affordable to existing tenants

on the New Era Estate, Petition', Change.org, as of 23 November 2014. https://www.change.org/p/new-era-should-not-become-the-end-of-an-era?recruiter=75607022&utm_campaign=signature_receipt&utm_medium=email&utm_source=share_petition

22. A. Johnson, 'Landlords on track to own £1 trillion of property next year', *Independent*, 6 November 2014. http://www.independent.co.uk/property/landlords-on-track-to-own-1-trillion-of-property-next-year-9843640.html

23. A. White, 'House prices: the north-south divide is now wider than ever', *Telegraph*, 14 October 2014. http://www.telegraph.co.uk/finance/economics/11161079/House-prices-the-north-south-divide-is-now-wider-than-ever.html

24. P. Dominiczak, 'Autumn Statement: stamp duty cut as George Osborne lays out grand designs for election', *Telegraph*, 3 December 2014. http://www.telegraph.co.uk/finance/autumn-statement/11272124/Autumn-Statement-stamp-duty-cut-as-George-Osborne-sets-sights-on-election.html

25. National Federation of Housing 'Broken Market, Broken Dreams: Home Truths 2014/15', 15 September 2014. London: National Federation. http://www.housing.org.uk/publications/browse/home-truths-2014/

Index

Diagrams and pictures are given in italics.